Siren City

Siren City

Sound and Source Music in Classic American Noir

ROBERT MIKLITSCH

Rutgers University Press
NEW BRUNSWICK, NEW JERSEY, AND LONDON

Library of Congress Cataloging-in-Publication Data
Miklitsch, Robert, 1953–
Siren city : sound and source music in classic American noir / Robert Miklitsch.
p. cm.
Includes bibliographical references and index.
ISBN 978-0-8135-4898-2 (hardcover : alk. paper) —
ISBN 978-0-8135-4899-9 (pbk. : alk. paper)
1. Film noir—History and criticism. 2. Motion pictures—Sound effects.
3. Motion picture music—History and criticism. I. Title.
PN1995.9.F54M55 2010
791.4302'4—dc22 2010013760

A British Cataloging-in-Publication record for this book is available from the British Library.

Visit our Web site: http://rutgerspress.rutgers.edu

Manufactured in the United States of America

For Catherine B. Miklitsch, poet laureate of Niagara Falls

Now listen. Was that a freight train or a 155 millimeter shell passing overhead? Now listen carefully. A door latch or the cocking of a .45 caliber pistol? A jungle bird or a falling bomb? Someone tapping on a champagne glass or Swiss bells?

—instructor administering sound test to O.S.S. agents in *13 Rue Madeleine* (1947)

GRETA BALLENTINE (SUSAN HAYWARD): You like music too, Miss Carlson?

VERNA CARLSON (RITA JOHNSON): I can take it or leave it.

GRETA: Didn't you like the polka? I think Shostakovich is so exciting.

TRENTON (TOM POWERS): I'm afraid Verna prefers the music of Harry James.

—*They Won't Believe Me* (1947)

Contents

Preview

I have wanted to write a book on film noir for some time, and since it is only upon some reflection that I have been able to determine the origins of my fascination with the genre as well as the text's main topics, sound and source music, I would like to begin with some autobiographical remarks before offering some additional comments on genre and methodology.

The most remote influence on *Siren City*, temporally speaking, was the music I listened to growing up in my parents' home. On Saturday nights and holidays (and, crucially, before the arrival of the Beatles, which forever changed the kind of music that my brothers and sisters listened to), my father would play big-band records, 78s—Harry James, Glenn Miller, Benny Goodman, the Dorsey brothers, Jimmy and Tommy—on the console phonograph in the living room. My parents would drink "highballs," we would drink "coolers" (ginger ale with vanilla ice cream) and munch on popcorn, which my father would make by vigorously shaking a beat-up pot on the electric stove until the corn was popped, whereupon he would add liberal amounts of salt and pan-warmed butter. At our prompting and to our immense amusement, my parents would also invariably jitterbug, a dance that in the early 1960s seemed hopelessly old-fashioned to us—compared, that is, to the twist.

A more recent source of my audiophilia has been my abiding interest in movie soundtracks. For example, at some point in the 1970s I became inordinately enamored with the "original motion picture" scores of *Chinatown* and *Last Tango in Paris* and, having bought the vinyl LPs, would listen to them over and over. While Jerry Goldsmith's period-perfect music for *Chinatown* has become a classic neo-noir score,[1] it now strikes me that Gato Barbieri's music for *Last Tango in Paris*, featuring the Argentine on solo saxophone, could be the soundtrack for some lost seventies neo-noir. The fact that Bernardo Bertolucci's film is set in Paris, where film noir might be said to have been born in 1946, and that the score includes tracks like "Para Mi Negra" or "Girl in Black" (Maria Schneider as femme fatale?), contributes to the noir-like aura of Barbieri's moody fusion of tango and jazz.

If forties swing and seventies soundtracks are two of the deep, autobiographical sources of *Siren City*, the most profound influence on this book was a thoroughly cine-sonic one: seeing *Apocalypse Now* in its first run at the Ziegfeld Theatre in Manhattan in 1979. At the time, I was visiting a college friend whose parents lived outside New York City and, on a whim, we decided to go into the city for the day and, as it turned out, the night. Propriety prevents me from offering full disclosure, but let's just say that *Apocalypse Now* was an eye- and ear-opening experience. My friend and I sat up front in the cavernous Ziegfeld and while the images were astonishing, Walter Murch's sound design was equally if not more so, simultaneously coming from behind our heads—I don't think I'll ever forget the *thwarp thwarp thwarp* of helicopter blades—and rapidly traveling from speaker to speaker to speaker to speaker. Murch has recounted how the sound of the helicopter "begins in the right back, travels to the left back, then travels to the left front and then to the right front."[2] Murch has also recounted how Francis Ford Coppola wanted the sound to be "true to the experience of being in Vietnam."[3] Never having served in Vietnam, I can't speak to the verisimilitude of *Apocalypse Now*, but seeing and hearing it in 70mm and in quadraphonic sound was so transformative that when I returned home, I wrote my first piece of journalism, a free-lance "review" of Coppola's film for the *Buffalo Evening News*. I can distinctly remember writing that *Apocalypse Now* was an "experience with a capital E," and a big part of that Experience was sonic.

Paradoxically enough, given my endless fascination, even obsession with film noir, I don't remember the first noir I saw, although it may well have been *The Maltese Falcon* on late-night TV in the basement of my parents' home. I do know, however, that in the early 1980s, while teaching part-time at a college in Boston, I was asked to pick up a course on detective fiction from a woman who had been mugged on Boston Common ("true crime" story). As a practicing poet at the time, I was spellbound by the language of "hard-boiled" fiction, a pulp poetry that is epitomized for me by the novels of Raymond Chandler.

Late Chandler: "Beyond the little hallway the room widened toward a pair of windows through which the evening sun slanted in a shaft that reached almost across the bed and came to a stop under the neck of a man that lay there. . . . I touched his neck. It was still warm. While I was doing it the shaft of sunlight moved away from the knob of the ice pick toward his left ear."[4] This passage from *The Little Sister* (1949) is something like the forties literary equivalent of John Alton's or Nicholas Musuraca's cinematography; to my ears, it's also a consummate example of sound and music or, in a word, audiovisuality.

Cues

Like the Maltese falcon—the statue, that is—film noir is a sublime object. As such, it's always already an "eminently lost object."[5]

The title of the essay in which this eminently sound proposition appears, Marc Vernet's "Film Noir on the Edge of Doom" (1993), is appropriately atmospheric, recollecting as it does Mark Robson's 1950 noir, *Edge of Doom*. Since for Vernet the sublimity of noir refers to the fact that "there's no there there," it's not surprising that in *Genre and Hollywood* (2000), Steve Neale contends that noir as a single phenomenon "never existed."[6] While it's possible to gain a foothold on this slippery slope, as I do below, by latching on to the word *single*, Neale's argument—on the sheer face of it—takes no prisoners. In the "provision of criteria," in the "construction of a corpus," and in "almost any interpretation of [its] contemporary socio-cultural significance," the concept of film noir "inevitably generates contradictions, exceptions, and anomalies" and is "doomed"—there's that word again—to "incoherence."[7]

Still, if the question of noir as a genre is ultimately less about the relative validity of Vernet's and Neale's claims (which are persuasive enough on their own terms) than about how we actually use genres, it might be more profitable to view film noir from a more pragmatic, less deconstructive point of view. In *More Than Night* (1998) James Naremore proposes just such a strategy, observing that the fact "film noir has no essential categories" is not an insuperable problem if we understand categories as "complex radial structures" which are a function of "forms of imaginative association that develop over time."[8]

There are any number of advantages to this radial point of view. One is that film noir as a genre can be defined more in centrifugal and inclusive rather than centripetal and exclusive terms. (I confess here to being haunted by Rick Altman's exclusion of *The Wizard of Oz* in his otherwise magisterial study of the American film musical.) Another advantage of defining film noir in non-essentialist terms is that it foregrounds the genre's discursive character where, to remember Roland Barthes, film noir is a myth or, as Elizabeth Cowie submits, fantasy.[9] Finally, yet another advantage of conceiving of film noir from an inclusive, centrifugal standpoint is its heuristic value. Practically speaking, this means that by assuming the style, canon, and history of film noir as it has developed imaginatively up to now, one can attend to other, more specific issues such as the expressivity of sound and music in forties noir, or the impact of other genres such as the musical or the Western.[10]

In fact, the issue of cross- or transgeneric influence is crucial to understanding classic noir since, as Neale notes, "hybridity is as common in old Hollywood as it is in the New Hollywood": "The strategies of the industry and its companies have always been plural and mixed, marked by an array of categories, formulas and combinations that overlap with, and often exceed, the categories that genre critics and theorists have tended to acknowledge."[11] In other words, as the continual recourse to song sequences in various forties films suggests, the "doom and gloom" of film noir and the "sunny," "happy-go-lucky" Hollywood musical may not be as antithetical as they at first appear.[12] Accordingly, one of the working premises of *Siren City* is that if all genres are "contingent, evolving, and transactional," the question is not, as Thomas Leitch writes in *Crime Films* (1997), "whether or not a particular film is a member of a given genre, but how rewarding it is to discuss it as if it were."[13]

If the notion of genre is an especially contentious one when it comes to film noir, the issue of what exactly constitutes its classical period is almost equally contentious. To be sure, the 1940s, whether understood as a strictly generic or historical period, is itself an arbitrary category. Writing at mid-century in their seminal text, *A Panorama of American Film Noir, 1941–1953* (1955), Raymond Borde and Étienne Chaumeton designate 1949–1950 as the moment of "decadence and transformation."[14] And in the almost equally seminal "Notes on Film Noir" (1972), Paul Schrader refers to the period from 1949 to 1953 as the "third and final phase" of the genre.[15] More recently, Andrew Spicer in *Film Noir* (2002) identifies the third cycle of noir, a period "dominated by semi-documentaries and social problem films," as extending from 1947 to 1952.[16]

The point is, since there's no standard or accepted periodization of classic noir, I have elected to cut the Gordian knot and think of the genre, as Danny Graydon and Alexander Ballinger do in *The Rough Guide to Film Noir* (2007), in terms of decades. I've decided, moreover, to restrict myself to films that were *released* in the United States between 1940 and 1949. This restriction has meant excluding some extraordinary films that were produced in 1949 and released in 1950 such as *Gun Crazy*, *D.O.A.*, and *The Asphalt Jungle*. But it has simultaneously freed me to attend to lesser known, peripheral films from the period, a "deep focus" approach that would have been impossible had I determined to write about classic noir as a whole—from, say, 1941 to 1958. (The other major and minor exclusions are international noir and forties Hitchcock.[17] See also "Note on Text" below.)

Although the main topics of *Siren City* are sound and source music in forties noir, the word "audiovisuality" perhaps best reflects my objective in this book, which is to illustrate how sonic effects and diegetic music work in concert with the image and narrative tracks. Film noir, of course, has been interpreted in terms of literary antecedents such as the detective novel (hard-boiled dialogue, private investigator, first-person narration, etc.)[18] as well as through a glass darkly—which is to say, in terms of its expressionist graphics. However, by concentrating on what Michel Chion calls "audio-vision," it's possible to show how, as a result of the collaboration of talented directors, sound designers, and music personnel, the sound track of film noir is frequently just as expressive as the genre's vaunted visual style ("Dutch" angles, chiaroscuro lighting, off-kilter compositions, etc.).

Hence my decision to focus on the sound track of classic noir which, with the exception of critics such as Richard Dyer and Robert Porfirio and, more recently, David Butler, Helen Hanson, and Jans Wager, has frequently been disregarded even by cinéastes.[19] Chion, for example, observes that "noises, those humble footsoldiers, have remained the outcasts of theory, having been assigned a purely utilitarian and figurative value and consequently neglected."[20] Yet even Chion goes on to pronounce that "noises" in film noir and the classical cinema are "scant" and "stereotypical": "with sound quality so acoustically impoverished, they all seem to be cut out of the same impoverished cloth."[21]

But as I detail in chapter 2 and as a close listening to the films makes clear, the noises or sonic effects of forties noir are both more complex and "colorful" than Chion suggests, a proposition that applies to the issue of source music as well. Thus, if one takes a "wide angle" on the genre—if, in other words, one examines a wide range of forties noirs—it becomes apparent not only that song sequences are a persistent trope of classic noir but that jazz performed by a combo in a nightclub is just one of the many forms of source music that is audible in the period. Indeed, in the form of popular music such as "hot" black jazz, audio technologies such as the radio and jukebox, and "big numbers" featuring iconic female performers such as Lauren Bacall, Veronica Lake, and Rita Hayworth, diegetic music is central to the noir aesthetic.

To complement this wide-angle perspective, I've adopted a corresponding "close up" or, more properly (to invoke the language of sound recording), closely miked approach to interpretation. While I've drawn on various critical approaches in the course of *Siren City*, my preferred method has been formal, sometimes shot-by-shot analysis with an attendant, novelistic emphasis on narrative. The book's particular, semi-nominalist "point of audition" has, needless to say, required making some hard decisions about methodology. For example, I engage the argument of Laura Mulvey's "Visual Pleasure and Narrative Cinema" (1975) in passing in chapters 6 and 7 since the notion of the male gaze is particularly relevant to the issue of female musical performance.[22] In general, however, I've tried to keep theoretical debates to a minimum. And here I must add that although I've endeavored to remain attentive to the tension between the 1940s and current theorizing about, among other things, race, nation, and gender, I've felt free to err—conscientiously, I hope—on the side of the films "themselves" (no phenomenological pun intended). My basic, even base assumption is that even lesser "works of art" are marked by contradiction and contingency and are therefore constitutively open to re-viewing and re-listening or, in a word, re-interpretation.

Finally, the unabashedly aesthetic approach that I take in *Siren City* has been dictated, like the book's discursive style, by the sort of general or common reader that I envisioned as the book's audience. (I've been duly educated by my sister Cathy, the "judge," who once told me—totally without malice—that she kept my first book, *From Hegel to Madonna*, on her nightstand and read one page every night to help her fall asleep.)

I might mention here that my no doubt fantasmatic sense of the common reader has been profoundly shaped by the "Tier 3" course on film noir, "Kiss Me Deadly," that I have taught at Ohio University over the last fifteen years. A capstone, cross-disciplinary class for juniors and seniors from across the university, it has vividly taught me the values of variety, accessibility, and, for want of a better word, entertainment. (I've long since embraced the lesson of "It Smells Like Teen Spirit": "Here we are now, entertain us.") My commitment to the above values has impacted the composition of *Siren City* in two important, if contrary, ways: first, this book is at least as much about film noir as sound and source music—in other words, the audio element serves to illuminate noir rather than vice versa—and, second, *Siren City* is not addressed only or even primarily to scholars in film or sound studies (although, as I hope it becomes clear, I have taken some pains to do justice to the extant literature).

The issue of address is delicate, even prickly. While I can't claim to have always hit the mark in terms of the appropriate pitch—the book's style, I recognize, is a sometimes uneasy hybrid of the high and low, the learned and the demotic—I wanted to write a fun and reasonably informative book about film noir as opposed to, say, a "rigorous," "sophisticated" analysis of sound and source music in the genre. The latter text when it appears will be a welcome addition to the rapidly expanding literature on film noir and sound studies, but *Siren City* does not pretend to be that book. Rather, my hope is that, since I very much enjoyed writing this book, readers will enjoy reading it.

Trailer

In the synopsis that follows, I preview the contents of *Siren City*. Readers who find such "trailers" either superfluous or pedestrian should feel free to fast-forward to the Introduction.

The Introduction to *Siren City* broaches the issue of sound and source music in forties noir that I develop in more detail in the body of the book. In the first part of the Introduction, I concentrate on sound in film noir understood not so much as music or dialogue as "noise." I take up a number of general issues here such as the distinction between diegetic and nondiegetic sound as well as the notion of point of audition (POA), a concept that suggestively parallels the idea of point of view (POV). For some additional historical perspective on the issue of film sound, the first part of the Introduction also includes a sidebar, "The Soundman," that reviews the process of sound recording and rerecording in Hollywood in the 1940s.

The second part of the Introduction explores the role of source and background music in classic noir. Since the accent in *Siren City* is on diegetic rather than nondiegetic music, I start with a short review of film noir composers, arguing that the scores of forties noir are neither as jazzy nor as avant-garde as has sometimes been suggested. I then turn to two topics central to the sound of classic noir: diegetic jazz music and the noir "songbird." In addition to showing how the fascination of an early hybrid horror-noir such as *Among the Living* (1941) is a direct function of its seminal depiction of jitterbug culture and the "big combo" of jazz and blackness, I situate the figure of the siren—typically, a female vocalist performing in a bar or nightclub and backed by a big band or orchestra—within its sociocultural context and in relation to another canonical figure of classic noir, the femme fatale. The key component here, as elsewhere in *Siren City*, is performance understood both as a musical act and complex signifier of subjectivity.

Chapter 1, "House of Sound," opens on a historical note with the birth of sound movies and the coincident birth of RKO studios. Although film noir would not emerge until well after the first "talkies," RKO has not only become synonymous with film noir and what many now consider the first film of the genre—Boris Ingster's *Stranger on the Third Floor* (1940)—but is coincident with the studio's apex: *Citizen Kane* (1941). Numerous commentators have noted the influence of Orson Welles's film—in particular, its use of flashback/voice-over narration—on the history of noir, but what is rather less known is that the personnel responsible for the sound track of *Citizen Kane*—recordist Bailey Fesler and recording mixer James G. Stewart—also designed the sound track for *Stranger on the Third Floor* and *Murder, My Sweet* (1944). Fesler's and Stewart's heretofore unrecognized contributions to these seminal films is, I argue, considerable since the interior monologue in *Stranger on the Third Floor* can be "seen" as the sonic antecedent of the first-person voice-over narration in *Murder, My Sweet*, the first film noir to marry this paradigmatic device with the figure of the private detective. Moreover, certain signature effects such as reverb and offscreen sound associated with the post-*Kane* RKO "house style" are integral to the evolving audiovisual language of classic noir: enhanced reverberation—courtesy of RKO's acoustic echo chamber—is mobilized in both *Stranger on the Third Floor* and *Murder, My Sweet* to heighten the hallucinatory character of their celebrated dream sequences, while offscreen sound is deployed in Ingster's and Dmytryk's films as an expressionist vehicle for one of the defining moods or affective modalities of classic noir: paranoia.

Chapter 2, "Sound and Fury in Forties Noir," begins with some preliminary remarks on hard-boiled dialogue before enumerating a range of sound effects in forties noir from discrete sonic phenomena such as screams and footsteps in the dark to the acoustic complexes associated with various modes of transportation such as the train and automobile. The aim of the chapter, however, is not so much to define the sound of noir—to paraphrase Chion, there is no noir sound track—than to indicate something of its sheer heterogeneity. So, while certain sounds are inextricably connected with the genre—one thinks immediately, as in the horror and crime film, of gunplay and sirens, the alpha and omega of the metropolitan environs—classic noir is also populated by the sounds of the country, whether it's the baying of blood hounds in the concluding chase sequence of *Moonrise* (1948) or, as in *Border Incident* (1949), the chuffing of a disc tractor as it inexorably bears down on a fallen federal agent.

Chapter 3, "Audio Technologies," considers the impact of communications and entertainment technologies—intercom and Dictaphone, telephone and radio, phonograph and jukebox—on the sound track of forties noir. Although the intercom assumes a pivotal role in *The Big Clock* (1948) and the Dictaphone is located at the narrational heart of *Double Indemnity* (1944), the most pervasive form of sound technology within the diegesis or fictional world of classic noir is undoubtedly the telephone, a uniquely audible presence that's reflected in the titles of such films as *Sorry, Wrong Number* (1948), *Call Northside 777* (1948), *Dial 1119* (1950), and *Dial M for Murder* (1954). The most significant medium in the period, though, is arguably the radio, which is utilized in forties noir to build suspense (in *Raw Deal* [1948], for example, it's part of a governmental apparatus that is intent on capturing an escaped convict), convey crucial narrative information and, occasionally, comment on the action. The radio, in fact, represents a bridge between technologies of communication such as the telephone to technologies of entertainment such as the phonograph or record player—with the proviso that, in the 1940s, the phonograph was also used as a recording device, as in *The Unsuspected* (1947). If a record player can be said to structure the operatic narrative of *House of Strangers* (1949) as well as the popular-musical backstory of *Black Angel* (1946), the synonym of the phonograph in the public sphere, the jukebox, performs a similar function in *Detour* (1945) and *Fallen Angel* (1945). Indeed, in Edgar G. Ulmer's and Otto Preminger's films, the jukebox is a coin-operated machine whose three-minute dreams not only intoxicate women but drive men to distraction and, sometimes, murder.

Chapter 4, "Blues in the Night," opens with a discussion of how instrumental source music in forties noir overscores scenes of physical violence.

While the music is transmitted via a live jazz band in *The Set-Up* (1949), a phonograph in *Crossfire* (1947), and a radio in *Born to Kill* (1947) and *Dead Reckoning* (1947), chapter 4 is less about technology per se than the way in which music, as in the classical Hollywood musical, motivates or "choreographs" action. In the ensuing section on instrumental source music, I switch gears, turning to what is commonly thought to be the quintessential music and format of classic noir: a black combo playing "hot" jazz in a nightclub. As Butler has been at pains to demonstrate, jazz, at least in the restricted sense of "modern jazz," is by no means the musical *lingua franca* of film noir, particularly in the 1940s, and this remains true for both diegetic and nondiegetic music. This said, the diegetic jazz sequences in certain forties noirs such as *The Dark Corner* (1946), *Kiss of Death* (1947), *Force of Evil* (1948), and *When Strangers Marry* (1944) constitute, I argue, a different, more nuanced portrayal of African Americans than is typical in film noirs of the period. The swing text here is Jacques Tourneur's *Out of the Past* (1947), a canonical film noir that includes an influential jazz scene set in Harlem in addition to, as in *Laura* (1944), American popular music in the form of diegetic variations on a single song. Since classical music is frequently used to counterpoint popular music in film noir, chapter 4 concludes by examining classical piano source music in the period, showing that despite or perhaps because of its high-cultural status, it is frequently linked, as in *Possessed* (1947) and *Undercurrent* (1946), with the discourse of madness and obsession.

Chapter 5, "Singing Detectives and Bluesmen, Black Jazzwomen and Torch Singers," explores the phenomena of vocal performance and instrumental self-accompaniment in forties noir. After an introductory section on *a cappella* singing, the most memorable of which is Gaye Dawn's (Claire Trevor) performance of "Moanin' Low" in *Key Largo* (1948), I spotlight musical sequences in which the principal characters sing and accompany themselves either on acoustic guitar—*The Postman Always Rings Twice* (1946), *Moonrise*, and *Gilda* (1946)—or piano—*The Glass Key* (1942), *House of Strangers*, *I Walk Alone* (1948), and *Road House* (1948). Like Rex Ingram in *Moonrise* and the jazz musicians I discuss in chapter 4, black singer–piano players such as Lillian Randolph in *The Glass Key* and Dolores Parker in *House of Strangers* complicate the standard conception of African American characters in forties noir. The musical numbers in *I Walk Alone* and *Road House* are notable in the context of female vocal performance since both Kay Lawrence (Lizabeth Scott) and Lily Stevens (Ida Lupino) occupy pivotal roles in their films, a narrative agency typically denied black female performers. Jean Negulesco's *Road House* is especially noteworthy because Lily, like Parker in *House of Strangers*, performs a cycle of popular American songs that is progressive in the strict sense of the term: it propels the narrative even as it comments on her character, a whiskey-throated torch singer who, as played by the fiercely independent Lupino, is as hard-boiled as the proverbial slouch-hatted detective.

Chapters 6 and 7—"Siren City" sides B and A, respectively—resume the prominence given to female vocal performance in chapter 5, reviewing what is arguably the cardinal musical conceit of classic noir: "the big number." Although not every musical sequence I discuss may deserve the appellation, each number, as in the classical film musical, is actively integrated into the narrative in which it appears. Marie Bryant, for example, is backed by a small band in *They Live by Night* (1948), but her performance of "Your Red Wagon" in Nicholas Ray's film showcases her jazz sensibility even as it highlights the young lovers' desperate plight. More generally, the very real interest of the most elaborate musical numbers in forties noir is the light *and* shadow they throw on the representation of femininity in the 1940s.

In fact, another look at and hearing of the noir "songbird" puts a performative twist on one of the genre's most sacred assumptions, the femme fatale, in the process torching the received wisdom about these women as, in the parlance of the period, canary *or* siren, "good girl" *or* "bad girl." The proposition that musical performance problematizes stereotypical *views* of femininity in the period informs my extended reading of the musical sequences that conclude chapter 7: Gilda's second, "striptease" version of "Put the Blame on Mame" in Charles Vidor's film and Elsa Bannister's performance of "Please Don't Kiss Me" in *The Lady from Shanghai* (1948). From the demonstrably vocal perspective of these films, women in forties noir, whether "bad girls" like Elsa or "good-bad" ones like Gilda, are singing their own tune.

By way of an afterword, *Siren City* concludes with an epilogue that acts as a bookend to the prologue on *Out of the Past* which introduces the body of the book. While the prologue ruminates on the opening of Tourneur's film and the signal interplay between Stefanos (Paul Valentine) and the Kid (Dickie Moore) as well as the sequence set at Marny's café, the envoi speculates about the "mute" rhetoric of the studio-imposed dénouement of Tourneur's film. This ambiguous happy ending may not be as bleak as some noirs, but it's an especially inspired and compelling one in its masterful evocation of the absolute other of sound and music: silence.

Note on Text

The extended case study on the fusion of sound and image in a quartet of Robert Siodmak films—*Christmas Holiday* (1944), *Phantom Lady* (1944), *The Killers* (1946), and *Criss Cross* (1949)—that originally constituted the second part of *Siren City* has been cut due to constraints of space. The names of certain actors have also been deleted. This is something of a judgment call since one person's bit actor is another person's cult figure ("I heart Percy Helton!"), but I have done so in the interests of making the text less cumbersome and more readable.

Finally, in the preceding Preview and throughout the course of *Siren City*, I use the word "soundtrack" in the contemporary popular sense as the recorded music associated with a movie and "sound track" for the totality of a given film's sounds—music, dialogue, silence, and effects.

Credits

I want to begin by thanking Leslie Mitchner at Rutgers University Press, who is the sort of editor one dreams of—witty, responsive, enthusiastic—and Murray Pomerance, whose own essayistic work on film is a welcome reminder that criticism and creativity are not mutually exclusive. For their unstinting assistance in the postproduction phase of *Siren City*, grazie to Marilyn Campbell and Katie Keeran. Grazie as well to Bob Brown for copyediting.

I also want to thank the various writers and critics, some anonymous, who have taken time to correspond or share forthcoming work: Rick Altman, Jonathan Auerbach, Vincent Brook, Mark Conard, Jennifer Fay and Justus Nieland, Philippa Gates, Julie Grossman, Frank Krutnik, Robert Porfirio, Jans Wager, and, in particular, James Naremore, who offered encouragement early on when I was finding my way. I'm also indebted to the organizers of the annual Screen Studies Conference in Glasgow for allowing me to preview work on classic and neo-noir. At the 2004 conference, I was fortunate enough to meet Richard Dyer, whose essay on "charisma through resistance" in *Gilda* is one of the sources of inspiration for *Siren City*, and Colin McArthur, whose work on "underworld" films and the Hollywood musical have been models of intellectual engagement and accessibility. At the 2006 Screen Studies conference, I was pleased to make the acquaintance of David Butler and Helen Hanson; my debt to Butler's *Jazz Noir*, the first book on noir and music, is manifest throughout *Siren City*, and Hanson's forthcoming book on sound styles in film noir and classic Hollywood cinema promises, together with Altman's on standardized sound practices during the studio years, to redefine our understanding of sound styles in both film noir and classic Hollywood cinema. Special thanks to Jay Beck and Tony Grajeda for the session on "Unheard Histories" at the 2009 Society for Cinema and Media Studies conference in Los Angeles where I was able to present work from the first chapter of this book. Finally, three trumpet blasts for Krin Gabbard, a truly magnanimous critic whose work on jazz and cinema I can only hope to emulate.

At Ohio University, both the dean and associate dean in the College of Arts and Sciences, Ben Ogles and Howard Dewald, were unusually supportive, offering, among other things, time off from teaching in order to jump-start the book. The chair of the English department during the period in which this book was written, Joe McLaughlin, has also been instrumental in its production. My colleagues at Ellis Hall continue to be a remarkably collegial bunch, especially Amrit Singh, who offered advice and guidance at opportune moments. Finally, I would be sorely remiss if I didn't acknowledge all the students at O.U. who've enrolled in my "Kiss Me Deadly" course over the years: they've enriched me and this book in ways that I'm not sure I'll ever fully comprehend.

For copies of obscure and out-of-print film noirs, I want to thank Bob Connors at eBay and Matthew Gladman, a real film noir buff who was kind enough to share with me his extensive collection of classic titles. I'm also grateful to computer-graphics whiz Rebecca Butorac for helping me download the digital illustrations used in the book.

In Columbus, Elizabeth Renker, fellow drummer, has supplied gourmet-quality food and sterling conversation, while the staff at the Bexley Public Library has been unusually solicitous: indeed, without the Bexley collection of noir titles, I would have been literally poorer.

My parents, Catherine and Robert Miklitsch, as well as my brothers and sisters—Cathy, David, Teresa, Fran, and Rose—remain, as always, a well-spring of love and affection.

Last but absolutely not least, this book may have been possible but it would not have been nearly as much fun without Jessica Jayne Burchard, who's been with me every step of the way. A devotee of true crime and vodka martinis (shaken, not stirred), she's the baddest "good girl" around, a pop chanteuse who seems to know the lyrics of every song and is happiest when singing them along with the car radio, out loud and with the window down.

Siren City

Introduction

SOUND AND (SOURCE) MUSIC

Sound

Despite the pervasive presence of musical numbers in classic film noir, not to mention the use of voice-over and hard-boiled dialogue, the genre—like the medium in general, *motion pictures*—has been viewed primarily in visual terms, whether it's high-contrast lighting or night-for-night shooting, oblique angles or claustrophobic framing, "dissonant" deep-focus compositions or the "archetypal noir shot": "the extreme high-angle long shot."[1] While film noir has also been defined in terms of, among other things, its mood and motifs, plot and mode of narration, sociocultural significance and conditions of production, the emphasis on visual style, an emphasis that's especially pronounced in Paul Schrader's "Notes on Film Noir" ("the theme is hidden in the style"[2]), has resulted in a corresponding disregard of the sonic or acoustic register.

One must therefore begin, to paraphrase Michel Chion in *Audio-Vision*, with the reality of "audiovisual illusion": "we never see the same thing when we also hear; we don't hear the same thing when we see as well."[3] One cannot perhaps emphasize this reciprocity between sound and image enough since, notwithstanding the advent of "talking pictures," the discourse of classical Hollywood cinema has historically been posed in terms of viewers and spectators. Although the word *audience*, with its residual sense of hearing, is salient in the context (hence my frequent recourse to it in the course of this book), it is preferable when discussing forties films to speak, as Chion does, of "audio-spectators."[4] The value of this portmanteau term, despite or because of its lack of felicity, is that it accents what Sergei Eisenstein calls "audiovisual cinema."[5]

Once one appreciates the fact that hearing or listening is the hidden key to what Eisenstein calls the "synchronization of the senses,"[6] one can begin to entertain the subject of film sound as such. Alas, even when one makes this "revolutionary" turn, one is immediately confronted with the hierarchical, asymmetrical character of the classic-realist sound track. Simply put, the sound track is rigorously regulated by the following "auditory hierarchy":

dialogue
music
effects
silence

Chion's term in *Audio-Vision* for the above valorization of dialogue as opposed to music and effects (in the industry, "M&E") is vococentrism. In other words, the human voice is the center or sine qua non of classical cinema: "it is the voice that is isolated in the sound mix like a solo instrument . . . for which the other sounds (music and noise) are merely the accompaniment."[7]

Chion's metaphorical recourse to music is wonderfully deconstructive since music, as the second term in the above hierarchy (dialogue/music), is the sonic element that most negatively impacts the intelligibility of filmic speech. (Note that classical Hollywood cinema, adhering as it does to a telephonic as opposed to phonographic model of sound, prizes acoustic clarity even at the expense of perceptual fidelity.[8]) So, rehearsing this normative practice, David Sonnenschein issues this caveat for future filmmakers and sound designers, "The entrance of music . . . can drown out the voice and detract from the understanding of dialogue."[9] At the same time, the subtitle of Sonnenschein's manual, *The Expressive Power of Music, Voice, and Sound Effects in Cinema* (note the primary placement of the word *music*) not only underscores the rhetorical force of Chion's conceit about the voice in classical Hollywood cinema but points up the "expressive," aesthetic ends to which music can be put.

Indeed, precisely because of its ambiguous status in classical Hollywood film, music illuminates a crucial aspect of cinematic sound, space. Since sound in film, as Chion reminds us, compels the audience to ask, "Where does it come from?," the answer typically involves locating its source.[10] The fundamental distinction in this "regard" is between *diegetic* and *nondiegetic* sound, a distinction that can also be formulated in terms of another question, Is the sound or music internal or external to the fictional world? If the sound or music—say, a song on a car radio—is internal to the story, it's diegetic; if it's external—an orchestral score—it's nondiegetic. In terms of diegetic sound, one can further distinguish between *onscreen* and *offscreen* sound which, as the nomenclature indicates, refers to whether the source —for instance, a radio—is visible or not. Chion's term for this phenomenon—"sound one hears without seeing its source"—is acousmatic.[11] (An early, locus classicus of offscreen sound is Beckert's [Peter Lorre] whistling of "In the Hall of the Mountain King" from Edvard Grieg's *Peer Gynt* in Fritz Lang's *M* [1931].)

Like diegetic/nondiegetic and on/offscreen sound, volume and the related notion of reverberation (direct vs. reflected sound) are also integral to forties sound as is "point of audition," which refers to a specific character's sense of hearing. In "Deep-Focus Sound: *Citizen Kane* and the Radio Aesthetic," Rick Altman summarizes the state of sound cinema circa 1941: "The clear separation of sound into foreground and background zones; foreground sound must be clear and spaceless; background sound may lack clarity and express space, but must be reduced in volume to assure communication of the foreground sound; only point-of-audition sound regularly links the two zones."[12] Although the originality of *Citizen Kane* (1941) derives in part from the degree to which Welles varies the volume and reverb to register the spatial distance between objects,[13] a number of forties noirs not only actively manipulate volume and reverberation to produce depth of sound but mobilize point of audition. In fact, POA sound is utilized to particular effect in such forties noirs as Lang's *Scarlet Street* (1945), Curtis Bernhardt's *Possessed* (1947), and John Brahm's *Locket* (1946) where it becomes, in tandem with signature visual flourishes, an expressionist device to capture the tortured interiority of the main character. Not so incidentally, it also represents a spectacular instance of audiovisuality.

If one turns from space to time, the most obvious and immediate issue is synchronization, the mechanical matching of sound and image, as in "lip synching," which is the "pivot point between onscreen and offscreen, diegetic and nondiegetic sound."[14] Chion's term for the "psychological" aspect of synchronization is *synchresis*; rather more suggestively, point of synchronization for Chion refers to a "salient moment of an audiovisual sequence during which a sound event and a visual event meet in synchrony."[15]

One of the most powerful examples of point of synchronization in forties noir occurs in Welles's *The Stranger* (1946). Inspector Wilson (Edward G. Robinson) of the Allied War Crimes Commission has brought Mary Longstreet (Loretta Young) to her father's house to confront her with the horrible truth about her new husband, Charles Rankin, a.k.a. Franz Kindler (Welles). While the projection light flickers on her face and a 16mm projector audibly whirs in the background, Wilson describes the images on the screen: massed dead bodies, a gas chamber, a lime pit. "All these things you're seeing," he tells Mary, are the "product of one mind, the mind of a man named Franz Kindler." As Wilson concludes his brief ("Now in all the world there's only one person who can identify Franz Kindler"), Welles caps the moment with a startling effect: the sound of the film running out and clacking loudly against the reel, the now filmless projector underscoring, like some abstract, atonal music, the terrible black-and-white images on the screen.

While asynchronous sound of the sort one associates with *Singin' in the Rain* (1952) is rare in classical Hollywood cinema, the dialectical twin of expressive synchronization is asynchronism or, more loosely, counterpoint. In a memorable collective statement, Eisenstein, Vsevolod Pudovkin, and Grigori Aleksandrov programmatically espouse the principle of counterpoint: "Sound must be directed along the line of its distinct nonsyncronization with the visual images. And only such an attack will give the necessary palpability which will later lead to the creation of an orchestral counterpoint of visual and aural images."[16] Eisenstein reiterates the importance of this "harmonic" principle in the "Music of Landscape," the culmination of his work on vertical montage and polyphonic structure.[17] After recapitulating the first two stages of cinema, the silent and the sound film, he declares that the third stage of audiovisual cinema will exploit the resources of rerecording in order to effect the "*organic fusion of sound and representations*."[18]

It's worth noting that Eisenstein composed "The Music of Landscape" in 1945 near the end of the first cycle of film noir when technical innovations brought about by the war were transforming both the genre and classical Hollywood cinema. As Altman observes, the "average film of the mid-forties . . . represented a significant improvement on the original efforts of the late twenties," but it was not until after the war that the "sound recording industry in general and the film sound track in particular [took] a quantum leap forward with the production of magnetic recording techniques."[19]

Although the "magnetic stereo" revolution, the second major one after the "talkies" (1927–1930), did not become standardized until 1952,[20] the semi-documentary film noirs at Twentieth Century–Fox such as *The House on 92nd Street* (1945), *13 Rue Madeleine* (1947), *Boomerang!* (1947), *Kiss of Death* (1947), *Call Northside 777* (1948), and *The Street with No Name* (1948) were "landmarks in sound practice" and constituted the "most extensive use of direct sound between the early 1930s and . . . the 'New Wave.'"[21] The semi-documentary cycle derived from, among other things, Italian neo-realism, Louis de Rochemont's "March of Time" newsreels, and advances in sound technology such as more portable, because smaller and lighter, mixing and recording equipment.[22] One momentous result of these varied influences was that movies moved out of the studio and onto the streets.

Since then, the arrival of "optical stereophonic sound-on-film" as well as the advent of the sound designer have radically altered the production and reception of film sound.[23] (While Dolby noise reduction originated in 1975, the title of sound designer can be dated to 1979 when Walter Murch received a credit for "sound montage and design" for *Apocalypse Now*.) The difference between the 1940s and now is well-nigh fantastic. For example, in the 1940s, "film sound was essentially a monaural, single-channel experience"; today, as the "role of sound designer has moved from the periphery to the heart of the filmmaking process," there are "multiple channels of sound information that envelop viewers in a dynamic, three-dimensional *sound field*."[24]

Indeed, from a contemporary perspective (say, 7.1 surround sound), forties films can seem "acoustically impoverished."[25] "Take a film noir . . . from the forties," Chion queries in *Audio-Vision*, "what do the noises come to?" The evidence for Chion is underwhelming: "A few discreet footsteps, several clinking glasses, a dozen gunshots."[26] Chion, to be fair, is attempting to revalorize the "repressed" of film sound, noise, but one working premise of this book is that the sound track of forties noirs is both more various and expressive than Chion suggests or that has heretofore been recognized.

DOCU-NOIR: *CALL NORTHSIDE 777*

One of the best, because most expressionistic, docu-noirs is Henry Hathaway's *Call Northside 777*, which was recorded by W. D. Flick and Roger Heman who worked together on a number of seminal semi-documentary films at Twentieth Century–Fox.

After a prologue ("the rise and fall of the bootlegging empire was written in blood and bullets"), *Call Northside 777* begins with an exterior shot of a Polish grocery store buffeted by winds (a "soundmark" for Chicago, the "windy city") followed by an interior shot of Wanda Skutnik (Betty Garde) serving an alcoholic beverage prohibited at the time (1932) to a purveyor of coal and ice who's just delivered his goods. A bell rings offscreen and, after a close-up of the bell ringing again as the door closes, a street cop comes into the back room for a quick shot of whiskey for his "cold." The bell rings again, but this time when the door closes, there's a close-up of a man's hand stopping it. As Wanda escapes out a side door, two armed men in dark hats and overcoats enter the store, open fire, killing the policeman.

Although the loud, gusting wind as the men exit is obviously post-synchronized, the documentary atmosphere of *Call Northside 777* is acoustically marked in various ensuing locations: the police station where one of the suspects, Frank Wiecek (Richard Conte), is interrogated; the deserted office building where the investigative *Chicago Times* reporter Jim McNeal (James Stewart) goes at night to interview Wiecek's mother, Tillie; and the foyer at the state penitentiary where we see Wiecek being brought in as McNeal waits with the warden in his well-appointed, wood-paneled office. In these "actual locales" (to invoke the opening voice-over), the "boomy," "bathroomy" sound, full of echoes and reverberation, reflects the hard, empty tone of these institutional spaces.

If the settings and sonic architecture foreground the documentary character of *Call Northside 777*, the film's noir aspect—first introduced by the cop killing—reemerges in the "production" sequence that follows McNeal's visit with Wiecek's ex-wife, Helen. After McNeal has returned to the newspaper to write up his interview, the film cuts from the clickety-clack of his typewriter to the roar of the printing presses ("Wiecek Is Innocent Says Ex-Wife"), a sound-image superimposed over a shot of McNeal turning restlessly in bed, "gnashing his teeth" (as his wife puts it).

The audiovisual properties implicit in this montage are more fully realized in the film's two extended sequences, the first when McNeal searches for Wanda Skutnik in Chicago's Polish district and the second when he finally finds the film's "phantom lady" (who, unlike Ann Terry in *Phantom Lady*, is anything but a lady). In the first sequence, McNeal emerges at night from a subway station to the beer parlors and saloons of Chicago's Polish district, the bright neon signs (Kingsbury Pale Beer, Fox De Luxe Beer, Schlitz on Draught) accompanied on the sound track by the jangle of jukeboxes and piano-players. (Note the bell-like sound at the very beginning of the sequence, an aural echo of the "grocery store" scene that opens the film.)

The second, even more expressionist sequence opens on a quintessential noir note with a low-angle long shot of an elevated train, whistle blowing and smoke billowing from its locomotive stack as it barrels above a streetlamp-lit sign for Honore Street (an allusion to Balzac?). After the camera cranes down to a shot of McNeal standing, hands in his pockets, looking up at the sign, it tracks along with him as he starts toward a run-down apartment building. Standing on the doorstep, McNeal bends down to read the address ("Wanda Siskovich #3"), then straightens up to peer inside the door window. In a stunning reverse-shot, his upper body is tightly framed by the bar-like wooden slats of the center windowpane while, in the left background of the frame, another train passes, its plume of smoke and lancing searchlight matched on the sound track by a whistle, warning bell, and the rhythmic click of wheels on railroad tracks.

Once McNeal enters the darkened, shadow-lined building, other ambient sounds —the reporter lighting and blowing out a match, a tenant furtively opening and closing a door—set up the audiovisual climax of *Call Northside 777*. McNeal knocks on the door of apartment #3 and lets himself in, but as soon as he identifies himself ("I'm from the *Times*"), Wanda Skutnik, her voice ravaged by booze, yells at him, "You're the one who wrote those lies about me." McNeal holds his ground—"I insulted you every way I could think of, and I'm gonna keep on doing it"—until a train whistles offscreen and, as the locomotive materializes in the frame of the open window, a man emerges with a gun. Wanda tells the man, Boris, to put down his weapon, although she adamantly refuses to change her eyewitness story, screaming at McNeal, "I ain't never gonna change my mind. Now get out of here!"

Later, by enlarging a newspaper photograph, McNeal is eventually able to get Wiecek released from prison. It's daytime, the sun is shining, and everyone is there—Wiecek's mother, his ex-wife, their son, and Helen's new husband. Wiecek exclaims, "It's a good world outside," and the narrator happily seconds this sentiment. The reality, however, is that Wiecek's friend and fellow suspect, Tomek Zaleska, is still "inside," Wiecek himself will never be able to get back the eleven years he spent in prison, and Wanda Skutnik "remains at large," as do the real murderers.[a] The last suggests the world can be a pretty bad place, a "sound" noir proposition atmospherically evoked in *Call Northside 777* by Flick and Heman.

[a] Joan Cohen, "*Call Northside 777*," in *Film Noir: An Encyclopedic Reference to the American Style*, ed. Alain Silver and Elizabeth Ward (Woodstock, NY: Overlook Press, 1992), 50. For an illuminating analysis of *Call Northside 777* and the semi-documentary cycle in general, see J. P. Telotte, "The Transparent Reality of the Documentary *Noir*" and "The Evolving Truth of the Documentary *Noir*," in *Voices in the Dark: Narrative Patterns of Film Noir* (Urbana: University of Illinois Press, 1989), 134–153 and 154–178.

(Source) Music: The Noir Score and Composer

Unlike sonic effects, which sometimes remain "invisible" even to savvy spectators, the music of film noir, in particular nondiegetic music in the form of scores, has attracted critics' attention. In fact, in *Reel Music*, Roger Hickman enumerates the various elements that typically constitute a film noir score: a "prevailing mood, generally dark and pessimistic"; "minimal musical cues"; "orchestration for small ensembles"; "prominent low-pitched instruments"; "emphasis on the lower registers of the strings"; "use of nontraditional orchestral sound"; "angular, disjunctive melodies"; and "harsh dissonant harmonies."[27]

In terms of formal analysis, the prototypical noir scores have been those for *Double Indemnity*, *Laura*, and *The Big Sleep* (1946), which were written by, respectively, Miklós Rózsa, David Raksin, and Max Steiner.[28] For instance, in *Overtones and Undertones*, Royal S. Brown states that Rózsa's music for *Double Indemnity* stands as a "quintessential example of the birth . . . of a new form of fiction that reversed 180 degrees the musico-cinematic tendencies" of a "golden age" film like Michael Curtiz's *Sea Hawk* (1940).[29] Unlike the Puccini-esque music composed by Erich Wolfgang Korngold that plays beneath *The Sea Hawk*'s opening credits, the title sequence of *Double Indemnity* begins with a trumpet "anti-fanfare" that's "peppered" with dissonances. (It should be noted, however, that when Rózsa arrived in Hollywood, the "only music [he] found in any way worthwhile was [that of] Erich Wolfgang Korngold."[30])

While Raksin's jazz-inspired music for *Force of Evil* may well conform more closely to the popular conception of the film noir score, it's his music for *Laura*, a "remarkable synthesis of the serious and popular," for which he's most remembered today.[31] (Its popularity is in no small part due to the hit song he composed with Johnny Mercer that appeared after the film's release.) The backstory of Raksin's "monothematic" score for *Laura* is justly memorable. The director Otto Preminger originally wanted the composer to use Duke Ellington and Irving Mills's "Sophisticated Lady" as the basis for the film's music (the same song was also supposed to grace both the jukebox and "Break O' Dawn" sequences in *Detour*), but Raksin argued that it was "wrong for the picture" because it conveyed a particular conception of the title character, whom Preminger bluntly referred to as a "whore."[32]

Raksin won the argument—no mean feat with Preminger—and the result was, in the composer's own words, "magical." A classic passage occurs when Mark McPherson (Dana Andrews) returns to the ostensibly dead woman's apartment late at night and, after searching her bedroom, pours a drink. In order to capture the detective's dreamlike state as he falls asleep beneath Laura's alluring portrait, Raksin turned to the "Len-a-Tone" process to produce a "slight waver" in the piano chord or, more precisely, in the *resonance* of the piano chord.[33] This unusual, otherworldly effect is one example, like Rózsa's use of the theremin in *Spellbound* (1945) and *The Red House* (1947), of the experimentation associated with the music of the more advanced noir composers. It's also a far cry from the "muted trumpet" and the rest of what Raksin called the "plague" of "prostitute" music that, at the time, was the prevailing orchestral "shorthand for representing female sexuality."[34]

If Rózsa's music for *Double Indemnity* and Raksin's for *Laura* illustrate something of the range of the film noir score, Steiner's for *The Big Sleep* (as well as, for that matter, Rózsa's affinity for Korngold) demonstrates the continuity between the noir and classical Hollywood score.[35] The motif for Philip Marlowe (Humphrey Bogart) in Howard Hawks's film is indicative: "part swashbuckling topic and part whimsical comment, the motif seems to be an amalgam of musical ideas" from post-Romantic composers such as Strauss and Mahler.[36] In fact, Marlowe's motif recalls the "great swashbuckling themes" from Korngold's scores for Errol Flynn's films of the 1930s.[37] The point is, the scores of forties noirs are, with respect to melody, harmony, and instrumentation, rather less dark and dissonant than—to pick an instance that is simultaneously exemplary and exceptional—Rózsa's for *The Killers*.

It's therefore not particularly surprising that the other major composer of forties noir, in addition to Rózsa and Roy Webb, is Victor Young, who wrote the music for *The Glass Key*, *Ministry of Fear*, *The Blue Dahlia* (1946), *Calcutta* (1947), *The Big Clock*, *I Walk Alone*, *Night Has a Thousand Eyes* (1948), *The Accused* (1949), and *Chicago Deadline* (1949). As one critic has observed, Young typifies "Hollywood musical techniques during the golden age of the studio system."[38] In fact, despite his very real gift for melody, Young's "musical ideas are never remotely avant-garde,"[39] so much so that Rózsa once remarked—not without pique—that he composed in the "Broadway-cum-Rachmaninoff idiom, which was then the accepted Hollywood style."[40] However, precisely because of its lyricism and popular appeal, Young's music is arguably just as representative of film noir music as the "more modernistic, 'urban' American sound" produced by Rózsa and Raksin.[41] (Just listen to Cyril Mockridge's score for the early Fox noir, *I Wake Up Screaming*

[1941], in which the romantic motif for the relation between Jill Lynn [Betty Grable] and Frankie Christopher [Victor Mature] is "Somewhere over the Rainbow.")

Before I turn to diegetic or source music, I'd also be remiss if I didn't mention Roy Webb at RKO, who scored such forties noirs as *Journey into Fear* (1943), *Cornered* (1945), *Crossfire*, *The Locket*, *They Won't Believe Me*, and *The Window* (1949). In *The Composer in Hollywood*, Christopher Palmer remarks that throughout the 1940s, Webb displayed "considerable sympathy with the world of film noir and skill in translating its nuances into musical terms—largely through a wide spectrum of modern harmonic resource and an understanding of the atmospheric properties of orchestral color, texture, and understatement."[42]

In addition to the above noirs, Webb not only scored two of the seminal films of the genre, *Stranger on the Third Floor* and *Murder, My Sweet*,[43] as well as, for many, the paradigmatic film noir, *Out of the Past*, but many of the classic Val Lewton features, including *Cat People* (1942). Jacques Tourneur's *Cat People*, according to Palmer, is a marvel of "musical chiaroscuro" in which Webb's music, complementing Nicholas Musuraca's cinematography, is the "precise aural equivalent of Lewton's half-heard sounds, half-seen shadows, and atmospheric lighting."[44] In fact, not unlike Webb's score for *Out of the Past*, which is based on the popular song "The First Time I Saw You," a similar practice of creative appropriation informs the score for *Cat People* where the traditional French nursery song "Dodo, l'enfant do" serves as its "thematic basis."[45]

Popular Music: Swing Jazz

As both *Cat People* and *Out of the Past* exhibit, popular music plays a prominent role in forties noir. Constantly referenced in the period's scores, it's perhaps most recognizable in the form of source music performed by a big band or heard via period technologies such as the radio, record player, or jukebox. Delmer Daves's *Dark Passage* (1947) is especially notable in the context because, in conjunction with its novel use of POA sound, POV camerawork, and "live" instrumental band music, it dramatically incorporates the various audio technologies associated with popular music in the 1940s.

However, if swing is the dominant form of popular music in the 1940s, one of the historical ironies of *Dark Passage*—embodied by Jo Stafford, who "exemplifies the postwar period more than any other songbird"[46]—is that by 1947 swing understood as big-band music was rapidly in decline. (This decline was a direct result of the rapid rise of the "solo" vocalist and a distinctly new form of jazz, bebop, both of which events were the result in turn of "war-time travel restrictions" and a "series of musicians' strikes."[47]) Irene Jansen's (Lauren Bacall) passing, seemingly innocuous reference in *Dark Passage* to "legitimate swing" can therefore be read as a symptom of the crisis swing music was undergoing at the time.

Still, in the previous decade (roughly 1935–1945), swing was not just a genre of popular music; it had become an "entire lifestyle."[48] In August 1935, Benny Goodman's band became an "overnight sensation" at the Palomar Ballroom in Los Angeles playing Fletcher Henderson arrangements,[49] and by the early 1940s, a moment that's synonymous with the advent of film noir, a "vast public flocked to hear the big bands," dancing to the music or encircling the bandstand to "listen to the music *as music*"—as, that is, a "certain kind of creative jazz."[50] Although the sort of jazz now associated with classic noir—say, a soprano saxophone solo—would not become common until the 1950s (see, for instance, Raksin's score for *The Big Combo* [1955]),[51] the affinity between forties noir and post-swing jazz has remained stuck in the public imagination, conjuring a scenario composed of "smoke, femme fatales, stormy nights, and weary detectives."[52]

The problem with this evocative, if highly stereotypical, scenario is its implicit valorization of noir's visual style at the expense of an attendant appreciation of the actual music performed *in* the films. The other problem is that despite the fact that music "arises out of the material circumstances of the people who made it and can work profound changes in those circumstances,"[53] it can also appear strangely immaterial, audible but invisible. In other words, the missing link in the royal history of swing is race where Benny Goodman rather than, say, Fletcher Henderson is the "King of Swing." It's an "ironic and sad truth," Gunther Schuller writes, "that the very style which succeeded with Goodman had already existed and flourished three or four years earlier in precisely the same form with Fletcher Henderson's orchestra."[54]

This said (and one cannot perhaps say it enough), the history of swing, however reified, is not simply a black and white thing. "Even if everyone was not aware that Benny Goodman's hugely popular band was playing the arrangements of Fletcher Henderson after 1935, they knew that many black bands played in similar styles," Krin Gabbard records, just as they knew that the "more exciting dance styles were derived from black vernacular dance."

In fact, while plenty of people, both black and white, deplored swing as "degenerate," many white Americans enthusiastically embraced the music because it displayed elements associated with black popular culture such as "spontaneity, transgressiveness, and, most importantly, sexuality."[55]

Illustration: *Among the Living*

A neglected film that illuminates the crossroads of jazz and noir circa 1941—not to mention, like *Cat People* and *Stranger on the Third Floor*, the historical relation between horror and noir—is *Among the Living*. Critics have commented on the role of Paramount, the director Stuart Heisler (who would go on to helm *The Glass Key*), and the cinematographer Theodor Sparkuhl (a veteran of both German Expressionism and French Poetic Realism) in the production of *Among the Living*, but its use of sound and source music is equally "brilliant" and "evocative."[56]

Paul Raden (Albert Dekker) has been presumed dead since childhood by his brother John (also played by Albert Dekker), though in fact he's been "among the living," protected by the family doctor Saunders and sequestered in the ruined family mansion where he's been faithfully cared for by a black servant, Pompey (Ernest Whitman). Traumatized as a child by his mother's death at the hands of his father, Paul puts his hands over his ears every time he hears someone screaming, a scenario that's invoked at the very beginning of *Among the Living* when John Raden returns home for his father's funeral and discovers Pompey dead with his hands over his ears.

After Paul escapes to a boarding house where he makes the acquaintance of the sexually flirtatious Millie Pickens (Susan Hayward), he's wandering downtown one night when he hears music issuing from a café, the camera tracking with him as he descends some steps and pauses to survey the couples drinking at tables and jitterbugging on the dance floor. A woman with blond hair and a hand on one hip, Peggy Nolan (Jean Phillips), stands looking up at Paul, but he doesn't register her gaze. (To paraphrase Geoff Mayer, she's a cruder double of the "mercenary" Millie.[57]) A dancing woman bumps into Paul and he starts to leave until a black waiter rushes over and encourages him to stay.

While the waiter, shuffling to the music, shows him to his table, Paul pauses again to touch a woman's hair ("That's such a nice perfume"). Peggy intervenes when the woman's male friend, Eddie, is about to punch Paul, but the ensuing three-shot in which the waiter pulls out a chair for Paul and Peggy inquires, "All by yourself?" mirrors his increasing entrapment. After Paul says he's hungry and Peggy orders two bourbons for them ("Aw, you shouldn't oughta eat on an empty stomach"), the action on the dance floor begins to parallel her seduction: a man twists a woman in place, her skirt flying, then after picking her up and touching her down, slides her between his legs.

Although Paul's clearly baffled ("What are they doing?"), he imitates Peggy and downs his shot, exclaiming, "It makes you feel kind of funny inside." The beat of the music suddenly picks up and the camera cuts to the dance floor, tilting down to a shot of the dancers' flashing legs. Paul rocks his head to a rhythmic series of trumpet blasts until, squinting his eyes, he becomes disoriented, an altered state of consciousness captured by a brief passage of dissonant music on the sound track. Noticing Paul's distraction, Peggy says, "What's the matter, don't you like my looks?" but when he says he prefers Millie, she gets up and starts dancing with another man, Frank, who laughs loudly in Paul's face. As the horns, climbing, begin to bleat (the music appears to be electronically distorted to mimic Paul's agitated point of audition), there's a violent montage—a man pushing his hand in a woman's face, another woman screaming offscreen—that's crowned by a close-up of Peggy laughing out loud like Frank.

Once Paul sits back down in his seat, there's another lightning montage—intercut with close-ups of Paul's face, the jukebox, and wildly dancing feet—of Eddie and his girl raucously laughing, a woman slapping her male partner, a man in a hat playing the harmonica, a woman throwing her arms drunkenly around a man's neck, and, most importantly for my purposes, the black waiter grinning and snapping his fingers. The sequence climaxes with a delirious mix of suggestive sound-images set to "hot" jazz: first, a male dancer performs an aerial with his female partner, flipping her over his back and baring her underwear, then, after Peggy laughs out loud again and Eddie punches a man in the face, another woman screams. Paul, terrified, puts his hands over his ears, then stands up, knocking the glasses off the table before stumbling drunkenly out of the club.

The jitterbug sequence in *Among the Living* lasts less than a minute and is composed of almost forty shots, but the open-mouthed, eye-bugging shot of the black waiter (played by Clarence Muse)—an image that echoes Pompey's death at the film's beginning and the townspeople's desire to lynch John Raden at the end—dramatically sutures the montage. Although it's impossible to determine the "color" of the musicians who performed the song on the jukebox, the stereotypical behavior of the waiter ultimately codes it as "black." This racial coding is not insignificant since the jitterbug sequence is succeeded by the equally seminal one in which Paul stalks Peggy as she walks home, her heels clicking on the rain-wet pavement, a passage that prefigures similar sequences in *Cat People*, *Phantom Lady*, and *The Seventh Victim* (1943).[58] In fact, precipitated as it is by a scream, Paul's murder of the "B-girl" at the end of the alley, composed in a deep-focus long shot that's a quintessential noir image of "terror, pathos, and alienation,"[59] not only links the jitterbug and street sequences but also associates jazz music, itself linked with blackness, with the spectacle of sexual violence.

While the jitterbug sequence in *Among the Living* indexes blackness, it's important to reiterate that jazz or swing music is also audibly and visibly performed by black musicians in such forties noirs as *When Strangers Marry*, a film that complicates the extant literature on the negative representation of African Americans in classic noir.[60] The key here is performance, which nevertheless remains a vexed issue in jazz given that the "grinning black man" was once the "most widely disseminated image of black musicianship in America."[61] There's also, of course, the related issue of cultural prejudice: "Negroes have always been a race of entertainers," the American composer Elliott Carter once opined, "whose tradition is outside that of serious music."[62]

Among the Living is again instructive. Clarence Muse, who plays the shuffling waiter, co-wrote *Broken Strings* (1940) and co-authored *Way Down South* (1939) with Langston Hughes, but after playing the "kindly Nigger Jim"—what Bogle calls the "archetypal tom"—in the 1931 version of *Huckleberry Finn*, he was subsequently typecast as a "tom" throughout the 1940s.[63] *Among the Living* is also symptomatic given that the Hollywood convention at the time for representing black music was the "grinning black man" in conjunction with jitterbugging dancers.

Still, the combination of a jitterbugging couple and "grinning black man" does not, as *Jammin' the Blues* (1944) demonstrates, a stereotypical film make (the grinning black man in *Jammin' the Blues* is drummer Jo Jones) since just such a judgment elides, among other things, the integral role of black vernacular dance in both jazz and swing culture.[64] Thus, although *When Strangers Marry* features a grinning black piano player *and* a black couple doing the Lindy Hop, the film's point of view and audition arguably turn the stereotypes, like a glove, inside out: not only are the white couple, who are on the lam, subject to the intense gaze of the black patrons, but the place is jumpin' while Paul and Millie can only sit on their hands, alienated and unhappy.

Noir Songbird

If the relation between music and blackness in classic noir is neither as simple nor as negative as some critics have contended, the reflexive association of noir with jazz is also misleading. A review of a wide range of forties noirs —rather than, say, a representative sample (which, frankly, all too often tends to be the same representative sample)—reveals a variety of instrumental source music, including, in addition to jazz, folk (*Desperate* [1947]), Chinese (*Sleep, My Love* [1948]), Latin (*Too Late for Tears* [1949]), and classical (see, for example *par excellence*, the Hollywood Bowl scene in *Double Indemnity*). In addition to showcasing strictly instrumental performances, forties noir is also studded with sequences where characters, sometimes featured ones, sing and accompany themselves on piano or guitar.

For most viewers, of course, the dominant image of source music in the period is not, say, a singer–piano player but a female vocalist backed by a big band. As Will Friedwald recounts, the age of the female big-band singer began on September 15, 1931, when Jack Kapp put Mildred Bailey—one of the three "white goddesses" (the other two were Connee Boswell and Lee Wiley)—"in front of the Casa Loma Orchestra," a band that, together with Benny Goodman's, can be said to have started the swing craze.[65] (The preeminent "femme fatale" of post–Bessie Smith jazz and blues is, of course, Billie Holiday.[66]) Little more than a decade later, around the time that bebop was brewing and Bird was playing "Cherokee" at the Savoy, the "Swing Era" became the "Sing Era." In September 1942, the year that Glenn Miller and other band leaders joined the armed services, "Frank Sinatra took a step that had not worked for any male singer since the Swing Era began: he went solo."[67]

Despite the eventual "conquest of the crooners" (not only Sinatra but Crosby ephebes like Perry Como and "black Bings" like Herb Jeffries), big-band male vocalists remain virtually absent in forties noir. (Ken Williams's character, David Street, croons the title song in *Moonrise* and the guitarist Tony Romano sings "If I Could Be with You" in the melo-noir *The Man I Love*, but the most memorable performance is arguably by Dick Haymes, whose rich baritone voice can be heard on the jukebox in *Fallen Angel*.) One reason for the relative absence of male vocalists in film noir no doubt has to do with the requirements of the genre. Men in film noir are supposed to be rough and tough, not "frail" like Sinatra, and detectives, pace Dennis Potter, don't sing—except perhaps Irish ones like Lieutenant Muldoon in *The Naked City*.

In the hard, rigidly demarcated world of noir, as the contemporary *Big Book of Swing* (1946) spells out, women are the songbirds: "The canaries, as they are called in the language of swing, are those lovely, lissome ladies who sing your favorite popular tunes."[68] If the diction here ("ladies"), not to mention alliteration (all those *l*'s), puts a candy-colored gloss on the phenomenon of swing "songbirds," their lives, as various autobiographies attest, were in fact closer to those of chorus girls than opera divas. (The best memoir is *High Times, Hard Times* in which jazz vocalist Anita O'Day chronicles how she had an abortion when she was twenty—this in 1939—and was the first "girl" singer to wear a band jacket and matching skirt and shirt instead of a dress.)

A complex "figure of modernity" like the Ziegfeld girl and her transatlantic peers, the chanteuse and the cabaret singer, the "canary" was "split between cutting edge and retrograde discourses: on one hand, the new female independence in mixed-sex working and leisure worlds and, on the other hand, the connotations of the oldest profession in the world."[69] In other words, if the canary, as the lone woman in an otherwise all-male band and working outside the sacrosanct precincts of hearth and home, signified sexual and economic autonomy, precisely because of this separation from the family and domestic sphere, she also conveyed sexual availability and emotional vulnerability—at least on stage. There, *up* there, female vocalists "decorated the fronts of swing bands like the figureheads on a ship" (Friedwald's review of the swing period begins, appropriately enough, with the "Hellenic era"—Helen Ward, Helen O'Connell, Helen Forrest),[70] a spectacular position or, more properly, pedestal that accorded with classical Hollywood's construction of women as objects of the gaze.

Still, pace Mulvey, female big-band vocalists were not simply looked at but actively *listened to*, an auditory register that endows their personas with a crucial performative dimension. At once visible *and* audible "icons of femininity," forties female singers were public custodians of "private emotion," whether it was the "blue," down-and-out travails of sex represented by the torch song, the hot urban thrum of the up-tempo swing number, or the "heightened promise of love" embodied by the sweet romantic ballad.[71]

Indeed, the complexity of this address—Are these women, like the songs they perform, slow or fast, hot or sweet?—captures the oxymoronic figure of the noir songbird who, at least for male characters, is at once unreadable and irresistible.

Given this ambiguity or undecidability, the female singers in forties noir who are protagonists or major characters—for example, Ellen Graham in *This Gun for Hire*, Abigail Manette/Jackie Lamont in *Christmas Holiday*, Vivian Sternwood in *The Big Sleep*, Veda Pierce in *Mildred Pierce*, Nora Prentiss in *Nora Prentiss*, and Elizabeth Hintten in *The Bribe*—are ultimately not so much femme fatales as "good-bad girls."[72] There are definitely "bad girl" singers in forties noir, but the real sirens—Kitty Collins in *The Killers*, Lili in *Scene of the Crime*, Coral Chandler in *Dead Reckoning*, and Elsa Bannister in *The Lady from Shanghai*—tend, despite the received wisdom, to be a distinct minority.

Even Coral Chandler, who's an even match for Bogart's postwar detective Rip Murdock in *Dead Reckoning* and the kind of woman who leaves burn marks on the men drawn to her hard flame, is redeemed in the deus-ex-machina coda, albeit not as an angelic thrush but—according to the film's exorbitant calculus—a male paratrooper, "Mike." This last-minute transubstantiation is why characters such as Lili in *Scene of the Crime* and, in a slightly different context, Elsa Bannister in *The Lady from Shanghai* are so compelling. While Lili remains unrepentant to the bitter end, a state of affairs that utterly dashes police detective Mike Conovan's (Van Johnson) "good girl" illusions about her, Elsa mocks Michael O'Hara's (Orson Welles) pretensions to goodness even as she's dying.

If there's a commonality between the "good-bad" and "bad girl" singers in classic noir, it's that the men in their lives, occasionally a husband and more often a nightclub owner, end up dead, if only indirectly. (The exception again is Coral Chandler in *Dead Reckoning*, who's directly responsible for the death of two husbands, one public and one private.) In the final analysis, though, what really unites these diverse women is their occupation as performers. Richard Dyer has observed that Gilda is the only femme fatale who dances,[73] which is not, strictly speaking, true (though it *is* true that nobody dances quite like Hayworth). Lili in *Scene of the Crime* does a "reverse" striptease that's just as tantalizing as it sounds, and Anna in *Criss Cross* (1949) is a whirling dervish on the dance floor of the appropriately titled Round Up.

But as Elsa Bannister in *The Lady from Shanghai* and Jackie Lamont in *Christmas Holiday* demonstrate, you don't have to physically move to be mesmerizing. In Welles's "mystery," Elsa, singing as she reclines like an odalisque on a yacht cruising the Caribbean, could make Neptune weep. And in Robert Siodmak's noir musical set at a New Orleans cat-house during Christmas, Jackie Lamont as channeled by Deanna Durbin and her coloratura chops is —to sample James Agee's description of *The Big Sleep*—a "smoky cocktail" of Saint Teresa and Saint Sebastian with a splash of Billie Holiday. For these sirens as for Sinatra, the song is everything.

Prologue

SMALL WORLD, BIG SIGN

While it might be appropriate to begin a book on sound and source music in forties noir with a film whose effects are exorbitant, I want instead to open with one that is arguably structured around its other: silence. The film is Jacques Tourneur's *Out of the Past*, and although it exhibits most of what might be called the genre's sonic semantics (music, effects, hard-boiled dialogue, voice-over narration), part of its uniqueness derives from the eloquent pantomime of the deaf-mute boy, the Kid (Dickie Moore), who has, as it were, the last word.

However, even before the Kid appears on screen for the first time, the film is not without acoustic incident. For example, Roy Webb's overture can be said to begin with the fanfare that accompanies the famous RKO logo where the letters—"A-n R-K-O R-a-d-i-o P-i-c-t-u-r-e"—materialize in sync with bolts of electricity emitted from a radio tower perched atop the revolving cloud-massed globe. The overture proper commences with the romantic theme that dominates both the narrative and the diegesis of *Out of the Past*, a "haunting theme song" that, as James Naremore notes, is played by the studio orchestra as well as "every jazz band and barroom pianist in sight."[1]

Naremore also notes that the theme song had been used the previous year in another RKO production, *Crack-Up* (1946), though the song in fact comes, true to the studio's rigorous policy of recycling, from an even earlier

RKO film, *The Toast of New York* (1937). In this Rowland V. Lee musical, Josie Mansfield (Frances Framer) is playing a harp and singing "The First Time I Saw You," the music and lyrics of which were written by Nat Shilkret and Allie Wrubel: "The first time I saw you / I knew at a glance / I was meant to be yours, yours alone." (Wrubel would later go on to pen the music for the central song of *I Walk Alone*, "Don't Call It Love," which I discuss in chapter 6.) The title sequence of *Out of the Past* consists of a series of still shots of the northern Sierra Californian landscape—from mountains and lakes to fields and streams—and Webb's overture, sans lyrics, sounds an appropriately bucolic, even idyllic note. This, it seems to say, is God's country.

Near the end of the title sequence, the camera pans to the right in order to capture part of a sign ("Bridgeport / 1 mile"), then pans again to the right in sync with a dark sedan traveling on a road that gently curves into town. As the music begins to crescendo (timed to coincide with the producer Warren Duff's name), the camera, mounted in the rear of the car, puts us behind the wheel of the convertible with a man who's dressed all in black: black hat, black gloves, black overcoat. This dynamic cut on action breaks the meditative spell produced by the natural tableaux and Webb's overture, thrusting us into the world of the film, as if we too are just now entering the precincts of this small town. Not so incidentally, this shot is signed by the film's director, Jacques Tourneur.

Consequently, we learn that the mysterious man in black, Joe Stefanos (Paul Valentine),[2] is an associate of a "big op" named Whit Sterling (Kirk Douglas). There's unfinished business between Whit and Jeff Bailey (Robert Mitchum) and, as in the beginning of *The Killers* (1946), Jeff's time, like the Swede's, is up. What Stefanos sees is simple enough but still cause for wonder, a proprietary sign for a gas station that reads "Jeff Bailey." (Another smaller sign—"Mono Motor Service"—reflects Jeff's solitary nature and monosyllabic manner of speaking.) The wide reverse shot of the first, slightly low-angled one is a high-angled shot that shows Stefanos standing in the left foreground and, in the middle ground, a boy squatting, completely absorbed in fixing a tire. In the silence, which is palpable compared to the opening credit sequence, Stefanos whistles at the boy. When the Kid doesn't look up, Stefanos takes out a pack of cigarettes and hits the car horn. When the boy still doesn't respond, he lights a cigarette, then throws the match at the tire, a rather callous act that nevertheless catches the Kid's attention and, of course, comments on Stefanos's character.

The first line of dialogue in *Out of the Past* is a question that, since Jeff

Fig. 1. Juke Gangster: Joe Stefanos (Paul Valentine) plays the jukebox while eavesdropping on Marny (Mary Field) and Jim (Richard Webb) in Jacques Tourneur's *Out of the Past*.

Markham has been hiding out in Bridgeport as Jeff Bailey, cuts right to the heart of the picture: "Where's Bailey?" In response to Stefanos's query, the boy smiles, then gestures to his mouth and ears, and Stefanos remarks, almost to himself, "Deaf and dumb, eh?" Just then, a car with a State of California seal on the door passes and first Stefanos and then the Kid turn their heads to look, at which point the man asks, "Can you read lips?" After the boy nods, Stefanos asks the question again, this time carefully pronouncing each word, "Where is Bailey?" and the Kid gestures to a place off in the distance. Stefanos continues, "Coming back today?" but when the boy doesn't answer quickly enough, he impatiently snaps his fingers. Finally, the Kid nods his head and Stefanos, satisfied for the moment, leaves for the diner across the street while the boy, a quizzical look on his face, starts off for the lake.

The exchange between Stefanos and the Kid is one-sided, although not so much because the boy is deaf and dumb as that he intuitively knows that this man, who is a stranger and asks a lot of questions, is not to be trusted. The scene at Marny's Café therefore represents a moment of restablization in the film: her running commentary, ceaseless as it is, returns us to a more familiar, less alien world, a small-town milieu where everybody knows everybody else's business. (The sign outside Marny's Café, right above the entrance, reads "Freeze Your Fish," which is at once familial and, like Marny [Mary Field] herself, oddly chilling.) The smallness of Marny's world is almost immediately counterpointed by the big-band music that Stefanos plays on the jukebox, which not only reintegrates the orchestral music played under the title sequence but, precisely because Stefanos has selected it, evokes the big city as well as the glamorous nightlife associated with it, the shows and clubs and bright lights.

The ensuing conversation between Marny and Jim (Richard Webb), a local game warden (it's his car that we saw earlier), speaks volumes about the differences between the city and the country. The composition, a three-shot, is equally eloquent: Marny stands talking with Jim who's sitting at the counter playing with a salt shaker while, sitting a few seats down, Stefanos smokes a cigarette and listens. (As Whit later says about Jeff, he knows when to stay inside himself.) In no time at all, we learn, along with Stefanos, that there are two things that Marny can "smell within a hundred feet": "a burning hamburger and a romance."

In fact, the conversation between Marny and Jim is as one-sided as that between Stefanos and the boy. The first time around, Jim tries, albeit awkwardly, to flatter her:

JIM: You dye your hair?
MARNY: Why?
JIM: I always keep thinking of you as a blonde.
MARNY: For all the thinking you do about me, I could be bald-headed.

Even though Jim is obviously no match for Marny, he continues to try bantering with her. Jim: "Did you miss me, honey?" Marny: "If you didn't, I can't think of anyone else who did." The third time around, Marny has him on the ropes:

MARNY: One thing's sure. That Bailey don't miss nothing.
JIM: Neither do you.
MARNY: She's your girl and he ain't my man, so it's no skin off my nose. I just see what I see.

Jim tries to counterpunch, but Marny's too quick on her feet:

JIM: Are you sure you don't see what you hear?

MARNY: Nothing can happen in this town that I don't hear about across this counter. I'm just saying what I see. Every day they go fishing together.

Trying to distract Marny, Jim says, "Look, the sandwich." Marny moves down the counter to take Stefanos's order, but before she gets his coffee and cream, she returns to Jim and, unhappily for him, picks up right where she left off, "First she's got you, now she's got you and Bailey, and the only thing I seem to get is older." After Jim, defeated, gets up and leaves, taking his half-eaten ham-and-rye sandwich with him (he's had quite enough repartee for one day), Marny wonders out loud, "I guess I must've said something." A cigarette stuck in his mouth, Stefanos answers her with laconic finality, "You talked enough."

The last bit of dialogue between Marny and Stefanos is, like the conclusion, signal. In the shadows of the inverted letters of the sign on the window through which Marny watches Bailey going about his daily business, Stefanos waxes philosophical, "I often wondered what happened to [Bailey]. Then one day I'm breezing through here, there's his name up on a sign." Marny for once is terse, "Small world," but Stefanos—who, unlike Jim, is versed in the ways of the world and can talk the talk and walk the walk—is pointed as a gun: "Or a big sign."

1

House Sound

REVERB, OFFSCREEN SOUND, AND VOICE-OVER NARRATION IN EARLY RKO NOIR

In the wake of Warner Bros.'s sound-on-disc *Don Juan* (1926) and *The Jazz Singer* (1927), "Hollywood scrambled on to the bandwagon of sound," Richard Jewell writes, "and gave birth to a new child of the revolution," RKO (Radio-Keith-Orpheum).[1] Another, related result of the sound revolution in American cinema was that, under the stewardship of President David Sarnoff, Radio Corporation of America (RCA) invented the Photophone system of optical sound-on-film to compete with the current, near-monopolistic Western Electric system and, to showcase it, acquired a "substantial interest" in Film Booking Offices of America, Inc. (FBO).[2] After FBO merged with the Keith-Albee-Orpheum circuit of vaudeville houses (movie theatres were a necessary component for the success of the Photophone formula), RKO was born, "legend has it," in a Manhattan oyster restaurant.[3]

Cut to 1941 and *the* pearl in the RKO oyster, *Citizen Kane*. Orson Welles's picture and the history surrounding it have also become the stuff of legend, but if *Citizen Kane* is one reason RKO has a special place in the history of film noir, another reason is Boris Ingster's *Stranger on the Third Floor* (1940), which, like *Citizen Kane*, began filming circa June 1940. Of course, in terms of production and reception, the two films couldn't be more different: whereas the making of the "A" *Citizen Kane* was a subject of intense speculation in

Hollywood and its reception even more tumultuous because of William Randolph Hearst's interventionist tactics, *Stranger on the Third Floor* was a "B" picture, albeit a "premium B" picture, that died a quick and quiet death at the box office.[4]

In fact, the production of Welles's and Ingster's films reflects the changing corporate structure at RKO. The departure of production chief Pandro S. Berman in 1939 represented the end of an era, one symbolized by the films of Fred Astaire and Ginger Rogers, "the most famous, profitable, and artistically ambitious series in RKO annals."[5] Incoming president George Schaefer, "the tiger," resolved to "turn RKO into a 'quality' studio" like M-G-M, which Berman had just departed for and which, unlike RKO, was recognized for "prestige" pictures rather than the "B-level melodramas, erratic comedies, and escapist musicals which had characterized its past."[6] Still, one of the legacies of the pre-Schaefer regime at RKO is that president Leo Spitz —who, along with Berman, had resurrected RKO after it declared bankruptcy in 1934—instructed B-unit producer Lee Marcus to make "some exploitation pictures" of a "topical and slightly sensational nature."[7]

One shining example of Marcus's "B" unit is *Stranger on the Third Floor*, "a premature *film noir*, [and] a picture that should, by all historical rights, have been produced in 1944 or 1943—not 1940."[8] I will return to 1944, the year in which film noir as a genre can be said to have blossomed like some *fleur du mal*, as well as yet another regime change and seminal "black film," *Murder, My Sweet*, but if *Citizen Kane* "introduced visual flourishes and narrative techniques that *noir* filmmakers would seize on later in the decade," it was the "unheralded director" Boris Ingster (who, I think it's safe to say, has not been confused with Orson Welles) and, until recently, the "largely forgotten" *Stranger on the Third Floor* that "first anticipated film noir."[9]

Given the intertwined destinies of *Citizen Kane* and *Stranger on the Third Floor* at RKO, it's no surprise the two films share a particular look—for example, art direction and special effects by Van Nest Polglase and Vernon L. Walker, respectively—as well as a standout sound design in the person of recordist Bailey Fesler, a veteran of radio who received his first credit in 1930 as a recording engineer on *The Pay Off*. While the extensive credits for *Citizen Kane* list Fesler as the production mixer and James G. Stewart as the dubbing mixer (the two also collaborated on *The Magnificent Ambersons* [1942] and the proto-noir *Fallen Sparrow* [1943]), *Stranger on the Third Floor*, befitting its lowly "B" status, has a truncated list of credits. In fact, in *Film Noir: An Encyclopedic Reference to the American Style*, the entry for Ingster's film (unlike the majority of those in this standard reference book) does not even include a credit for sound.[10]

Two things are pertinent here: one, the division of labor at RKO, and two, Stewart's role at the studio. With respect to the organization of personnel at RKO, as early as 1930 Carl Dreher, the director of the Sound Department, had distinguished between the "first recordist" (who corresponded, in Dreher's words, to the "first cinematographer") and a rerecording "specialist" who supervised the "production of sound effects."[11] In a prescient passage, Dreher, anticipating the increasing specialization of cinematic sound (re)production, allowed that although it is a "moot point . . . whether the re-recording should be done by a specialist or by the first recordist who originally made the sound for the picture," the "best *system* is probably to assign re-recording to a specialist who knows the capabilities of his equipment and the best method of adapting the final sound version of the film . . . with consulting service by the original recordist, the cutter assigned to the picture, and the director or his deputy."[12]

With respect to Stewart and the studio system, in 1931 he left RCA Photophone—where he "designed, installed, and maintained some of the very first sound systems, including Radio City Music Hall"—for RKO where he was hired to "develop a noise reduction system."[13] However, due to Depression-related financial constraints, he became instead a "stage man" or boom operator, then, after suffering sun stroke in 1933 shooting John Ford's *Lost Patrol* (1934) in the Yuma desert, he was asked to sit in on some dubbing sessions at the studio and, soon after, became the chief rerecording mixer at RKO. In fact, Stewart, who is officially credited as the dubbing mixer on—to note only his forties noirs—*Journey into Fear*, *Experiment Perilous* (1944), *Johnny Angel* (1945), and *Deadline at Dawn* (1946), not only embodies the historical shift in classic Hollywood cinema from recording to *re*recording but RKO's distinctive house sound.[14] As Robert Carringer has written, "the high quality of sound for which RKO product was generally known can be attributed to him."[15]

As Stewart himself recollects in "The Evolution of Cinematic Sound," in the immediate period before his move to RKO, the "major emphasis" in the motion-picture industry—a "holdover from the days of radio"—was on production sound with "little thought given to the possibilities of improving the sound after the original recording had been completed."[16] Simply put, almost all sound was produced on the set: "the track recorded on the set was the track used on the film."[17] When it eventually became obvious, though, that there was a decided "advantage in putting sound effects and music into the product *after* it had been completed on the stage and edited in the cutting room," the emphasis gradually began to shift from recording to rerecording.[18] One net effect of this increased emphasis on *post*-production ("We'll fix it in rerecording!") was that almost overnight dubbing mixers "became the heroes of the recording process," so much so that by 1935, the "supervising dubbing mixer on a production attained about equal rank with the editor of the picture" and even, occasionally, the director.[19]

Stranger on the Third Floor

Although Stewart is not listed in the credits for *Stranger on the Third Floor*, he may well have been involved in its production since "unlike some department heads who were only nominally involved . . . Stewart worked on virtually every RKO film" from 1937 to 1945.[20] More specifically, Ingster's film, like *Citizen Kane*, features montage and voice-over narration, which are typically the province of the dubbing mixer.[21]

Whatever Stewart's exact role on *Stranger on the Third Floor*, the sound track is remarkable for its time, a fact recognized by Bosley Crowther, the reviewer for the *New York Times* who opined not only that Ingster's film appeared to derive inspiration from "radio drama" (cf. *Citizen Kane*) but that the "notion seems to have been that the way to put a psychological melodrama across is to pile on the sound effects and trick up the photography."[22] Crowther was not especially enamored of *Stranger on the Third Floor*, but his pejorative précis of Ingster's picture—piled-up sound effects and tricked-up photography—captures the audiovisual one-two punch of early RKO noir.

Though the technique has become virtually "invisible" because of its prominence in film noir, the most striking sonic device in *Stranger on the Third Floor* is voice-over or, to invoke its audiovisual format, flashback/voice-over narration. In *Invisible Storytellers* Sarah Kozloff has traced voice-over narration in fiction film to, among others, Fritz Lang's *M*. However, it was not until 1939 and the convergence of several factors such as newsreels ("The March of Time"), documentaries (*The City* [1939]), and radio drama ("The Mercury Theatre of the Air") that voice-over narration began to flourish with the release of *Juarez*, *Wuthering Heights*, *The Roaring Twenties*, and *Confessions of a Nazi Spy*. "The ice was broken," the "stream of narrated films deepened into a flood," and the "1940s became the technique's golden age."[23] As for the visual axis of voice-over narration, Maureen Turim in *Flashbacks in Film* has identified two major types of noir flashback, the "investigative," as in the early Fox noir, *I Wake Up Screaming* (1941), and the "confessional," as illustrated by *Stranger on the Third Floor*.[24]

Flashback/voice-over narration is not, as Kozloff and Turim recognize, unique to film noir, but *Stranger on the Third Floor* is arguably central to its development in terms of both this technique and the use of expressionist dream sequences (which are indebted, as the first epithet indicates, to German Expressionism). Frank Krutnik summarizes this creative synthesis, writing that *Stranger on the Third Floor* "is now generally regarded as the first film noir of the 1940s [and] contains several flashbacks, voice-over narration, and an extended dream sequence."[25] In her historical account of noir during the war years, Sheri Chinen Biesen also refers to the film's "voice-over narration" and "haunting voice-over,"[26] although as Turim suggests ("the form of the flashbacks . . . tries to mimic interior thoughts"), the enunciative mode of *Stranger on the Third Floor* is not, strictly speaking, voice-over narration but interior monologue.[27]

Whereas voice-over narration tends to produce a "temporal dislocation of the voice with respect to the body," in interior monologue, according to Mary Ann Doane, "the voice and the body are represented simultaneously, but the voice, far from being an extension of that body, manifests its inner lining. The voice displays . . . the 'inner life' of the character."[28] In other words, interior monologue in *Stranger on the Third Floor* is a "primitive" form of voice-over narration and, in its intimate association with paranoia, can be said to anticipate this technique as it appears in its classic, mature form in *Double Indemnity* and *Murder, My Sweet*.

Unlike *Double Indemnity* and *Murder, My Sweet*, which are based on the first-person, hard-boiled fiction of, respectively, James M. Cain and Raymond Chandler (Chandler of course also co-authored the screenplay of *Double Indemnity* with Billy Wilder), *Stranger on the Third Floor* was adapted by former newspaper reporter Frank Partos from his own original story and "polished" by Nathanael West. (Partos also worked as a screenwriter on another, early proto-noir, John Brahm's *Rio* [1939] and later collaborated with Chandler on *And Now Tomorrow* [1944].) While the influence of *The Cabinet of Dr. Caligari* (1920) on *Stranger on the Third Floor* can be traced to Ingster's tenure at UFA, the film's trial scenes and critique of the criminal justice system as scripted by Partos reflect not only the influence of Lang's first sound film, *M*, as well as his American films *Fury* (1936) and

You Only Live Once (1937) but another, early proto-noir directed by Brahm, *Let Us Live* (1939), a "wrong man" film that, like *You Only Live Once*, stars Henry Fonda.[29]

However, as opposed to, say, *M*, psychopathology in *Stranger on the Third Floor* is associated less with the film's ostensible villain, The Stranger, than with its working-class hero, Mike Ward (John McGuire), whose psyche deteriorates in the course of the narrative to the point where it doubles that of the criminal asylum escapee played by Peter Lorre. Hence the import of Ward's interior monologue in *Stranger on the Third Floor* which, in Ingster's film, becomes the vehicle for what Freud called the psychopathology of everyday life and its various affective disorders: anxiety and alienation, obsession and paranoia.

In concert with Nicholas Musuraca's "mystery" lighting, the sound track of *Stranger on the Third Floor* utilizes the full panoply of classic Hollywood sound—music and dialogue, silence and effects—to stage the psychodrama that befalls Ward, a *New York Star* reporter who's consumed by guilt after getting his first byline when he witnesses a taxi driver, Joe Briggs (Elisha Cook, Jr.), murdering a coffee-shop proprietor named Nick (an act which, not so incidentally, earns him a twelve-dollar raise that will allow him to finally marry his fiancée, Jane [Margaret Tallichet]).

Consider, for example, the silent pantomime that is the film's opening credit sequence. The camera pans up from the street to the third floor of an apartment building where a silhouetted man is shown smoking, typing, and talking on the phone. In retrospect, we take this figure to be Ward, although the silhouette not only recalls the initial, shadowed appearance of Beckert in *M* but intimates, true to the rampant Doppelgänger theme, that it's Ward who is "the stranger on the third floor."

The first prominent sound effect in *Stranger on the Third Floor* occurs when Briggs takes the stand at his own trial and the public defender stops him in mid-sentence to alert the judge, who himself appears to be snoozing, that a juror is snoring, "It's your duty to stay awake." If the farcical nature of the proceedings foreshadows the courtroom sequence in *The Lady from Shanghai*, the tragic and dramatic implications of this gross miscarriage of justice are underscored when Briggs, his voice rising to a scream, appeals first to the judge, then the jury, "I didn't kill him! I didn't, I didn't, I didn't!" Ward proceeds to the pressroom to call his editor, and although we do not see him smoking, the offscreen sound of typing and the sight of him on the telephone animate the opening, "dumb show" credit sequence.

Since the word of a "gentleman of the press" will always trump a taxi-driver's (the former being, according to the prosecutor, a "trained observer of men"), Briggs is preemptively found guilty. But while being led away, he directly petitions the man whose key eyewitness account has convicted him, "Mr. Ward, I didn't do it. You know I didn't do it. He was dead." Ward returns to the pressroom, it's evening, and the deepening shadows on the wall engulf the reporter, who sits alone and despondent at a desk. The subsequent scene, one of the most sonically evocative in the film, anticipates the picture-puzzle sequence in *Citizen Kane*: after Ward exits the pressroom, the camera cuts to a wide shot of him crossing the hall, his footsteps reverberating in the empty, cavernous space, then to a deeper POV shot of the now vacant courtroom accompanied by a sonic flashback of Briggs's screaming, "I didn't do it!"

In addition to severing Briggs's voice from his body and annexing it to Ward's point of audition, thereby radically subjectivizing it, this sonic flashback precipitates Ward's interior monologue. Paradoxically enough, given the connection between noir voice-over narration and hard-boiled masculinity, Ward's interior monologue can be said to feminize him since it's associated with Jane who, unlike Ward, sympathizes with Briggs's plight: when Briggs violently protests the verdict, she puts her hands over her ears and runs crying to the hall outside where she asks her fiancé point blank, "Suppose, for just one minute, he's telling the truth."

Ward tries to buck himself up—"What's the matter with me? I'm getting soft. He did it. Of course, he did"—but his "tough" voice-over is almost immediately countered on the sound track by Jane's disembodied voice: "he's telling the truth." The location of this second sonic flashback on the street (RKO's "New York" set) is especially conspicuous since the ambient noise is drastically muted. Indeed, Fesler almost completely fades down the traffic to italicize Ward's sudden, steep fall into self-consciousness. The reporter's prolonged reverie is interrupted only when he sees that the sign for Nick's All Nite Coffee Pot has already been changed to "Jack's" ("Business as usual") and when, as the romantic motif of Webb's score swells on the sound track, a newspaper boy calls out, "Paper, Mr. Ward." Coupled with the exterior shot of the coffee shop which for Ward is associated with Jane (the film opens with the two meeting cute for breakfast), the newspaper boy's voice is a harsh reminder that his big "break," the byline, now threatens to break up their relationship.

The intrusion of the real world into Ward's reverie sets up our first vision of The Stranger: while Ward's crossing the street lamenting his predicament ("Why did I have to live across the street?"), he sees a small man in a dark hat sitting outside his Riverside Drive apartment fingering his scarf. Sensing Ward's presence, the man looks up, then wanly smiles in recognition, his muteness indexing his uncanny status—he could be a homeless person—as well as Ward's own feeling of being metaphysically unhoused. The latter sentiment is forcefully expressed when the reporter enters the building and, pausing at the third-floor landing, thinks to himself, "What a gloomy dump! Why can't they put in a bigger lamp." (As Biesen remarks, it's as if the film, in the distempered voice of Ward, is self-reflexively commenting on its own impecunious "B" status.[30])

Ward is also seriously aggravated by the sounds of low-income urban housing. Passing the apartment of his neighbor, Albert Meng (Charles Halton), Ward hears him loudly snoring and, even when he's inside his apartment, the cramped studio only seems to magnify the sounds of the "snoring animal next door." Meng's snoring, in fact, is the sonic pretext for the film's first flashback: it's night and Ward is working on a newspaper story, pounding away at a typewriter, when Meng and the landlady knock and enter ("What's the idea of breaking in that way?"). Although Meng claims he can't sleep because of the racket the reporter is making, Ward tells the landlady he's paid his rent, just like Meng, and the flashback ends without, it appears, further ado.

However, when Ward opens the door to go to the washroom, he sees The Stranger peeking out of his apartment, "Who's that?" Pretending to close the door, Ward hides until The Stranger appears again: first we see his hand, snow-white against the black sleeve of his jacket, creeping up the door, then, as he steps out, the camera cuts to a shadow of him theatrically tossing his scarf around his neck. Ward chases him down the stairs, peppering him with questions—"Looking for somebody? What do you want? Who are you?"—but The Stranger, resolutely mute, escapes out the front door. Although Ward surveys the scene—there's a slow, panoramic POV pan from left to right of the empty, silent street ("Where'd the devil he go?")—The Stranger has vanished, hidden in the shadow of the stoop.

Returning to his room, Ward notices Meng isn't snoring—"Why is he so quiet? I can't hear a sound. Is there something wrong with him?"—and instinctively reaches for the knob of his neighbor's door until the prosecutor's voice—in another, even more alarming sonic flashback than Briggs's or Jane's—stops him cold, "You forgot that fingerprints always give you away." Ward quickly retreats to his apartment where, pressed up against the wall, his hand outstretched like The Stranger's, he knocks to see if Meng is still alive. Hearing nothing, he considers knocking again until he realizes he might "wake the whole house": "Why should they think I had anything to do with it? Why did I believe Briggs was guilty? That was different. He said himself he'd kill [Nick] if only he had a gun."

The ornamental knife that Ward picks up ("I've never said anything like that") is the prompt for the second flashback in which Ward is dining at Nick's café with a colleague, Martin. Meng comes in and, after purchasing a bottle of milk, pauses to admire the bared leg of a young woman who has just discovered a run in her stocking. Suddenly, seeing Ward, Meng comes over to his table and chastises him for drinking coffee before bed: milk, according to Meng, "makes you sleep like an innocent babe." When Martin disparages Meng's not-so-innocent behavior ("It looks as though his mind could stand a little laundering"), Ward picks up a dinner knife and asks Martin if he's ever thought of killing a man, adding that "it would be a real pleasure to cut [Meng's] throat."

The violence of Ward's fantasy here, tinged as it is with sadism, reveals the dark, violent side of his personality and sets up the third and final flashback. This flashback, preceded by an oblique mirror shot, provides supplemental motivation for Ward's "crime"; not so incidentally, it also comments on both Meng's voyeurism and Ward's feelings of sexual frustration. It's raining and, since Ward and Jane can't rendezvous as usual in the park, they return to his room where he removes his fiancée's wet shoes before instructing her to take off her stockings. There's a knock at the door and it's Meng and the landlady again: Ward has previously told Jane it's okay to have friends in his room, but in fact he's broken the "rules." The scene climaxes when Meng, ostensibly aghast (but, we surmise, secretly titillated), points out Jane's bare legs, enraging Ward, who threatens to kill him—"I oughta wring your neck!"—until Jane and the landlady intercede.

In the second and third flashbacks Meng is constituted as a "grotesque projection" of Ward's own sexual desire: while Ward is "blocked by circumstances" (and by Jane who is very much a "good girl"), "Meng is 'doubled' with Ward as a figure who can not only frustrate any intimate contact between Ward and Jane but who can openly express sexual interest."[31] (Later, when Ward and Jane are reluctantly leaving his apartment, he whispers to her that Meng must have his "ear glued to the wall.") Consequently, the dream sequence, which enacts Ward's intense, masochistic desire to be punished, is a function of his fantasy of murdering Meng and possessing Jane as well as the "guilt he feels in profiting from the misfortune of Briggs," whom he identified as the murderer of Nick for a "scoop."[32]

Like the "drug" sequence in *Murder, My Sweet*, the dream sequence in *Stranger on the Third Floor* is a stunning "example of one of film noir's . . . 'explosive' [audio]visual set pieces."[33] As such, it's marked by a combination of sonic and cinematographic devices. While offscreen sound is mobilized in *Stranger on the Third Floor*, as in *M*, to articulate the theme of "paranoid obsession,"[34] the heavily reverbed dialogue, a form of aural expressionism courtesy of RKO's acoustic echo chamber, accentuates the hallucinatory quality of the sequence. The first sonic effect fuses, in fact, the use of reverb and "pre-lap," offscreen sound.[35] The camera inexorably tracks in on Ward who, dead tired, has settled back into a wingback chair and, hands over his eyes, is desperately trying to allay his suspicion that Meng is dead. After a man offscreen intones as if from a distance, "Wake up!," another, closer offscreen male voice demands, "Why did you do it?" (Volume and reverberation are masterfully manipulated here in order to suggest the gradual onset of Ward's dream.) The camera stops on a medium, high-angle shot of Ward sitting in a chair encircled by bowler-hatted, cigar-smoking men whose interrogative animosity is amplified by the choker close-ups and echo-enhanced voices, "Speak up! Why did you do it? Why did you kill him? C'mon, come clear. Confess and we'll go easy on you."

Like Briggs, Ward vehemently maintains his innocence—"I didn't, I didn't, The Stranger did it!"—but after a knife materializes from the bottom left-hand side of the screen, a newspaper boy cries out offscreen "Extra! Extra! Read all about it!" and the film dissolves via a ring of fire to an ultra-low-angle shot of Jane, dwarfed by towering skyscrapers (the perspective is forced as in *The Cabinet of Dr. Caligari*), screaming at the headlines of the newspaper in her hands: "Reporter Indicted for Meng Murder." The mode of the dream sequence is montage (Ingster worked as an assistant director on Eisenstein and Aleksandrov's avant-garde surrealist classic, *Romance sentimentale* [1930][36]) in which, as the above two passages of the dream sequence exhibit, the expressive synthesis of sound and image, audio and vision, mirrors Ward's "dislocated perspective."[37]

This phantasmagorical perspective, underscored by Webb's swirling string and brass-punctuated score, is extravagantly on display in the Kafkaesque trial sequence. After the prosecutor laughs in Ward's face when he confesses he's thought about killing Meng, the reporter approaches the jury who, to his abject horror, are fast asleep like the juror at Briggs's trial: "Please, your honor, they're not listening. Make them hear me!" Ignoring Ward, the judge asks the jury for their verdict and, suddenly waking, they stand and point at Ward, chanting in unison "Guilty!" Ward points in turn to The Stranger (who, tossing his scarf around his neck, has miraculously appeared in the gallery), but the judge, composed in a low-angle shot against a cyclorama-swirled background, sentences him to death and Ward can only gaze up helplessly as the judge transforms into the statue of Justice, now with a scythe instead of a sword in her right hand.

In the ensuing execution scene at the state prison, Ward is desperately pleading with the chaplain ("Please, say you don't believe I killed him") when the camera cuts to Briggs laughing at him from behind the bars of a deeply shadowed cell, "Did you believe me?" The final coup de cinéma occurs while Ward is being strapped into the electric chair, a massive silhouette of which is exceeded only by the enormous, diagonal shadows that constitute the chamber's architectural space: Meng suddenly appears, the sound of the metal door clanging after him reprising the audience's last vision of him alive, shutting his door after gleefully watching Ward and Jane exit the reporter's room. The dream sequence ends with the camera fatefully closing in again on Ward who, seeing Meng, screams, "He's alive!"

Familiar from the seminal Universal horror film, *Frankenstein* (1931), this interjection is the bridge from the dream sequence back to everyday life which, in *Stranger on the Third Floor*, mimics the twisted, paranoid logic of the dream. In fact, the exclamation produces a double movement: first the film cuts from a close-up of Ward closing his eyes to a reverse tracking shot of him still asleep in his chair, then cuts again to the reporter waking up and, rubbing his arms (which were strapped to the electric chair at the end of the dream), exclaiming, "Of course, he's alive!" If the second exclamation signifies the objective end of Ward's nightmare, the third time—"Of course, he's alive!"—represents his realization, like Professor Wanley's in *The Woman in the Window*, that his execution was only a dream.

Since it represents the conclusion of Ward's interior monologue, the last exclamation appears to denote a return to reality as opposed to fantasy. However, one of the estranging ironies of *Stranger on the Third Floor*—signified by the command "Wake up!" at the beginning of the dream sequence—is despite the fact that Ward's finally awake, reality itself has become a nightmare. Thus, after wondering out loud "Then why don't I hear [Meng]?," Ward rushes out and knocks on his door. Although this time he's not stopped by the prosecutor's voice, when Meng doesn't answer, he enters the unlocked room to find his neighbor "dead," his jugular slashed like Nick's.

As opposed to the pre-dream part of *Stranger on the Third Floor* in which Ward's thoughts are conveyed via interior monologue, in the post-dream part his monosyllabic utterance "dead" punctuates the triple rhyme of "He's alive!" It also sonically points up Ward's predicament: because he's on record having physically threatened and attacked Meng, he's now in the exact same circumstances as Briggs. The uncanniness of Ward's situation is accented when the reporter, accompanied by a police lieutenant, has to wake the district attorney who, yawning loudly, interrogates Ward about his sanity, "Do you often have nightmares? Tell me, was there ever any insanity in your family?" Ward insists he's as sane as the D.A. ("If you thought I had anything to do with it, you're crazy"), but the D.A., razor in hand, remands him to headquarters as a "material witness."

The scene set in the district attorney's bedroom is the last time we hear Ward's voice until the film's coda. When he calls Jane from the police station to tell her he's been arrested, she's taking dictation from her boss (like another secretary turned detective, Kansas in *Phantom Lady*) and, from this point on, it's not Ward—who is ultimately more victim than hero in *Stranger on the Third Floor*—but Jane who assumes the burden of the film's action, a "courageous" "steno-detective" who "saves her reporter sweetheart from the electric chair."[38]

Jane's perseverance and esprit are featured in a montage that, at least initially, appears pedestrian compared to Ward's dream. Hitting the streets like a seasoned reporter or private detective, Jane queries various working-class people—a cab driver, a man hosing down his garden, a mailman, a woman cleaning a window—about The Stranger, whom she describes as having "big protruding eyes" and a "funny looking, off-white scarf." After an off-kilter shot of a man with a cigar saying "Sorry, lady," the montage, however, begins to accelerate: the wipes turn into dissolves, and close-ups of Jane's legs ascending and descending staircases are superimposed over shots of people silently shaking their heads.

Jane's search appears to have come to a dead end when she stops, exhausted, at a coffee shop where she sits at the counter making small talk with the owner. The door opens and a man offscreen orders a couple of raw hamburgers. Jane looks over and we see The Stranger, speaking for the first time in the film. Since he has been emphatically mute in his previous appearances—on the stoop and stairs of the rooming house, in the courtroom in the dream sequence—the sound of his voice has an express acousmatic charge. At the same time, the moment of deacousmatization when The Stranger speaks is strangely disorienting, not to say disenchanting.

Part of the effect is doubtlessly due to Peter Lorre's peculiar, Hungarian-accented voice which, coupled with his heavily lidded eyes and moon-round face, is not the sort one immediately associates with a throat-slashing murderer. Indeed, unlike the tough-talking characters who populate classic noir, The Stranger is decidedly soft-spoken with an unassuming, even meek demeanor that's reinforced when Jane follows him outside, where we see him feeding the hamburgers to a stray dog, "Here you are, you poor little devil. Don't eat too fast, you'll get a tummy ache." (The Stranger's pathos is reinforced when he tells Jane he can't keep the dog because he has "no home.")

The climax of *Stranger on the Third Floor* inverts one of the classic tropes of both the noir and horror film: when The Stranger says goodnight to Jane, she begins to follow him rather than vice versa. As the two walk down a deserted street at night, the sound of their footsteps ricocheting against the buildings, The Stranger wonders if the asylum has sent her, then confesses he killed Nick and Meng because they were going to report him to the authorities. Seizing her chance to clear her fiancé's name, Jane tells The Stranger that the brownstone they're standing in front of is her apartment, but when she rings the bell and the woman who comes to the door says she's going to call the police (it's clear she's been rudely awakened), The Stranger realizes what's happening and starts to strangle her.

Although Jane manages to break free, running into the street crying for help, The Stranger pursues her until the sudden sound of a horn and screeching tires, punctuated by Jane's scream, marks his foreordained demise. The concluding dialogue of the sequence, unlike the film's coda, is downbeat and strangely recursive: while the driver proclaims his innocence à la Briggs and Ward (he claims it's not his fault), Jane agrees to be a witness to the accident and The Stranger, defiant to the end, vows, "I'll not go back."[39]

Intermission

I will return to *Stranger on the Third Floor* in the conclusion of this chapter, but suffice it to say that its audacious dream sequence, pervasive atmosphere of paranoia, and inventive use of interior monologue pave the way for what we now consider classic noir. The "investigative" voice-over flashback structure of *Citizen Kane* is clearly an influence on the genre (see/hear, for example, *The Killers*), but the "confessional" nature of the interior monologue in *Stranger on the Third Floor* can be said to presage not only Walter Neff's Dictaphone-mediated "confession" to Barton Keyes in *Double Indemnity* but the equally quintessential voice-over narration of private investigator Philip Marlowe in *Murder, My Sweet*. (Although *Laura* was released by Twentieth Century–Fox slightly earlier in 1944 than *Murder, My Sweet*, Preminger's film is narrated by the film's "antagonist," Waldo Lydecker, not the police detective Mark McPherson.)

Although the point of view of Cain's *Double Indemnity* is first person (the narrative is the notarized statement that Walter Huff has agreed to write for Keyes so he can catch a steamer out of San Pedro), the key to the film's voice-over narration is Raymond Chandler, who had famously exploited the device in his novels. RKO, as I've noted, was nothing if not opportunistic. It was the first studio to adapt a Chandler novel to the "silver screen" (it made *Farewell, My Lovely* into *The Falcon Takes Over* in 1942), jumping on the "red meat," "crime and romance bandwagon" initiated by Paramount's *Double Indemnity*[40] when the Chandler-Wilder script for *Double Indemnity* received Joseph Breen's imprimatur in September 1943. While RKO did not submit the new script for *Farewell, My Lovely*, as it was then titled, to the Production Code Administration (PCA) until April 1944, Breen had already endorsed the project in 1941 when, ironically, he was head of production at RKO. (In a tenure marked by rash decisions, Schaefer's decision to hire Breen as head of production remains the "most unbelievable": to paraphrase Jewell, Breen might have had some vague notion about what didn't go into pictures, but he had absolutely no idea what went into them.[41])

As with *Stranger on the Third Floor*, the ever-changing corporate structure at RKO in the early 1940s was instrumental in the development and production of *Murder, My Sweet*. In 1942, Charles Koerner replaced George Schaefer as head of production at RKO and Koerner, unlike the "notorious micromanager" Schaefer, "took a hands-off approach to running the studio," relying on, among other things, small, independent production units.[42] One such unit was spearheaded by Adrian Scott, a former screenwriter who had been "promoted to the rank of producer" at RKO in December 1943.[43] Scott was looking for a project to produce, but with only a "modest A" budget—roughly half that of *Citizen Kane* or *Double Indemnity*[44]—he realized that RKO owned the rights to Chandler's *Farewell, My Lovely* and enlisted the services of staff writer and former New York theater scribe John Paxton.

Scott and Paxton were passionately committed to retaining the spirit of Chandler's *Farewell, My Lovely*, something that had definitely been lost in translation in *The Falcon Takes Over*. As another key member of the Scott unit, director Edward Dmytryk, recalled, "I looked at *The Falcon Takes Over* before making *Murder, My Sweet* [and] thought Chandler's novel had been gutted by forcing it to conform to the Falcon formula."[45] "After all," he added, "I directed a Falcon picture myself, *The Falcon Strikes Back*" (1943).[46] Dmytryk's contribution to the success of *Murder, My Sweet* remains, as Chandler himself recognized, considerable, but a "first-rate script" was sine qua non, and both Scott and Paxton agreed that one of Chandler's principal assets was his "adroit use of first-person narration."[47] In fact, earlier in his career as a screenwriter at RKO Scott had used a flashback frame in *Mr. Lucky* (1943). In the new film version of *Farewell, My Lovely*, though, the narration would not so much serve the "purposes of direct story-telling" (as was the custom at the time) as punch up the subjectivity of protagonist Philip Marlowe. Moreover, the voice-over—what Paxton referred to as "syncopated narration" —would be "indirectly related to the images . . . on the screen."[48]

The latter element of in- or misdirection assumed additional resonance with the casting of Dick Powell as Philip Marlowe. In the 1920s Powell was a singer and bandleader and, in the 1930s, a song-and-dance man, appearing in such musicals as *Footlight Parade* (1933), *42nd Street* (1933), *Gold Diggers of 1933* (1933), *Hollywood Hotel* (1937), and *Naughty but Nice* (1939). By the end of the decade, however, he had rebelled at being typecast as a "pretty boy" tenor and, when he was turned down at Paramount for the part of insurance investigator Neff in *Double Indemnity*, he left Paramount for RKO. In *It's a Hell of a Life but It's Not a Bad Living*, Dmytryk recounts that when Koerner suggested Powell for the role of Marlowe in *Murder, My Sweet*, Paxton and he thought, "Dick who?"[49] Scott and Dmytryk's original choice was Humphrey Bogart, who had made an indelible impression as Sam Spade in *The Maltese Falcon* (1941), but since Bogart was already making *The Big Sleep* at Warners with Howard Hawks, they decided to meet with Powell, whom they found to be "huskier and more masculine than he looked in the musicals."[50]

The difference between Bogart's and Powell's interpretation of, respectively, Spade and Marlowe is substantial. Commenting on Powell's performance in *Murder, My Sweet*, Paxton suggestively observed that the actor's "casual, off-beat type of playing . . . was his defense against trying to be

Bogart."[51] Paxton also acknowledged that Powell "developed a flip detective, which I hadn't intended at all and I don't think Chandler had ever intended."[52] This flipness is most apparent in Marlowe's narration which, as voiced by Powell, is inflected by the light, even "feminine" tone of the film musical and counterpoints both the hard-boiled discourse of film noir and, as Paxton intended, the dark, violent images on screen. In fact, Powell's performance as Marlowe in *Murder, My Sweet* is the vanishing mediator between *Stranger on the Third Floor* and the maturation of film noir as a genre in 1944.

Although there are a number of crucial differences between *Stranger on the Third Floor* and *Murder, My Sweet* such as interior monologue versus voice-over narration, the special effects in Ingster's and Dmytryk's films were designed by Vernon L. Walker and the sound track of both films features the work of Webb, Fesler, and Stewart. Moreover, the dominant psychic trope of *Stranger on the Third Floor* and *Murder, My Sweet*—and, perhaps, the genre as a whole[53] —is paranoia. Hence (and here we return to Paxton's characterization of Powell's performance) Jonathan Buchsbaum's characterization of *Murder, My Sweet* as a "modal example of paranoia in *film noir*," where paranoia is understood as the "defensive denial or expulsion of . . . feelings of weakness in the main character and represents the flip side of . . . excessive masculinity."[54]

Murder, My Sweet

What Buchsbaum calls the "supple paranoid structure"[55] of *Murder, My Sweet* is conveyed, as in *Stranger on the Third Floor*, via voice-over narration and, in particular, offscreen sound. Indeed, *Murder, My Sweet*, like *M*, provokes the "audience to infer unseen, offscreen presences and actions" and, in so doing, equates the "spectator's relation to the events in the film . . . to the detective's relation to the clues."[56]

Consider the first two, justly celebrated sequences of *Murder, My Sweet*. The film opens on an image of a white, saucer-like globe accompanied, as in the beginning of the dream sequence of *Stranger on the Third Floor*, by hectoring offscreen male voices: "I remember you as a pretty noisy fellow, son. All of a sudden you get quiet." "You lost your book of answers, or you just waiting for your lawyer?" "Maybe you think murder don't look so good on you." There's a dissolve and the camera pulls back to a medium shot of a man, his eyes bandaged, being questioned by three police detectives. The man is Philip Marlowe and, not unlike Briggs or Ward in *Stranger on the*

Third Floor, he's a suspect in a murder case, "Boys tell me I did a couple of murders."

The initial image, it turns out, is a "reflection of an overhead light in the polished surface of the table," an "optical trick" that implies that "our desire for a certain *insight* might well depend on what remains *out of sight*, offscreen."[57] In his insightful reading of *Murder, My Sweet*, J. P. Telotte concentrates on the issue of vision, but the fact that Marlowe is blindfolded like the statue of Justice in *Stranger on the Third Floor* indicates that his sense of hearing may well be "more reliable than his vision."[58] This proposition is confirmed in the initial interrogation scene when Marlowe, hearing a door open, says "Randall?" and the man answers, "Uh huh." The aggressive offscreen voices and the sound of the opening door also suggest that Marlowe's point of audition is privileged in *Murder, My Sweet.*

Randall is Lieutenant Randall (Donald Douglas), and since he wants a statement "on the record," he cues the male stenographer; Marlowe, cigarette smoke drifting across his face, begins to tell his story—"from the beginning." As he recounts a case involving a barber "whose wife wanted him back" (an anecdote that introduces an early note of romantic cynicism), the camera tracks toward a window that looks out on Los Angeles in all its neon-lit, nighttime glory. Marlowe acknowledges he never "found the barber" but did find out "how big the city is," a rueful admission that comments not only on his limited abilities as a private detective but the size of Los Angeles which, like California, is big—too big, perhaps, for any one man to comprehend.

Voiced over a brief montage of the metropolis at street level, Marlowe's self-deprecating quips about his sore feet and empty bank account foreground, like the investigative montage in *Stranger on the Third Floor*, the pedestrian—and, in this case, impoverished—life of the private eye. A canted, low-angle shot of buildings and telephone wires is the subtle, expressionist segue to a slow track-in to an exterior, window-framed shot of Marlowe at his desk, talking on the phone after having consulted his "black book." If the neon sign flashing in the window emphasizes his reflective nature, the vision of the private detective sitting alone in his darkened office calling a woman for a date evokes, despite the jokey remark about his "morale," a feeling of isolation, even loneliness.

Once Marlowe hangs up ("soft shoulders" has a date but will call back), he lights a cigarette and the film cuts from an exterior to interior shot of his office: "There's something about the dead silence of an office building at night. Not quite real." The sudden cutting out of the sound of traffic outside magnifies the silence, while the phantasmagorical aspect is captured in a highly expressive visual device: when the sign across the street blinks off, a "stolid, brutish face, the massive features carved out by the dim light,"[59] appears in the top half of the windowpane. The man in the window is Moose Malloy (Mike Mazurki) and, like the city of Los Angeles, he's big and its presiding locus genie.

The fact that Moose's image appears when the sign is off and Marlowe's remains visible in the bottom half of the window intimates he's an apparition or phantasm the detective has conjured out of the metropolitan night. The irony, as the script indicates, is that the big man's voice is "soft"—"I like you to look for somebody"—and Marlowe himself speaks "quietly." Marlowe no doubt doesn't want to antagonize this moose of a man who has materialized, it seems, out of the blue, but as Dmytryk has noted, the volume of Malloy's voice speaks to the "big man's vulnerability as well as Marlowe's."[60] In other words, for all their obvious physical and intellectual differences, Moose and Marlowe, as the matched voices and window shots indicate, complement each other. Both men, for instance, are looking for romance (and for Moose, as we'll see, in all the wrong places). The big man can also be seen as a compensatory figure for Marlowe: not unlike Meng vis-à-vis Ward in *Stranger on the Third Floor*, Moose can do what Marlowe can only dream about.[61]

The sequence set at Marlowe's office concludes with an audiovisual conceit that offers a comic transition to the following scene at Florian's, the Central Avenue nightclub where Moose's ex-girlfriend, Velma Valento, once sang. The phone rings—it's "soft shoulders" again, calling back about the date—but when Marlowe sees the two twenties Moose has tossed on the desk, he forgets about the phone and gets up to go. As the two exit his office, the camera pans to a "burping" water cooler. In his primer on the concept and practice of cinema, Dmytryk elaborates on this technique, revealing in the process just how mindful he was of the audiovisual properties of the medium: "Accompanied by its distinctive sound, the shot . . . provides both an audible and visual 'springboard' into the next scene. Here the image of the amorphous bubble is augmented by the shot of the sputtering neon, and its vulgar 'burp" enforces the tawdriness of the sign and the enterprise it advertises."[62] While the "distinctive sound" of the "burp" is in fact drowned out by the ringing phone, the latter effect is fraught with significance and demonstrates the importance of *on*screen sound in *Murder, My Sweet*.

For instance, the ringing phone terminates the initial office sequence on an enigmatic note (since the mystery associated with "soft shoulders" remains unresolved at the film's end); it also anticipates a slightly later scene where Marlowe visits Jessie Florian (Esther Howard) to inquire about Velma. As he departs Florian's house, a train whistles in the distance and he accidentally kicks a can (the latter sonic "trash" a not-so-oblique commentary on Florian's squalid, alcoholic life), then, looking in a window, sees the suddenly sober widow making a phone call: "She was cool like somebody making funeral arrangements for a murder not committed."

The dramatic use of both on- and offscreen sound is audibly on display in the sequence set at Florian's. As soon as Moose opens the doors of the club, honky-tonk music can be heard wafting from upstairs, but the low-angle shot of the narrow stairwell and the tangle of shadows at the top, like the flickering neon sign outside, endow the place with a menacing air. Played by ex-wrestler Mazurki,[63] Moose is a very big man, towering over Marlowe in the initial office scene and in the one on the sidewalk outside Florian's. Consequently, when he comes barging through the swinging doors, the piano player stops "right in the middle of a phrase."[64] Once the bartender and the owner get a good look at Moose, the conversational din in the bar also dies down, as if "somebody [was] making funeral arrangements for a murder not committed." In Chandler's novel, Moose in fact kills the owner when he pulls a Colt .45 on him in the back room; in Dmytryk's, the owner tries to placate Moose—he explains "no show, no noise"—but Moose picks him up like a laundry bag and throws him crashing across the room. Although Moose speaks softly, he carries a big stick in the form of his outsized, Brobdingnagian body.

The second client who shows up announced at Marlowe's office is preceded, not unlike Joel Cairo in *The Maltese Falcon*, by his "perfume" (the elevator attendant tells Marlowe "he smelled real nice") and his clipped, British accent as well as silk ascot and camel-hair coat set him apart from both Moose and Marlowe. His name is Lindsay Marriott (Douglas Walton), and while Marlowe is put off by his finicky, effete manner, he agrees to act as the man's "twin": to drive, in Marlowe's loaded locution, "to a nice dark petting spot . . . to buy back some jewelry for a lady friend."

As they drive up together to the secluded canyon, Marlowe's uncharacteristically apprehensive voice-over—"We were watched. I didn't see anything. I felt it in my stomach"—foreshadows the film's recourse to offscreen sound. Marlowe instructs Marriott to sit tight, then ventures out alone into a fog-shrouded forest glade that, pierced by shafts of moonlight, appears just as ominous and surreal as the mean streets of Los Angeles. A branch breaks offscreen, then again, closer. Marlowe, his gun drawn, poised for action in fedora and trench-coat, points his flashlight . . . and a deer, startled, looks up. After Marlowe returns to the car—there's a wide, low-angle shot of it sitting still as a hearse in the mist and moonlight—he starts talking to Marriott, "Looks like a tryout to see if you'll obey orders." There's another noise offscreen and Marlowe, sapped hard from behind, falls like a tree. A black stain begins to spread like oil or blood across the screen: "I caught the blackjack right behind my ears. A black pool opened at my feet. I dived in. It had no bottom. I felt pretty good, like an amputated leg."

If this blackout, the first of three in the film, testifies to just how tough, not to mention hard-headed Marlowe is, the castratory simile ("I felt like an amputated leg") emphasizes his fallibility even as it casts doubt on his reliability as a narrator. In fact, the first "fall" concludes with an extraordinary dissolve that blurs the line between subjective and objective points of view: while Marlowe is unconscious, a point of light appears in the blackness and begins to grow brighter. The vision appears to be from Marlowe's POV but it shifts into an objective, high-angle shot of him groggily waking to a flashlight in his face. After a female voice offscreen asks, "Are you all right? What happened?" there's a reverse shot from Marlowe's POV of a young woman with a scarf tied around her head, but, blinded by the light, he can only watch, stunned, as she runs off down the road.

It's only much later—after, among other things, Marlowe has discovered Marriott's body in the back seat of the car ("He was curled up on his face in that bag-of-old-clothes that always means the same thing")—that he realizes the mysterious woman with the flashlight was the same one, Ann Grayle (Anne Shirley), who had come to his office disguised, complete with "cheaters," as investigative reporter "Miss Allison." As Buchsbaum observes, "Marlowe cannot see Ann's face at the scene of the murder for his vision is still affected by the blow to the head. He places her at the scene only when she repeats the question, 'Are you all right?' "[65] In other words, it's not Marlowe's sense of vision but of hearing, jarred by another "fall," that finally enables him to place Ann at the scene of the crime.

The scene where Marlowe makes the connection between the mysterious woman in the scarf and Ann is revealing on a number of counts. Marlowe has gone to Ann's apartment after being drugged within inches of his death only to be revived with digitalis by Dr. Sonderborg (Ralf Harolde). "What were you doing out in the canyon that night Marriott was killed? You found out something was going to happen out there that night. Knowing your methods [a reference to her 'Miss Allison' disguise] I'd say you overheard Marriott . . . making some sort of arrangements about the jade." If Ann's eavesdropping allies her, on one hand, with the figure of the detective, on the other hand, her offscreen presence at the canyon associates her with whoever murdered Marriott and sapped Marlowe.

In *Noir Anxiety* Kelly Oliver and Benigno Trigo submit that Ann in *Murder, My Sweet* "is not all good": she's "deceptive, a snoop, and an eavesdropper."[66] In other words, despite her good-girl persona, Ann is a good-bad girl. (It's not for nothing that her hair is red like Velma's.) This distinction is critical since one of the constitutive differences between *Stranger on the Third Floor* and *Murder, My Sweet* is that the former proto-noir does not feature a bad girl or femme fatale, only the good girl Jane who assumes the investigative or "romance" quest typically associated with the male detective "hero." Although Ann in *Murder, My Sweet* assumes some attributes of the "private ear,"[67] Marlowe, as the opening sequence at the police station in Dmytryk's film attests, is an equivocal figure.

Ann's ambiguity is highlighted in a scene set at the Grayles' beach house (they've leased it to Marriott) where Marlowe returns to the issue of her involvement in his death: "All I can do about you is guess. You haven't told me anything except you went out to the canyon because you like your father. When you found me out there with my face in the mud you thought I was your father." After Marlowe compliments Ann, the "snoop," on her nose ("You know that's a cute nose, even if it's crooked"), the two embrace and kiss, though he continues to dissect her motives, "When I came along you were afraid I might become another Marriott, so you tried to buy me off. It didn't work. . . . A real tough guesser might say that when [your father] couldn't buy me off either, you decided to be nice to me."

Offended, Ann proceeds to recite a monologue on men ("Sometimes I hate men, all men, old men, young men, almost heels who are private detectives") only to be rudely interrupted by a woman laughing offscreen. It's Helen Grayle (Claire Trevor), wife of Lewin Lockridge Grayle (Miles Mander), stepmother of Ann, and "lady" friend of Marriott and self-admitted "quack" Jules Amthor (Otto Kruger). Dressed in a trench coat like the proverbial private dick, Helen patiently listens to Ann give the second half of her speech—"I hate their women too, especially the big-league blondes, beautiful, expensive babes who know what they've got, all bubble bath and dewy morning and moonlight and, inside, blue steel, cold, cold, but not that clean"—then cuts her to the quick, "Your slip shows, my dear." As Helen's barb suggests, Ann is a little too fond of her father, a complex, Electra-like attraction that explains, in part, her hatred of her stepmother.

While Mrs. Grayle might be said to be "all bad" (Marlowe at one point compares her to a "cancer" and Ann in the end describes her as "evil, all evil"), Ann herself remains an enigma and continues to be associated with offscreen sound, as in the first sequence set at the Grayle residence. As Ann drives up to the house, Marlowe describes it in his usual, hyperbolically understated terms ("It was a nice little front yard. Cozy, okay for the average family, only you'd need a compass to get to the mansion"), then, while Ann "sells" him to the "folks," he waits alone in the hall, an enormous marble-floored foyer decorated with marble pillars and statuary. Marlowe's droll voice-over—"it was like waiting by a crypt in a mausoleum"—captures the ubiquitous aura of decay and corruption that hangs like a cloud over the Grayle family. The deathly, crypt-like coldness of the family manse is atmospherically evoked when Ann calls out to Marlowe and her voice reverberates in the voluminous space, as does Marlowe's quick dance step on the patterned tile as he skips toward her, a comment on Mr. Grayle's age—Marlowe later cracks that his "two step's getting a little stiff"—as well as a sly allusion to Powell's days as a Hollywood hoofer.

Mr. Grayle expounds on the value of the missing jade necklace, but when he begins to tire, he turns the issue over to his considerably younger wife, who's sporting a midriff-baring white playsuit and gardenia in her hair and whose bared leg attracts Marlowe's attention like a magnet. He eventually joins her on the couch for cocktails until a door opens offscreen and Ann walks in to see the two sitting close together holding hands like lovers. Later, having concluded his "business" with Mrs. Grayle, Marlowe is exiting the house when he spots Ann in the foyer and calls out to her ("Hey!"), his voice reverberating in the canyon-like space as she vanishes behind a door.

Unlike Ann, Helen is not shy around either guns or men. Having played patty-cake with Marlowe at the Grayle residence, she shows up at his spare, one-bedroom apartment and, when the laundry boy leaves the door open, walks in on the detective standing in front of a mirror in a state of semi-undress, "You don't mind my sizing you up." If her unblinking gaze and black formal evening dress reflect her dominance even here in Marlowe's private space, the subsequent sequence at the Cocoanut Beach Club links her, like Ann, with offscreen space. The sequence opens on a beam of light cutting a bright swath through a veil of cigarette smoke. Propelled by Webb's bewitching orientalist motif, the camera cranes across and down to a pair of hands snaking rhythmically in the air, then descends, following the hands, to the headdressed face and spangled body of an Asian female dancer and, finally, pulls back to a wide shot of the house band playing in the background.

The gradual, teasing revelation of the undulating dancer dramatizes the play of presence and absence in the sequence. First Marlowe finds Ann hiding in the corner of a dark booth, sporting, not unlike Helen, a bejeweled outfit and flowers in her hair. After the music ends, she tells him, as if on cue, that Helen's already left, then, sinking back into the booth, her face crosshatched by shadows, she tries to buy him off, "Whatever she was willing to pay you, I'll up it." Marlowe banters—he says she reminds him of someone in his dreams (an allusion to Ann's fleeting appearance at Marriott's murder scene)—until he sees Moose standing by the bar.

The two men go outside to the ocean-view deck where—again, as if on cue—the music starts up and Moose tells Marlowe he wants him to "meet a guy." (The "guy" turns out to be Amthor, the "psychic consultant" who, among other things, has treated Helen's "centers of speech.") On the way out Marlowe stops by Ann's booth to say goodbye but, like Helen, she's already disappeared, leaving in her wake a Cocoanut Beach Club coaster with her address on it. Marlowe rejoins Moose who's dreamily watching the Asian dancer, "You do go for the showgirl type, don't you?" Moose's reply—"Cute, huh?"—recollects his demotic description of Velma ("cute as lace pants") and suggests, together with the offscreen Oriental music and dancer, that the missing jade and girl are somehow connected.

The complex play of doors and offscreen sound is repeated in the sequence at the Sunset Towers, the de luxe, art moderne apartment building where Amthor resides. Moose and Marlowe use the basement "back door" entrance, and the hard reverberation of the space as well as the neon "Service" sign above the elevator link Amthor with the Grayles and the elite world of the rich, a world that Moose and Marlowe—one an ex-con, the other a private dick—patently do not belong to. Not surprisingly, given the sinister connotations of offscreen sound in horror and suspense films, we hear Amthor before we see him when, offscreen, he comments on Marlowe's view from his penthouse apartment, "On clear days, you can see the ships and harbor in San Pedro." (Noir aficionados can see as far as *The Usual Suspects* [1995].)

As Marlowe interrogates Amthor about his relationship with the police, the precariousness of his situation is reinforced by the sound of doors opening and the appearance first of Amthor's chauffeur, then Moose. In fact, offscreen sound—here, opening doors—signals, as in the Marriott murder scene, Marlowe's imminent loss of consciousness. Since Amthor has earlier misled Moose, telling him that Marlowe knows the whereabouts of Velma, when the private detective pleads ignorance, the big man starts to strangle him. Amthor stops him just in time, but when Marlowe punches Amthor, "foxy grandpa" knocks him down with the butt of his gun. The oil-black stain reappears accompanied by the now familiar, almost comic refrain, "A black pool opened up at my feet again, and I dived in."

This, the second blackout mimics the first one except it suddenly morphs into what Marlowe calls a "crazy cold-cut dream." In his text on film editing, Dmytryk differentiates between "European" and "Hollywood" montage. Although the former is associated with Russian filmmakers of the 1920s such as Kuleshov, Eisenstein, and Pudovkin, it can be utilized, according to Dmytryk, "as a means of exposing a character's unconscious thoughts, or to pictorialize his subconscious experience, as in dreams or nightmares."[68] The dream sequence in *Murder, My Sweet* was originally supposed to be a "concoction of surrealistic scenes" in the style of Salvador Dali à la *Spellbound* (1945),[69] but in its insistent recourse to expressionist sonic effects, it ultimately has more in common with the dream sequence in *Stranger on the Third Floor*.

The sequence itself, which is comprised of twenty-three shots and lasts eighty-six plus seconds,[70] is an allegory of Marlowe's "crazy" experience. First, Marlowe is dragged and dumped into an elevator, then, after falling into space, he climbs a staircase to nowhere where he's accosted by a monstrous image of Amthor whose voice ("Where's the necklace?"), like those in the dream sequence in *Stranger on the Third Floor*, is thick with reverberation. A canted image of Amthor turns into one of Moose raising his hands as if he's about to strangle Marlowe, but when Marlowe tries to back down the stairs, they melt into thin air and he's suddenly falling again. Next, Marlowe approaches a series of increasingly smaller doors only to look back over his shoulder to see Moose whose voice, like Amthor's, is thick with reverberation ("You shouldn't have hit me").

In the second part of the sequence—scored, as in *Stranger on the Third Floor*, by bruised horns, piercing woodwinds, and tremulous strings—a "ragged cobweb" appears superimposed over the screen as Marlowe traverses the doors while being steadily pursued by a man in a white lab coat holding a hypodermic syringe.[71] Although Marlowe is able to squeeze through the final door (Dmytryk borrowed this image from a recurring nightmare), the man in the white lab coat is waiting for him on the other side. Cut to a gigantic syringe rapidly plunging toward the camera as Marlowe falls into a whirling black vortex that resolves into a rapidly spinning saucer of light.

Since the spinning saucer of light resolves, in turn, into a ceiling fixture, this image can be said to represent a return, as in a vicious circle, to the film's beginning. The difference is that Marlowe is not sitting in a police station but lying on a bed in a locked room hopped up on drugs. As he gradually regains consciousness, his voice-over resumes: "The window was open but the smoke didn't move. It was a gray web woven by thousands of spiders." (The not-so-subtle insinuation is that Marlowe's trapped like a spider in Helen Grayle's web.) Marlowe paws helplessly at the smoky cobweb, then screams for help. The fact that the smoke remains after the male nurse and Moose check up on him—Marlowe tells them the "doors are too small" and the "stairs are made of dough"—accentuates the fine line between fantasy and actuality: "The dream is waking reality, and waking reality is a dream."[72]

In addition to anticipating the dream sequence in *Vertigo* (1958), *Murder, My Sweet* can be said to synthesize the interior monologue in *Stranger on the Third Floor* when Marlowe gets up from bed and says to himself, "Okay, you cuckoo, walk and talk. What about? Anything, everything, just talk and keep walking." Here, Marlowe's interior dialogue, nestled like a Chinese box within the frame of the voice-over narration, effectively "calls into question the origin of his voice-over."[73] In fact, Marlowe's bewilderment continues even after he's talked and walked the cobwebs out of his head ("I walked I don't know how long") when he bursts in on Dr. Sonderborg, "Speak up, Dr. Jekyll, I'm in a wild mood tonight!" The more he talks, though, the crazier he becomes ("I wanna go dancing, I hear the banshees calling, I haven't shot a man in a week") until his voice suddenly drops to a whisper and the pall of smoke reappears like a veil.

It's only in the last part of the film, after Marlowe has managed to escape Dr. Sonderborg's "fun house" (see *The Lady from Shanghai*), that his voice-over becomes more authoritative: when he goes to Anne's house where, in the aforementioned scene, he realizes she was present at Marriott's murder; when he returns to Amthor's apartment to find him strangled to death ("He wasn't hurt. He was just snapped, the way a pretty girl would snap a stalk of celery"); and when, after leaving Moose on the surf-loud beach ("That was like lighting a stick of dynamite and telling it not to go off"), he returns to the Grayles' beach house to rendezvous as planned with Helen who, as befits her labyrinthine machinations, is lounging in the smoke-plumed dark, the "dragon lady" incarnate.

After Marlowe unlocks the door and turns on the light (note his startled look when Helen appears behind a lamp), she hands him a box that contains the missing jade necklace—significantly, we never see it—and confesses it was in her possession all along: that, as Marlowe puts it, "the necklace was never stolen, there wasn't any holdup, [and she] faked the whole thing." Embracing him, Helen sheds some crocodile tears for Marriott (Amthor, like Marriott, has been using his knowledge of her déclassé past as a show-girl to blackmail her), but when she realizes Amthor is dead, she pulls a gun on the "grubby" detective. Marlowe appears to be a goner until there's a crash offscreen and, in a reversal of the first scene at the beach house, Ann appears accompanied by her father. Although Mr. Grayle obeys his wife and takes Marlowe's revolver, in yet another reversal, a gunshot sounds off-screen and the "duchess," Mrs. Grayle—not the "duke," Marlowe—falls, mortally wounded.

This is the climactic moment when, at least according to the conventions of classical Hollywood cinema, Marlowe should assume control of the narrative, but in the conclusion to the "body" of the film he remains, as in the beginning, fallible. Moose belatedly appears on the scene to find his beloved Velma dead and to offer an impromptu paean, "She hardly changed, just like always, only more fancy. Cute as lace pants, always." Moose in fact seems strangely reconciled to Velma's death until Mr. Grayle admits he pulled the trigger, at which point the big man starts walking trance-like toward him ("Shouldn't have killed her") and the old man shoots again. True to form, Marlowe is unable to prevent Mr. Grayle from shooting Moose; he's also blinded by the gun blast. Ann screams. Two more offscreen shots later, the familiar oil-black stain reappears—"That old black pit opened up again right on schedule. It was blacker than the others and deeper. I didn't expect to hit bottom. I thought I was full of lead"—and Marlowe's now literally in the dark.

It's entirely apropos that the last diegetic sound of the narrative proper is offscreen since, not unlike the ringing phone at the beginning of *Murder, My Sweet*, it reintroduces the hermeneutic code just when everything appears to have been definitively resolved. To echo Ann, "What happened?" While

Fig. 2. Private Ear: Philip Marlowe (Dick Powell), "scorched" eyeballs bandaged, talking to Detective Nulty (Paul Phillips) and Lieutenant Randall (Don Douglas) in Edward Dmytryk's *Murder, My Sweet.*

Marlowe's "eyeballs" are "scorched," his sense of hearing is fine, "I heard the shots, I didn't fire the gun, I don't know who got hit. It wasn't the kid?" Randall leaves the room with the stenographer and Marlowe calls out his name. When he returns, Marlowe's "sprung" but not before he questions the lieutenant about what happened, "Who backed me up? Who got shot? I heard three." Although Marlowe correctly surmises Ann has vouched for him, Randall remains mum about whether she's okay ("I didn't say"), the camera panning to Ann who's been in the room all along, sitting on the sidelines, listening—from the beginning.

Marlowe's final question to Randall—as if the tables have turned and now he's interrogating the police—is about Ann, "She here now?" Ann silently mouths the word "no" and Randall's corresponding "white lie" sets up the comic coda to *Murder, My Sweet.* Randall tells Nulty to see Marlowe home and, as the police detective escorts Marlowe to a taxi, Ann trails behind while the two banter, as in the beginning of the film ("Is [Randall] holding the kid?" / "I don't know"), like an old married couple:

MARLOWE: What you know about the redhead pitching for me. How'd she take it about the old man?
NULTY: I wouldn't know.
MARLOWE: Cute figure, huh?
NULTY: I wouldn't know.

At the last moment, right before Nulty gets into the cab with Marlowe, Ann grabs his arm and gets in instead. The two are sitting silent in the back seat when the driver takes a hard turn and Ann, her fur loose around her shoulders, leans into Marlowe. Marlowe sniffs the air, then, as Webb's romance theme rises on the sound track, announces, "Nulty, I haven't kissed anybody in a long time. Would it be all right if I kissed you, Nulty?" Ann leans in again and they start to embrace until Marlowe stops and, taking a cue from Helen Grayle, removes the gun from his holster. Then, at long last love, they kiss.

Coda

The conclusion of *Stranger on the Third Floor* is superficially similar to *Murder, My Sweet*. When Jane and her fiancé, Mike Ward, meet as usual at a coffee shop for breakfast, he tells her the "judge and D.A." are waiting for them. She looks momentarily alarmed until he pulls out a marriage license. The happy ending is secured once they leave the coffee shop. A cabdriver yells "Taxi!" and Mike calls out "City Hall." Jane begins to remonstrate—"Oh, no, we're not going to start out like that. From now on, we save"—until, offscreen, the cabbie says, "It's all right, lady," and the camera cuts to a beaming Briggs who, holding open the door, adds, "This one's on the house!"

Although at the end of *Stranger on the Third Floor* we may still wonder about Ward's mental stability, not to mention violent tendencies, the external causes of his ostensibly acute case of paranoia have been eliminated: both Nick's real murderer, The Stranger, and Ward's nemesis, Meng, are dead and the "wrong man," Briggs, is not only alive but back on the streets, happily working again as a cabdriver. The conclusion to *Murder, My Sweet* is, by contrast, shadowed with ambiguity. First, when Marlowe removes his pistol from his holster, it recalls—albeit on a humorous note—"his close death at the hands of Ann's stepmother."[74] Second, the film offers up—at the "very moment of heterosexual communion"—"a homosexual joke that suggests an unlikely couple."[75] Finally, neither Nulty nor Ann herself ever answers Marlowe's pointed question about her father's death ("How'd she take it about the old man?").

It's in the last unspoken context that Ann's silence at the end of *Murder, My Sweet* assumes particular resonance. During the opening and closing sequences at the police station, Ann is present, first off-, then onscreen, but not unlike The Stranger, she remains steadfastly mute. Nor does she speak in the coda. Given Ann's silence and penchant for eavesdropping, the ultimate destination of Marlowe's voice-over narration is therefore not Randall but Ann. Hence the fairy-tale ending where Moose is the giant, Mrs. Grayle the wicked stepmother, Mr. Grayle the benign but benighted father, and Marlowe the Chandlerian knight who, although tested and even tarnished, renounces the bad grail (the jade necklace and Helen) for the good one, Ann. In other words (and here *Murder, My Sweet* resembles those "romance" noirs in which an intrepid working woman finds her mate), "The final test is Ann, her presence unknown, hearing what Marlowe thinks about her so that she may judge accurately the genuineness of his lovemaking."[76]

Still, if Marlowe remains marked, as his bandaged eyes intimate, by the physical and psychic abuse he's endured in the course of the investigation, Ann has not only witnessed the concluding bloody action at the beach house but been seriously traumatized by her neglectful father, for whom she was —despite her very obvious devotion to him—an afterthought. (Mr. Grayle to Marlowe after being interrupted by Ann and him while contemplating suicide: "I have two interests in life—my jade and my wife." Pause as he notices Ann, "And, of course, my daughter.") Marlowe presumably represents a resolution of Ann's Electra complex, but given the darkness of her family romance, how sound is she? If, as Michel Chion observes, the "presence of a mute character clues us in to the fact that there is a secret,"[77] at the end of *Murder, My Sweet* it's as if Ann is a spelled princess, her lips sealed with a kiss.

2

Sonic Effects

SOUND AND FURY IN FORTIES NOIR

Hard-Boiled Dialogue

With respect to sound I think it's safe to say that, in addition to voice-over narration, the most distinctive aspect of film noir is, as a number of compilation volumes attest, its hard-boiled dialogue.[1] For example, one of my favorite exchanges in *Out of the Past* occurs late in the action when Kathie Moffat (Jane Greer), having killed Whit Sterling, tells Jeff Bailey, "Don't you see you've only me to make deals with now?" Jeff's response couldn't be harder, "Build my gallows high, baby," a line that echoes the film's original title, *Build My Gallows High* (filched, according to Daniel Mainwaring, from a "Negro's poem"[2]), which the producers promptly changed when Dr. Gallup's Audience Research, Inc., reported that preview audiences found it too "morbid."

One reason Jeff's retort is so compelling is Robert Mitchum's jazzy delivery, Mitchum being, in the words of Eddie Muller, the "slow, rolling piano beneath Kirk's bass and Jane's sexy saxophone."[3] In fact, as Greer herself once observed, Mitchum "would arrive for work in the morning" (no doubt already high on "gage") and announce, "Where are the lyrics?" His musical modus operandi was a perfect match for Tourneur's method, which was that the "actors should be tuned to the same key" and that since the "film was based around Mitchum's character, the other cast members should adopt his pace and tone."[4]

Of course, delivery is nothing if the "lyrics" aren't there and the screenplay for *Out of the Past*—written by Geoffrey Homes, a *nom de plume* of Daniel Mainwaring, who adapted his own novel and later scripted a number of other noirs including *The Big Steal* (1949), *The Hitch-Hiker* (1953), and *The Phenix City Story* (1955)—remains a marvel of wit. Although Frank Fenton has been credited with much of the lively dialogue, the screenplay for *Out of the Past* was also rewritten by one of the seminal writers of hard-boiled detective fiction, none other than James M. Cain, the author of *The Postman Always Rings Twice* (1934), *Double Indemnity* (1936), and *Mildred Pierce* (1941).

However one allocates the credit, the dialogue of *Out of the Past* reveals a complex set of rhetorical registers. Consider the film's opening sequence. If the conversation between Stefanos and the Kid is largely built on silence, on what is *not* said (in this, the Kid represents an implicit rebuke to Stefanos's blunt manner), the film's real hard-boiled stuff does not surface until Jeff (duly notified by the Kid who signs from a distance that someone wants to see him) returns from the lake where he's been fishing with Ann (Virginia Huston). Given the magnificent country setting, the exchange between Ann and Jeff is appropriately pastoral. Ann: "They say the day you die your name is written on a cloud." Jeff: "Who says?" Ann: "They." Jeff: "Never heard of them." Compared to this poetic speech, the initial, mano-a-mano exchange between Jeff and Stefanos is hard as the nails in a flat tire:

STEFANOS: You have fun pumping gas?
JEFF: Yeah, me and the kid laugh all the time.

Like Dizzy Gillespie, who strategically underplayed in cutting contests with younger, less experienced but overly ambitious musicians, Jeff's deadpan reply trumps his interlocutor's ostensibly bright repartee.

At the same time, Jeff's discourse in *Out of the Past* is frequently counterposed to stereotypical hard-boiled speech. So, at the beginning of the flashback when Jeff goes to meet Whit, his partner Jack Fisher (Steve Brodie) says out loud at one point, "You know, a dame with a rod is like a guy with a knitting needle." After Whit puts Fisher in his place ("What's he doing here?"), he praises Jeff's laconic manner—"You just sit and stay inside yourself. You wait for me to talk"—a compliment that highlights the difference between the two men. It's therefore no surprise when Fisher is later gunned down by Kathie, since his cliché-ridden speech betrays both inexperience and a certain witlessness.

Jeff's first-person voice-over evinces another, altogether different tonality. In *Flashbacks in Film* Turim describes noir voice-over as a "bleeding wound which bandages a temporal wound," a description that deconstructs any easy opposition between masculine hard-boiled and feminine melodramatic narration.[5] *Out of the Past* is particularly illustrative in the context since the dominant tone of Tourneur's film is anything but "clipped and cynical."[6] Indeed, the fact that Jeff Bailey confesses his past history with such "pathetic relish," as Paul Schrader puts it in "Notes on Film Noir," can be seen as just another facet of the voice of "romantic narration" that distinguishes *Laura, Double Indemnity, The Postman Always Rings Twice,* and *The Lady from Shanghai.*[7]

This heightened narration is also one of the things that differentiates *Out of the Past* from *Murder, My Sweet,* both of which films were made at RKO and bear the studio's unmistakable imprint. Marlowe, especially as played by Dick Powell, is never as "romantic" or, for that matter, as "hard" as Mitchum's character. (It's thus surprising to learn that Powell instead of Mitchum was originally slated to star in the film.) Another, subtler aural difference between the two films is the sound track. While Roy Webb's music for *Out of the Past* is infinitely more lyrical than his score for *Murder, My Sweet,* Clem Portman and Francis M. Sarver's recording of Tourneur's film, produced in the wake of the war and the recording advances realized in docu-noir (see Introduction), is less studio-bound and therefore more naturalistic than Fesler and Stewart's for *Murder, My Sweet.* Which doesn't mean, as I indicate below, that it's any less atmospheric.

Consider the sequence in *Out of the Past,* to pick up where we left off, in which Jeff, notified by the Kid, returns to town to meet with Stefanos. Stefanos is standing near some gas pumps looking into the distance when a car pulls up offscreen. A door slams and Stefanos, without taking his hands out of the pockets of his black trench coat, turns around. The sound of gravel crunching underfoot can be heard as Jeff, trailing twin plumes of smoke from the cigarette stuck in his mouth, strides toward Stefanos. The two exchange pleasantries—Stefanos: "Everybody sure missed you, Jeff." Jeff: "Wish it was nice to see you"—then Jeff, after taking the cigarette out of his mouth and tossing it to the ground, says as he exhales, "I owe you something?" Stefanos, guarded as usual, asks how far the Kid can read and Jeff suggests they go "inside" (note the reverberation when they enter the garage) where he informs Jeff that Whit wants to see him.

As Stefanos gives out the directions—"Lake Tahoe. Turn right at Emerald Bay. Big house on the hill. You won't miss it. [Pause] You can't"—bird song can suddenly be heard in the background. Although it seems oddly out of place given the automotive setting, this ambient sound not only recalls the unspoiled natural world from which Jeff has just come (and from which he'll shortly be banished), it also serves as the transition to the following scene where Jeff pulls up outside Ann's house at night—he honks the horn twice to her parents' obvious vocal displeasure—for the drive to Tahoe, a drive during which he'll try to explain to Ann the mystery that is Jeff Bailey.

The Sounds of the City

Ambient sound may not be as identifiable a feature of film noir as voice-over narration or hard-boiled dialogue, but one could not imagine the genre without it. Of course, since noir is synonymous with the urban environs, the most characteristic sounds of the genre are the sounds of the city,[8] the symphonic ambience created by the various metropolitan means of transportation—subway and automobile, train and bus—intermixed with domestic racket and pedestrian traffic as well as all manner of enterprise, newspaper hawker and hot-dog vendor, taxicab hack and nightclub promoter.

A sonic locus classicus is Jules Dassin's *The Naked City* (1948), which begins with the sound of tolling church bells and in which the heterogeneous sounds of New York City recorded by Leslie I. Carey and Vernon W. Kramer, together with Rózsa's "spacious," "Copland-like" score,[9] provide the sonic backdrop for Mark Hellinger's celebrated docu-verité voice-over:

> Ladies and gentlemen, the motion picture you are about to see is called *The Naked City*. My name is Mark Hellinger. I was in charge of its production. And I may as well tell you frankly that it's a bit different from most films you've seen. . . . We're flying over an island, a city, a particular city. And this is the story of a number of people and a story also of the city itself. It was not photographed in a studio. Quite the contrary. [The actors] played their roles on the streets, in the apartment houses, in the

> skyscrapers of New York itself and along with them a great many New Yorkers played out their roles also. This is the city as it is. Hot summer pavements, the children at play, the buildings in their naked stone, the people without makeup.

As the narrator, "Mr. New York," observes, "there is a pulse to a city and it never stops beating," an observation mirrored by the wingtip lights of the American Airlines plane blinking on and off.

The ensuing montage, which may well owe something to Ruttmann's *Berlin: Symphony of a Great City* (1927),[10] encapsulates a series of discrete activities, each associated with a particular sound: a man oiling a machine; a woman pushing a mop across a floor ("Sometimes I think this world is made of nothing but dirty feet"); another man typing newspaper copy ("It's wonderful working for a newspaper company. You meet such interesting people"); a night disk jockey with one ear on the Guy Lombardo–style music playing in the background ("You put on a record, you take it off, you put on another one. Does anyone listen to this program except my wife?"); formally dressed men and woman partying in an upscale apartment; a couple studying a menu at a Latin nightclub; and, finally, as the camera tracks in to a window whose blinds are open, an ex-fashion model named Jean Dexter "at the close of her life." The sequence, which is positively symphonic, concludes with a sonic flourish, a match-on-action cut from one of the killers turning on the faucet of a tub (Dassin's film was based on the "Dot King Case," the so-called "Bathtub Murder") to a truck spraying water as it washes down a city street at dawn.

As the prologue to *The Naked City* suggests, certain sounds in film noir are virtually inseparable from the life of the metropolis. Where there's a body (and there's almost always a body), sounds such as gunshots and footsteps in the dark are as inevitable as canted angles and jalousie lighting. In fact, as I illustrate in the course of *Siren City*, gunshots litter the narratives of forties noirs whether, to adduce two of the most celebrated, it's Kathie Moffat unexpectedly shooting Jeff's partner while the two are fighting in *Out of the Past* or Treasury Agent Dennis O'Brien (Dennis O'Keefe) silently witnessing the execution of his partner in *T-Men* (1947).

The most spectacular firefights, however, tend to occur at the beginning or end of a film. For example, *The Street with No Name* (1948) opens with a bang when six masked men, guns pulled, stick up a road house called the Meadowbrook and kill an innocent housewife who just happens to be at

Fig. 3. "Traffic Ticket Stuff": Tommy Udo (Richard Widmark) empties another round into Nick Bianco (Victor Mature) in Henry Hathaway's *Kiss of Death.*

the wrong place at the wrong time. Shots also ring out at the beginning of *Mildred Pierce* when Monte Beragon (Zachary Scott) is gunned down at his beach house by an unknown assailant. Although Monte blurts out "Mildred" as he stumbles toward the camera—shot through the heart—we learn at the end that he was murdered not by Mildred (Joan Crawford) but by her homicidally jealous daughter, Veda (Ann Blyth).

If numerous noirs open with gunplay, even more conclude with it. *The Big Sleep* famously ends when Marlowe makes gambler Eddie Mars (John Ridgely) walk out of Geiger's house and into a "hail of bullets that were meant for him."[11] Similarly, in the brutal conclusion to *Kiss of Death*, Nick Bianco (Victor Mature) walks out of an Italian restaurant and right into Tommy Udo's (Richard Widmark) line of fire, taking five shots to the body in order to put Udo away and secure the safety of his new wife and children. In *The Strange Love of Martha Ivers* (1946), in a twist on the double shooting that concludes *Double Indemnity*, Martha Ivers (Barbara Stanwyck) helps her husband pull the trigger on her before he turns the gun on himself. (The second shot is from Sam Masterson's [Van Heflin] point of audition as he walks away from the house and the couple's hopelessly corrupt lives.) And in the genuinely spooky dénouement of *Night Has a Thousand Eyes* (1948), John "The Mental Wizard" Triton (Edward G. Robinson) fulfills his own fatal prediction when, at the appointed hour, he's mistakenly shot and killed by a policeman.

While Triton in *Night Has a Thousand Eyes* is coming to the aid of a young woman, some of the most explosive conclusions feature "girls with guns." If Lily Stevens (Ida Lupino) is forced against her will to shoot Jefty (Richard Widmark) at the end of *Road House*, in *The Dark Corner* Mari (Cathy Downs) —poised at the top of the stairs that lead down to a vault where her husband keeps a Raphael look-alike portrait of her—has no such compunctions, blasting him in the back before he can shoot private detective Brad Galt (Mark Stevens).

Still, the most expressive, reverberant gunshots in forties noir are arguably those rooted in trauma or psychosis, as in *Cornered* (1945) where Laurence Gerard (Dick Powell), an ex-Royal Canadian pilot released from a prisoner-of-war camp, is haunted by the shooting death of his young French bride at the hands of a Nazi sympathizer. Thus, in *Possessed* (and in a reversal of the narrative logic of *Mildred Pierce*), it's only at the very end that we witness the immediate cause of Louise Howell Graham's (Joan Crawford) breakdown. Manic and dressed all in black like a grieving widow, Louise shows up at her ex-lover David's (Van Heflin) apartment to ask for help. (She wrongly believes that her husband has fallen out of love with her and wants her committed.) David tries to reason with her, but when she finds out he's engaged to her stepdaughter, she pulls out a revolver. True to his "cruel to be kind" character, David remains cool as can be, "Mathematically, your chances of killing me are slight." Famous last words. When he tries to take the weapon from Louise, the camera cuts to a tight close-up of the gun—bang! David lurches toward the camera (he can't believe she's actually gone and done it) as she continues to fire away—bang! bang! bang! bang!—until, on the sound track, the gunshots dissolve to Louise, hands over ears, attired now all in white and surrounded by attendants in the "psycho" ward of a hospital, screaming, "David! David! David!"

If film noir is a visual art, it's also a black art, an art of darkness. That is to say, since our sense of hearing tends to be more heightened when visibility is an issue, gunshots are even more audible when it's dark, as in the climactic shoot-out in *Railroaded!* (1947). In Anthony Mann's Producers Releasing Corporation (PRC) "quickie" (71 minutes from opening beauty-parlor holdup to final shoot-out), Sgt. Mickey Ferguson (played by a pre–*Leave It to Beaver* Hugh Beaumont) tracks down Duke Martin (John Ireland), a cold-blooded murderer who likes to perfume his bullets, to a deserted nightclub. In a fire fight Mann has orchestrated for maximum audiovisual effect, Ferguson, realizing Martin has cornered the sister of a man wrongly accused of murder, hurls a trash can through the glass entrance to the nightclub, setting off the alarm. While a bell rings insistently in the background, Ferguson shields himself with the trash-can lid as Martin fires away from behind a cocktail table that he rolls across the floor. The sequence ends on an appropriately dissonant musical note when, having run out of bullets, Martin tries to escape and crashes into a piano as Ferguson guns him down.

Gunshots in the dark also emblazon the sound track of Byron Haskin's noir/gangster hybrid, *I Walk Alone*. Caught in the dark with his girl, Kay Lawrence (Lizabeth Scott), ex-con Frankie Madison (Burt Lancaster) taunts Noll "Dink" Turner (Kirk Douglas), an ex-bootlegging partner who's cheated him out of his share of their nightclub business while he was in prison. Frankie counts out Dink's shots:

> Missed, Dink. You only got five shots left. [Dink shoots again, then Frankie throws a book and there's another shot] You're pretty lucky, Dink. I only threw a book at the door. You got three shots left. [Frankie stands up and Dink shoots and misses] Two shots left, Dink. You oughta be more careful. It's hard to hit the sound of a voice in the dark.

From the City to the Country

Although *I Walk Alone* is notable in the context of forties noir for its recourse to various forms of source music (black combo, female piano-player, orchestra-backed female vocalist), it features another classic sonic effect—footsteps on the pavement in the dead of night—when Dink shadows Dave (Wendell Corey), an accountant who has just gone over to Frankie's side and is about to pay the ultimate price for his transgression: gunned down alone in a dark alley.

The sound of someone walking—alone, at night, in the "naked city"—is a recurring sonic figure in forties noir.[12] But the most suggestive example of this effect, outside of *Cat People* in which Irena Dubrovna (Simone

Simon) stalks Alice Moore (Jane Randolph), "Irena's heels clicking loudly and rapidly, Alice's sounding more muted and measured,"[13] is arguably the least literal. In *Double Indemnity*, Walter Neff, having contrived with Phyllis Dietrichson to knock off her husband for the insurance money—double the money, double the pleasure—muses to himself as he heads back alone to his bachelor apartment at night, "I couldn't hear my own footsteps. It was the walk of a dead man."

Like footsteps in the dark, another sonic effect common to both the noir and horror film—illustrated, appropriately enough, by the "noir-horror," *Cat People*[14]—is the scream. In Tourneur's film, Alice, after snubbing Irena at the museum, returns home to the YWCA where she lives. (Right before Irena gets out of a taxicab at the YWCA—she's stalking Alice—Irena's shown standing alone on the stairs of the museum next to a "jackal-headed anubis."[15]) No doubt "intending to fit a quick swim into her busy life,"[16] Alice asks the female attendant for the keys to the basement pool, then, accompanied by a kitten, goes down to the locker room to change. Something spooks the kitten, but Alice turns off the light and proceeds to the deserted pool. However, when something growls, she quickly dives into the water. A large cat appears to be prowling the perimeter of the pool, its sinuous black shape lost among the shadows rippling on the wall. Treading water, Alice becomes increasingly terrified until she lets out one loud, high-pitched scream after another, the sound reverberating in the room's closed, ceramic-tiled quarters—claustrophobic as a "shoebox," as Tourneur noted[17] —until the attendant arrives and turns on the lights: there's no panther, just Irena, dressed in black from head to foot, standing innocently by the side of the pool.

Although screaming informs the title of another, seminal forties noir, *I Wake Up Screaming* (1941), the most evocative use of the sound occurs, as with gunshots, in films like *Among the Living* where it's not so much an isolated effect as a complex, psychologically motivated phenomenon. A classic example is *Nightmare Alley* (1947). Edmund Goulding's film, photographed by Lee Garmes, recorded by E. Clayton Ward and Roger Heman, and set in the "dark, shadowy world" of second-rate carnivals and the "moneyed, jeweled rooms of bright nightclubs,"[18] might be said to commence when Pete "the Geek" Krumbein (Ian Keith) suffers an attack of what Stanton Carlisle (Tyrone Power) calls the "heebie jeebies." Pete needs a bottle of moonshine every evening in order to forget his daytime job eating live chickens. One fateful night, Stan gives Pete a bottle of booze he's just bought, but Pete inadvertently dies when he drinks a bottle of wood alcohol instead. The good news is now that Pete's dead, Stan can hit on his widow, Zeena (Joan Blondell), for the Code, a sideshow con devised to separate the suckers from their hard-earned moola.

With this secret and the help of a fresh-faced carnival girl, Molly (Coleen Gray), Stan leaves behind the small-time life at the Heatley and Henry Carnival for Chicago and the big time as a mind reader of the rich. However, after a surprise visit from Zeena, his luck changes when she picks up the very same Tarot card, the Hanged Man, she previously turned over while reading Stan's future and, out of the blue, he hears the sound of Pete the Geek screaming. Later, while Stan receives a post-performance rubdown, the smell of "pure alcohol" conjures Pete's ungodly scream again—at least in his own, now guilt-stricken mind—and the Great Stanton begins his downward slide to becoming the lowly thing that, at the beginning of the film, he could never have imagined being, a geek.

While some of the most characteristic sound effects in film noir have their origin, like *Nightmare Alley*, in the abnormal, not all of them are associated with criminal activity. Some, like the sound of girls gaily skipping rope at the beginning of *The Naked City*, suggest that the urban environment is, if not exactly innocent, a space where normal human activities occur. Sometimes, prototypical innocent behavior is used as aural counterpoint, as in Hathaway's *Kiss of Death* where the sound of Nick's girls roller-skating is set against the not-so-silent threat represented by Tommy Udo, whose high-pitched, psychopathic laugh is the stuff of nightmares.

As *Kiss of Death* demonstrates, home itself can change in a moment's notice from haven to prison. Thus, once Nick leaves prison, his life quickly goes from bad to worse when the Assistant D.A. Louis D'Angelo (Brian Donlevy) tells him that Udo, whom Nick has been persuaded to testify against in order to be with his children, has been acquitted and is back on the street. Now that Udo is free, every sound that Nick hears at night—say, a back screen door opening and closing—is fraught with menace. The suspense reaches a breaking point when Nick sends his family away and then, nursing a glass of milk, waits up alone at night for Udo to show. He hears a car pull up outside and, as David Buttolph's score builds in the background, we expect the worst—Udo, guns blazing, coming through the front door. Instead it's the D.A. come to tell Nick they've somehow lost track of Udo and that Nick should come in for his own good. (Like the home-as-prison trope, the law as sinister double of the outlaw is a persistent figure of both the noir and gangster genres. So, in *Kiss of Death*, D'Angelo is just as sadistic in his own way as Udo. As Nick remarks at one point, "Your side of the fence is almost as dirty as mine.")

In fact, interiors in classic noir are frequently just as charged, acoustically speaking, as exterior ones. Quotidian domestic sounds—say, a ticking clock combined with a ringing phone—can acquire extraordinary dramatic intensity as, for example, in the believe-it-or-not conclusion to Fritz Lang's *The Woman in the Window*. Professor Richard Wanley (Edward G. Robinson) has unsuccessfully counterplotted with an unwitting femme fatale, Alice Reed (Joan Bennett), to poison Heidt (Dan Duryea), the young man who's blackmailing them. In a beautifully paced sequence, Wanley tells Alice he's "too tired too think about it any more," then proceeds to the bathroom to take the remainder of the "pep pills" a solicitous doctor-friend has given him. (As Wanley walks down a hallway, Lang's set-up—"a doubly framed, entrapping composition"[19]—is a perfect formal analogue for the scene's poignant gravity.) Meanwhile, after Heidt is shot down by the police outside Alice's apartment, she races back to her apartment to call Wanley.

Cut to a medium shot of Wanley slumped in a chair, a pendulum clock ticking down the final moments of his life as the phone on the nightstand next to him rings and rings and rings. A clock chimes, there's the sound of a man's voice, "It's 10:30, Professor Wanley," and (this is the big reveal) he's never left his chair, it's all a dream. It's an exhilarating moment, one scrupulously set up by Lang at the film's outset by having Wanley fall asleep at a men's club with a copy of "The Song of Songs" in his lap, the faint but unmistakable sound of a clock ticking like a bomb in the background.

I will return to *The Woman in the Window* and its recourse to radio technology in the next chapter, but it's important to note that the noir soundscape encompasses the natural world as well, and never more so than in the conclusion to *The Gangster* (1947) in which, as in the film's opening, thunder and lightning foreshadow the cleansing, cathartic death of local gangster Shubunka (Barry Sullivan) who's mowed down by machine-gun fire as he stands alone in the middle of a street in the pouring rain. Nature in all its tropical glory—rain and thunder and shutter-shaking winds—is also violently on display in the opening scene of *The Bribe* (1949) in which federal-agent Rigby (Robert Taylor) stands in front of a window in the Hotel Marlin in Carlota, somewhere "off the coast of South America," contemplating whether he should sell out in order to spare the life of an American dealer in illegal war surplus, Tug Hintten (John Hodiak), and his ravishing, if duplicitous wife, Elizabeth (Ava Gardner). Complementing the spectacular fireworks that light up the landscape at the film's close, the storm is a sonic "objective correlative" for the tempestuous circumstances in which Rigby, once the very embodiment of governmental probity, finds himself.

Then there's the tropical, storm-scored consummation scene in *Out of the Past*. Not unlike a similar sequence in *Double Indemnity* where Walter and Phyllis appear to consummate their affair in the blink of an eye (and, remarkably, without taking off their clothes or getting their hair mussed), in Tourneur's film everything happens, true to the PCA protocols of the day, between the lines. Laughing and soaking wet, Jeff and Kathie race back from the beach to her place, what Jeff calls a "nice little joint with bamboo furniture and Mexican gimcracks." With the "rain hammering on the windows," he roughly begins to dry her hair, then, when she complains, kisses her on the neck and throws the towel at a lamp, knocking it over. As if by magic, the door suddenly opens and, as "The First Time I Saw You" swells on the sound track, the rain blows in with the wind. When we next see Jeff and Kathie—she's lifting the needle off the record player, he's putting on his jacket—we know that something has transpired, something momentous.

Pet Sounds

Although the natural world has more audio play in forties noir than is commonly assumed (see, for example, the raging wind storms in *The Brasher Doubloon* [1947] and the gothic "farm" noir, *The Red House*), nature in the form of animal sounds is also audible at key moments in various films, whether it's the loon in *Leave Her to Heaven* (1945), a sound that can be said to comment on Ellen Berent's (Gene Tierney) severely disturbed personality, or the snorting black "devil" horse associated with the missing Michael Garroway (Robert Mitchum) in *Undercurrent* (1946), the chirping birds high in a nest where the secret microfilm is hidden in *Ministry of Fear* or the roaring tiger that represents the return of Joan Alris Ellis's (Phyllis Thaxter) murderous alter ago, Karen, in *Bewitched* (1945).

Often, as in the horses' hooves that startle the ménage à trois making camp in *Raw Deal* (1948), the natural world is less a "breath of fresh air," as ex-con Joe Sullivan (Dennis O'Keefe) puts it, than a place where outlaws flee to escape the authorities, a theme accented in Mann's film by the bloodhounds unleashed by the police to track down another escaped convict. (The keening sound of bloodhounds also distinguishes the conclusion to Borzage's *Moonrise* [1948] in which the police, with the help of Mose, are trying to capture suspected murderer Danny Hawkins.) What criminals fear in the country are not so much the animals, like the enormous stuffed bear in the back room of the taxidermy shop in *Raw Deal*, as the long arm of the law.

Animals, of course, are sometimes a criminal's best or only friend. In the notorious opening scene of *This Gun for Hire* (1942), Philip Raven (Alan Ladd) leaves an open tin of milk for a hungry cat meowing in a window before—in a scene that's still shocking—slapping the maid across the face for "mistreating" his pet. (The scene is justly famous because Raven, who's about to leave for a contract killing, appears to care more about the cat than the maid.) Similarly, in the concluding sequence of *The Crooked Way* (1949), Petey (Percy Helton), wheezing throughout the film like someone in the late stages of emphysema, is shot and killed when he abandons his attic hideout with Eddie Rice (John Payne) to rescue one of his beloved cats caught in the crossfire. By comparison, the crying cat that the tap dancer Tom Quinn (Don Castle) throws a "magic" shoe at in *I Wouldn't Be in Your Shoes* (1948) fatefully implicates him in a murder, and the blood-curdling scream of the cat electrocuted in *The Postman Always Rings Twice* tacitly comments on the cold-hearted nature of its adulterous lovers.

Occasionally, an animal's sound reflects its master's malefic disposition. In Arthur Ripley's *The Chase* (1946), based on Cornell Woolrich's *Black Path of Fear*, Eddie Roman (Steve Cochran) has a penchant for fine wine and killer dogs. When rival businessman Emmerrich Johnson (Lloyd Corrigan) turns down an offer he shouldn't refuse, Eddie graciously encourages him to check out his wine cellar. Escorted there by Eddie's right-hand man, Gino (Peter Lorre), Johnson ends up trapped inside with Tony, the big man's attack dog. Although Eddie expects everyone, including his wife, to accede to his imperial wishes (hence his surname, Roman), his dog, even more so than the servile Gino, is the purest instrument of his will, the sound of Eddie's mastiff snarling a sign that Johnson's good as dead. In fact, "the moment the dog pounces," Johnson, terrified, "drops a bottle of Napoleon brandy,"[20] the liquor running across the floor like blood.

THE SOUNDMAN

Today sound is an integral part, not an adjunct of, a motion picture. Sound effect notes on the margin of a shooting script no longer suffice. In the modern conception of sound, musical scores and sound effects are part of the total construction of the story.

—Frederic Thrasher, " 'You Ain't Heard Nothin,' " *Okay for Sound* (1946)

What, exactly, did a "soundman" do in the 1940s?[a]

The first thing to be said about the recording and rerecording of film sound in the 1940s is that Hollywood, in the words of the Research Council of the Academy of Motion Picture Arts and Sciences, was an "entertainment factory": "In many respects it is an organization on the same principles as those followed in any other type of manufacturing plant."[b] The analogy is somewhat misleading (M-G-M, Adorno aside, was not organized like General Motors except in a very general way), but the point is that the typical Hollywood studio was profit-oriented: "Regardless of artistic desires which are its foundation, the commercial end is of manifest importance."[c]

As the corporate language suggests, the names listed for "Sound" at the end of a film are a metonym for the studio itself and its various departments (art, music, sound, etc.). Accordingly, on a production set, the soundman—with the "whole department" at his back—worked within very real limits: "The individual recordist may then go out on the firing line—the set—with a system at a command which is carefully maintained and adjusted for him and he is free to work out and to coordinate the many details which arise there."[d] While this passage, at least from today's post-classical Hollywood perspective, may appear to circumscribe the creative latitude of the "individual recordist," the manual in fact remarks that, precisely because of his extensive technical training and basic knowledge of the other fields of filmmaking, the soundman has the "reputation of being 'high brow.' "[e] This is a striking admission, although it's important to add this designation is not so much a cultural as a technical one. Which is to say that even at the beginning of the 1940s, the "decibels, gammas, and equalizers"—the soundman's lingua franca—remained "entire strangers to the rest of the motion picture world."[f]

[a] Although a "traditional Hollywood term" for the gender-inflected "soundman" was, as Handzo notes, "sound mixer" ("Glossary of Film Sound Technology," *Film Sound*, ed. Elisabeth Weis and John Belton [New York: Columbia University Press, 1981], 401), the term "soundman"—in addition to that of "recorder" and "recordist"—was also used. For the latter, see, for example, George Groves, "The Soundman," *Journal of the Society of Motion Picture Engineers* 48 (March 1947), 220–230. See also James G. Stewart's reminiscence ("During all this [the late 1920s and early 1930s] the soundman had his day!") in *Sound and the Cinema*, ed. Evan William Cameron (Pleasantville, New York: Redgrave, 1980), 44.

[b] Wesley Miller, "Basis of Motion Picture Sound," *Motion Picture Sound Engineering* (New York: D. Van Nostrand, 1938), 5.

[c] Ibid., 4.

[d] Ibid., 6.

[e] Ibid., 5.

[f] Ibid., 5.

With this caveat in mind (with the advent of electronic technology, the production and reproduction of film sound has become even more specialized), the (re)production of motion picture sound circa 1944 may be understood as a three-phase process: preproduction, production proper, and postproduction. As for sound and music, the primary activity in the preproduction phase was "pre-scoring" or making "playback" recordings for the song and dance numbers. While it was not uncommon for musical sequences to be recorded *during* and even *after* a shoot, as I mention in chapter 7 with respect to *Gilda* and *The Lady from Shanghai*, music was generally prerecorded for vocal and dance numbers in order to achieve "fidelity" of tone and tempo and, rather less obviously perhaps, in order to take advantage of special sound stages that were "acoustically treated to make it as perfect as possible for music recording."[g]

Prescoring and scoring are both critical aspects of the production process, but in terms of dialogue and sound effects, the bulk of the soundman's work took place during production recording and then in postproduction rerecording. On a shooting set (generally a sound stage), the soundman was responsible for "sound pick-up"—that is, adequately recording "dialog" and other "incidental" noises such as "footsteps" and "door slams."[h] The key to accomplishing this task—which was no mean thing even on a sound stage, not to mention a real location—was so-called "acoustic lighting" (a term that, given the valorization of sight over sound in classical Hollywood cinema, not so subtly subordinates the sonic to the photographic register).[i] Ironically enough, acoustic lighting refers primarily to "microphone placement." Since the microphone, according to *Motion Picture Sound Engineering* (1938), is a "robot" that picks up sound with no particular sense of discretion or selection, "the soundman is the brain of the microphone."[j] Whether "carbon" or "condensed," "ribbon" or "crystal," the microphone itself was attached to a "boom" or "fishpole" which the operator, sometimes from a wheeled "dolly," would pan, tilt, lower, or elevate to obtain the best results in terms of volume and perspective ("Preservation of the proper sound perspective is probably one of the greatest single factors in the successful production of the required illusion").[k] Meanwhile, the on-set mixer, equipped with an "ear bug," would control the volume and quality of the sound.[l]

Of course, inasmuch as the most important element in the classical Hollywood

[g] Bernard B. Brown, "Prescoring and Scoring," in *The Technique of Motion Picture Production* (New York: Interscience, 1944), 65.

[h] For a diagram and detailed description of on-set recording in early sound cinema, see Carl Dreher, "Sound Personnel and Organization," in *Recording Sound for Motion Pictures*, ed. Lester Cowan (New York: McGraw-Hill, 1931), 344–345.

[i] Homer G. Tasker, "The Technique of Production Sound Recording," *The Technique of Motion Picture Production*, 54. But for rerecording as not only analogous to but, with respect to "artistic and commercial advantages," "greater than" trick photography, see Kenneth Morgan's comments on "dubbing" in Helen Hanson, "Sound Affects," *Music, Sound, and the Moving Image* 1, 1 (2007), 34.

[j] Miller, "Basis of Motion Picture Sound," *Motion Picture Sound Engineering*, 6.

[k] J. Maxfield, "Sound Perspective," in *Recording Sound for Motion Pictures*, 215.

[l] Frederic Thrasher, *Okay for Sound* (New York: Duell, Sloan and Pearce, 1950), 229–230.

(*continued*)

sound hierarchy was dialogue (hence the use of "automatic limiting devices" to "fade down music and sound effects whenever dialogue came in"[m]), "best results" ultimately translates to intelligibility. (Most sound mixers, however, were not insensitive to what might be called "depth of sound": "If an actor is walking toward someone from a distance, his voice must be fainter than that of someone in the foreground."[n]) In general, in order to record usable, intelligible dialogue, the soundman's immediate aim was to minimize the acoustic reflections relative to the size of the recording space ("barrel" [small], "roominess" [medium], "reverberant" [large]) via a number of techniques and strategies such as: 1) proper microphone placement, 2) "damping" or blanketing in order to absorb excessive reflections, 3) utilization of microphone properties, and 4) "proper choice of materials or designs"—for example, insulated walls in order to reduce external noise such as traffic and machinery (camera, wind machines, etc.).[o]

Given that these techniques and strategies tend to be preventive, it's fair to say that the soundman's main enemy was noise. "Noises occurring within the motion picture set," as *The Technique of Motion Picture Production* (1944) insists, "are objectionable except in rare instances when they are in keeping with the character of the action."[p] Consequently, if cinematography, as in acoustic lighting, can be said to govern the practice of on-set recording in the 1940s, then theatricality, as in "good theatre," was the guiding principle in terms of "volume control": "In actual life, a dance band will produce more than ten million times the sound energy of a quiet scene in a murder mystery. This is a 70-dB [decibel] difference, but if the murder scene were recorded 70-dB lower in level than a properly chosen dance band level, the dialog would be completely inaudible in the theatre."[q] The interest of this passage from *The Technique of Motion Picture Production* is that it not only highlights the difference between sound heard in real life as opposed to dialogue produced on a sound stage but that it effectively underscores the whole issue of exhibition and projection.

Before a motion picture could be released for exhibition in a theater, though, on-set production sound had to be *re*recorded, and this *post*production phase, even in 1944, was equally, if not more complex than "location audio" or "field recording" (to use contemporary parlance). Thus, after principal photography was completed, a "cutting [sound] track" separate from the "picture track" was sent in the form of 1,000-foot reels to the rerecording supervisor and his crew, which typically comprised a rerecording mixer, two sound-track editors, a sound-effects editor, and a projectionist. After the sound-track editors checked their reels for problems with dialogue and synchronization, sound-and-picture "dupes" were printed for dialogue

[m] Handzo, "Glossary of Film Sound Technology," 413.

[n] Thrasher, *Okay for Sound*, 229.

[o] Tasker, "The Technique of Production Sound Recording," 59.

[p] Ibid., 59.

[q] Ibid., 60.

"looping" (now accomplished via "Automatic Dialogue Replacement" [ADR]) and to allow the music department to begin scoring the picture.

While the "musical director and his associates" (composer, arranger, etc.) spotted the dupe picture print for musical cues, the sound-effects editor would do the same for the sound track, incorporating those "direct" or "sync" sounds already recorded during production (in addition to—again, in contemporary parlance—non-sync "wild" location sound or "pfx"), scouting the library for stock sound effects ("laughing," "applause," "street" and "crowd noise") as well as creating original sound effects on the Foley stage.[r] Then, once the music department completed its work, the "dubbing" or rerecording mixer utilized the detailed cue sheets for dialogue, music, and effects provided by the respective editors to remix the various tracks for contrast and balance, using the tricks of the trade—filters, amplifiers, etc.—in order to "sweeten" the overall sound and to "heighten [the picture's] dramatic presentation."[s]

It's here, in the mixing stage, that the "artistry rather than the technical ability of the mixer comes into play."[t] As *Elements of Sound Recording* (1949) puts it, the rerecording mixer, under the supervision of the managing sound editor, was able to "change at will the volume and character of any of the sound components and blend them into a harmonious whole that will reflect the mood of the accompanying photographic scene."[u] If the end point of motion picture sound (re)production in classical Hollywood cinema is predicated, as the above passage indicates, on a Romantic notion of the organic work of art, the emphasis in the same passage on transformation ("change") and volition ("at will") also anticipates the contemporary sound designer's ability to radically manipulate aural phenomena and, in the process, fabricate another, sonic field, a world of noise unto itself that does not merely accompany but rivals that of the image. As Kenneth Morgan lyricized about rerecording in 1931 at the dawn of the sound era, "it is an acoustical art in itself and represents a new form of composition in sound where the artist's keyboard commands the sounds of the universe."[v]

[r] In *Okay for Sound*, Thrasher enumerates: "unusual sounds such as the motor of a fast, special type racing boat, a delicate clock tick, and a rare bird call are all on file as well as the widely used handclap, hoof-beat and crowd noise" (242).

[s] L. T. Goldsmith, "Re-Recording Sound Motion Pictures," in *The Technique of Motion Picture Production*, 43. For example, just as sound tracks were run at different speeds to generate special aural effects, circuit equalizers were employed to simulate various types of sound such as the radio, telephone, and Dictaphone. Silence was also, if you will, part of the "mix": "Silence is used constantly as counterpoint against sound to intensify the emotional content of a scene" (Thrasher, *Okay for Sound*, 256).

[t] Thrasher, *Okay for Sound*, 229. And here it should be noted that a mixer was also present, whether on or off the set, during shooting. That is, the ostensibly "raw" sound picked up by the microphones on the set was transmitted to a recording machine: "with a number of microphones placed around the set, the sound from on location comes to the mixer panel at the volume established by the mixer" (Thrasher, *Okay for Sound*, 228–229). On the rerecordist simultaneously mixing eight tracks like an organ player, a conceit that is musical rather than, say, cinematographic, see also K. B. Lambert's remarks circa 1941 in Hanson, "Sound Affects," 37–38.

[u] John Frayne and Halley Wolfe, *Elements of Sound Recording* (New York: J. T. Wiley, 1949), 505.

[v] Morgan, "Dubbing" (1931), quoted in Hanson, "Sound Affects," 35.

If the most visually expressive animal imagery in forties noir is the aquarium sequence in *The Lady from Shanghai*, the most acoustically impressive is the zoo sequence in *Kiss the Blood off My Hands* (1948). (Executives at Universal-International found the title of Norman Foster's film needlessly "gruesome," but in retrospect it's one of the most inspired in the classic canon.) Recorded by Leslie I. Carey and Corson Jowett, *Kiss the Blood off My Hands* stars Burt Lancaster as Bill Saunders, a "casualty" of the Second World War whose "wounds" of the mind, to cite the discursive prologue, are as raw as the bombed-out London locales photographed by Russell Metty.[21]

Saunders's fate is sealed, true to the axiomatic logic of noir, at the film's start: when he doesn't leave a pub fast enough at closing time, the proprietor threatens to get rough. Indignant, Saunders knocks him down, but the proprietor accidentally hits his head against a piano leg and dies. Seeking refuge, Saunders breaks into the apartment of Jane Wharton (Joan Fontaine) and, when she doesn't report him to the authorities, pursues a relationship with her. However, when they meet again—she's getting out of work and he's just purchased a suit—she politely asks him to leave before she enters a zoo.

After Jane stops among schoolchildren to watch some barking seals, Saunders suddenly appears at her elbow. Although he gets her to smile by making a monkey face, the hopeful mood is shattered when a zoo attendant prods a hunk of meat at a lion (it's feeding time) and the growling rouses the other animals. A montage of wildly cacophonous sounds—bear, panther, leopard—reflects Saunders's increasingly unbalanced mental state. Finally, when a chimpanzee begins to bang its feet against the bars of its cage, Saunders, sweating profusely, confesses he "can't stand to see anything caged up" because he was incarcerated for two years behind barbed wire in a Nazi prisoner-of-war camp.

The full implications of Saunders's confession are dramatically reenacted when he's arrested for robbery and violent assault, then sentenced to "six months hard labor on each count," plus "eighteen strokes of a cat o' nine tails." The subsequent "whipping" scene is a tour-de-force of audiovisuality. After a guard ties Saunders's wrists to a metal hanger attached to a pulley and places a cloth brace around his neck, the pulley is raised and the camera cuts to a shot of Saunders, arms above his head, the shadows of the cell bars imprinted on the floor behind him like zebra stripes. While one guard counts the strokes and another in black leather gloves cocks the whip, the film cuts successively closer to Saunders's face as it distorts with pain, the periodic crack of the cat o' nine tails signified on the sound track by a musical "stinger."

Death Drive

Since the police in forties noir tend to appear more in patrol cars than on foot, the sound most associated with the law tends to be not so much a whip as a siren. In fact, the concluding action of many a film noir is punctuated, as in *The Big Sleep*, by the sound of a police siren. Hence the originality of Rudolph Maté's *The Dark Past* (1948), a scrupulous remake of Charles Vidor's *Blind Alley* (1939) in which the blaring siren at the end signals not the restoration of order, as in *The Big Sleep*, but the persistence of crime. In the final moments of Maté's film, after police psychiatrist Andrew Collins (Lee J. Cobb) has psychoanalyzed escaped convict Al Walker (William Holden) so that he's unable to use his handgun (the redemptive interpretation centers on a recurrent nightmare Walker has about being deluged with thundering "sheets of rain"), Dr. Collins stands watching from the window of his office as a siren screams below, marking the arrival of yet "another Al Walker."

Like Pete the Geek's scream in *Nightmare Alley*, a siren can also assume alarming, even hallucinatory proportions. In Goulding's "carnival" noir, Stanton Carlisle rises to the top of his racket entertaining people with his prowess as a mentalist until he meets his match in Dr. Lilith Ritter (Helen Walker), a psychoanalyst whose "icy intelligence" is matched only by her "soulless ambition."[22] Although Lilith has been feeding Stan inside dope about her clients, she uses her clinical knowledge of his dark past to ensnare him in her mercenary plans. Thus, when Stan wakes Dr. Ritter in the middle of the night to warn her about talking to the police, she counters by throwing the Freudian book at him, "All these things that you think you have done lately, or that have been done to you, are merely the fantasy guilt of your past life projected on the present. You must regard it all as a nightmare." Stan, who's spent his whole life conning other people, isn't buying: "Listen, [you] can't bluster me with that baloney." A siren wails in the distance. Is it a patrol car to take the Great Stanton to jail or an ambulance to cart him off to the sanitarium?

The siren sounds genuine enough, but Dr. Ritter has one more trick up her dirty sleeve, her insidious suggestion that the sound itself is a hallucination:

STANTON: Don't you think I got ears? What about that?
LILITH: What about what?
STANTON: That police siren.

Cut to a reaction shot of Dr. Ritter listening intently to Stan as if she were speaking to a child, then raising her limpid eyes and telling him calmly, "I don't hear anything." It's one of the most arresting, disorienting moments in classic noir since for a split second we too wonder, like Stan, whether what we're hearing is real or not.

Although car horns are by no means as prevalent as sirens in forties noir, they're employed to equally dramatic effect in various classic films. For example, in *Double Indemnity*, Phyllis honks the horn to signal Walter, who's hidden in the back seat of the car, that it's time to kill her husband. The scene is especially chilling since the camera stays on Phyllis's impassive face as the honking drowns out her husband's death throes. (In the context of sonic effects, it's also worth noting the slightly later scene—novel in 1944—where Phyllis cannot start her car and we anxiously wait for the ignition to catch. Finally, after she pushes the starter button three times, a sonic rhyme with the honking that masks her husband's murder, Walter calmly reaches over and the car, unlike Mr. Dietrichson, comes to life.)

In *The Postman Always Rings Twice*, sounds, as the wonderfully suggestive title intimates, possess an even more uncanny aspect than they do in *Double Indemnity*. Tay Garnett's film opens on a conspicuous audiovisual note when Cora Smith (Lana Turner), dressed in white like some roadside angel, "accidentally" drops her lipstick. As it rolls toward Frank Chambers (John Garfield), a drifter who's come looking for a little work, he has little choice but to stop and admire her shapely legs. And once he's seen them, he won't be able to leave, even if it means having to help Cora kill off her husband, Nick (Cecil Kellaway).

Oddly enough, it's the sound of a trailer-truck horn that first gets Frank thinking about what Chandler called the "simple art of murder." Nick is drunk to the gills and driving back to his diner one afternoon when a blast from an oncoming trailer-truck momentarily startles him into sobriety and he swerves out of the way. Frank, who's watching with Cora from inside Nick's roadside diner, The Twin Oaks, mutters, "That was close," then thinks out loud to himself, "I'd like to see him get plastered like that some night and drive off a cliff." Later, Frank's wishes come true when the three take a little road trip. Nick is drunkenly singing "There Is a Tavern in the Town" and the last thing he hears—right before Frank hits him over the head with a bottle—is his voice echoing in the canyons. To cover up the crime, Frank and Cora send the car over the cliff, but when it doesn't fall far enough, Frank has to scramble down to give it a push and becomes trapped inside. As it careens down the canyon, Cora's anguished screams for help reverberate in the desolate night air, providing a pathetic coda to Nick's happy-go-lucky singing.

While the inside of an automobile, particularly one equipped with a radio, is a popular setting for romance in forties noir (see, for instance, the kiss-me-once, kiss-me-again scene in *The Big Sleep*), cars in the period are associated more often than not, as in *The Postman Always Rings Twice*, with death and destruction. They're also, as in the gangster film, a "status symbol and instrument of power and control."[23] Thus, even though Eddie Roman hires Chuck Scott (Robert Cummings) as his personal chauffeur in *The Chase*, he's able to manipulate the speed of the car whenever his dark heart desires —and to Scott's considerable dismay—via another accelerator in the back seat. In *Dark City* Eddie Muller remarks that *The Chase* is "spellbinding as a car wreck,"[24] no doubt because of the spectacular dénouement where Roman, chasing Scott and Eddie's wife Lorna (Michèle Morgan), crashes his speeding limousine right into a train.

In fact, as the car-train collision that concludes the fantastic, Schumann-inspired overture to Edgar G. Ulmer's *Strange Illusion* (1945) epitomizes, car wrecks are almost as common in classic noir as fist fights or gunplay. Automobiles, in addition to being smashed into other cars (*They Live by Night* [1948]), are driven into poles (*The Strange Love of Martha Ivers*), ditches (*Moonrise*), bridges (*Desert Fury* [1947]), and police barricades (*Out of the Past*). Sometimes, as in *They Won't Believe Me*, *Impact* (1949), and *Thieves' Highway* (1949), they crash and burn. Occasionally, they're accoutrements of torture, as in *Border Incident* (see below), or shooting galleries, as in *White Heat* (1949) in which Cody Jarrett (James Cagney), munching on a drumstick, knocks off a fellow gang-member who crossed him in prison but is now locked in a trunk. Parker: "It's stuffy in here. I need some air." Cody: "Oh, stuffy, huh, I'll get you a little air." Bang. Bang. Bang. Bang. Bang.

Then there's *Manhandled* (1949), an end-of-the-line noir like *White Heat* and *Border Incident* that sonically showcases the sadistic potential of the American automobile. In this Lewis R. Foster film, a corrupt private detective, Karl Benson (Dan Duryea), uses a car to terminate a colleague. When Dr. Redman (Harold Vermilyea), a psychiatrist who moonlights as a jewel thief, double-crosses fellow burglar Benson, Benson jumps in a car and, zig-zagging, shadows the doctor down a back street. The climax is as violent as any in classic noir, the film crosscutting between Redman desperately running for his life and the car inching closer to his body until, caught in the car's headlights, Redman's pinned against a brick wall, his arms raised in the air like a suspect's. After gunning the engine, Benson drives the car right into Redman's body and, as the doctor screams bloody murder, the camera cuts first to Benson's gleeful face, his foot pumping the gas pedal, and, finally, the screeching tires. If cars are symbols of the masculine will to power, Benson, maniacally chewing gum while he grinds the psychiatrist into mincemeat (this is negative transference with a vengeance), is every bit as lunatic as Tommy Udo in *Kiss of Death*—a private dick gone bad, he's the mad, inhuman face of the death drive.

Tunnel of Hate

Although only 700 passenger cars were produced for private consumption in 1945 due to the war, by 1949 the number had risen to five million and the American automobile was "modestly priced and offered freedom of movement to everyone."[25] Accordingly, the sedans, coupés, and convertibles of the period—Ford, Chrysler, and General Motors as well as Nash, Kaiser, Frazer, Crosley, Packard, and Studebaker—populate not only the side streets and avenues of the "dark city" but, as dramatized in films such as *Detour* (1945), *The Devil Thumbs a Ride* (1947), and *They Live by Night*, the spaces *between* cities.[26]

Unlike *They Live by Night*, which is mostly set in rural America and whose romantic opening credits feature the traditional Scottish ballad "I Know Where I'm Going," *Act of Violence* (1948) captures the alienated sounds and spaces of modernity, a soundscape in which a car tunnel can be said to lead straight to a train station. In Fred Zinnemann's film, ex-bombardier Joe Parkson (Robert Ryan) has come to the picturesque Southern California town of San Lisa looking for his former CO, Frank Enley (Van Heflin), a "respected contractor and civic-minded man." While Enley was interned in a prison camp during the war, he became, as Parkson bitterly tells Enley's wife Edith (Janet Leigh), a "stool pigeon for the Nazis," informing on his fellow starving Americans who were planning to escape the camp via an underground tunnel.[27] (Enley did it, or so he's told himself over the years, to "save lives" but he was "paid": "They gave me food and I ate it.") Only Parkson, crippled and deranged by the experience, survived the attempted escape. Describing the aftermath in graphic detail to Edith, he recounts that "one of the [men] lasted till morning": "By then you couldn't tell his voice belonged to a man. He sounded like a dog that had been hit by a truck."

Parkson wants Enley to pay for his betrayal with his life, but Enley can't go to the police because he's "made a new life for himself" and the publicity would jeopardize his standing in the community. Instead, with the help of Pat (Mary Astor), a down-and-out prostitute whom he meets at an L.A. bar after attending a builders' convention there, he makes the acquaintance of an unsavory "attorney," Mr. Gavery, who suggests—for the tidy price of ten grand—the services of a "private cop," Johnny (Berry Kroeger). Although Enley is ultimately horrified by the idea, he's haunted by Gavery's voice when he rests briefly outside the bar ("You're the same man you were in Germany. You did it once, you'll do it again") and then again when he stops at the entrance to the Third Street Tunnel, "What do you care about one man? You've sent ten along already."

Enley, distraught, starts walking toward what one can only call the darkness at the end of the tunnel. As the camera tracks behind him and André Previn's music rumbles on the sound track, he's bombarded by fragments of conversation from his traumatic past as a prisoner of war:

PARKSON: Tonight the tunnel's through, the north corner . . . we make the break tonight.
ENLEY: You haven't got a chance. Remember what happened to the others.
PARKSON: We're not gonna starve any longer.
ENLEY: Don't do it, Joe, don't do it!

This waking nightmare, an involuntary auditory hallucination rendered in stream-of-consciousness, is succeeded by the voices of the camp commandant ("You have nothing to be ashamed of, Captain Enley. An officer's responsible for his men. They'll be treated with all possible leniency"), Parkson ("Tonight the north corner, you'll find the tunnel"), and a Nazi officer ("Achtung!"). Unable to take it any longer, Enley screams, "Don't do it, Joe! No, no, don't, no!" before rushing headlong toward the camera and out of the car tunnel, "whose roadway disappears into the vanishing point of the horizon."[28]

Once the voices stop, Enley leans against a chain-link fence (a visual allusion to his incarceration), then heads toward a train yard, the camera cutting to a shot of him standing in the middle of the tracks as a locomotive bears down, its whistle blaring, until he leaps out of the way and falls to his knees, weeping. If the tunnel sequence represents a repetition of Enley's painful experience in the prisoner-of-war camp, the "train yard" scene suggests that the past for Enley is not so much behind as directly in front of him. At the deserted Southern Pacific Station where the only sound is the wind whipping across the tracks, the "private cop" Johnny pulls up in a car while Enley and Parkson walk straight toward each other as in a Western showdown—at the very last second, Enley sees that Johnny's about to shoot Parkson and throws himself in front of Parkson's body, saving his life.

Like the car tunnel, a vertiginous space in which the "resonances of the past erupt with explosive force,"[29] the train station in *Act of Violence* becomes the vehicle for a traumatic past that, in the avenging form of Joe Parkson, can no longer be suppressed. Enley's act of atonement, figured by his dying scream, is the junction between the crack of Johnny's gun and the passing train associated with Parkson, a sonic effect that reveals the hidden continuity between two worlds: the patent violence of the prison camp and the violence hidden right below the surface of the seemingly peaceful, suburban post-Holocaust world.

Stranger on a Train

Although by the 1940s American railroads, "once associated with progress and expansion, had lost much of their place in the American psyche,"[30] they began to reclaim some of their cultural cachet during the war years in noirs such as *Berlin Express* (1948) and *Sleep, My Love* in which they become a charged setting for romance and intrigue. (Subway trains also offer a gritty sonic backdrop in a number of forties noirs such as *Cornered*, *The Window*, *The Gangster*, and *The Dark Corner*.) However, it's in Irving Reis's *Crack-Up* (1946) even more so than in *Act of Violence* that the various sounds associated with trains—whistles, crossing signs, the persistent clicking of wheels on railroad tracks—are deployed to maximum expressionist effect.

Crack-Up, a "key thriller in the noir cycle,"[31] stars Pat O'Brien as George Steele, a New York art curator who's a passionate opponent of modern art —in particular, surrealism, which he calls "nonsense"—and an equally passionate advocate of popular painting: "If knowing what you like is a good enough way to pick out a wife or a house or a pair of shoes" (these activities are apparently commensurate), "what's wrong with applying the same rule to painting?"

One night George, drunk and disorderly, breaks into the Manhattan Museum and, while fighting off a security guard, accidentally topples a classical male torso. Although he later claims his actions were the result of a train accident, he has absolutely no recollection of "what happened between the time of the wreck and his appearance at the museum" and, moreover, there's "no record of the accident."[32] In a classic psychoanalytic scenario (George is supine on a couch), Dr. Lowell (Ray Collins) asks him about the "crack-up" and the film flashes back to Joe's Place where George and his girlfriend Terry Cordell (Claire Trevor) are listening to "The First Time I Saw You" on the jukebox. (It's the song that was playing when they first met; it's also the song that provides the main musical motif for *Out of the Past.*)

After a waiter interrupts the couple to tell George he has a call (he learns that his mother has suddenly fallen ill), he leaves immediately for Grand Central Station. Cut to George sitting in a window seat aboard a train, his face doubled in the glass, a Doppelgänger effect that suggests psychic division. A whistle blares in the distance and when George looks out, he sees that the oncoming train, racing around the curve at full tilt, is on the same track as the train he's on. The alternation between subjective and objective shots—the interior reflecting the locomotive's beam growing brighter in the passenger window, the exterior capturing the train's exhaust drifting like clouds across the windowpane—builds to a rapid track-in to George's bewildered face, a shot of a random passenger, and then, as the trains collide, an explosion of white light, screams and, finally, darkness.

Although the experience is truly harrowing (the sequence itself is a dynamic fusion of music, montage, and sound effects[33]), George is determined to repeat it in order to understand what's happened to him. Not unlike the ex-servicemen protagonists of other amnesia noirs such as *Somewhere in the Night* (1946) and *The Crooked Way*, he becomes a "detective investigating his own past," engaged in a desperate search to reclaim his now shattered identity.[34] (The theme is made explicit when George, who aided the Allies during the war by exposing Nazi forgeries, says, "Seen a lot of good guys crack up in this war.")

Retracing his steps, George purchases another train ticket and takes the same seat as before, even going so far as to ask a professorial man, burdened down with books, to move. Everything seems fine until the steadily clicking sound of the tracks becomes louder and, suddenly, it's déjà vu all over again: the other train, its searchlight lancing the night, is racing around a curve bearing down fast . . . then rushes by, the light from the windows flashing strobe-like across his terrified face. Relieved, George pushes his hat back on his forehead, but when the conductor comes on the intercom to announce the next stop, his voice sounds strangely garbled and, in an optical dissolve, George's head—detached, as in the classical nude, from his body—reverse-zooms into a dark vortex and the screen goes black.

It's only when the conductor clearly enunciates the word "Marlin" that George snaps out of his trance, getting off at the next stop where he discovers an unidentified "drunken" man had gotten off the previous week. That man, of course, was George Steele, who later discovers he was doped because some famous paintings on loan at the museum that he planned to X-ray are fakes. The mastermind of the art forgery ring is Dr. Lowell who, unlike George, believes that art is for the select, discriminating few: "museums have a habit of wasting great art on dolts."

The bang-up conclusion of *Crack-Up* turns on a quotidian, everyday sound. After George is knocked unconscious by Lowell's henchmen and taken to his house where, as in the film's opening, he's laid out on the couch like a corpse, the doctor administers sodium pentothal, then plans to shoot George at the exact moment the Chicago train is passing to muffle the sound of the gunshot. However, an undercover Scotland Yard detective arrives just in time to shoot the doctor and it becomes clear that Lowell's "devilishly brilliant plan" was to use what the detective Traybin (Herbert Marshall) calls the "handy" sound effects of the train, combined with the power of suggestion, to simulate a "crack-up." "He'll be all right when the injection wears off," Traybin nonchalantly remarks to Terry, "He'll just think he's been in another train wreck." Easy for him to say.

While the use of narcosynthesis associates fine art, as in *The Dark Corner*, with villainy, the new technologies of "truth," the X-ray and sodium pentothal, are ultimately subordinate in *Crack-Up* to the film's central audiovisual event: the train wreck itself, which becomes an exquisite sonic trope for the psychic dislocations of the postwar world. Hence the bravura opening of Reis's film, a smash cut from a head-on shot of a locomotive hurtling toward the camera to George Steele shattering the plate-glass entrance to the Manhattan Museum.

Borderlands

If it's unsurprising that the sonic effects associated with cars and trains are omnipresent in forties noir, it's something of a surprise to learn that one of the most resonant soundscapes in the period involves, of all things, a disc tractor. If it's also unsurprising that the film, *Border Incident*, was directed by Anthony Mann, whose forties films are virtually synonymous with the genre, it's also surprising to learn that the sound track was supervised, like *Act of Violence*, by Douglas Shearer who was responsible not only for making Leo the Lion roar at M-G-M but for the sound on some of the most celebrated musicals in the history of Hollywood, including *The Wizard of Oz* (1939), *Meet Me in St. Louis* (1944), *Singin' in the Rain* (1952), and *The Band Wagon* (1953).

The premise of *Border Incident* is a unique and, at the moment, highly topical one: criminals are smuggling *braceros*—"those who work with hands and arms"—across the Mexico-California border as cheap labor for what the omniscient, stentorian narrator describes as the "vast farm empire" located in the Imperial Valley (the penultimate word of which has the appropriate colonialist inflection). The *braceros* are not merely exploited—they're only paid half-wages on this side of the border—but killed and robbed of their meager earnings once they try to cross over to Mexico. The scenes where the *braceros* are murdered for their money are, true to Mann's dark aesthetic, typically swift and savage: in a montage set in the aptly titled Valle de Muerte, they're ambushed, then knifed to death and dumped in a bog into which their bodies slowly sink and disappear. In the persons of Captain Pablo Rodriguez (Ricardo Montalban) and Inspector Jack Bearnes (George Murphy), the Policia Federale and the Immigration and Naturalization Services decide to join forces to break the continuing cycle of "human suffering and injustice." As Colonel Raphael Alvarado says at the film's outset, if the smugglers "work together to break the law," then (and here he's speaking for both the Mexican and American authorities) "we will work together to enforce the law."

This noble sentiment, though, is subject to an increasingly corrosive irony in the course of *Border Incident* since the federal agents, unlike the smugglers, must work undercover and, all too frequently, alone. For example, no sooner are the agents given the go-ahead by their superior than they're split up. While Rodriguez pretends to be a *bracero* and is transported across the border together with another *bracero* he's befriended, Juan Garcia, Bearnes adopts the alias of Jack Bryant, a fugitive wanted by the FBI for stealing illegal immigration permits, in order to infiltrate the "border slave trade" overseen by Owen Parkson (Howard Da Silva).

The perilous nature of Bearnes's assignment is conveyed in a number of scenes that are acoustically earmarked. For instance, it's established early on in the film that for Parkson the *braceros* whom he buys and sells mean no more to him than the miniature pigeons he practices shooting with a toy pistol in his "game room." The fact that he shoots at these targets from across the room while sitting behind his desk comments on the long-distance nature of his operation: in a very real sense, he's spatially divorced from the implications of his criminal operation, in particular the slaughter of the *braceros* when they try to return to their native country. Whether it's the walkie-talkie that Parkson's runners use to communicate with each other to evade the border patrol or the recording machine in his office that his Mexican subalterns marvel at ("Dear Tom. . . . I hope to be able to fulfill your labor requirements"), Parkson's mastery of the new communications technologies reflects his desire to remain as unsullied as possible by his farm-labor racket.

Bearnes's assignment to pretend to be a pawn in Parkson's predatory game is underscored when his superiors outline his mission and, before he gets up to leave, the T-man describes himself as "Pigeon, Clay Pigeon." Bearnes's eventual fate—"one of the most grisly in this period of film history"[35]—is foreshadowed when he's found out by Hugo Wolfgang Ulrich (Sig Ruman) and his henchmen, Cuchillo (Alfonso Bedoya) and Pocoloco (José Torvay). In order to extract information about Bearnes's identity, Hugo's men bind his arms in front of his body, slip a metal rod through them, then connect the rod via a wire to a running truck. The torture is as ingenious as it is simple: each time Bearnes refuses to answer one of Hugo's questions, he's violently shocked, his face straining with pain as the electricity courses through his body.

The torture scene is particularly disturbing since Bearnes has to endure a certain amount of pain to convince Hugo's men he's telling the truth when he finally gives up his false identity as Jack Bryant, which he eventually does ("I'll tell ya! I'll tell ya!") by telling them about the FBI Wanted List hidden in his left shoe. At this point Bearnes makes his move, offering Parkson the packet of illegal immigration permits in exchange for money. Bearnes now appears to have the upper hand, a position of superiority emphasized when he casually picks up Parkson's air pistol and, in one motion, shoots over his shoulder and hits the target. But in an unexpected reversal, he's caught out when Parkson calls Kansas City and, learning that "Bryant" is a federal agent, orders his foreman, Jeff Amboy (Charles McGraw), to take care of him and "make it look like an accident."

In her early monograph on Mann, Jeanine Basinger remarks that "every film Mann made between 1947 and 1950 takes place in the modern urban world."[36] Although this is true for the majority of Mann's films in this period, *Border Incident*, anticipating the way the director would use the "craggy formations and vast nocturnal landscape" in his fifties Westerns,[37] is set—as the film's narrator says—in the "great agricultural empire of California." Mann's bleak, unsparing vision of cultivated nature—a no-man's land between nature and culture, the city and the country—is exhibited in the "disc tractor" sequence in which the idea of man's elemental aggression, what one critic calls an "original dictionary of the ways in which to punish the human body,"[38] is graphically documented.

It's the dead of night and Amboy, armed with a shotgun and accompanied by a Mexican farmhand, marches Bearnes to the middle of a field that's empty except for a disc tractor. Garcia and Rodriguez, having escaped from their captors, are positioned at the field's edge, waiting and watching. Sensing time is running out, Bearnes knocks down Amboy and the farmhand, but when he tries to escape, he's gunned down, then smashed in the head with the butt of a gun. Stunned, Bearnes lies immobile in the foreground of the frame, his body inert like that of an infant trying to lift his head off the ground.

The heart of the sequence begins when, in an echo of the earlier torture scene, Amboy starts up the tractor, the engine's whine slicing the night air as the film cuts to a ground-level shot of the rotating disc attached to the rear of the tractor, its enormous curved blades caked with dirt. While the Mexican farmhand stands over Bearnes and Garcia and Rodriguez watch from a distance, Amboy steers the tractor toward Bearnes, its diesel engine chuffing, its two headlights lit up like enormous eyes. After Garcia and Rodriguez, desperate to help Bearnes, run up and throw themselves on the ground (the fixed camera position reinforcing their utter futility), the film cuts to a complementary two shot—man versus machine—with Bearnes pinned down in the left foreground and, in the near background, the tractor looming larger and larger. Garcia and Rodriguez inch closer as Bearnes, his face smeared with soil, frantically digs his fingers into the earth, pathetically trying to crawl out of the way.

Fig. 4. Mulch: I.N.S. agent Jack Bearnes (George Murphy) face to face with the disc tractor driven by Jeff Amboy (Charles McGraw) in Anthony Mann's *Border Incident*.

Its engine laboring, its massive grill blotting out the screen, the tractor continues to bear down on Bearnes until in an extremely tight close-up from his point of view, the undercarriage of the tractor passes over him and he's face to face with the disc's giant blades. There's a snapshot of Bearnes's face pushed up against the camera, his mouth twisted into a grimace, eyes wide with fear, then another equally brief shot of the disc slicing into the soft, rich earth, and, finally, a cutaway to Garcia and Rodriguez looking away, their foreheads pressed down on their clasped hands, as if in prayer.

"If one scene were chosen to illustrate the violence of film noir," Basinger writes, "Murphy's death in *Border Incident* would surely be the best choice."[39] One reason the disc tractor sequence remains so shocking is that it's "good old Murphy"[40]—rather than his Mexican "buddy," Montalban—who's killed off. Murphy in fact was familiar to postwar audiences from the musical comedies he had made over the previous decade from *Kid Millions* (1934) to *This Is the Army* (1943), in the latter of which he played Irving Berlin. Although Montalban also appeared in various musicals such as *Neptune's Daughter* (1949) and would go on to star as a police detective in *Mystery Street* (1950), it was a "generic axiom" at the time that the minority figure would eventually meet his "gruesome demise" in the course of the picture, while the white male "Americano"—to quote the xenophobically "normal" Oliver in *Cat People*—would survive to save the day and pontificate on his *partner*'s sacrifice.[41]

It's in this generic context that the infantilization of Murphy's character assumes a subtly subversive charge in *Border Incident* given that the only thing more shocking than watching an All-American hero die, chewed up like mulch, is seeing an adult red-blooded male reduced to a baby, his face soiled with "pablum." As Jonathan Auerbach remarks, "Jack's final glimpse of the underside of the tractor is a purely *noir* moment of recognition that reveals the terrifying underbelly of the American farm industry . . . and [its] ruthless exploitation of Mexican labor."[42]

The radicality of the disc tractor sequence in *Border Incident* has, I suspect, been obscured by Murphy's later career à la Ronald Reagan as a politician. (And here I must add that it's always best to trust the character, not the actor.[43]) Thus, Eddie Muller, comparing Mann's film to another "agri-noir," *Thieves' Highway* (whose impeccable liberal credentials are underwritten by its director and screenwriter, Jules Dassin and A. I. Bezzerides, respectively), casts *Border Incident* in a "Republican" light: "*Border Incident*, like *T-Men*, is undermined by its association with the Federal government. In exchange for the imprimatur of the Justice Department and the Immigration and Naturalization Services, the film was obligated to show criminal labor practices as the work of a few small renegades—not corporate America."[44]

Muller is no doubt correct about the overt politics of *Border Incident* vis-à-vis *Thieves' Highway* (the representation of, inter alia, the Mexican "coyotes" is also open to criticism). However, to invoke Janey Place on the femme fatale, what one takes from *Border Incident* is not so much its compromised narrative as certain searing sounds and images. From this audiovisual perspective, Bearnes's brutal subjection—and, by implication, the audience's—to the law of the genre constitutes a radical gesture, all the more so for being subsidized by M-G-M. (In retrospect, Mann conceded the film was not "Metro's cup of tea": "They were flabbergasted. It wasn't anything they thought a motion picture should be."[45]) To paraphrase Muller, the "dull" conclusion of *Border Incident* is no match for Mann's "cutting edge" and Shearer's razor-sharp sound track.

3

Audio Technologies

INTERCOMS AND DICTAPHONES, TELEPHONES AND RADIOS, PHONOGRAPHS AND JUKEBOXES

As Nicholas Christopher observes in *Somewhere in the Night* (1997), there is an "ongoing fascination in film noir with electrical devices," a "galaxy of new machines and luxury" accoutrements such as the radio and hi-fi phonograph that rapidly became essential to the lives of Americans in the postwar period and that, in the "hands of both criminals and the police, altered the urban landscape in a way that could be *heard*."[1]

Of Intercoms and Dictaphones

In John Farrow's *The Big Clock* (1948), the "noir universe *is* the office building."[2] The Janoth Building becomes the labyrinthine space or maze in which George Stroud (Ray Milland), the managing editor of *Crimeways*, a magazine that's the publishing equivalent of a tabloid detective agency, finds himself in a paradoxical but paradigmatic noir predicament: the object of his crack team's investigative powers is none other than Stroud himself.

Telephones are omnipresent in *The Big Clock*. For example, the flashback narrative begins with George's secretary informing him, even as he's striding past her toward his office, that he has two calls, one from his wife and one from a source in Salt Lake City about an ongoing case. The most distinctive sound technology in the film, however, is the intercom. It makes its first, unremarkable appearance in a scene where Earl Janoth (Charles Laughton), having made his grand entrance from a private elevator at 11:00 A.M. on the dot, is presiding over a business conference and, right in the middle of one of his underling's reports, informs his secretary, "Hold the call from Boston."

The intercom's status as a mode of domination as well as surveillance is reinforced in the following scene when Janoth, who has just been surprised by a visit from his mistress, Pauline York (Rita Johnson), listens in on a private conversation between Stroud and Janoth's right-hand man, Steve Hagen (George Macready). Stroud has been deferring his honeymoon for five years and his marriage is now on the rocks: "I've been working twenty-six hours a day, Christmases, Fourth of Julys, Mother's Days. What does Janoth think I am, a clock with springs and gears instead of flesh and blood?" After Hagen tells Stroud that their employer expects loyalty from everyone —"from the top right down to the bottom"—Janoth tells Pauline, "Shut that thing off."

Later, Janoth, informing Hagen via intercom that he's decided to talk to Stroud himself about his decision to quit ("When does he think he's leaving?"), displays his micro-managerial mania: "Steve, on the fourth floor in the broom closet, a bulb has been burning for several days. Find the man responsible. Dock his pay." Janoth is a white-collar monster, but his dominion over Stroud takes an unexpected twist when George shares a drink with Pauline after work. A quartet is playing "I'm in the Mood for Love," and Pauline, describing herself as a "woman of mystery," reads his palm, correctly guessing that he has recently quarreled with a "very unpleasant man" about working "twenty-six hours a day." No femme fatale, Pauline admits she was listening in on Stroud's conversation with Hagen in Janoth's office, at which point the couple realize that they're both under the big man's thumb.

However, when Janoth sees a man leaving his mistress's apartment that night (he doesn't recognize Stroud), he murders her with a sun-dial (a sign, given his obsession with time, of a primitive regression) and then has Hagen clean up the mess. Now partners in crime, Janoth and Hagen decide to pin the murder on the unidentified person leaving Pauline's apartment. The noose begins to tighten for Stroud when Hagen buzzes him on the intercom to stand by for a call from the "communications czar": "George, I want this man smoked out. Use the guard. Mobilize everyone. Floor-by-floor search.

Follow through in person, understand me?"[3] Stroud, Janoth's best, most aggressive editor, is now at the mercy of the very same machinery he manages every day to bring criminals to justice.

In a reversal of the aural surveillance that signifies his enslavement to the Janoth regime, Stroud eavesdrops on a conversation between Janoth and Hagen on the intercom, then, seizing the means of communication, uses it to set them up: "I'm in Hagen's office, Mr. Janoth. I've nailed our man. He'll be here as soon as you and Hagen get here." Since Stroud and his long-suffering wife, Georgette (Maureen O'Sullivan), have found a handkerchief in Hagen's office that implicates Janoth's right-hand man, they decide to put the screws to him. But confronted with the evidence, Hagen refuses to take the rap for his boss and instead gives him up. Although Janoth tries to shoot his way out, he falls to his death in his private elevator shaft crowned by a clock that symbolizes the vertiginous, rapidly upward and downward world of forties corporate culture.

As Lutz Koepnick notes, "Whether they transmit, record, or amplify linguistic expression, voice machines abound in Hollywood's dark cinema."[4] In *The Big Clock*, George Stroud's strategic recourse to the intercom, an audio technology associated with the corporate world and its infernal affairs, enables him to outwit his antagonists. It also enables him to answer the question that, trapped inside the big clock, he asks himself in voice-over at the very beginning of the film, "How did I get into this rat race anyway?"

The intercom and Dictaphone are interpersonal means of communication common to the corporate sphere in the 1940s, but unlike the intercom, the Dictaphone was designed not to transmit but to record memoranda. While it has a complex function in terms of both narrative and narration in Billy Wilder's *Double Indemnity*, it does not appear in the novel on which the film is based. In Cain's novel, the head of the Claims Department, Barton Keyes, instructs Walter Huff to write up a statement detailing his criminal activities before he and Phyllis leave on a steamer "for Balboa and points south."[5] (Although Keyes has made the travel reservations for Huff and Phyllis Nirdlinger, his confederate in the murder-for-insurance-money scam, he knows the two will never make it because Walter is bleeding internally and Phyllis no longer has the will to go on. In fact, she's decided to "meet her bridegroom," Mister Death, by jumping off the stern of the ship.[6])

The difference in narration between the novel and film version of *Double Indemnity* is substantial. Whereas in Cain's novel we learn only in the final chapter that what we've just read is Huff's statement, in Wilder's film the

Fig. 5. *Apologia pro Vita Sua*: Walter Neff (Fred MacMurray) confessing into the Dictaphone in Billy Wilder's *Double Indemnity*.

Dictaphone is introduced near the beginning of the action. A car runs a red light, the bell clanging as the sign changes to "Stop," then careens wildly around a honking truck before pulling up outside an office building. A man in a hat with his overcoat thrown over his shoulders walks up to the glass doors of the All-Pacific Risk Insurance Co. and knocks. A night attendant arrives and takes the man in an elevator to the mezzanine floor where there's a wide-open, panoptic view of the workplace below—desk after desk after desk—deserted now except for the black janitorial staff emptying waste baskets. Once inside his office, the man slips out of his coat and turns on a desk lamp, dispelling the Venetian-blind shadows, and we see Walter Neff: "Thirty-five years old. Unmarried. No visible scars—until a while ago, that is."

Loosening his tie as he settles into a chair, Walter uses his one good hand to pull out a pack of cigarettes and, in a bit of business that will continue to accrue meaning in the course of the film, strikes a match with his thumbnail and lights a cigarette. After inhaling deeply, he wheels over to the Dictaphone, takes out a recording cylinder and inserts it into the machine. When it buzzes, he begins to speak:

> Office memorandum: Walter Neff. Department: Keyes, Claims Manager. Los Angeles, July 16, 1938. Dear Keyes, suppose you'll call this a confession when you hear it. Well, I don't like the word "confession." I just want to set you right about something you couldn't see because it was smack up against your nose. You think you're such a hot potato as a claims manager, such a wolf against a phony claim. Maybe you are. Let's take a look at that Dietrichson claim. Accident in double indemnity. You were pretty good in there for a while, Keyes. You said it wasn't an accident. Check. You said it wasn't suicide. Check. You said it was murder. Check. You thought you had it cold, didn't you? All wrapped up in tissue paper with pink ribbons around it. It was perfect except it wasn't because you made one mistake. Just one little mistake. When it came to picking the killer, you picked the wrong guy. You want to know who killed Dietrichson? Hold tight to that cheap cigar of yours. I killed Dietrichson. Me. Walter Neff. . . . Yes, I killed him. I killed him for money and for a woman. I didn't get the money and I didn't get the woman. Funny, isn't it?

This "confession"—wry yet full of heart—is performed in the film by Fred MacMurray, a "second-tier Paramount star" who "had been a saxophone player in an orchestra where the talent scouts spotted him."[7] However, as Wilder once remarked ("I didn't say he was in a choir. That was a dance band he played in"[8]), there was more to MacMurray than met the eye. Beneath the gray-flannel manner was another, more cynical self, the MacMurray who "knew something about the hard and slippery life—one-night stands, shady nightclubs, wise-guy managers."[9]

Therefore, although the voice-over starts out on an appropriately professional note ("Office memorandum . . ."), it almost immediately comes alive with the demotic patter of the door-to-door life-insurance salesman ("smack up against your nose"). This street sensibility, the persona of a guy who's "just a little too smooth, a little too quick, a little too salesman-sleazy" for his own good,[10] is reflected in Walter's tone, which is full of the sort of false bravado that comes when you've just gambled everything and there's nothing left to lose. Then there's the poetry, which comes through in the lively metaphors ("wolf for a phony claim," "hot potato"), antistrophe

("You said. . . . Check"), and mocking rhetorical questions ("You thought you had it cold, didn't you?"). In fine, a soliloquy masquerading as an office memo, Walter's voice-over is laced with the "rhythms of ordinary American speech," only it's just a little jazzier, like the banter between Walter and Phyllis, "than we are likely to hear in life."[11]

Of course, the initial Dictaphone scene, as well as the five succeeding ones, is also a device—like Jeff and Ann's car ride to Lake Tahoe in *Out of the Past*—to anchor the first-person point of view. Call them rest areas on the highway to hell that is *Double Indemnity*. Consequently, whenever we see Walter sitting at that desk speaking into the Dictaphone, "we know we have returned to the present time, temporarily rescued from the dark events of the past."[12] At the same time, despite the darkness that descends like nightfall on Walter and Phyllis's plans, there are occasional moments of light and lucidity or, at least, reprieve along the way.

Thus, after Walter and Phyllis have murdered her husband, Neff is worried about what Keyes knows and searches his office. After rifling through the papers on the desk, Neff spots the Dictaphone and turns it on. What he hears is music to his ears since at the All-Pacific Risk Insurance Co., Keyes's word is as good as gold:

> Memo to Mr. Norton. Confidential. Dietrichson file. With regard to your proposal to put Walter under surveillance. I disagree absolutely. . . . I've known Neff intimately for years and I personally vouch for him without reservation.

This Dictaphone recording, which occurs in the past tense of the film and exonerates Walter of any possible wrongdoing, grounds the later, present-tense voice-over scenes. In fact, as evidenced by the initial voice-over's direct address ("Keyes") and mock injunctions ("Hold on to that cheap cigar of yours"), there's genuine affection between the two men. That is, the real "love story in the picture," as Wilder himself remarked, is not between Walter and Phyllis or even Walter and Lola but between Walter and Keyes.[13]

Since Walter in the voice-over scenes might be said to be talking to his father, his confession also retroactively illuminates his overriding desire not simply to crook the house and get the girl but best Keyes and his "little man." In this sense, the horn of the Dictaphone is a double of the matchstick that Walter, ever ready, uses to light Keyes's perpetually unlit cigar, a conceit that's consummated in the final scene of the film. It's 4:30 in the morning and Walter's wrapping up his story with tissue paper and pink ribbons ("I want you to take care of [Lola] and that guy Zachetti so he doesn't get pushed around too much") when he finally sees Keyes and hangs up the Dictaphone. Keyes in fact has been standing by the door for some time, but when he moves to phone a doctor (Walter's "leaked a little blood on the way in"), Neff tries to stop him, saying he doesn't want to get patched up for the gas chamber at San Quentin and is leaving for Mexico. Keyes warns him he'll never make it to the border, let alone the elevator, but he lets him leave and Walter collapses on the threshold of the office.

Finally out of gas, his dream of escaping to Mexico gone like his dream of the perfect score—of getting the money *and* the girl—Walter pulls out a pack of cigarettes. As he fumbles around trying to light his cigarette, Keyes is there to strike the match:

WALTER: The guy you were looking for was right across the desk from you.
KEYES: Closer than that.
WALTER: I love you, too.

In *Double Indemnity*, the Dictaphone is at once near and far, close as another person's heartbeat and distant, as in *D.O.A.* and *Sunset Blvd.*, as a dead man's voice.

Dial N for Noir

Although the immediate postwar period "represented an era of on-going stability for the telephone and its basic meaning and functions,"[14] it continued to be imbued with all sorts of affect. Alfred Hitchcock, for example, once confessed that the sound of a ringing phone made him jump —"It's like a knife through the shoulder blades"[15]—and in "an age of telephones," as David Thomson observes, "we are made more attentive to ambient sound."[16]

This heightened attention to ambient sound is foregrounded in *Force of Evil* (1948), a celebrated film noir in which the telephone, according to director Abraham Polonsky, "is a dangerous object."[17] In fact, in *Force of Evil* the telephone represents the link between the legitimate corporate world represented by attorney Joe Morse (John Garfield) and the "numbers racket" that's "conducted almost exclusively over the phone wires."[18] Ben Tucker

(Roy Roberts) is the kingpin of a syndicate that Joe's trying to legalize but which his brother, Leo (Thomas Gomez), the owner of a small independent "bank," stubbornly refuses to join.

In the film's penultimate sequence—before Joe, carried by Raksin's score, makes his way down to the East River where his brother's body lies on the rocks below the Manhattan Bridge—he outwits Bill Ficco (Paul Fix), a rival racketeer who's ordered his death, by sneaking a tapped phone out of his desk and lifting the receiver from its cradle so that the police and the prosecutor Hall can listen in. Telling off Tucker ("I'm not going to end up on the rocks in the river like my brother"), Joe, phone still in hand, sweeps the lamp off his desk, plunging the room into darkness. While the phone steadily hums, "alive, open, talking to Hall" (to cite Polonsky's super-literate script), Joe, a "black figure in the blackness," shoots Ficco, then walks over to the phone and, picking up the receiver, says, "This is Joe Morse. Tell Mr. Hall and the police I'll be down to see them in an hour."[19] As with George Stroud in *The Big Clock*, Joe turns the means of communication—here, the telephone—on his adversaries, in the process arresting the spreading web of corruption.

In "Two or Three Things about the Telephone," Jean-Luc Godard essays that the phone reminds us "we are very selfish, very isolated, so curious to know. Every phone call might transform our lives. It's all liberty or slavery."[20] In Anatole Litvak's *Sorry, Wrong Number* (1948), adapted from a radio play by Lucille Fletcher that was originally heard on the popular and "prestigious mystery anthology series," *Suspense*, it's all slavery.[21] A written prologue superimposed over a shot of women working the telephone switchboards sets the scene:

> In the tangled networks of a great city, the telephone is the unseen link between a million lives . . . It is the servant of our common needs—the confidence of our inmost secrets . . . life and happiness wait upon its ring . . . and horror . . . and loneliness . . . and *death*!!!

After a panoramic view of the New York City skyline, the film dissolves to a tracking shot that glides across an empty office at night to a door marked "Henry Stevenson/Vice President" and then through the door to a desk where a phone, still humming, lies off the hook. The person on the other end of the line is Stevenson's wife, Leona (Barbara Stanwyck), the "cough drop queen" of New York high society who mans her phone in her Sutton

Park apartment overlooking the East River with the "authority of a general dispensing orders."[22]

The main premise of *Sorry, Wrong Number*, evoked in the opening titles by the busy signal and "huge menacing shadow phone looming above its ordinary counterpart,"[23] is positively telephonic: due to some crossed wires, Leona has inadvertently overheard a conversation between two men about a murder that's supposed to occur at 11:15 that night. However, when she tells her father who's called from Chicago, he brushes the whole thing off, saying it's probably some kind of "gag"—"a couple of actors on a radio program." Deeper into the film, flashbacks embedded within flashbacks occur during a single phone call Leona has with her doctor in which we learn that her mother died from heart failure but that her own condition is "mental."[24] There's also a phone call within a phone call: while Leona is conversing with Sally Hunt Lord (Ann Richards), the film flashes back to Sally overhearing her district attorney husband talking on the phone with a colleague about setting a trap for Leona's castrated husband, Henry (Burt Lancaster).

Although Leona, not unlike Louise Howell Graham in *Possessed*, suffers from a cardiac neurosis—according to her doctor, her heart is "sound as a bell"—she manages via phone call after phone call to discover the dark secret behind the original, crossed-wire conversation: that Henry has not only been ripping off her father's company, Cotterell Pharmaceuticals (from which, of course, she derives her considerable wealth and position), but that a blackmailer has forced him to agree to have Leona murdered in a "simple robbery" while he's away on business.

The final sequence, embroidered by a passacaglia composed by Franz Waxman, is "one of the most frightening in film music."[25] As designed by Gene Merritt and Walter Oberst, it's a masterpiece of sonic architecture. Following a 360-degree pan around Leona's room that accents the constricted space in which she operates (the inventive camerawork is by Sol Polito), the film cuts between a man breaking into the house and Leona talking on the phone with Henry who, having belatedly changed his mind about having his wife murdered, tells her to do the one thing she appears constitutionally unable to do: "get out of bed." The shadow of a man approaches and, though Leona screams, it's drowned out by the roar of a subway train crossing the bridge outside her open window. Suddenly, the phone rings and there's a close-up of a leather glove picking up the receiver. Henry's calling again, frantically asking for Leona, but on her end of the line, there's only the sound of a man gruffly saying, "Sorry, wrong number."

Fig. 6. Dial M for Murder: Advertisement for Anatole Litvak's *Sorry, Wrong Number* featuring Henry (Burt Lancaster) and Leona Stevenson (Barbara Stanwyck).

Chapter 3

Radio Noir

"Radio's golden age is generally considered to have lasted from the 1920s until the 1950s," but its apex occurred during the 1940s when the holy trinity of programming—news, music, entertainment—was established.[26] While television was clearly "The Future," radio's utter dominance of the nascent mediascape can be gleaned from a comment David Sarnoff, the "father of American broadcasting," made about TV in a speech at the RCA Pavilion at the 1939 World's Fair, "Now we add radio sight to sound."[27]

The Set-Up (1949), whose sound track designed by Phil Brigandi and Clem Portman is a veritable showcase of sonic effects, might be said to add "radio sound to sight." Early in the film, Julie (Audrey Totter), the wife of over-the-hill boxer Stoker (Robert Ryan), is wandering the streets at night. At one point, contemplating attending her husband's fight, she approaches the arena, but the bloodthirsty roar of the crowd inside sends her scurrying in horror. Pausing by an open-air tobacco store, she listens with increasing dread to the match being announced on the proprietor's radio, "The old man keeps coming back for more. One-two to the jaw. He's down. He's out like a light. The referee's counting him out. Four, five. It's just a formality. He might as well count up to a hundred. Nine, ten, out." When Julie realizes the announcer is talking about another fighter, she turns away in relief, returning to the radio-wired streets.

Radios in fact appear throughout the short, brutish course of *The Set-Up*. For example, in the boxing sequences, which are as graphic as anything in *Raging Bull* (1980), the camera occasionally cuts to a man in the crowd with a radio glued to his ear, a sonic detail that connects the interior world of the boxing match with the exterior world of the streets where boxing, in the form of the radio announcer's ongoing, animated narration of the fight card, is as inescapable as the smell of fried food.

Although radio as a complex form of communications technology materializes in various formats in the decade's noirs, it's primarily employed as a vehicle for popular American music. A classic example is the conclusion to *Double Indemnity*. In a reprise of the film's beginning, Neff shows up at the Dietrichson house and walks into the living room where Phyllis, having hidden a gun under the cushion, is waiting for him. An instrumental version of "Tangerine," the Victor Schertzinger and Johnny Mercer song that first appeared in the 1942 musical *The Fleet's In*, plays in the background: "Tangerine, she is all they claim / With her eyes of night and lips as bright as flame /

Tangerine, when she dances by / Señoritas stare and caballeros sigh." Right before the gunplay begins (which, in *Double Indemnity*, is just another form of foreplay), Leo Robin, Richard Whiting, and Newell Chase's "My Ideal" comes on the radio—"Will I ever find / The girl in my mind / The one who is my ideal?"—and Neff, hearing the song, asks Phyllis if he can close the window: he doesn't like the music anymore, and no wonder. Phyllis is not like the ideal girl in the song, waiting "Just around the corner" for him. She's right there in the darkened parlor, ready, willing, and able to use the loaded gun in her hand.

While radio technology in classic noir is utilized for the most part to provide atmospheric background music, it also functions occasionally as a source of breaking news. *Lady in the Lake* has become notorious for its audacious use of point-of-view camerawork, but its Shearer-supervised sound track—in particular the Christmas music that plays, as in Siodmak's *Christmas Holiday*, under the opening credits—is oddly upbeat for a Chandler-inspired film noir. For example, in one especially outré bit, bad cop Lieutenant DeGarmot (Lloyd Nolan) forces Philip Marlowe's (Robert Montgomery) car off the road and douses him with liquor in order to frame him for drunk driving. However, when Marlowe comes to, it's to the sound of a pickpocket caroling off-key, "O Santa Claus, O Santa Claus."

After Marlowe punches the man out and exchanges identities with him, he crawls to a phone booth to call Adrienne Fromsett (Audrey Totter), the editor-in-chief of a company that publishes *Black Mask*–style crime magazines such as *Lurid Detective* and *True Horror Tales*. When he later wakes, dazed and confused, at Fromsett's apartment, it's to the very first radio report of the holiday: "It's one minute past midnight Christmas morning and police revealed that, so far, for the first time on any Christmas eve in years, death has taken a holiday." This news is, to say the least, ironic. It's not simply that Marlowe has earlier in the night discovered the bullet-riddled body of Chris Lavery—the existence of which corpse is signaled, as with Ida Sessions's in *Chinatown*, by the sound of a dripping faucet—but that DeGarmot himself, the very embodiment of the law, is responsible for this "holiday" homicide.

Not unlike Marlowe's teasing voice-over in *Lady in the Lake* ("You'll see just as I saw it. You'll meet the people, you'll find the clues, and maybe you'll solve it . . . and maybe you won't"), the radio commentary in Robert Montgomery's film has a distinct satiric edge. More often than not, though, the radio in forties noir is used to generate dramatic as opposed to comic irony. For example, in *The Blue Dahlia* (1946), returning serviceman Johnny

Morrison (Alan Ladd) has promised to wait for "friend" Joyce Harwood (Veronica Lake) so they can go for a "walk along the beach and look for moonstones" when a radio report suddenly catches his ear:

> The discovery occurred early this morning when neighbors complained about the loudness of the radio. [The radio's volume increases] The cause of death has so far not been definitely established. Wanted for questioning is Lt. Commander John Morrison, recently returned from the South Pacific. Lt. Commander Morrison is described as about twenty-eight years old, weight 160 pounds, light brown hair, light brown or blue eyes. When last seen, he was wearing civilian clothes with a navy raincoat and was carrying a civilian suitcase.

In *The Blue Dahlia*, a film whose narrative incessantly revolves around sound technology, the radio can be said to constitute a form of audio surveillance, as if Johnny is subject, no matter where he goes, to the omnipresent ear of the law.

The radio as a technology of surveillance is even more explicit in *Raw Deal*, an Anthony Mann film recorded by Leon S. Becker and Ear Sitar that commences when Joe Sullivan, aided by the masochistically loyal Pat (Claire Trevor), escapes from the state penitentiary to the cacophony of alarms. Later, even as he's trying to talk his former prison counselor Ann Martin (Marsha Hunt) into helping him get out of the city, the police reports on the radio, preceded by sirens in the distance (what Joe calls the "whole brass band"), track his every move. The fact that the reports occur at regular intervals during the brief time he's inside Ann's apartment heightens the sense of entrapment:

> Repeat. The escapee is Joseph Emmett Sullivan, six feet one, sandy red hair, blue eyes. Known to have changed clothes. He's desperate. Armed. All cars broadcast. That is all.

Ann tells Joe he doesn't "stand a ghost of a chance" of evading the authorities, but he ignores her and, as the radio continues to play in the background, shuts the window blinds:

> Calling Sheriff car 12 on US 50 going east. . . . Gray Plymouth sedan. Escaped convict reported in it. That is all.

Since there's now a dragnet "tight as a fist" around the city, Ann tries to persuade Joe, who as a boy risked his life to save eight other children from a fire, to turn himself in to the police. But Joe's cynical reply, "Maybe he became a fireman," suggests, together with the radio updates, just how desperate Joe has become:

> Sheriff substation to state trooper control. All covered at points. Oak Creek Canyon, Lincoln Park to the cutoff.

Listening intently, Joe studies a map for escape routes:

> KROX to state trooper control. Highway 12 covered. State route to Florence covered. Also Cripple Creek Junction covered. Highway Cripple Creek covered. That is all.

In *Raw Deal*, the radio seems particularly oppressive because Joe's wanted by both the authorities and the murderous Rick Coyle (Raymond Burr). While Coyle eventually falls screaming in a cocoon of flames to his death, payback for his earlier fiery crimes against humanity, Joe is captured by the police and ends up in Corkscrew Alley (musically evoked at the beginning of the film by a bluesy piano riff) where he dies in Ann's arms ("I got my breath of fresh air") and with Pat's blessing, "In my heart I know this is right for Joe. This is what he wanted."

Although *White Heat*, unlike *Raw Deal*, "is not notable for its expressionist lighting or doom-laden camera angles," its "nerve jangling sound track represents the beginning of the modern assault upon the ear."[28] In fact, Raoul Walsh's film constitutes something like a cinematic primer on the advanced audio technologies associated with modernity. These technologies of surveillance—radio, teletype, and oscillator—are arrayed against the film's larger-than-life antagonist, Cody Jarrett, the last of the great Warners gangsters who, in the person of James Cagney, harks back to the glorious thirties.

Although Jarrett is linked at the outset of *White Heat* with locomotion, leaping off a bridge onto a train he's about to hold up, his ambiguous relation to technology is emphasized when one of the members of his gang, Zuckie Hommell, is badly scalded by a blast of steam from the train's engine. On one hand, as the wind that whips around his hideout shows, Cody is a force of nature. On the other hand, the fact that he learns a "storm is coming" from a gang member who, despite Cody's express wishes, has been outside listening to a car radio, suggests that his natural dynamism, even when supplemented by gun-power, is no match for the law's superior technology.

The efficacy of this technology is foregrounded throughout the dynamic trajectory of Walsh's film. Thus, after Cotton Valletti leaves a pack of cigarettes for the severely burned Zuckie, whom Cody callously abandons when the gang decamps, the teletype provides Philip Evans, the head of the Treasury Department's investigation, with crucial information: "prints on cellophane of cigarette pack belong to Cotton Valletti, a known member of the Jarrett gang." Later, Cody escapes to a motel court and the police use the "ABC method" to shadow Cody's mother's car and discover where he's hiding out. However, not unlike Cody's "Trojan horse," a gas truck retrofitted to house his gang so they can slip undetected into an oil refinery, the critical weapon in the police arsenal, the oscillator, is a repurposed radio. "That little thing," a T-man says at one point, "you can make one out of a radio."

Not so incidentally, this is precisely what undercover agent Hank Fallon, a.k.a. Vic Pardo (Edmond O'Brien), is doing the evening before the big heist. After Cody carries his moll, Verna (Virginia Mayo), off to bed to the strains of big-band music, Vic sets to work transforming the radio into an oscillator whose signal will allow Evans and his agents to track the progress of the gas truck. In fact, Evans and Pardo's original plan is to utilize the oscillator to track Cody when he breaks out of prison, a breakout initiated by the feds. Their well-laid plans go seriously awry, though, when Cody learns in the mess hall his mother has died: "news of [her] death travels down the table from a lip-reader, who acts as a semaphore, along the row of prisoners until it reaches Cody, and the inaudible whispers seem like sparks from a fuse."[29] In one of the rawest, most visceral passages in forties cinema, Cody, crazed with grief, clambers onto the dining table where he scatters dishes and utensils, then drops to the floor, knocking down one guard after another like so many bowling pins until he's finally subdued and straitjacketed.

Riveting as this sequence is, the most expressionist sequence in *White Heat* occurs after Ma Jarrett (Margaret Wycherly) tells her son during a prison visit that his right-hand man, Big Ed Somers (Steve Cochran), has been cozying up to Verna. His mother's words ("I'll get him") ricocheting in his skull like loose marbles, Cody is working in the machine area when the film suddenly cuts to a shot of the ceiling lights, then, short-circuiting, goes out of focus. The ensuing split-second montage of pumping drill, pneumatic press, and grinding machine—an audiovisual rebus that reflects the "white

Fig. 7. Trojan Electronics: Vic Pardo, a.k.a. Hank Fallon (Edmond O'Brien), transforming a radio into an oscillator in Raoul Walsh's *White Heat*.

heat" coursing through Jarrett's brain like a "red-hot buzzsaw"—captures both his galvanic life-force and its destructive, self-canceling power.

The self-destructive aspect is spectacularly on exhibit in the electrifying finale of Walsh's film as an armed and wildly dangerous Cody climbs to the top of a gas tank. Unwilling to turn himself in to the authorities and already wounded like an animal by Fallon's long-distance rifle fire ("What's holding him up?"), Cody turns his handgun on the gas tank, setting off a series of sky-high, semi-nuclear explosions that are a fitting sonic tribute to Jarrett's incandescent death drive: "Made it, Ma! Top o' the world!"

Photographed by John Alton, recorded by Leon S. Becker and Hugh McDowell, Jr. and directed in part by Anthony Mann, *He Walked by Night* (1948) represents—with the possible exception of *White Heat*—the most overt expression of the themes of mass communication and audiovisual surveillance in forties noir. The film begins on a semi-documentary note with an "objective" voice-over that, in sync with an establishing shot of Los Angeles City Hall, zeroes in on the "communications division" of the LAPD where the "ears and voices" of the law are located and where, "minute by minute, the orders go out to the radio cars in the far-flung divisions" of Watts and Wilshire. The relay itself travels from the public at large, which calls in the crimes ("the lights on the complaint board flash twenty-four hours a day"), to the communications bureau, which then sends out radio instructions to the mobile police force.

The narrative proper kicks in when an officer in one such patrol car is killed by a man, Roy Morgan, a.k.a. Roy Martin (Richard Basehart), who's trying to break into an electronics shop. (The shop's neon-bright sign reads "Radio Television Supply Co.") The location of the shooting ("5057 State Street") is promptly transmitted to "all units," but Martin, a former "police department employee who monitors the activities of officers on patrol over a police radio receiver,"[30] is listening to the report, which includes a detailed description of himself: "white male, age twenty-six or twenty-seven, 5 feet 10 or 5 feet 11, 155 to 165 pounds, brown hair, regular features, pencil mustache." In fact, while Martin's listening, he shaves off his "pencil" mustache.

Martin's *métier* is an unusual one for the time: he steals electronic equipment, then, after tweaking it, consigns it to a man named Paul Reeves who unwittingly sells it at his retail store. The neon sign for Reeves's company, prominently displayed in the film, acts as a virtual advertisement for state-of-the-art electronics:

Reeves Electronics
Laboratories
Sound Equipment
Radio * Public Address * Radar

Although Reeves doesn't realize Martin's equipment has been stolen, it's clear in the paranoid context of the film that there's not only a fine line between the legitimate and illegitimate uses of the new technologies but that the public sphere must be policed by society lest criminals like Martin become more powerful than the lawmen paid to surveil them.

A "brilliant, technically adept young man," Martin continually eludes the police, but despite his mastery of disguises and scientific wizardry (he's a techno-terrorist *avant la lettre*), he's no match for the LAPD and its vast telecommunications "dragnet."[31] (The "thick" procedural handling of this theme in *He Walked by Night* anticipates, among other things, the popular radio and television series created by Jack Webb, who plays a lab technician in the film.) Eventually, Martin meets his fate in the same subterranean spaces that have served as his preferred means of escape. The "underground man," flushed from his home by the police, flees to his default safe house, the cavernous drainage tunnels of Los Angeles which loudly reverberate with the sound of dripping water and the echoing footfalls of the police. Stripped of his technological armature and cornered like a sewer rat, Martin tries to resurface through a manhole, but when he's blocked by a car, he's hung out to dry on the ladder, the boom of his machine gun answered by a thundering rain of police bullets.

If the radio in *Raw Deal*, *White Heat*, and *He Walked by Night* can be said to operate as the voice of the Big Other, it also makes its presence felt in forties noir in the form of advertisements, a device that Fritz Lang employs to particular dramatic effect in his "American" noirs. For instance, in *The Woman in the Window* (recorded by Frank McWhorter), Professor Wanley (Edward G. Robinson) has returned home after getting rid of the body of a man, Claude Mazard, whom he's inadvertently killed. As swing music plays in the background on the radio, Wanley sits down in his den to write his wife a letter: "I am lonelier tonight than I have ever been . . ." Unable to put his thoughts down on paper, he glances at his watch and, as if on cue, the music comes to a close and an announcer beams:

> Twelve o'clock and the midnight news from station WPQ through the courtesy of Castolorex, that tangy, bracing acid remedy for that tired feeling. But first a word about Castolorex. Wise Mother Nature has balanced the chemical contents of the gastric juices so carefully that heartburn, acid stomach, or an upset digestive system resulting from overindulgence in food and drink can blight a person's whole outlook on life. But why suffer when Castolorex, Mother Nature's own helping hand, is available at your nearest drugstore? Try it today and every day.

Although the commercial appears to mock Wanley, a middle-aged man who's found himself in dire circumstances due to a fleeting infatuation with "the woman in the window," the object of Lang's satire is the radio, a medium that owes its very existence to corporate sponsorship. This coruscating critique of the culture industry and, by implication, American capitalism and its peculiar form of optimism—the bromide that one can change one's "whole outlook on life" by purchasing a commodity—is brought savagely home when, as Mazard's boat hat burns in the fireplace, Wanley learns that the man he has killed in self-defense was "founder of the fabulous public utilities empire, World Enterprises, Inc." and, worse yet, that there's a $10,000 reward for any information relating to his "mysterious disappearance."

A similar, critical use of commercial radio appears in Lang's *Scarlet Street* (1945). The difference is that whereas Wanley in *The Woman in the Window* seems to be happy in his marriage, in *Scarlet Street* Christopher Cross (also played by Robinson) is dominated by a woman, Adele, who worships at the altar of her missing husband. Although Cross's only escape from his stifling marriage is, to his wife's manifest chagrin, painting in the bathroom, her favorite pastime is the radio soap "Hilda's Hope for Happiness." According to the show's sponsor, "Happy Household Bubble Suds," a commercial for which product can be heard emanating from a downstairs apartment, "no soap gives you more happiness, more washings, and more suds per package than Happy Household Bubble Suds." The postscript to the commercial—"Ask your nearest grocer for the Large Economy Size today"—conveys what Walter Benjamin called the "dream wish" at the very heart of consumer culture: that the sort of transcendent happiness which Cross fantasizes about and which he thinks he can find with Kitty March (Joan Bennett) can be purchased as easily as a box of detergents.

The conclusions to the two Lang films represent a study in contrast: while the happy-to-be-alive dénouement of *The Woman in the Window* comically reframes the earlier radio commercial for antacids, the ending of *Scarlet Street* features one of the bleakest passages in forties noir. When Chris belatedly realizes that Kitty, with the aid of "pimp" Johnny Prince (Dan Duryea), has not only been passing off his suddenly successful paintings as hers but actively despises him, he stabs her to death with an ice pick. However, in a bizarre twist of fate, Johnny, not Chris, is executed for the crime and Adele's former police husband turns out to be alive. After Chris loses his cashier's job for embezzling funds to subsidize Kitty's luxurious lifestyle, he returns alone to his new home, a shabby hotel room illuminated by a blinking neon sign.

There, mournfully whistling Kitty's favorite song, "Melancholy Baby," he's mercilessly battered by the pulsing neon light and voices from his past —Johnny calling Kitty "Lazy Legs," Kitty crying out "Johnny, O Johnny" —until, despondent, he tries to hang himself. Cross (the surname is telling[32]) survives this dark night of the soul only to wander the streets of the metropolis in the dead of winter, the festive, seasonal sounds of the outside world eventually giving way to Kitty's impassioned voice repeating in his head like a broken record, "Johnny, O Johnny . . ."

Although the critical use of sound that informs Lang's films is relatively rare in classic noir (but see the savagely ironic scene in *I Wouldn't Be in Your Shoes* in which Ann Quinn, after her husband's been wrongly imprisoned, listens to a radio commercial about "footwear"), poetic and discursive commentary is rarer still. Preminger's *Laura* is justly famous for its music, but the violent climax where Waldo Lydecker tries to kill Laura (Gene Tierney) and is killed instead by Mark McPherson is arguably scored not by David Raksin, the composer, but a radio. (The sound is supervised by two of Fox's premiere recordists, Harry M. Leonard and E. Clayton Ward.) Laura is standing in front of a vanity mirror brushing her hair when a clock chimes and she crosses the room to turn on a wall radio. As she returns to brushing her hair, Lydecker's prerecorded program unspools in the background: "And, thus, as history has proved, Love is eternal. It has been the strongest motivation for human actions throughout centuries. Love is stronger than life. It reaches beyond the dark shadow of death." Unlike Professor Wanley in *The Woman in the Window*, Lydecker feels he's directly responsible for the transformation of Laura into the work of art she is.

The poem that Lydecker proceeds to recite, Ernest Dowson's "Brief Life" ("Vitae Summa Brevis Spem Nos Vetat Incohare Longam"), is even more disturbing than his discourse on love since it's matched by a shot of him loading a shotgun while standing in front of a ticking clock, a duplicate of the baroque one in his house that chimes at the film's beginning. (Laura was originally mistaken for the deceased woman found in her apartment who was literally de-faced by a shotgun blast.)

> They are not long, the weeping and the laughter,
> Love and desire and hate;
> I think they have no portion in us after
> We pass the gate.
> They are not long, the days of wine and roses:
> Out of a misty dream
> Our path emerges for a while, then closes
> Within a dream.

There are numerous ways to parse these lyrics. One is that Lydecker has finally realized his romance with Laura, "the days of wine and roses," is now irrevocably over. Another is that if Laura represents, as he later says, the "best part of him," then killing her is akin to killing himself, as Arthur

Bannister says to his wife, Elsa, in the concluding "magic mirror" sequence of *The Lady from Shanghai*.

But perhaps the most subversive interpretation of Lydecker's poetic recitation is that Laura, not unlike Madeleine Elster in *Vertigo* (1958), is herself a dream—as in fact she was in the original version of *Laura*. (In the original script, the entire second half of the film is a dream, from the moment McPherson falls asleep in the living room beneath Laura's seductive, Mona Lisa smile to the violent dénouement.[33]) Lydecker's poetic recitation receives a final, ironic twist when he enters Laura's boudoir just as his radio program is about to conclude and, shotgun in hand, blithely says, "That's the way it is, isn't it, Laura?" But before Laura can respond, a radio announcer intervenes, "You have heard the voice of Waldo Lydecker by electrical transcription," a pre-mortem communication (since McPherson arrives just in time to rescue Laura) which intimates that Waldo, not Laura, is the ghost who haunts the film's narrative, broaching another, different love that cannot speak its name.

Radio (Re)Recording

A noir that owes something of its story to *Laura* and, like Preminger's film, features the portrait of a beautiful young woman who's apparently dead but is in fact alive, *The Unsuspected* (1947) actively integrates radio technology into its melodramatic narrative. As in *Hollow Triumph* (1948), *Whirlpool* (1949), and *Nightmare Alley*, film noirs in which a psychiatrist employs a phonograph to record patients' conversations and, in the last two films, extort them, Michael Curtiz's film, showcasing the work of "soundmen" Everett A. Brown and Leslie Hewitt, illustrates the malevolent uses to which *private* recording technology can be put.

The Unsuspected opens with radio producer Jane Moynihan reading an article in an industry magazine, *Radio Semi-Weekly*, about the apparent suicide of Alexander Woollcott–like radio personality Victor Grandison's (Claude Rains) "attractive young secretary," Roslyn Wright. After a cue—"on the nose"—for the show's sponsor ("This is the United Motor Company"), the studio orchestra plays the show's fanfare and the announcer says, "Starring your genial host, the renowned writer, art collector, and teller of strange tales, Victor Grandison."

As Jane and other personnel observe from a control booth, Grandison stands before a microphone, script in hand, "Good evening, ladies and gentlemen, Grandison speaking. Tonight, I bring you from the files of the nation's unsolved crimes a story of one the most brutal and yet the most cunningly conceived murders ever committed, a murder of rare delicacy and wondrous ease that was called suicide." Looking to the control booth, Victor pauses for Jane to cue the music, then continues, "Yes, suicide the police called it, yet the murderer walks among us, free. But is he really free? Can he escape from the evil that he has done? No."

The camera slowly tracks over and into a loudspeaker high up on the wall to the right of the control booth—"By day it follows him like a shadow. The cold hands of death awaken him from a thousand nightmares"—then the screen fades to black and a rushing locomotive appears, the beam of its headlight piercing the night, whistle blowing, boxcars flashing by in a blur. There's a brief cut to a close-up of a portable radio, the camera pulling back to reveal a well-dressed man, Steven Howard (Michael North), lighting a cigarette and listening to Grandison's monologue: "And so, day and night, he is driven on with the dead forever haunting him, pursuing him. Or perhaps he isn't running away but is hiding in some dark hole listening with terror to the voice of his own conscience."

The subsequent sequence, one of the most celebrated in all of film noir (the DP is "Woody" Bredell), begins on another "aural cue,"[34] an ambiguous passage in Grandison's script—"There is no escape for one who has committed murder"—that introduces us to a suspect who in fact appears to be the direct object of Victor's address. While the train pulls into a city, Howard's reflection in the train window dissolves to a rapid forward-tracking shot that, driven by the train-like rhythm of Franz Waxman's score, hurtles down a street past a parked sedan before stopping in front of a vertical neon sign, "Hotel Peekskill." The score dies down and the camera pans left from a neon-lit window to a man lying propped up in bed:

> They say that drowning men relive their lives in seconds. The guilty, too, relive their crimes a thousand times a day . . . every unexpected sound, every glance that turns their way, and a thousand fears that have no form. The guilty must go on and on, hiding his evil behind a mask, the calm and often smiling mask of the unsuspected.

Crushing his cigarette in an ashtray, the man turns toward the nightstand to get another, then turns back toward the window, which now shows only the bottom half of the sign, the neon-illuminated letters spelling out the word "Kill."

This bravura sequence not only displays Curtiz's consummate mastery of the audio and visual codes of classic Hollywood cinema but concludes with a montage that neatly ties together the narrative's various, multi-colored threads: Detective Richard Donovan listening to the broadcast, one hand on Grandison's radio, as he examines his friend's mail with a letter opener ("Yes, the unsuspected is anywhere, everywhere, so be on your guard. He might be the man who calls you friend, who visits frequently at your home"); a bartender listening to the same broadcast on a bar radio at a surprise birthday party for Grandison at his Groton, New York, home ("And yet his day of reckoning must come"); alcoholic Oliver Keane listening as the bartender puts down a napkin and drink for him ("He is tormented by fear that some day he will make one false move, one slip"); and, finally, Althea Keane (Audrey Totter), Oliver's wife, the hostess of the party, and Grandison's "capricious, acerbic niece,"[35] sitting on an couch ("that will betray him, and when he does, the lightning of justice will strike the unsuspected") until the broadcast ends, at which point she stands up and turns off the radio, loudly remarking, "Victor's the only man I know that can turn my blood to ice water."

Although this extended, radio-driven sequence poses the fundamental hermeneutic question, Who is the unsuspected?, the answer, oddly enough, lies less with the medium foregrounded in the first part of Curtiz's film, the radio, than with record(ing) technology itself—in this case, "a phonograph that records on vinyl."[36] Hence the significance of Grandison's first name, Victor, as in Victrola. In a scene set in "Grandee"'s office after the ostensibly dead woman in the portrait, Matilda Frazier (Joan Caulfield), boards a plane in Brazil, Victor uses a recording machine to practice his delivery so that, as he smugly puts it, his "listeners have the benefit of every full, rich tone." Later, when the guilty-looking man in the hotel room, Press (Jack Lambert), shows up unannounced at Grandison's house complaining that the radio program points to him as "the unsuspected," Victor explains that the technology has "other uses" and plays back Press's confession ("I swear, Mr. Grandison, I didn't mean to kill her") which, unbeknownst to Press, Victor has recorded.

The climax of *The Unsuspected* turns on Victor's sole possession and mastery of the means of sound reproduction. When Oliver decides to leave his wife, Althea, and they begin to quarrel, Victor secretly records Oliver's threat to kill his wife, then sends him away and shoots her. As Althea slumps to the floor, a high overhead shot of the record player is succeeded by a track-in to a reflection of Victor's gloved hand lifting the arm off the phonograph. (This upside-down mirror shot, which recurs throughout *The Unsuspected*, recollects the very beginning of the film when an image of Roslyn Wright's hooded, anonymous killer is reflected in the polished veneer of the desk over which her lifeless body hangs.)

Later, Grandison sets the phonograph volume on high, replays the acrimonious conversation between Oliver and Althea, then, pretending it's live, goes upstairs to tell Howard and Matilda. Although they've already discovered Althea's body, Howard manages to foil Grandison when he sneaks into his study and, locating the incriminating recording, calls the police. Grandison, meanwhile, contacts Press to eliminate Howard and tries to poison Matilda with a champagne cocktail, but to no avail: the "lightning of justice" eventually strikes down the genial host in the midst of recording one of his popular radio mysteries.

The concluding sequence of *The Unsuspected*, even more so than the opening one set at the radio station, can be said to acoustically "bare the device." After Grandison stutters when he sees Lieutenant Donovan enter the control booth, he touches the microphone as if to steady himself, the camera cutting to the control booth (the decrease in volume is realistically rendered) where the lieutenant agrees to let him continue his confession before arresting him:

> Ladies and gentlemen, you're about to experience something unprecedented in the history of our program or, for that matter, of radio itself. And you, who have followed my adventures in the half-world of crime for so many years now, you are listening to my last broadcast. . . . For a time the unsuspected wore his mask safely—not for long, however. Soon he found it necessary to commit two murders more, a young woman who shared his ominous secret and her husband. You begin to see how enmeshed he became in his own incredible folly. Would you like to know who the unsuspected really is? It is I. I am the unsuspected, your genial host, Victor Grandison.

The Unsuspected appears to end on an appropriately high-minded note, with Grandison becoming a victim of his own malignant enunciative authority.

However, if the gloved hand that holds the radio script in the opening credit sequence is in fact Grandison's and he can therefore be said to be the film's author just as we, the audience, are "caught up in the play of its discourse,"[37] in this Brechtian "happy end" Victor's ingenious manipulation of recording technology is not so much the product of a criminal mind as the work of a gifted recording artist, one who endeavors to make the world over into a portrait, not unlike *The Unsuspected* itself, of the "sensual beauty of sight and sound."[38]

Noir on Record

In the late 1940s, around the same time as the advent of tape recording and high-fidelity reproduction, the long-playing 33⅓ microgroove disc began to replace the 78 rpm shellac record. But even before the annus mirabilis of 1947, Americans were freely disposing of their booming postwar incomes and "buying music to listen to in their homes."[39] (For example, twice as many records were sold in 1946 as in 1945.) In addition to its trenchant recourse to radio technology, *Laura* provides a prime example of just how familiar and unfamiliar, just how uncanny, record technology can be.

Early on in Preminger's film Mark McPherson goes to Laura's apartment with Waldo Lydecker and Shelby Carpenter (Vincent Price) and plays a record. It turns out to be "Laura's theme," a "string-laden symphonic arrangement" that Waldo immediately asks him to turn off but that Shelby characterizes as "not exactly classical, but sweet."[40] Although strings and melody are not typical of Raksin's style, one reason his music for *Laura* is so significant is that it "introduced elements of popular music into the vocabulary of the Hollywood score."[41] In other words, if classical music in the form of orchestral scores is a ubiquitous aspect of film noir as well as, more generally, classical Hollywood cinema, popular music, whether played on radio, phonograph, or jukebox, is almost equally ubiquitous.

While the opening of *Journey into Fear* showing the Nazi assassin Banat playing a scratched recording of "C'est mon coeur" is typical of Welles's acerbic wit (Banạt's cracked like the record, both assassin and sentimentalist), a more conventional "romantic" example appears in *Mildred Pierce*: Mildred has gone to the beach house of Monte Beragon and Monte, setting the mood for a seduction, puts on a recording of "It Can't Be Wrong." However, in the middle of their first passionate kiss (Mildred can't quite believe that Monte wants her and, as she later finds out, she's right—it can be wrong), the record ends and Mildred stops him, saying, "The record, Monte, the record." Since music in the film is associated with her wayward daughter, Veda (whose piano lessons are a testament to her mother's hard-won embourgeoisement), the fact that Mildred notices the record's skipping says something about her; that, unlike Veda, she won't allow herself to be carried away by her feelings—unless, of course, they involve her precious, criminally spoiled daughter.

As opposed to *Mildred Pierce* in which record technology plays a slight, if telling role, *Scarlet Street* plays up the relation between Kitty, a "loose" woman, and the music she listens to on her phonograph. (In Renoir's film *La Chienne* (1931), on which Lang's film is based, Lulu [Janie Marèse] is a prostitute plain and simple.) I've already discussed the penultimate sequence of *Scarlet Street* whose hallucinatory, expressionistic force is conveyed not so much by distorted sets or camera angles as by imagined voices in concert with the neon sign's pulsing rhythm,[42] a sequence that draws on Lang's earlier presentation of Kitty as an object of desire who is not herself without desire.

This motif appears for the first time in a scene where Kitty's introduced in her environs, lying on a couch in her apartment reading a magazine and listening to a recording of "Melancholy Baby." The needle sticks on the line "in love," but Kitty, unlike Mildred, remains nonplussed, too lazy to get up and change the record. Hence Johnny's nickname for her, "Lazy Legs." The ironic implications of this scene eventually rebound on both Chris and Kitty —Chris because he's hopelessly in love with Kitty, Kitty because she's hopelessly in love with Johnny. Consequently, as soon as Chris is released from his marriage, he rushes over to Kitty's apartment where he pauses outside an Art Deco window: when the recording of "Melancholy Baby" begins to skip, Chris hears Kitty sing offscreen for Johnny ("O Johnny, Johnny . . ."), then watches as she walks into the frame and right into his arms. The sequence is sutured with a "nearly explosive bang" as Chris, sickened, "drops his suitcase to the floor."[43] For the determinist Lang, desire is not an escape from but an inescapable aspect of the Destiny-machine, and love is not unlike a broken record: it's only a matter of time before the hook becomes stuck in your throat and the groove becomes a grave.

As in Lang's ultra black *Scarlet Street*, a specific record is also central to the plot of *Black Angel* (1946). Directed by Roy William Neill, adapted from a Cornell Woolrich novel, and recorded by the talented Universal duo of Bernard B. Brown and Joe Lapis, *Black Angel* begins on an audacious note with a boom shot originating from the point of view of Marty Blair (Dan Duryea) that rapidly ascends from the street to a high window of the Wilshire Hotel, then sails straight through the blinds and into the lavish penthouse apartment, accented by an ornate cut-glass chandelier, of Mavis Marlowe (Constance Dowling). The doorbell rings and the maid Flo brings Mavis a wrapped box that contains a ruby, heart-shaped brooch, an anniversary gift sent up by her estranged husband, Marty, whom she's previously barred from her apartment building.

Seemingly moved by the gesture, Mavis asks Flo to "put on some soft music," but when it begins, she barks, "Must you play that song?" and, ignoring her maid's entreaty ("But you sing it so beautifully"), takes the record off and tosses it into a wastebasket. Meanwhile, Marty, rejected again, has retired to a piano bar where, inspired by cigarettes and copious amounts of hooch, he plays "Heartbreak" over and over with delirious abandonment. As one patron remarks before Marty's head hits the keys like a pillow, "He sure can play the piano."

Cut to Mavis's apartment where, mid-song, the camera pans from a close-up of a mantle clock adorned with mermaids past a vase of flowers and a monogrammed-framed photo of Mavis to a door that's been left ajar: "I try to pretend / Saying that I don't mind it / But everyone knows behind it / I'm trying to mend / A heartbreak." As the camera tilts down to a shot of a fur rug caught in the door, a man whom we later learn is one of Mavis's ex-lovers, Kirk Bennett (John Phillips), enters the apartment. He removes his hat, calls out her name, then looks for something to light his cigarette: "That's what you get when you set love so high / I gave it a try, then kissed it goodbye."

After a close-up of the record player and the sound of the needle sticking as the song ends, the arm automatically lifts, returns to off, then back to play: "Not much to regret / Finding your arms so thrilling / And finding myself too willing / So what do I get? / A heartbreak." Bennett picks up a matchbook ("Crestview 2111"), but before he can light his cigarette, he hears a noise. Calling out Mavis's name as he opens the door to her bedroom, he sees her body reflected in the bottom corner of a vanity mirror: she's been strangled with her own monogrammed scarf, the heart-shaped brooch pinned to her chest like a medal. Bennett grabs his hat and is about to depart when he thinks better of it and turns off the phonograph to call the police. A close-up of the stopped record ("Express") reads: "Heartbreak / By Martin Blair / Sung by Mavis Marlowe / With the Composer at the Piano."

Although Bennett immediately becomes the main suspect in Mavis's murder, he explains to his devoted wife, Catherine (June Vincent), that she was using their illicit affair to blackmail him. (One of the ironies of *Black Angel* is that "Heartbreak"—composed for the film, like "I Want to Be Talked About" and "Time Will Tell," by Edgar Fairchild and Jack Brooks—is performed on the sound track by Vincent, who appeared in a series of forties musicals from *Honeymoon Lodge* [1943] to *Here Come the Co-Eds* [1945] and who later became typecast as the "other woman.") Convinced of her husband's innocence, Cathy enlists the help of Marty Blair whom, in the words of a Hollywood bit player Cathy overhears in a commissary, Mavis treated "like dirt": "And after he wrote that beautiful song for her, 'Heartbreak.' " Under the alias of "Carver and Martin," Cathy and Marty become a duo—Marty on piano, Cathy on vocals—in order to investigate Marko (Peter Lorre), the owner of a nightclub called Rio's where they perform "I Want to Be Talked About." One afternoon, as they rehearse a new song Marty has composed for her, "Time Will Tell," fate begins to "reveal its designs":[44] Marty has fallen hard for Cathy. However, when she rebuffs his advances, the composer goes on a world-class drinking binge during which he bumps into a woman wearing the same ruby, heart-shaped brooch that Phillips found on Mavis's body (and that, disturbingly, the woman claims Marty gave her one night).

In a wildly expressionist sequence that recalls the film's opening boom shot, Marty, unlike Stan in *Nightmare Alley*, ends up in a sanitarium where the fog of his alcoholic blackout lifts just long enough for him to remember he killed Mavis. (The dipsomania is vintage Woolrich, a reflection of his own life after "he discovered John Barleycorn": "the empty days and nights . . . echoed and re-echoed with the typical *miseria* of broken appointments and paranoiac harangue."[45]) The music on the sound track morphing from a boozy-woozy horn solo to a piano-spiked crescendo, Marty, handcuffed to the posts, flails about in bed as the image track, rippling like a sheet of water, records his dark, now suddenly unrepressed past: strangling the "black angel" who inspired him to write "Heartbreak."[46]

Radio/Record Player/Jukebox: *Dark Passage*

If *Black Angel*'s exploration of the phenomenon of the contemporary pop-music composer can be said to turn on a record, *Dark Passage* exhibits the full spectrum of audio technologies at play in forties noir, progressing from (car) radio to record player to jukebox and beyond ("live" band music performed in Peru). Delmer Daves's film is also striking for the way in which it mobilizes point-of-audition sound effects to complement its daring use of point-of-view camerawork. In fact, unlike Marlowe in *Lady in the Lake*, Vincent Parry (Humphrey Bogart) is a fugitive from the law and, perhaps because his head's swathed in bandages, his sense of sound is heightened to an almost hallucinatory degree, his only salve the lyrical sounds of "Too Marvelous for Words" he seems to hear everywhere he turns.

The first POA sound in *Dark Passage*—a phalanx of police motorcycles zooming across a bridge under which Vincent's hiding after his escape from San Quentin in a trash barrel—sets up the film's first use of radio technology. In the 1940s, the radio was the preeminent medium for news and entertainment. *Dark Passage* reflects this dual function when Vincent hitchhikes a ride from a man named Baker who's driving into San Francisco. Initially, the big-band music playing on the car radio (Vincent Rose's "Avalon" with a telling reference to "E lucevan le stelle" from Puccini's *Tosca*) suggests Vincent has managed to evade the authorities and find temporary refuge, but a news "flash" on the radio exposes him:

> We interrupt this program to warn all listeners in the North Bay area. Be on the lookout for a convict who escaped from San Quentin fifteen minutes ago . . . on an outbound truck. His description follows: the escaped convict is 5 feet 10, hair dark, eyes brown, last seen wearing gray prison trousers, black shoes. His name is Vincent Parry sentenced to life for the murder of his wife three years ago.

This news flash, which relays crucial narrative information (Parry murdered his wife three years ago), is a favorite device of scriptwriters and filmmakers in the 1940s. In *Dark Passage* as in *The Blue Dahlia*, it also functions as a form of aural surveillance, one that, not so incidentally, confirms Vincent's paranoia.

Desperate, Vincent knocks out Baker, but before he hits him with a rock he's just picked up, Irene Jansen (Lauren Bacall) appears and offers to help him escape. Later, safely ensconced in her apartment, Vincent asks why she stopped and, while she climbs the staircase, she says, "Oh, and turn on the music if you like." Vincent turns on the phonograph, then, as she descends the stairs with a newspaper clipping, says, "I see you like swing music." The song, a big-band version of Cole Porter's "Just One of Those Things," first appeared in *Jubilee* (1935); Irene's response ("Yes, legitimate swing") speaks to the sort of person she is, both an artist (she paints) and someone with class or taste who distinguishes between "good" and "bad" swing.

"Just One of Those Things" can also be heard in the background as Vincent reads Irene's letter to the editor: "I think it's time someone spoke up on behalf of Vincent Parry. . . . I don't know this man but I for one protest your scandal-sheet tactics." When Irene leaves to buy Vincent some clothes, he plays the phonograph again, but the moment he turns it on, there's a knock at the door and it's Irene's neighbor, Madge Rapf (Agnes Moorehead), whose testimony sent Vincent to prison. (Rapf was jealous of his wife.) Vincent persuades her to go away, then goes upstairs where he discovers a newspaper clipping about Irene's father having been found guilty, like Vincent, of murdering his wife.

In the following scene, while Irene and Vincent share a cup of coffee and an instrumental version of "Too Marvelous for Words" plays in the background, she tries to explain how she came to find him by the side of the road outside San Francisco: "I don't believe in fate or destiny or any of those things because I know it wasn't destined for my father to die in prison." The film's turning point, the passage from dark to light, occurs when Irene suddenly reverses herself—"I guess it was something like fate to make me go out to Marin County to paint"—and, for the first time in the film ("Maybe it was simply because I was thinking of you"), we hear Jo Stafford singing "Too Marvelous for Words": "You're much too much and just too very very / To ever be in Webster's dictionary / And so I'm borrowing a love song from the birds / To tell you that you're too marvelous for words / Too marvelous for words." Although the song's romantic and sexual undertones are underscored when Vincent lights Irene's cigarette, he tells her he has to leave because Madge may have heard his voice.

The cabdriver who picks Vincent up outside Irene's apartment building recognizes his face, but in another reversal, he also tells him about a plastic surgeon. After a hallucinatory sequence in which Vincent is anaesthetized and has his face refashioned (the "surgeon" says he might end up looking "like a bulldog or monkey"), Vincent returns to the apartment where he's been staying to discover his friend George Fellsinger has been murdered. The scenes set at George's apartment begin and end on a musical note: when Vincent first shows up, he sees a trumpet on a music stand and asks George, "Still practice on the trumpet?" Later, kneeling over his friend's body as a church bell tolls in the distance, he cradles the heavily dented trumpet in his hands and laments, "Only thing he ever wanted was to go to South America with me and play that trumpet. That's all he wanted out of life. Go to Peru and play the trumpet."

Vincent, his head now bandaged like a mummy's, returns to Irene's apartment where during a candlelit dinner "I Guess I'll Have to Change My Plan," the Schwartz and Dietz standard that can be heard in the "horse racing" sequence in *The Big Sleep* (and, in a rather different context, in *The Band Wagon* [1953]), plays softly on the phonograph. After Irene removes his bandages, Vincent comes down the stairs in his new face and suit to the strains of George Gershwin's "Someone to Watch over Me," then, when the record ends, he asks Irene if he can "play the other side once more." It's Jo Stafford again, this time singing the opening verse of the Richard Whiting and Johnny Mercer song that first appeared in the 1937 Warners musical *Ready, Willing and Able*: "You're just too marvelous, / Too marvelous for words / Like 'glorious,' 'glamorous,' / And that old standby 'amorous.'" (Stafford's "pure," honeyed rendition is a long way from the exuberant, Busby Berkeleyesque number staged in *Ready, Willing and Able* where Pinky Blair [Lee Dixon] and Jane Clarke [Ruby Keeler] tap out the song's lyrics on a giant typewriter.)

Vincent and Irene finally kiss, but as Jo Stafford's voice rematerializes on the sound track, he tells Irene, yet again, that he has to go. Not surprisingly, "Too Marvelous for Words," what Alec Wilder calls a "model of pop song writing,"[47] haunts the conclusion of *Dark Passage*. At the bus station, after Rapf has committed suicide by jumping out a window, Vincent overhears a single woman with two children talking to a single, sympathetic man who complains about having "nothing to look forward to." Vincent goes over to the jukebox and plays "Too Marvelous for Words" before calling Irene, who asks, "Do I hear music?" "I picked it out on the jukebox," Vincent replies, adding, "I'm just beginning to realize it's better to have something to look forward to."

Cut to crashing waves and a "little café on a bay" in Peru where the bartender is pouring a crushed ice drink and Latin music burbles in the background. A waiter serves the drink to Vincent who sits alone at a table, sipping it through a straw—as he did when he was staying with Irene recuperating from facial surgery. Suddenly, the band begins to play a slow, "sweet" version of "Too Marvelous for Words" and, looking up, Vincent sees Irene standing near the band. He goes over to her and, wordless, they begin to dance.

Juke Noir

In the 1940s, after the jukebox "went into mass production, turning anyone with a few nickels into a purveyor of contemporary music," its influence on American culture and society was so great that the music editor of the *Washington Times Herald*, Glen Dillard Gunn, claimed radio and movies were mere "extensions" of it.[48] In this pre-JD period circa 1942, Glenn Miller was the "king of the jukes," followed by Harry James, Tommy Dorsey, and Kay Kyser. Yet if Aristocrats, Rock-Olas, and Wurlitzers could be found, it seemed, in every café and tavern, cocktail lounge and ice-cream parlor, the music was not always sweet to the ear. For the nerve-wracked servicemen at the USO centers and canteens who just wanted to relax, the "sound of a hot trumpet or a three-minute drum solo could put them on edge."[49]

The Blue Dahlia opens on just such an edgy note. Back in L.A. after having served their country overseas, Johnny, Buzz (William Bendix), and George (Hugh Beaumont) step off a bus, then make a beeline for the first bar and a "goodbye drink": "bourbon with a bourbon chaser." (How else would Chandler, who wrote the script, have these veterans jumpstart their postwar lives? The film's circular conclusion reprises this beginning with Buzz asking George, "Did someone say something about a drink of bourbon?") After a bartender serves the men, another serviceman plays the jukebox until Buzz, who has a plate implanted in his skull from an injury he sustained during the war, loudly complains, "We gotta have that monkey music in here?" Apparently, the monkey music being played on that "thing," the jukebox, gives Buzz the sort of headaches that send tough, combat-hardened men like him off the deep end.

In fact, the distortion on the sound track suggests Buzz not only suffers from auditory hallucinations but may well be plagued by some sort of psychosis. Consequently, when Johnny's wife, Helen (Doris Dowling), is murdered, it's easy to think, especially given the cultural codes of the day, that Buzz—not Johnny, whom the police suspect—is the real culprit. (As in fact he was in Chandler's original script before the navy intervened, objecting to the author's depiction of Buzz as an ex-bomber with a head full of lead.[50]) The most expressionistic moment in *The Blue Dahlia* involves a memorable sound-image: Johnny, George, Joyce, and the police have gathered in Eddie Harwood's (Howard Da Silva) office at the Blue Dahlia to determine who killed Johnny's wife. (Note the "cheeky" cue when Buzz and George enter Harwood's club: a canary warbling "It's Easy to Remember.")

Provoked by some music coming from the club's dance floor via one of the office speakers, Buzz suddenly remembers hearing a record being played over and over again, "beating in [his] head," while Johnny's wife compulsively picked at a blue dahlia. (This flower, a neon version of which adorns Harwood's club, is seeded early on in Marshall's film: Johnny, arriving stateside at his wife's apartment to the sound of Harold Arlen and Johnny Mercer's "Ac-cent-tchu-ate the Positive," sees some dahlias Harwood has sent and remarks, "I didn't even know these things were blue."[51]) As in *Possessed* and *Sorry, Wrong Number*, Buzz's disorientation is expressed on *The Blue Dahlia*'s sound track as an amplified heartbeat. Traumatized by his war experiences, Buzz is now sensitive to the point of insanity to the sounds of everyday life: what's a swinging good time for everyone else is hell on earth for Buzz.

Although the jukebox scene in *The Locket* (1946) is a minor one, it's an early, revealing episode in a memorable John Brahm film—sonically engineered by John L. Cass and Clem Portman—whose complicated, Chinese-box narrative not only turns on music (in this case, as in *High Wall*, a musical cigarette box) but on a female protagonist who, like Buzz in *The Blue Dahlia*, is not completely right in the head. On Nancy Blair's (Laraine Day) wedding day, her former husband, psychiatrist Dr. Blair (Brian Aherne), comes to John Willis to tell him about his prospective wife's troubled past. As Dr. Blair starts relating the story of her first husband, the artist Norman Clyde (Robert Mitchum), the film flashes back to his story.

It's at this point in *The Locket*—with Norman going to Dr. Blair to warn him about Nancy, just as Blair himself has gone to Willis—that the film flashes back for a second time. After attending a party where a diamond bracelet is stolen and Norman's portrait of Nancy as Cassandra wins an award (the soiree also serves as a private exhibition), the couple retires to their favorite haunt, an Italian restaurant, to celebrate. Nancy, sliding into a booth, says, "Let's play some music," but the restaurant owner Luigi tells them the jukebox only plays "Body and Soul." In order to play another song, he explains, "You have to drop a coin here and run fast like a deer to press the button for the song there." Nancy, fast on her feet in more ways than one, replies to Norman, "You be the dropper, and I'll be the deer." However, while she runs to press the button, Norman realizes he doesn't have the proper change and looks inside Nancy's purse where he discovers the stolen bracelet.

In a final, head-spinning twist, the film flashes back again for a third time—that's a flashback within a flashback within a flashback—when Norman presses Nancy to try to remember why she stole the bracelet. A diagonal black shadow cuts a swath across her tear-streaked face as she confesses, "My father had just died. He was a painter like you, Norman, only he was a failure. My mother . . . got a job at a home for a rich family. When you're a housekeeper's daughter, you see the world through half-opened doors."

Nancy is best friends with the rich family's daughter, Karen, but she's not allowed to attend her birthday party because, according to Mrs. Willis—in one of those common-sense pronouncements common to the discourse of class—she's the "housekeeper's daughter." Later, Karen steals away from the party to give Nancy the heart-shaped, diamond-studded locket she's just received from her mother and Nancy is ecstatic, "Thank you, God, I will never ask you for anything again." Mrs. Willis, however, not only asks for the locket back but, when it goes missing, forces Nancy to confess to stealing it. The latter, dramatic scene is the turning point of *The Locket*: although Nancy's mother eventually finds the locket among Karen's clothes, Mrs. Willis decides to demonstrate "how to get the truth out of a child." Insisting Nancy took the locket, Mrs. Willis violently pushes her up against a wall until Nancy, screaming, accidentally knocks over a musical cigarette box. The ensuing, disorienting shot—an extreme low-angle one from the tinkly music box's point of view—shows Nancy's shocked, pained expression. (For an even more twisted scenario, see *The Dark Mirror* in which psychopath Terry Collins [Olivia de Havilland] uses a music box to try to make her "good" twin sister, Ruth [de Havilland], think she's going insane.)

The Locket returns to this traumatic moment in a dénouement that is worlds away from the light, uplifting conclusions typical of the Hollywood musical. John Willis patiently listens to Dr. Blair's damaging story about Nancy, but when he confronts her, she attributes it to his stay in a sanitarium and, before that, the London blitz. (While she's away from the party, a woman entertains guests by singing a ditty about the bride-to-be, "Nancy, Nancy, what'll you do to him now? / He's only a fish on a gilded dish / About to be fried and how.") Ultimately persuaded by Nancy's version of events, Willis prepares to marry her and, in an unexpected gesture of kindness, his mother—perhaps because of the earlier death of her only daughter, Karen—presents her with the locket she had forcibly taken away so many years ago. Nancy closes her eyes as if in prayer, "Thank you, God, I won't ask you for anything again."

However, when a bridesmaid enters calling her name (an echo of the above ditty), Nancy accidentally knocks over the very same cigarette box whose music haunted her in the past. This time, though, the extreme low-angle shot highlights the lace from the bride-to-be's white veil, which flies out in the sunlight like stars from her startled face. After the bridesmaid rushes over and closes the box, stilling the music, Nancy, terrified, asks, "Did you close it tight?"

Moments later, having apparently regained her composure, Nancy walks down the garlanded staircase to the triumphal sounds of a wedding march, but the insidious music from the cigarette box returns, distorting the march and transforming it into a dirge. Assaulted first by hallucinations in the form of faces superimposed on the Oriental carpet, then, like Chris Cross at the end of *Scarlet Street*, by voices from the past, including Mrs. Willis ("You stole that locket"), Norman ("You stole it, remember?"), and her own mother ("If you want things badly enough, some day you'll have them"), Nancy somehow manages to make it to the front of the room where her future husband stands and where, taking his extended hand, she collapses with a scream.

Although it's never entirely clear what's encrypted inside the musical cigarette box, there's obviously a lock, as in "lock it," on the terra incognita that is Nancy's psyche.[52] What is the cause of her psychosis? Is it the evil mother, Mrs. Willis, insuperable class barriers, or latent lesbianism? What *is* clear is that the cigarette-box music, what Nancy calls "the tune," represents the full force of the return of the repressed: once released like some evil genie, it can't be put back. A happy-ever-after ending hovers over the conclusion of *The Locket* when, in the final scene, John defies his mother, who now wants nothing to do with Nancy, and says he'll stand by his wife. Nancy, however, seems beyond repair, her ear secretly tuned to a distant melody, forever adrift—as Dr. Blair predicted—in the lost, impenetrable world of childhood.

In *Detour* (1945), Al Roberts (Tom Neal) is neither a returning serviceman like Buzz in *The Blue Dahlia* nor a kleptomaniac traumatized by the past like Nancy in *The Locket*, though he's equally alienated. At the beginning of Ulmer's film, shot in only six days for the grindhouse Producers Releasing Corporation (Ulmer being the "Capra of PRC"[53]), Al is sitting alone at the counter in a roadside diner in Reno. A truck driver tries to befriend him, but when Al sarcastically says his "mother taught [him] never to speak to strangers," the truck driver asks the waitress for some change to play the jukebox. The song starts and the camera cuts to a close-up of Al's face, scrunched up with displeasure:

AL: Hey, turn that thing off. Will you turn that thing off?

OWNER: What's eating you now?

JOE: Yeah, what's eating ya?

AL: That music, it stinks.

OWNER: You don't like it, huh?

AL: No. Turn it off.

JOE: Wait a minute, pal. That's my nickel, see. It's a free country and I play whatever I want to.

AL: OK.

OWNER: If you don't like it, you don't have to listen to it. And you can leave here any time you want to. First good piece played tonight and you don't like it.

AL: OK, OK, I'm sorry I asked.

OWNER: Some people just don't got any good taste.

While the song on the jukebox, "I Can't Believe That You're in Love with Me," may not be a model of "good taste" (we later learn that Al in fact has pretensions to becoming a classical pianist), it doesn't stink either. (Billie Holiday, for one, recorded it as well as Frank Sinatra, not to mention the likes of Benny Carter and Coleman Hawkins.) What is it about this "piece" that makes Al feel so bad, splitting his head like an ax?

Suddenly, the lights go down, we're inside Al's head, spot-lit like a raccoon's around the eyes, and it's a very crowded place:

> That tune, *that tune*! Why was there always that rotten tune, following me around, beating in my head, never letting up. Did ya ever wanna forget anything, did you ever wanna cut away a piece of your memory or blot it out? You can't, you know. No matter how hard you try. You can change the scenery, but sooner or later you'll get a whiff of perfume or somebody will say a certain phrase or maybe hum something. Then you're licked again.

The camera tilts down from Al's hooded face to a close-up of a coffee cup that looms surreally in the foreground,[54] then dollies in to the lighted jukebox where the record turns in circles like the tracks of Al's mind:

> I used to love that song, once. So did the customers back in the old Break O' Dawn club in New York. I can't remember a night when I didn't get at least three requests for it. Sue, she was always selling it too. Those were the days.

In a stunning match-shot, the camera cuts from the spinning record to a "brightly lit circular object so abstract as to be virtually unidentifiable,"[55] which—when the camera pulls back—turns out to be the bass drum of the combo that Al and Sue Harvey (Claudia Drake) play with at the Break O' Dawn club.

After Al puts the finishing touches on a piano solo, Sue steps onto the stage to sing their song, Jimmy McHugh and Hugh Gaskill's "I Can't Believe That You're in Love with Me" (which, for financial reasons, Ulmer used instead of "Sophisticated Lady"): "I have always placed you far above me / I just can't imagine that you love me / And after all is said and done / To think that I'm the lucky one." Although the lyrics, together with her sidelong glances, make it seem as if it's Sue who can't believe her good fortune, the fact she's standing over Al while he's seated at the piano gazing "adoringly up at her" suggests it's the other way around.[56] It's therefore no surprise when she later breaks it off with Al, cementing his own dawning realization he won't be seeing himself up on stage like Paderewski at Carnegie Hall any time soon. Down but not out, Al decides to follow Sue to the West Coast, but not before punishing Chopin's Waltz in C Minor and Brahms's Waltz in A Major with "maniacal, boogie-woogie" improvisations.[57]

Al, in fact, never does make it to L.A. First, he finds himself in a world of trouble when "hymnal salesman" Charlie Haskell (Edmund MacDonald) picks him up hitchhiking, then when Charlie suffers a fatal heart attack while Al's behind the wheel *or* hits his head on a rock falling out of the passenger side of his own car—or, not improbably in Ulmer's absolutely absurd world, both. "That's life," Al waxes philosophically in voice-over, "Whichever way you turn, fate sticks out its foot to trip you."

Assuming Haskell's identity, Al drives off only to pick up the dead man's previous passenger, Vera (Ann Savage), the hitchhiker from hell and the femme fatale to end all femme fatales. Al initially sees Vera—in profile—through rose-tinted glasses: "She looked like she had been thrown off the crummiest freight train in the world, yet . . . I got the impression of beauty." Then she turns her face and his fantasies about her, like Jeff Markham's about Kathie Moffat in *Out of the Past*, come crashing down like a bullet-shattered mirror.[58]

Despite the abuse Vera heaps on Al ("Shut up! You're a cheap crook!"), the two play cute, or at least try to (their momentary cohabitation a vicious parody of forties domesticity), until she threatens to call the cops and he accidentally strangles her to death in the most grotesque manner imaginable

—with a phone cord. All Al can do is ruminate again on the twists and turns of fate that have brought him to this god-forsaken place, a run-down motel with a dead woman in the other room, a phone cord wrapped around her throat like a boa: "All I could think of was the guy with the saxophone and what he was playing. It wasn't a love song anymore, it was a dirge." Al, taking a cue from the music, puts on his hat and splits.

The concluding sequence of *Detour*, a bleak, utterly disenchanting coda, returns to Al sitting alone with his thoughts in the same Reno diner: "But my problems weren't solved. I had to stay away from New York for all time because Al Roberts was listed as dead and had to stay dead. And I could never go back to Hollywood. Someone might recognize me as Haskell." After the camera reframes to include the jukebox in the background, the lights come up as if a bulb had suddenly gone on inside that dim, not very well lighted place that is Al's head: "Then, too, there was Sue. I could never go to her with a thing like this hanging over my head. All I could do was pray she'd be happy." And with this sentimental fare-thee-well, Al walks out of the diner and straight into the abyss. A highway patrol car, like some ghastly apparition, pulls up beside him. A copper gets out and says something to Al who, as he obediently slips into the backseat, famously opines, "Yes, fate or some mysterious force can put the finger on you or me for no good reason at all."

Juke Lust: *Fallen Angel*

Since its release in 1945 *Detour* has, over the years, become the most acclaimed "B" noir. However, the ultimate "juke" noir is an "A" feature released the same year, Otto Preminger's *Fallen Angel.* A roadside diner bookends Ulmer's film, but the seaside one into which Eric Stanton (Dana Andrews) stumbles after being unceremoniously dropped off in Stanton, California, by a bus driver because he doesn't have the fare to continue on to San Francisco is "*almost* the quintessential noir set": "exterior, night, deserted street; neon on wet paving."[59] The word *almost* is italicized because despite the fact that *Fallen Angel* is a remake of one of the quintessential forties noirs, *Laura* (it's virtually the same Fox personnel with the exception of Bernard Freericks, Roger Heman, and Harry M. Leonard on sound), it's suffused with passages of *film gris* and *film rose.*

Among the various extra-noir influences that inform Preminger's film, the musical is perhaps the most important and is manifest in two ways: in the casting of Alice Faye, "a top musical star at the studio" who by then was in "her mid-thirties and seeking to promote a career as a dramatic actress,"[60] and in the film's repeated recourse to the jukebox-played song "Slowly" (composed by David Raksin and Kermit Goell). As for Faye, in the previous ten years from *George White's Scandals* (1934), her debut film with Rudy Vallee, to *Four Jills in a Jeep* (1944), Faye was—to paraphrase Stanley Green—Fox's "reigning queen": "the blond, throaty-voiced singing actress with the snub nose, pouting lips, and hourglass figure."[61] If the key film in Faye's career is arguably *Alexander's Ragtime Band* (1938) where she played Stella Kirby, in *Fallen Angel* she's June Mills, the light angel to Linda Darnell's dark one, Stella.

Darnell appeared in the Fox musicals *Rise and Shine* (1941) and *Sweet and Low-Down* (1944), but in *Fallen Angel* her mere presence inspires people—read "men"—to play "Slowly" on the jukebox. (Faye in fact chose "Slowly" from a number of compositions Raksin played for her and, although Preminger originally shot a scene where she "sang a complete version along with the radio," it was decided the song was better suited to Darnell's character and Faye's number was cut.[62]) Hence the conceit that informs the first scene at Pop's Diner. After Eric enters to the sound of a ringing bell, a traveling operator tells Pop the jukebox is "way down this week" and Pop (Percy Kilbride) replies that "nobody plays them with Stella not around"—songs, that is. (As we later learn from the policeman who's talking to Pop when Eric arrives, Stella has unaccountably disappeared for three days.)

In the subsequent scene at the diner, "Slowly" plays in the background (it's well back in the mix) while Eric tries to talk Pop into pushing tickets for a séance that he and his confederates, Joe Ellis and Professor Madley, are sponsoring. (In its depiction of the "spook" business, *Fallen Angel* recollects *Ministry of Fear* and presages *Nightmare Alley*.) In the flip side of the scene, the focus turns from Eric and his "spook promotion" to Mark Judd (Charles Bickford), a habitué of Pop's Diner who happens to be an ex-cop from New York City. After paying Stella for his coffee, Judd takes his change and, on the way out, puts a nickel in the jukebox, casting a backward glance at his muse as the bell rings. In response, Stella opens her eyes wide and smiles: "Slowly I open my eyes / Hazy with mist / Slowly my lips realize / They have just been kissed." The transition from the first "instrumental" part of the scene to the second "lyrical" one—a difference marked on the sound track by a dynamic increase in the song's volume—is a cue that there's more going on here than meets the eye.

The most obvious thing is petty theft. After erasing and changing the figure on Judd's bill, Stella opens the cash register, takes out a dollar bill, and sticks it in her bra:

> ERIC: That the only song on the jukebox?
> STELLA: I like it.
> ERIC: He knows what you like.
> STELLA: That's for his wife to worry about.

In the context of this combative exchange, the lyrics of "Slowly" (sung by Dick Haymes) assume a determinate ambiguity. On one hand, it's pretty clear that despite his stolid manner, Judd is mad about Stella, the Delilah of Pop's Diner: when he plays her song, it's his way of paying tribute to this Formica-counter goddess. On the other hand, the fact that Eric sees Stella pinch a dollar bill but only complains about the song suggests his eyes, like Stella's, are wide open. At the same time, the implication is that Eric's falling for her, not slowly but fast, precisely because she's a con artist just like himself.

This theme is dramatized in two sequences, one set in a nightclub and the other on the beach outside. While Eric wants to sleep with Stella (when she tells him she would like to have her fortune told, he immediately invites her up to his room to "read her horoscope"), she replies she wants a "ring" and a "home." In the sonata-like sequence set at the nightclub (dance, talk, dance), they dance to swing music—Stella: "I like the way you talk" / Eric: "I like the way you dance"—then sit down for a drink while he reads her palm: "There's a man in your life and you just met him. Tomorrow he's going to San Francisco and you're gonna lie awake at night unable to forget him." In the eloquent long take that follows, Joseph LaShelle fluidly moves the camera from a medium shot of Eric and Stella dancing to an extreme close-up of them kissing, a kiss initially interrupted when the band stopped for a break.

It's a heady, voluptuous moment, the prelude, it appears, to the consummation of the lovers' whirlwind affair. Thus, when the couple leaves the nightclub, Eric, hearing the "sound of the ocean," asks Stella if she likes the "sound of far-off places." Unlike Judd, who's married to a woman who won't give him a divorce, Eric can take Stella away from the stultifying, small-town life she's stuck in. (Is it any accident that the striped outfit Stella wears in Pop's Diner looks like a prison uniform?) Fighting off Eric's sexual advances, Stella has only one question for her ardent mind-reader, "Do you see me with a ring on my finger?"

As the following scene of Eric waking up in his hotel room without Stella to a ringing church bell confirms, it's a stalemate, not kismet, between the two. In fact, the church bell not only echoes the ringing bell at Pop's Diner and Stella's marital stipulation but foreshadows Eric's later seduction of June at the very same church. In the meantime, when Eric returns to Pop's Diner to tell Stella he's leaving on a bus in fifteen minutes (he's joining the Professor's traveling show), her only response is to ask for a nickel to play "Slowly" on the jukebox. Exasperated, Eric says "goodbye for good," but he can't get Stella, like the song, out of his mind and, in a parallel scene, the film cuts to her saying goodbye to a slick coin-slot operator named Atkins (Bruce Cabot). Eric's "proposal": he'll marry June, then once he's "got the cash" (she's due to collect $12,500 from her father's inheritance), he'll divorce her and marry Stella.

Although Eric's seduction of June mirrors his amorous pursuit of Stella, the difference is that instead of going to Pop's, whose sole charm is provided by the big-band music playing on the jukebox, he goes to June's church, a bright airy place reverberating with the fervent sound of her organ playing.[63] In fact, while June in *Fallen Angel* is associated with literature and classical music, Stella is symbolically linked with popular music and its pleasures, what June calls the "little things" of life such as drinking and dancing, going to the beach or the movies. Therefore, when Eric compliments June on her performance ("Beethoven never sounded so good") and she answers she was merely "improvising," the allusion to jazz suggests that the world with which each woman is identified—June with the classical and Stella with the popular-musical—can't be separated out so easily.

June and Eric's *débat* about music sets up the later sequence where he takes her out drinking and dancing to the same nightclub he took Stella. When June proves to be a slow learner, dismissing her "first Scotch," Eric smartly asks, "Did you learn to play Beethoven in one night?" For Eric, the payoff comes in another rhyming scene, this time on the beach with the surf lightly crashing in the background when he teases her with the prospect of seeing Toscanini conduct the San Francisco Symphony: "When you see them up on the stage all dressed with their fiddles and horns, people right up to the roof, ten thousand of them waiting for the music to begin, that's a concert."

June soon finds out, when there's no concert, that it's just Eric's ploy to

Fig. 8. Roadside Delilah: Stella (Linda Darnell) selects "Slowly" as Eric Stanton (Dana Andrews) looks on in Otto Preminger's *Fallen Angel*.

get her out of Walton and away from her diffident sister long enough to marry her. However, Eric's plans backfire on the very first night of their honeymoon. He rushes to the diner to tell Stella who, pocket mirror in hand as she applies lipstick for a date, is standing in front of the jukebox, the romantic strains of "Slowly" a testament, like the opening shot of her framed in the doorway, to her sexual allure. What Eric can't know is that it's the last time he'll see her alive.

The emotional and audiovisual climax of *Fallen Angel* occurs in the wake of Stella's sudden, violent death at the hands of an unknown assailant. Since Eric, like Atkins, is a suspect, he flees with June to San Francisco where, in a threadbare hotel room, he bitterly tells her off—"I don't need your dough. If I had been alone, I could have kept right on going"—before walking out on her. When he gets to the hotel bar, though, the swing music playing in the background—Harry Warren and Leo Robin's "Paducah," originally performed by Benny Goodman and His Orchestra in *The Gang's All Here* (1943)

—is a harsh reminder Stella is dead and, with her, his dream of a life of simple pleasures. Returning to the hotel room with a book and toothbrush for June, Eric confesses he only married her for her money. To his very real surprise, though, she tells him—twice—she loves him and, for the first time, Eric begins to see her not as some bookworm or as a way to win Stella back but as a real woman with her own needs and desires.

As in *Double Indemnity* and *Out of the Past*, the straight cut—from Eric and June kissing to Eric sitting on the windowsill recounting his life story—can be interpreted as a sexual ellipsis, an interpretation reinforced by the two hats sitting side by side on the dresser. After Eric concludes his monologue by acknowledging he's a "wash-out at thirty," June encourages him to lie down on the bed where he repeats his mantra ("Why don't you just go home?") and June repeats hers ("We're married, remember? You're my husband and I'm your wife"), at which point Eric, a cigarette still burning in his hand, mumbles, "Right out of a book, again."

Softly repeating what Eric has said ("Out of a book"), June looks up and begins to recite a poem from memory:

We were born to tread the earth as angels
To seek out heaven this side of the sky
But they who race alone shall stumble in the dark and fall from grace
Then love alone can make the fallen angel rise
For only two together can enter paradise

Once the poem works its magic, putting Eric to sleep like a lullaby, June takes the burning cigarette from his hand. Turning off the light, she unfolds the blanket at the end of the bed and drapes it over his body, then walks over and opens the window. In the warm darkness, the large neon letters spell "Hot," but when she returns to bed, the camera tracks in to the window where a breeze stirs the curtains and, not unlike a similar sequence in *House of Strangers*, the light gradually changes from night to day, the neon letters dissolving in the morning glare to a reflected view of San Francisco below and, in the distance, the Bay Bridge. The camera pans back across the room to Eric and June fast asleep in bed, her face illuminated by a wedge of light, his body dappled with shadows.

The police capture June the next morning coming out of a restaurant, though Eric manages to escape and returns to the "scene of the crime": Pop's Diner. There, as the jukebox stands silently in the background like a witness, he confronts Judd with Stella's murder. The ex-detective pulls a gun on Eric, then begins to reminisce about Stella—"Two years I came here to drink coffee just to get a look at her"—until Pop wrestles the gun away from him. A policeman who's been waiting outside enters and handcuffs one of Judd's hands, but not before the die-hard romantic uses the other hand to put a nickel in the jukebox one more time.

The conclusion to *Fallen Angel* is something of an anticlimax, especially compared to the masterly and deeply moving hotel sequence that precedes it. However, it must also be said that critics sometimes make too much of the endings of forties films, as if their value, not to say pleasures, were incumbent on a dramatically convincing or, in the case of a film noir's bona fides, suitably dark dénouement. Sometimes, as is frequently the case with Preminger (a self-described "foreman for a sausage factory"[64]), the ending is a sop thrown to the studio.

In fact, what one can only call the director's "screen memory" of the film's conclusion is, in the context, tonic: "I was dressing for dinner and *Fallen Angel* was on television. I watched it and I got quite involved; then I finished dressing and never saw the ending. I still cannot recall the ending!"[65] Sometimes, as in *Fallen Angel*, it's not about the "plot." Sometimes, the end is not all and the real action is elsewhere, like the play of music and poetry, mise-en-scène and camera movement, or the resonance of a popular song played over and over again on a jukebox, its melody haunting the air like cigarette smoke.

4

Blues in the Night

POPULAR AND CLASSICAL INSTRUMENTAL SOURCE MUSIC

Violent Interludes

In the form of scores as well as emanating from various sources, radio and record player and jukebox, music in forties noir and classical Hollywood cinema more generally is employed to accent almost every conceivable kind of action. One of the most distinctive, though, is the use of diegetic music to underscore scenes of physical violence. "Beatings are interludes of spectacle, like song-and-dance numbers in musicals," Manohla Dargis writes in her BFI volume on *L.A. Confidential* (1997), "and as in the musical, they have a subtextual function."[1]

Robert Wise's *Born to Kill* (1947) is an "excellent example" of the early RKO film noir, marrying the "atmospheric style of Welles and the moody, Gothic atmosphere of Lewton,"[2] but it's also notable for its unique marriage of music and violence. Laury Palmer (Isabel Jewell) and her boyfriend, Danny (Tony Barrett), have returned to her apartment after a night out on the town in Reno. What Danny doesn't know is that Laury has recently met another man, Sam Wild (Lawrence Tierney), and is only continuing to see Danny in order to "needle" her new beau. Laury gushes about Sam, "he's the quiet sort," then adds, not without admiration, "And yet, you get a feeling if you stepped out of line, he'd kick your teeth down your throat."

While Laury goes to the bedroom to freshen up, Danny switches the radio on as he strolls to the kitchen to fix some drinks. Whistling along with the swing music, he breezes through the kitchen door (he's clearly done this before) and pivots as he flips on the lights. In doing so, however, he doesn't see Sam still wearing his hat and placidly sitting on a barstool. The ensuing scene, shot in the full, high-key light usually reserved for musicals, is fraught with menace: in the foreground, Danny's body is blocked by the fridge door; in the background, Sam, having taken the final puff off a cigarette, stands with his hands ready at his sides. Sam tells him to get out and, for a moment, Danny tries to reason with him ("Let's talk this out over a couple of drinks"). But when Sam says, "There's no man big enough to cut me out," Danny pulls out a switchblade.

Mistake number one. Sam handily disarms him, then hits him four straight times, the last an upper cut to the chin that sends him crashing to the floor. Danny grabs a stick of broken furniture and gets up. Mistake number two. Sam disarms him again and, with a single punch, sends him flying across the room. Danny, still game, wipes his mouth and gets up again. Mistake number three, his final one. Danny rushes Sam and, for an instant, it's as if they're dancing—until, that is, Sam throws him down like a sack of coal and beats him to death.

Suddenly, Laury's voice can be heard offscreen, "Sounds like you're tearing the house apart, the racket you're making!" Since Sam has turned off the lights and is hiding behind the door, Laury doesn't see him when she comes into the kitchen; instead, she sees Danny's lifeless body crumpled on the floor. Backing up in horror, she bumps into Sam and is momentarily relieved until she sees the look on his face, then her eyes fill with terror. As the radio drones in the background, Sam proceeds to "knock her teeth down her throat"—or so we imagine, since in fact we see nothing. We only hear the big-band music, the sickening sound of flesh on flesh, and Romeo, Laury's dog, whimpering.

The working title of Wise's film, *Deadlier Than the Male*, refers to Claire Trevor's character, Helen Brent, who, such is her lust, remains completely unfazed by Wild's brutality. "The adopted sister of a newspaper heiress" whose life of wealth and leisure she envies,[3] Helen, like Sam, is "born to kill," her overpowering sexual attraction to him eventually eroding her veneer of civility and revealing a base strain of greed and aggressivity. Still, we're ultimately transfixed not so much by Helen as by Sam who, as played by the mesmerizing, tight-lipped Tierney, is the ultimate homme fatal. (See as well Tierney's louche, lubricious performance as Steve Morgan in the contemporaneous RKO film, *The Devil Thumbs a Ride* [1947].) "There are many examples of masochistic males exploited by ruthless women in the 1940s and 1950s," as one critic has observed about the classic period of noir, but "*Born to Kill* reverses this pattern."[4] In other words, despite all the ado about femme fatales, Sam Wild is deadlier than the deadliest female.

There are numerous forties noirs in which physical violence is set to music as, for example, *Scene of the Crime* (1949) in which police investigator Mike Conovan (Van Johnson) accidentally turns on a radio, waking up a suspect and precipitating a knock-down, drag-out fight scored, like *Born to Kill*, to blaring big-band music. But perhaps the most expressionistic interlude of violence occurs during the conclusion to *The Set-Up*. Bill "Stoker" Thompson has improbably won a fight he's supposed to have lost. (In fact, Stoker is such a has-been even his own manager doesn't bother to tell him before the fight that it's a set-up.) Now, his left eye black and blue, sporting a bandage on his brow like a red badge of courage, Stoker tries to sneak out of the Paradise City A.C. without being noticed by Little Boy (Alan Baxter) and his thugs waiting outside for him. Cornered in a dingy alley enlivened only by the sound of the hot jazz band playing next door, Stoker fights back with every last ounce of his rapidly dwindling strength, the furious exchanges between the clarinet and horns brightly shadowing the sound of flying fists and Stoker's muffled cries of pain. Eventually, as Little Boy looks on, three men pin Stoker down as if he were being crucified, one holding his right arm, one his left, and one his feet. However, when Little Boy grabs him by the shirt to hit him in the face, Stoker hits him first, drawing blood. "You'll never hit anybody with that hand again," Little Boy spits. After a smash cut from a low-angle shot of Little Boy to a close-up of Stoker's right hand, the music jumps in volume, the camera panning sharply to the left where a live-action hieroglyph is imprinted on the brick wall of the coliseum: a silhouette of a trumpeter and drummer, the shadows of the drummer's hands and sticks pounding away at a shadow snare drum. (This audiovisual passage, perhaps even more so than James Edwards's bit part as the black boxer Luther Hawkins, echoes the film's source material, Joseph Moncure March's 1928 Jazz Age verse narrative, "The Set-Up," in which the boxer-protagonist is an African American.[5])

As in *Born to Kill*, we can only imagine what's happening, but we know it's not pretty. Mercifully, the scene shifts to the run-down Hotel Cozy where Stoker's long-suffering wife Julie is periodically checking the window as she prepares her husband's post-fight supper. A clock in the right foreground ticks loudly and, in the distance, there's the sound of honking cars and the steady pulse of jazz music. When the film returns to Stoker after what seems like an eternity, he's struggling to stand up, his left hand climbing the wall like a tendril while, above him on an iron balcony illuminated by swirling crystal-ball lights, a couple kisses to the soft romantic music issuing from within. Desperately calling for his wife, Stoker drags the dead carcass that's his body to the street where, from her second-story window, Julie finally sees him and rushes out. In the painfully mean time it takes her to reach him, we watch in long shot from her now-absent perspective as Stoker collapses in a heap under a sign big as life for a chop suey joint, "Dreamland." When the ending comes it's happy enough (since Stoker can't fight any more, Julie has theoretically won), but even the sweet music on the sound track can't rinse the bitter taste out of our mouths. In *The Set-Up* life is a fight that, sooner or later, everybody loses.

A kind of "barbarous poetry," to invoke Raymond Borde and Étienne Chaumeton, also suffuses *Ride the Pink Horse* (1947).[6] Produced for Universal-International by Joan Harrison from a script by Ben Hecht and Charles Lederer, Robert Montgomery's film represents a substantial advance on his earlier, technically adventurous *Lady in the Lake*. An ex-serviceman, Lucky Gagin (Montgomery), arrives in the small New Mexican town of San Pablo looking to avenge the death of his friend Shorty. Gagin is instantly befriended by an Indian girl, Pila (the extraordinary Wanda Hendrix), who entrusts him with a doll of Ishtam for good luck. (Just back from the war, Gagin mistakenly thinks his "soldier gun" is his lucky charm.)

When Gagin walks into the De Las Tres Violetas cantina looking for Hugo (Fred Clark), a mobster who talks a big game but wears a hearing aid, everything comes to a standstill, including the music. Seeing Gagin's plight, Pancho (Thomas Gomez), the owner of the local tiovivo, intercedes and, after Gagin buys a round of tequila for the patrons, Pancho exclaims, "La musica, la musica," explaining that the man is singing because the next day during the Pasatiempo carnival the townspeople will burn Zozobra, the "god of bad luck": "no more Zozobra, no more bad luck." Later, when Pancho finds out that Gagin has no place to sleep for the night (hence his nickname, "the man with no place"), the two retire to the tiovivo and the adjoining shack that Pancho calls his home.

Pancho falls fast asleep, but when Pila shows up, Gagin asks her if she wants a ride on the carousel. Although Pancho, waking, says it's too late

—he never gives rides for free and "music wake the peoples"—he eventually relents and starts up the machine. Since Pila has never ridden the tiovivo, she asks "Which one?" and, without hesitating, Gagin walks over to a horse, takes off the blanket and, pointing, says, "Try the pink one." According to Alain Silver, it makes no difference to Gagin which horse Pila rides because they "all travel in the same circle," but for Pila "it makes all the difference."[7] Mounted on the silently turning merry-go-round, the camera captures Pila's face as her countenance gradually transforms from somber to animated.

This carousel scene, devoid of music, sets up the pivotal sequence near the end of *Ride the Pink Horse* when Pila brings the half-dead Gagin, who's been stabbed in the back by one of Hugo's torpedoes, to the tiovivo. After Pancho tries to shield Gagin by giving free rides to all the children and putting him in a carousel chair draped by a horse blanket and safeguarded by Pila, Hugo's men finally appear. However, when Pancho refuses to talk, the men savagely beat him, the camera cutting to the merry-go-round turning round and round to the music (a tinny, prerecorded piano tune, not unlike the theme music of *Shoot the Piano Player* [1960]), his cries of pain mirrored in the children's frightened faces.

In *A Panorama of American Film Noir*, Borde and Chaumeton write of the film's "chill violence of events," referencing the "punishment inflicted by two hoodlums on the old Mexican . . . while the wounded hero remain[s] spread out on the merry-go-round that [goes] on silently turning."[8] In fact, the second carousel scene, unlike the first one, can be said to turn on music and, to echo Silver, it makes all the difference. It may not wake up the people, but associated as it is with the fiesta that follows in the wake of Zozobra's fiery death, it represents a reawakening for Gagin. On one hand, "Hugo, 'burned,' awaits punishment";[9] on the other, Gagin finds redemption in the unlikeliest of places, a tiovivo. Thanks to some good luck in the person of Pancho and, in particular, Pila, the young girl who sees something in him that he's incapable of seeing, Gagin finds himself still among the living, having survived the classic noir merry-go-round of life and death.

While the use of recorded music in *Crossfire* (1947) to highlight the spectacle of physical violence may be more conventional than in *Ride the Pink Horse*, it's equally dramatic. Dmytryk's film, produced like *Murder, My Sweet* and *Cornered* by Adrian Scott for RKO, begins with four soldiers—Montgomery (Robert Ryan), Keeley (Robert Mitchum), Floyd (Steve Brodie), and Mitchell (George Cooper)—waiting to be demobilized and "crawling," as Keeley puts it, in the nation's capital. There, they make the acquaintance of Joseph Samuels (Sam Levene) who befriends the former WPA muralist, Mitchell, then invites him to dinner with his girlfriend. But before they go out, the men return to Samuels's apartment (the girlfriend goes to hers to change) and, although uninvited, "Monty" and Floyd follow.

The critical sequence occurs in the second flashback narrated by "Mitch" who, despite being drunk, remembers the moment "everything began to get fuzzy." It's his POV, so the image gets "fuzzy" when the phonograph automatically changes the music from the majestic codetta of "The Blue Danube" to an up-tempo, Benny Goodman–style number. (The Johann Strauss selection is significant since in an earlier draft of the screenplay Samuels mentions his preference for classical recordings such as Sergei Prokofiev's score for *Lieutenant Kijé*.) Inebriated, Mitch decides it's time to get some fresh air, but Monty demands another round of drinks and when "Sammy" says there's no time, he bellows, "What's the matter, Jew boy, you afraid we'll drink all your wonderful, stinkin' liquor?" Enraged at Samuels's "civilian" behavior (we later learn he in fact received a medical discharge after serving in Okinawa), Monty proceeds to beat him to death.

In the conclusion to *Crossfire*, the investigating detective Finlay (Robert Young) shoots Monty dead in the street from a second-story window, a conclusion that not only "transforms the New Deal detective into a cowboy" but makes Monty look like a "helpless rat in a maze executed from on high by an all-seeing authority."[10] As in *Dead Reckoning*, the war may be over "over there," but "over here" it's still very much alive. As for Monty, his bigotry and homicidal instincts, stoked by his combat experiences in the South Pacific ("The snakes are loose," as Keeley says), appear to have been triggered by the sudden change from Strauss's famous waltz to the "hot," clarinet-driven sound of jazz swing. (The nationalistic associations of "The Blue Danube" with Austria may be a cue as well.) In fact, the association in *Crossfire* between jazz and violence—which is not, unlike the film's racial politics, progressive—recalls Theodor Adorno's influential critique of jazz as "animalistic": classical music soothes the savage beast, big-band jazz releases it.[11]

Chapter 4

Encore: Scoring Sadism

As in *Crossfire*, *Brute Force* (1947), produced by Mark Hellinger and photographed by William Daniels, tenders a clear equation between music and violence. In response to the sadistic regime spearheaded by captain of the guards Munsey (Hume Cronyn), the convicts of cell R17 at Westgate Penitentiary are planning a breakout masterminded by Joe Collins (Burt Lancaster). However, when the inmates are unable to procure dynamite, Gallagher (Charles Bickford) instructs the star prison reporter, Louie (Sam Levene), to procure a pass in order to tell Collins, who's laboring along with other inmates on a drainpipe to nowhere.

Instead of receiving a pass as promised, Louie is taken straight to Munsey's office where the captain, clad in a white t-shirt, is polishing his prized shotgun to the strains of Richard Wagner's *Tannhäuser*. Before a guard ushers Louie in, the camera cuts from a shot of Munsey, who's washing his hands like Pontius Pilate in a sink, to the spinning record reflected in the top of a phonograph above which hangs a lithograph of Michelangelo's "Rebellious Slave." Munsey asks Louie why he wants to do a story about the drainpipe, but when Louis balks, Munsey slaps him across the face, an act of violence that recalls his earlier slapping of the humanitarian doctor Walters (Art Smith).

As the overture to *Tannhäuser* spirals higher and higher on the sound track (the fact that it's "The Venusberg" invests the sequence with a perverse, libidinal undercurrent), Munsey walks over to the windows, pulls down the blinds and, after telling the guard to leave, takes out a rubber hose and lays it on the desk. All business now, Munsey repeats his question about the drainpipe, but when Louie says he doesn't know anything, the captain slaps him again, harder. As the camera tracks in low, Munsey walks behind Louie and, lifting the hose in the air like a hammer, brings it down again and again on his head. Stirred, Munsey goes over to the phonograph and turns up the volume, the action climaxing with the music: a rapid-fire montage of the spinning record, a gun rack next to a planter, and, finally, a formal portrait of the captain in full-dress, standing at attention, his arms crossed like swords.

In both Dassin's *Brute Force*, which was scripted by Richard Brooks, and Dmytryk's *Crossfire*, which is based on Brooks's novel *The Brick Foxhole*, music can be seen as a catalyst for the song-and-dance of violence. The difference between the two films, while slight, is significant: whereas in *Crossfire*

Montgomery's murder of the Jewish Samuels appears to be caused by a phonograph that mechanically changes the music from classical to jazz, in *Brute Force* the record has been personally selected by Munsey. In other words, Munsey plays *Tannhäuser* not simply to drown out the sound of the beating but to mirror his own mythic, exalted sense of himself as an Übermensch: unlike the weak-willed warden, Munsey knows that strength, "brute force," is what separates him from other men.

At the same time, if the recourse to Wagner in *Brute Force* (which may have been suggested by the film's composer, Miklós Rózsa) reflects Munsey's fetishistic sense of ritual, it also depicts the captain as a crypto-Nazi. (I'm thinking here of Wagner's well-documented anti-Semitism as well as Hitler's "enthusiastic" embrace of the composer.[12]) As Michael Tanner has commented, remembering Nietzsche, the "noble" appearance of Wagner's heroes tends to conceal an "underlying insecurity and egoism, not to mention pusillanimity,"[13] a verdict that can be equally applied to the vicious, vainglorious Munsey.

In his entry in *Film Noir*, Blake Lucas observes that the "magnificent brutality of the abortive prison break" in *Brute Force* contrasts with the "stylized tortures" performed by Munsey,[14] a counterpoint that's also audible on the sound track of Dassin's film. For example, at the beginning of *Brute Force* the men hammer their tools against their machines to mask the execution of the captain's informer, who's forced at the point of blowtorches into an enormous machine press where he's crushed. And at the conclusion of Dassin's film as Collins and his men are about to break out, Gallagher encourages the convicts assembled in the prison yard to raise their voices in protest to distract the authorities.

But perhaps the most eloquent moment in *Brute Force* occurs in the coda when a lone voice on the sound track answers Munsey's dehumanizing, Wagner-inspired "brute force." In the aftermath of the rebellion, the Molotov cocktails and machine-gun fire, order has been restored at the prison, and the camera tracks past the second-tier cells at Westgate where someone can be heard humming. The tune is a calypso and the inmate is played by Victor Edward Pinard, a.k.a. Sir Lancelot, the famous Trinidadian singer who, before touring with Lionel Belasco's band, appeared in *Cat People* and *I Walked with a Zombie* (1943).

Earlier in *Brute Force*, in a brief but memorable bit, Sir Lancelot's character sticks his head into cell R17 to announce in his mellifluous cadence: "White tails and tie for the movie tonight / The boy gets the girl and that's all right."

Although the song is not without irony (the men in R17, as any number of critics have noted, have been incarcerated because of the women in their lives), it recollects another, not-so-ancient site of discipline and punishment, the plantation, and its abiding music, the blues. Hence the complex resonance of the mise-en-scène in the "operatic" beating scene where, in a dialectical collision of music and image, master encounters slave, Wagner meets Michelangelo.

Like *Ride the Pink Horse*, *Crossfire*, and *Brute Force*, forties noirs all audibly marked by their historical moment, *Dead Reckoning* mobilizes source music to reconfigure the traumatic terrain of postwar masculinity. A Columbia production, John Cromwell's film is about ex-serviceman Rip Murdock (Humphrey Bogart) after he's mysteriously abandoned by Johnny Drake (William Prince) on their way to the capital to be decorated. In an attempt to understand why his buddy left without a word, Rip travels to Gulf City, the "Paradise of the South," where he discovers that Johnny's been reduced to a "lump of coal" from a car accident that his former girl, Coral "Dusty" Chandler (Lizabeth Scott), may well have been involved in.

Tipped off by a bartender, Rip eventually makes his way to the office of Martinelli (Morris Carnovsky), the Nietzsche-quoting owner of the nightclub where Coral sings, to obtain the coded letter Johnny has left for him. Before Rip can read the jasmine-scented letter, though, he's sapped. In one of those spectacular moments in classic noir that appear out of nowhere but are the very essence of the genre, Rip is confessing in voice-over to an ex-paratrooper priest in a church. (The stunning montage was edited by Gene Havlick and shot by Leo Tover, who also photographed *I Walk Alone* and *The Set-Up*.) After he describes "going out the jump door" of a plane during the war, the camera shows him "falling through space" until he pulls the rip cord and the parachute opens like an enormous flower against the black sky, Rip counting down—"one thousand, two thousand . . ."—as the lights of the ground batteries below grow "brighter and brighter," blinding him.

Although the war's over and Rip is back on American soil, he wakes up to the enemy—the Italian Martinelli and his right-hand man, the German Krause (Marvin Miller)—gazing down at him. (The source of the whirling, vortex-like lights of the batteries in Rip's dream comes from the lamp Martinelli has shone on his face.) Krause's first words—"Go ahead and make with the music, friend, we love it"—are enigmatic, but the word "friend" is not since we know from his heavy, German-accented pronunciation that he really means "foe." Rip struggles to his feet, but when he won't disclose the

Fig. 9. "All Tuned Up": Rip Murdock (Humphrey Bogart) turns the tables on Martinelli (Morris Carnovsky) and Krause (Marvin Miller) in John Cromwell's *Dead Reckoning*.

contents of the letter, Martinelli leaves him to Krause who, as the camera follows his boss to the door, knocks Rip down. As in *Born to Kill*, we don't see what Krause has done; we only hear Rip being slugged and his body falling to the floor with a thud.

Then the real fun starts, for Krause. "The rest is to dance time, friend," he says with barely suppressed glee (and not a little homosexual frisson). After turning on the radio and wrapping his right hand with a handkerchief, he bends down next to the still unconscious Rip and continues his spiel, "You like music, friend? I like music, I love music." The volume of the "cocktail" swing on the radio surges in the background and, as the camera cuts to an extreme low-angle shot of Krause, he methodically begins to work Rip over, punching him again and again in the head.

Naturally, turnabout in *Dead Reckoning* is fair play since Krause is a "Kraut" and associated with the easy, "civilian" life that Rip is contemptuous of (hence the import of Martinelli's passing comment that his nightclub stocks only "pre-war" wine and paté). So, when Rip returns to Martinelli's office (right after Coral repeats Johnny's code-word "Geronimo" as she slips out a side door), his one overriding desire is to "dance" with Krause. Turning on the radio (the big-band music here is positively "sweet"), he tells Martinelli's man to "come a little closer"—"How's the tempo of the music, friend, suit you?"—then savagely pistol-whips him. In a final flagrant gesture, he tosses some "creeping jelly" in the form of a fire grenade at the two ("Here's a little melody for you, one of my favorite tunes"), a stunt that avenges Johnny's earlier, untimely demise and sends Krause to his death, not unlike Rick Coyle in *Raw Deal*, in a "cocoon of fire."[15]

If, keyed by Krause's radio number, Rip in *Dead Reckoning* has turned Gulf City into a battlefield (it's only a matter of time before Coral, corrupted by the "lush life," will have to pay the piper too), Rip and Krause's song-and-dance routine has transformed Martinelli's nightclub into a backstage musical in which Rip plays Astaire to Krause's Rogers, and vice versa, a strangely violent interlude where, to echo Dargis, subtext is everything.

Jazz in Black and White

The recourse to diegetic music to underline physical violence understood as a mode of performance is not uncommon in forties noir, as the above "song-and-dance" films suggest. However, the most common way in which source music appears in the period is, of course, the de rigueur nightclub scene in which a jazz combo or swing orchestra is playing. Although these set pieces may be stereotypical, they can be said to possess a performative aspect in that the music bears a symbolic relation to the featured "players," a relation that becomes especially pronounced when the band is black.

In this performative context, it's worth remembering that black musicians in the 1940s were primarily cast as popular entertainers. Moreover, as David Butler has argued, the recurrent use of nightclubs as settings in film noir "enabled jazz to be included in a way that made narrative sense,"[16] a strategy that, not so incidentally, allowed exhibitors in the South to excise certain scenes. This said, not every noir nightclub is "dark and smoky" nor a space of "potential sexual transgression."[17] (For instance, the white-run establishments in *Kiss of Death* and *Force of Evil* are anything but saturnalian.) The black musicians may be there to provide entertainment (and, given the status of popular, big-band jazz at the time, *dance* music), but they're not merely entertainers. More emphatically, while jazz is represented in a primitivist, if not racist, manner in a canonical film such as *D.O.A.*, black performers in forties noir possess a certain dignity that reflects their professional status as musicians.

The Dark Corner (1946), starring Mark Stevens and Lucille Ball, features a jazz sequence that's at once typical and atypical of forties noir. It's typical because, outside of the opening passage, Eddie Heywood's band remains off-screen; it's atypical because the opening number set in an up-scale white nightclub not only foregrounds the musicians but plays out in real time. (Heywood's appearance in *The Dark Corner* is contemporaneous with his Commodore recordings with Billie Holiday and Signature ones with Coleman Hawkins.)

Bradford Galt (Stevens) is a free man in New York City after being released from prison for manslaughter—"two years plus time off for good behavior." (Why he was incarcerated is part of the enigma that drives the film's action: when Galt accused his previous partner, Tony Jardine, of blackmail, Jardine framed him by loading him up with Scotch and putting him behind the wheel of a car, whereupon he proceeded to hit a truck, killing the driver.) Now, despite the fact that Galt has moved all the way from San Francisco to set up a new private-detective agency, he's being tailed by a man in a white suit, Stauffer, a.k.a. Fred Foss (William Bendix). Galt senses—correctly, it turns out—that he's being set up for another frame, although he doesn't know who's doing it or why: "I'm backed up in a dark corner and I don't know who's hitting me."

The jazz sequence begins with an establishing shot of the High Hat Club outside of which "White Suit" sits in a parked car, then—in a dramatic dissolve that anticipates *The Set-Up*—cuts to an enormous silhouette of a top-hatted pianist. After tilting down to a close-up of Heywood's percussive fingerwork, the camera pans away, pausing on the stand-up bass player thumping his instrument before gliding out to the couples on the densely packed dance floor. The lighting, supervised by Joe MacDonald, is as lively as the drummer's beat, segueing seamlessly from the stark high contrast of the silhouette and the rich low-key hues of the bandstand to the brightly lit table where Galt and Kathleen sit drinking cocktails. (The costumes and décor are as jazzy as the music, Galt's striped black tie and Kathleen's matching dress reflected in the bright-white lampshades of the cocktail lamps decorated, like the club's walls, with black top hats.)

Drumming her hands on the table, Kathleen exclaims, "Oh, boy, music like that does something to me," but Galt's perfunctory reply—"Yeah,

Fig. 10. "Heywood Blues": Top-hatted, pre-paralysis Eddie Heywood playing the piano at the High Hat Club in Henry Hathaway's *The Dark Corner*.

they're OK"—indicates his mind's on something besides the music. When she asks why, he lies, bantering about the Tahitian girl he was viewing through a kinescope at the Penny Arcade:

GALT: Maybe you won't be around for very long. I've been thinking about that Tahitian secretary.
KATHLEEN: Well, you won't like her.
GALT: Maybe not. Those grass skirts rustle.
KATHLEEN: I told you before, they're a fire hazard.
GALT: So are you.

Kathleen pretends to be offended ("Please, Mr. Galt"), then asks him to dance, but Galt continues to warn her off, "I gotta feeling I'm behind the eight ball. Something's gonna happen and when it does, you're gonna end right in the corner pocket." Even after Galt drops Kathleen off at their table so he can talk to a police detective who, like White Suit, has been tailing him, the band continues to cook in the background, Heywood's energetic playing punctuated by blasts from the horn section. It's only when Galt returns to the table and finds Kathleen still there that the song comes to a close, "I decided to wait. I don't want you to be in that corner pocket all alone." In fact, Kathleen announces that her "maternal instinct" has been "aroused" ("I want to look out for you"), at which point the band breaks into a slightly brighter, up-tempo number and Galt reaches across the table, putting his hand on hers.

The sequence, not unlike the film's tough, hard-boiled tone, concludes on a measured note that reflects the mutual give and take between the two characters. Kathleen, who's committed to cracking the "steel safe" that is Galt's heart, asks what Jardine has on him and Galt says nothing until, tapping her hand before withdrawing his own, adds, "Not you either." Refusing to be put off by his gruff manner, Kathleen gives back as good as she gets, "All right, but remember I can get brand-new tough guys for a dime a dozen." Galt pulls out a couple of dimes (an echo of the roll of quarters White Suit uses as brass knuckles) and pushes them across the table, "Here, get yourself two dozen," but Kathleen continues to push back, "I'd rather pick you up in a rummage sale. I'm a sucker for bargains."

While Michael Keaney asserts that "Ball, as Stevens' secretary, doesn't have much to do except look beautiful" (which may nevertheless be something of a revelation for viewers familiar only with *I Love Lucy*),[18] Kathleen becomes, like Kansas in *Phantom Lady*, "the driving force in the investigation to clear [her boss's] name."[19] In fact, *The Dark Corner*, like Siodmak's film, not only stars a strong female character but "ingeniously incorporates [jazz] music."[20] Although jazz can be heard "playing in the background of nearly all of the film's crucial scenes,"[21] its dynamic presence derives from the fact that it's juxtaposed with other kinds of music such as Beethoven's Minuet in G Major and Brahms's *Wiegenlied*.[22] For example, in the "cocktail party" sequence that precedes the one set at the High Hat Club, the guests are dressed in evening clothes and dancing to "champagne" music. Even in this sequence, though, the music dramatically shifts after Jardine goes to a dressing room to conclude some blackmailing business (a society matron exchanges an envelope of cash for a packet of letters), the camera cutting on action from a close-up of the woman's gloved hand clasping the packet to a shot of the tuxedoed band members putting a Latin number through its paces.

As the camera pans out to Hardy Cathcart (Clifton Webb) dancing with his wife Mari, the Laura-like figure who's the still point of his art-enshrined world, it's clear that the *au courant* music is a mere façade for Cathcart's machinations, his ardent desire to eliminate Jardine for carrying on with his beloved wife. Accordingly, the vibrant jazz milieu of the High Hat Club offers a keen musical contrast to the vulpine, rarefied world in which Cathcart moves. Indeed, precisely because of its association with the " 'positive' female figure" of Kathleen, jazz might be said to be aligned in *The Dark Corner* with the "failure or impossibility of masculinity," where the fantasy of being "hard" is one of the matrices of film noir.[23] It's not so much that Galt is passive ("I may be stupid but I know I'm licked") or that, because she "can raise his spirit and provide shelter from the turmoil of the masculine arena of crime and detection," Kathleen is active; rather, it's that Kathleen "persistently criticizes Galt's profession as a private eye," not only "encouraging him to abandon the 'tough,' masculine regime" but chastising him when he insists on maintaining his persona even when it's patently not in his interest to do so.[24] In *The Dark Corner*, Kathleen will not be silenced. Like Kansas in *Phantom Lady*, she's all jazzed up about a world where men are more "soft-boiled" than they care to admit and women are the "hard," "tough" ones.

As in *The Dark Corner*, a central scene in Hathaway's *Kiss of Death* features a white nightclub fronted by a black band as well as a white character who's a fan of "jive" music. Fresh out of prison, Nick Bianco has contrived to meet Tommy Udo, a hot-headed hood, in order to assist the police and thereby facilitate his reintegration into mainstream society. The two go to a boxing match, during which Tommy is characteristically blood-thirsty ("Rip the other eye!. . . . Tear it out of his head!"), then to the Club 66 where they're obsequiously shown to a table. (Tommy likes to come here when he's sprung because they treat him like the big man he thinks he is.) Tommy, however, can't sit still. Glancing at the band, a black combo, he brags the place will be "jumpin' in a couple hours," and it's obvious from his manic behavior he can scarcely wait.

After ordering a bottle of champagne, Tommy turns around in his seat to take in the music, all the while snapping his fingers. Cut to a medium shot of the band with the stand-up bass player in the rear, the pianist to the right, and the drummer, a double of the hyperactive Tommy, in the near foreground, his mallets rapidly shuttling between the snare, tom, and floor tom. (The band on the sound track is J. C. Heard, playing "Beautiful Moods" and "Congo Conga," but the drummer is "Papa" Jo Jones, an influential member—minus the war years—of Count Basie's rhythm section

Fig. 11. The Man Who Threw a Cymbal at Charlie Parker: "Papa" Jo Jones plying the mallets at Tommy Udo's favorite post-caboose joint, Club 66, in *Kiss of Death.*

from 1933 to 1948.[25]) "How do you like that music, man?" Tommy asks Nick before turning back to the band, "Right upstairs. C'mon, send it, Jack!"

Nick, however, isn't jazzed by the music the way Tommy is, and when the band downshifts, it's clear that his mind, like Galt's in *The Dark Corner*, is on other things, like his new wife and two young daughters and the fact that their lives are jeopardized by the violently unpredictable man sitting right across the table. It's also clear that Nick, who was nabbed after robbing a jewelry store at the Chrysler Building to buy Christmas gifts for his kids, inhabits a totally different world than the hip, thrill-seeking Tommy. For Tommy, as for Steve Morgan (Lawrence Tierney) in *The Devil Thumbs a Ride* who, paranoid at one point about a news report, stops a woman from changing a radio station, "I like that jive," life is all about getting kicks, sometimes violent ones, and jazz music, like "shavin' a guy's ears off his head" or pushing a wheelchair-bound old woman down a steep staircase, gets his blood going.

While the correlation in *Kiss of Death* between the hopped-up Udo and the jumpin' combo appears to demonize jazz, not to mention urban black musicians, more than one critic has preferred Udo's character to Nick's. Unlike Nick, who's something of a Christ figure (see the scene where, waiting for his kids at an orphanage, he sits beneath a mural of Jesus "suffering the little children to come unto him"[26]), Tommy Udo, like the music he admires, is absolutely alive to the vagaries of the moment.

Although Udo's completely authentic in his own quite twisted way, a rather different, more salutary use of a black jazz combo for dramatic punctuation can be heard in *Force of Evil*. Bookkeeper Freddie Bauer has just been murdered in cold blood after trying to escape from a restaurant where he set up his employer, Leo Morse. (In addition to David Raksin's score, which borrows liberally from Beethoven's late String Quartet op. 131, no. 14, the sequence is distinguished by an Eisensteinian shot of the eye-glassed Bauer peering up from the stairs right before he's executed.) While Leo is being kidnapped by Ficco's goons, his brother Joe returns to his law office to empty his safe, then leaves for good, walking out onto Wall Street where his footsteps echo among the cavernous buildings (the location photography is by George Barnes). The next time we see Joe he's sitting at a table with his girlfriend, Doris Lowry (Beatrice Pearson), at the Iron Door; in the background, against the backdrop of a giant flower, a jazz combo is desultorily playing.

Since Joe's drunk, Doris tells him to go home. Instead he calls the manager over and, shoving a crushed bill into his hand, asks him to tell the band to play louder because he "has something private to tell the lady." After the band picks up the tempo and a couple begins to dance, Joe explains he's celebrating because his life will be taken away from him in the morning —that, debarred, he'll be "dead, done for, finished, kaput." Then he pulls Doris onto the dance floor and, kissing her, confesses:

> You don't know what it is to wake up in the morning and go to sleep at night and eat your lunch and read the papers and hear the horns blowing in the streets and the horns blowing in the clubs and all the time, wherever you are, whatever you're doing, whatever you're seeing . . . you're afraid in your heart. Is that what life is?

Doris breaks away from Joe's embrace and returns to their table. The band pauses to watch until Joe once again orders them to play louder and they start into a bluesy New Orleans number. As the three horn players take the lead (an allusion to Gideon's trumpet?), Joe continues his confession, bragging that he's "running away with a pocket full of money." Doris, however, seeing the trap he's in, says that "somehow" he has to fight and that "somehow" she loves him.

A boy enters the club and hands the evening paper to the manager who, signaling the band to stop, goes over and gives it to Doris. Lifting his head, Joe sees the headline, "Tucker–Ficco War! 1 Dead; 1 Kidnapped," then stands up and, throwing the paper away, bolts for the nearest door. Doris's words still ringing in his ears, Joe Morse—"a great force" having taken hold of him[27]—has finally decided the time to act has come.

In *Kiss of Death* and *Force of Evil*, diegetic band music not only sets the mood for a scene, it acts as a barometer of a character's psychological state. While in *Kiss of Death* the jazz combo reflects Udo's "jive" character (Nick, by comparison, is hopelessly square), in *Force of Evil* it comments on Joe's inner turmoil: confronted with the fact of his brother Leo's death, he's on the verge of an act that will change his life forever. The two characters are different in other, more fundamental ways. Whereas Joe endeavors to conduct the band and his failure to do so comments on his utter futility (in this the combo and, in particular, the horns can be said to function as a chorus), Udo completely identifies with the music, so much so that he appears to be not so much a fan as fanatic.

Praised at the time of its release by James Agee and Manny Farber, *When Strangers Marry* is memorable for its director, William Castle (whom Orson Welles lionized), its executive producer Maurice King of the King Brothers (in a witty bit early in the film a porter hails a Mr. King), and a raced music scene set in a black nightclub that's as seminal in its way as the jitterbug sequence in *Among the Living* and that provides an apt point of comparison with the black jazz scenes in *The Dark Corner*, *Kiss of Death*, and *Force of Evil*.

The studio is Monogram, not M-G-M, and the film is only 67 minutes long, but it opens with a lion's roar. In fact, the roar sounds as if it comes from a real lion, although the source turns out to be a drunken businessman, Sam Prescott (the always amiable Dick Elliott) who, after attending a Lion's Club Convention at the Philadelphia Hotel (itself an established jazz venue at the time), is sporting a papier mâché lion's head and proclaiming he's the "King of the Jungle." Later, in a startling sound match, the film cuts from a maid screaming upon finding Prescott dead in his hotel room still sporting the lion's head (minus his $10,000 bankroll) to the "roar" of a train on which Millie Baxter (Kim Hunter) is en route to meet her new husband, Paul (Dean Jagger).

Anxiously waiting at the hotel for Paul to show (he's a traveling salesman), Millie is lying in the dark staring at the phone and alarm clock when her night vigil is interrupted by the raucous sound of jazz coming from the nightclub across the street. In a bravura audiovisual passage of the sort Welles admired, Millie goes to the window to lift the shade, and the blinking neon sign alternately illuminates and darkens her single room. If the music reflects Millie's alienation, the truncated sign—"Danc"—mocks her romantic naiveté: this is not Grantsville, Ohio, but the big city, a nocturnal world in which nobody is who he or she appears to be, including, perhaps, herself. In fact, in the flashing illumination, Millie is a "creature half of darkness, half of light—part angel, part woman of the shadows."[28]

While Millie suspects her husband, with whom she's just been reunited, has murdered the "lion king," she decides, despite her suspicions, to accompany him on a "Share-a-Car" ride out of town. (The other passengers are a single mother and crying baby—so much for nuclear-family fantasies.) However, when Paul, the very embodiment of noir paranoia, thinks the driver has recognized him, the two get out in Harlem. Reminiscent of the famous and, for some, notorious opening of *Farewell, My Lovely* (1940), the married couple find themselves stranded in, to recollect Chandler, an alien world. When a siren wails nearby, Paul and Millie try to duck into a pool hall until they're scared off by a black man blocking the entrance; the siren still wailing, they walk further uptown, picking up their pace until, hearing music, they see a sign for Big Jim's.

The ensuing cut plunges us into the club's sprightly milieu: a bartender pours a cocktail for a black woman sitting at the bar with her male companion, then, in response to the clapping patrons and boogie-woogie piano music, the couple gets up to dance, the camera tracking along with them as they sweep arm-in-arm across the floor, pausing only to converse with the piano player. Miming the couple's gaze, the camera tilts up to frame the legs of a white woman descending the stairs, a descent marked by two reaction shots, a black man standing at a table who looks up surprised and another black man who appears to be dismayed when he sees it's a white couple.

Although the reverse shot from Paul and Millie's point of view is no doubt meant to suture the scene from their perspective (and thereby elicit our sympathy), the sequence as a whole establishes them as outsiders: here in Harlem, it's the white couple who are the object of the black gaze. Unlike

Paul and Millie who are on the lam and estranged from each other, the patrons at Big Jim's are happy and relaxed, a contrast in mood that's heightened when the camera pulls back to a wide shot of the now even more enthusiastically dancing black couple, succeeded by close-ups of Paul and Millie sitting uncomfortably at a table against the wall like a couple on their first date.

A siren wails again. Everything stills until a black boy, his arms full of papers, comes bounding down the stairs, yelling, "He's won! He's won! The champ's here!" Amid the tumult, Paul and Millie steal away, but when they step outside, it's to two black policemen sitting on their motorcycles. Paul and Millie stop dead in their tracks, but the cops are too busy ribbing each other about that night's fight to notice them, "One more round and he would have killed him." "Your luck can't hold out forever." Relieved, Paul and Millie start walking, a quickening montage of street signs—137th and Lennox, 134th and 7th Avenue, 128th and St. Nicholas Avenue—marking their progress as they work their way downtown.

If the jazz music and neon sign in the hotel sequence mirror Millie's loneliness and estrangement, the jitterbugging couple and happy-go-lucky patrons at Big Jim's counterpoint the newly married couple's abject fear and desperation. In fact, bearing "witness to a self-contained social world that possesses a vitality and cohesion lacking in the America that [Paul and Millie] know," the jazz sequence in *When Strangers Marry* can be said to comment on the "containment of blacks as a servile minority in US society, a situation personified by the porter who assists Millie on the train to New York."[29] Like Bowie and Keechie in *They Live by Night* (who find themselves in a similar predicament), Paul and Millie cannot find sanctuary in a black nightclub not because it's dangerous but because, paranoid from being on the run, they're cut off from the simple pleasures of life like music and dancing. In *When Strangers Marry*, the police in Harlem are benign; it's the white people who are on the wrong side of the law.

Mex-American Popular Music

Unlike the black clientele in *When Strangers Marry* who clearly register Paul and Millie's entrance, the patrons in the Harlem nightclub sequence near the beginning of *Out of the Past* remain oblivious to Jeff Markham's presence, a sign perhaps of his "hipness" and "familiarity with black culture."[30] Tourneur's film, however, remains exemplary not simply because of its provocative jazz sequence (which provides an introduction of sorts to an "intensely eroticized and deadly world"[31]) but because of its continuous recourse to popular instrumental source music.

The Harlem nightclub sequence appears in the immediate aftermath of something like the navel of the film's labyrinthine plot, the moment when the private detective, unconcerned about the details, makes a deal with the devil. Jeff and his partner, Jack Fisher, have just left Whit Sterling's office where they've agreed to his very generous terms of $10,000 plus expenses—an offer neither can refuse—to find his ex, Kathie, and bring her back. (The details: she's stolen, or so Whit claims, $40,000 as well as taken four pot shots at him with a .38.) The scene dissolves from a shot of Jeff and Fisher getting into an elevator to a tight close-up of a black trumpeter belting out a series of notes followed by a swish pan to a nightclub filled with dancing black people, the "phallic" thrust of the music "almost immediately mellow[ing] into a dance swing groove."[32]

Jeff strolls up to a table where two black couples are sitting and, as they're about to be served, he tells the owner the drinks are on him. After the owner informs them that "Jeff's an old friend," he asks about Eunice Levin (Theresa Harris), at which point one couple gets up and leaves. Although part of the scene's beauty derives from its masterful execution of the genre's conventions—the detective assiduously tracking down leads—the action as choreographed by Tourneur has a well-nigh musical rhythm. (I'd also be remiss if I didn't note that both Harris, who played the waitress Minnie in *Cat People* and the maid Alma in *I Walked with a Zombie*, and her partner, Caleb Peterson who, among other things, sang "Ol' Man River" in *Till the Clouds Roll By* [1946], "play their bit parts with easy sophistication."[33])

Eunice was Kathie's maid, but here in the club she's dressed like Billie Holiday, "upswept hair coiffed with a veil of white camellias, black dress accented with white trim."[34] In other words, the femme noire Eunice "sings" to the white detective about Kathie Moffat, the dark woman or femme fatale whom Whit holds a torch for. "It wasn't no cold place," Eunice, doing her "colored maid turn," slyly tells Jeff in response to his questions about Kathie's whereabouts, "she was lookin' for sun."[35]

Since, Jeff concludes in voice-over, "you don't get vaccinated for Florida," he heads straight for Mexico City, then south to Taxco ("How hot can it get?") and, finally, Acapulco. There, he ends up in a little café called La Mar Azul across the street from a movie house that broadcasts Latin music from two speakers mounted above its entranceway. In one of the most evocative passages in film noir, Jeff sits at a table waiting, not unlike the refugees in *Casablanca* (1942), for something—anything—to happen: "I sat there in the afternoon and drank beer. I used to sit there half-asleep with a beer and the darkness, but the music next door kept jarring me awake."

Classical film music is supposed to be invisible, but Jeff's voice-over draws attention to the movie-house music and thereby lays bare the film's status as a fiction or illusion. The irony, of course, is that if Kathie is associated by way of Eunice with the "dark" jazz music in the earlier nightclub sequence, she's also the movie-like fantasy that sustains Jeff's beer-induced reverie. When Kathie eventually appears, like a figment of Jeff's imagination, framed by the arch under which she walks ("And then I saw her coming out of the sun, and I knew why Whit didn't care about that forty grand"), she's all in white—white dress, white purse, white hat—and cool as the day is hot.

Now wide awake, Jeff immediately goes over and sits down across from her. She doesn't say much, nor does she want the silver and jade earrings that he buys from José Rodriguez, but before she departs, she leaves him with a little something to think about: "If it gets too lonely, there's a little cantina down the street called Pablo's. It's nice and quiet, the man there plays American music for a dollar. Sit and drink bourbon and shut your eyes. It's like a little place on 56th street. . . . I sometimes go there." And then, with Jeff left holding the earrings, Kathie walks back out into the sunlight, the music from the Cine Pico abruptly coming to a close as it resolves into the minatory sounds of Roy Webb's score.

Although he's just seen Kathie, Jeff does not, as he's been instructed, send a telegram to Whit. Instead he goes, as we know he will, to Pablo's, a place that recollects both the uptown club in Harlem where popular American music is played and the little café where you can hear Mexican music all day long even as you try to get a little shut-eye. At Pablo's Jeff sits all alone at the bar while, in the next room, a violinist strolls from table to table playing "The First Time I Saw You." Jeff's drink of choice at Pablo's is bourbon, not beer, but he hasn't lost his head—yet: "I sat there and drank bourbon and I shut my eyes, but I didn't think of a joint on 56th street. I knew where I was and what I was doing."

As the camera pans to the left and piano notes cascade on the sound track, the film dissolves to a medium shot of Jeff—not unlike the earlier one at La Mar Azul—sitting alone at a table, flicking a match with his thumb, waiting. Time passes. The camera pans again to the left, then pauses as Jeff, enthralled, narrates Kathie's entrance, "And then she walked out of the moonlight, smiling." When he sits down next to her ("Well, this is a coincidence"), Kathie, nodding at the musicians as she takes out a cigarette, responds, "American music." The implication is that everything is just as she said it would be—the bourbon, the American music, the little cantina ambiance—but it's clear from Jeff's slightly exasperated tone she's kept him waiting. "I've been sitting here for three hours," he mock-complains, nodding like Kathie at the band, "I thought the guy was going to break out with 'Melancholy Baby.' "

Since Jeff is neither lonely nor melancholy, his reference to the Tin Pan Alley standard (which, as I've discussed in chapter 3, is used to very different effect in *Scarlet Street*) is obviously sarcastic. However, the number that the house band is playing, "The First Time I Saw You," is not only a diegetic version of the film's romantic theme but, performed on piano and violin and cued by Kathie's arrival, lyrically counters Jeff's earlier sardonic voice-over ("What a sucker I was"). Moreover, if the Latin movie-house music at La Mar Azul is, at least before Kathie arrives, jarring, reflecting Jeff's ennui and alienation, now the music is "American" but performed by Mexican musicians as if it's Kathie who's lonely for the States—as if, even in Acapulco, a veritable paradise on earth, she too cannot resist the pull of the past.

Although they've just met or perhaps because Jeff senses how charged the situation is, he tells Kathie he wants to leave, dryly adding he's "just not ready to settle down." She offers to take him someplace else and, downing a shot, he's happy to go. (In fact, for a while, he's happy to follow her anywhere.) During a brief stop at a gambling joint where Jeff, in one of the great exchanges in the film, tries to tell Kathie how to play roulette—

JEFF: That isn't the way to play.
KATHIE: Why not?
JEFF: 'Cause it isn't the way to win.
KATHIE: Is there a way to win?
JEFF: Well, there's a way to lose more slowly—

they end up at the beach where, in the glimmering moonlight, surf breaking softly on the shore, Jeff hears Kathie's side of the story: that she didn't steal the $40,000, that she doesn't want anything of Whit's. In another extraordinary exchange, Kathie asks, "Don't you believe me?" and Jeff, about to kiss her, replies, "Baby, I don't care." In the half-light, fishing nets loom ominously.

Later, after another rendezvous at the beach, Jeff and Kathie consummate their relationship (see chapter 2). However, before they sail north to San Francisco, he sits alone again at La Mar Azul, this time outside at a sidewalk table, the music from the Cine Pico still blasting from the speakers:

> I never saw her in the daytime. We seemed to live by night. What was left of the day went away like a pack of cigarettes you smoked. I didn't know where she lived. I never followed her. All I had to go on was a place and time to see her again. I don't know what we were waiting for. Maybe we thought the world would end. Maybe we thought it was a dream and we'd wake up with a hangover in Niagara Falls.

As the movie-house music suggests, Jeff knows perfectly well, even as he's doing it, that he's chasing a dream, that the odds are against them, but unlike Kathie, he knows there's a way to lose more slowly and, for the moment at least, he's enjoying losing.

Consequently, after the sequence where he sits outside La Mar Azul contemplating his future with Kathie, Jeff's in his hotel room packing to go off with her—not so incidentally, right before Whit shows up unannounced with Stefanos wondering if he's found her—and happily humming "The First Time I Saw You." It's an ingenious passage since Jeff's impromptu performance contrasts with Kathie's earlier mechanical one in the bungalow when she puts on a recorded version of the same song, a difference that suggests not only that she's doing the seducing but that he's falling for her. In retrospect, of course, Jeff should have heeded the movie-house music, a reminder that the sort of life he's now living—night by night, drink by drink, cigarette by cigarette—can only end one way, badly. In the end (see Epilogue), he won't wake up with a hangover in Niagara Falls, married to the woman of his dreams; he'll be dead, slumped over in a sedan, shot point-blank by the very same dream woman.

Don't Shoot the Piano Player

Not unlike *Out of the Past* in which Jeff Markham can't help humming the film's romantic theme, forties noir is peopled with characters, including cops and killers, private eyes and femme fatales, for whom musical performance of one sort or another is as unremarkable as a shoot-out or romantic liaison.

While the piano tends to be the instrument of choice with respect to strictly instrumental source music (the solo guitarist in the Havana nightclub sequence in *The Chase* is a memorable exception), it also "registers a distinct gender ambivalence": "Played in public, for money or show, it's mostly a manly affair; played in private, for pleasure or its sublimations, a decidedly feminine, even emasculating one."[36] Given these connotations, the sight and sound of a man playing the piano in public—at, for instance, a bar or nightclub—should therefore come as no surprise. What's surprising is that both *Detour* and *Black Angel* feature male protagonists—Martin Blair and Al Roberts, respectively—emotionally exposing themselves at the keyboard. If it's also something of a surprise to see a woman playing an instrumental number on the piano in public, as at the beginning of *I Walk Alone* in which Kay Lawrence catches the ear of the recently paroled Frankie Madison, the conventions remain in place for women who play the piano in private.

So, in John Stahl's super-saturated color noir, *Leave Her to Heaven* (1945), Ruth Berent's (Jeanne Crain) piano playing testifies to her aesthetic affinity with her cousin Ellen's novelist husband, Richard Harland (Cornel Wilde). The piece is Chopin's Nocturne op. 27, no. 2, and the composition, with its "vocal" inflections, speaks to the deep, if unspoken harmony between Ruth and Richard. Ruth's piano playing is also one of those things, like gardening, that differentiates her from her otherworldly cousin. Ellen, played by the impossibly beautiful Gene Tierney, has no need of anything so mundane as music or gardening since Love with a capital L, a love so "all-consuming that she must murder to retain exclusive possession of her husband,"[37] is her sole reason for being. Compared to such romantic *Sturm und Drang*, Ruth's mini-recitals are pacific interludes, temporary oases of sanity and well-being.

Paradoxically enough, the gender trouble associated with the piano manifests itself in forties noir not so much with female as with male characters. While a penchant for the piano can be a positive masculine attribute, as it is in *Undercurrent*, *The Chase* (where, in the remarkable "porthole" sequence, Chuck Scott woos Eddie Roman's wife Lorna), and *Johnny Angel* (in which Hoagy Carmichael's character, Celestial O'Brien, plays the film's theme, "Memphis in June"), it often indicates a criminal sensibility. Indeed, in forties noir, a man playing the piano in private is less a sign of emasculation than a form of musical masquerade, a deviance epitomized by Zachary Scott who plays the louche Monte Beragon in *Mildred Pierce*, the elusive, enigmatic

Dimitrios in *The Mask of Dimitrios* (1944), and the suave, smooth-talking lady-killer Ronnie Mason in *Danger Signal* (1945). But perhaps even more remarkable than the fact that certain criminally minded men play the piano in private (like the mobster Alec Stiles [Richard Widmark] in *The Street with No Name*) is the recourse to classical instrumental source music in forties noir as an expressionist device.

A "classic" example is Curtis Bernhardt's *Possessed*, which not only foregrounds diegetic piano performance but exploits the film's various audio and visual cues to communicate the protagonist's tortured psyche. After Louise Howell Graham is found wandering the streets of Los Angeles hysterically crying for someone named "David" (see chapter 2), she's rushed to the "psycho" unit at a local hospital where she's diagnosed as suffering from a "catatonic stupor." In order to get her to talk (she's also suffering from a form of mutism), Dr. Willard induces narcosynthesis and she immediately begins, as in a dream, to speak, "Someone's playing Schumann on the piano. Yes, oh yes, listen. There, hear it?"

As in John Brahm's "period noir" *Hangover Square* (1945) in which sonic and musical point of audition is used to articulate classical composer George Harvey Bone's (Laird Cregar) homicidal blackouts, *Possessed* invites the spectator to participate in Louise's mental condition by "presenting her auditory fantasy as the reality of the sound track."[38] In other words, we first hear the Robert Schumann piece, then when Louise says she doesn't like it ("Make them play it softer"), the volume is accordingly lowered ("That's better, that's nice").[39] The reduction in volume prompts a flashback to a lakeside house where, après swim (read "sex"), Louise and David Sutton are deep in conversation. Dressing to leave, Louise laments they "never seem to have enough time together," but when she notices David doesn't appear to be listening, he replies he's "making love to the piano," telling her that while he plays Gershwin or "something light and frivolous" like Mozart for "other women," for her it's the "tenderness" of Schumann. (The "little scene" that David's playing from *Carnaval* is titled, ironically enough, "Chopin," though it's in *agitato* and, in a buried allusion, Chopin was a member of Schumann's imaginary, anti-Philistine society the *Davidsbündler* or "League of David" celebrated in *Carnaval*.)

Encouraged by this musical compliment, Louise plunks down next to David at the piano and, resting her head against the back of his neck, announces she wants a "monopoly" or, as she puts it in rather alarmingly possessive terms, "whatever it is that people have when they don't want anyone else to have any of you." As his "smooth, expert handling of the piano suggests," David is a "self-confessed master of many tunes."[40] Hence his terse response to Louise's declaration of love: after telling her he likes "all kinds of music except a little number called 'O, Promise Me'" ("It's a duet, but I like to play solo"), he takes her by speedboat back across the lake to the house where she works as a nurse for Dean Graham's (Raymond Massey) invalid wife. After David departs on a business trip and Mrs. Graham (whose demanding personality is epitomized by the electric buzzer with which she summons Louise) is found drowned in the lake (she mistakenly believed her husband was having an affair with Louise), David decisively rejects Louise and she reluctantly agrees to marry Mr. Graham.

Although things appear to be looking up for the new Mrs. Graham, in fact they're about to take a baroque, incestuous turn. First, David arrives uninvited at Louise's wedding and flirts with her stepdaughter, Carol. (She's fresh out of college and he's just plain fresh.) Then, at a musical concert, Carol sees David in the audience and signals him to join Louise and her in their private box. The pianist starts to play Schumann's *Carnaval*, whereupon David and Louise exchange looks. But since it's not the look of love (David, the composition makes clear, is with Carol), Louise reverts to memory, the film flashing back to the opening scene set at the lakeside house.

While her superimposed face floats ghost-like on the earlier "primal scene," the sound track suddenly becomes distorted as if the music were being heard under water. (In fact, in *Possessed* water links the two traumatic events that are at the origin of Louise's mental condition—Mrs. Graham's drowning and David's rejection.) The version of Schumann's *Carnaval* that the audience hears at the concert—the remembered one, as Franz Waxman has noted, "omitting all the sharps and flats"[41]—is also what Louise hears. In other words, it's not only from her specific, fantasmatic point of audition but suggests she's becoming increasingly psychotic.

The startling audiovisual climax of *Possessed* builds on the above concert sequence. Louise, feigning a headache, leaves the concert early to return home. Just as Mrs. Graham suspected Louise was romantically involved with her husband, now Louise believes that Carol and David are having an affair. Robert Porfirio has called Bernhardt a "past master of Stimmung or atmosphere," the "dreamlike tone that is a seminal character of film noir,"[42] and nowhere is this more apparent than in the scene where a neurasthenic Louise waits, distraught, for Carol to return.

The scene begins with a close-up of a loudly ticking clock on the nightstand next to Louise's unmade bed. It's storming outside and, as the wind howls, the camera tracks counterclockwise around the room, Schumann swirling on the sound track, until it stops on Louise slumped in a chair. Momentarily rousing herself, Louise walks toward an open window where she buries her face in the curtains, the wind rising as if channeling her storm-tossed spirit. After a disorienting high-angle shot of Louise falling back onto her bed, the camera cuts to a low-angle one of the clock ticking on the nightstand, the sound growing louder and louder. Louise puts her hand on the pendulum to stop the noise, but—in an amazing, and amazingly expressionistic, sound match—it's picked up and amplified by a loud tocking sound: Louise frantically looks to the window, the camera swiftly tracking along with her gaze to the sash where the rain is falling, drop by audible drop.

After the film cuts again, this time to an external, objective shot of the bedroom window, Louise walks over to shut it, her face pressed, eyes closed, against the cool surface. When she opens her eyes, a car pulls up and she secretively watches from the second floor as David and Carol come in from the rain and kiss ("We fooled her"). Disturbed by what she's seen and heard, Louise tells Carol to stay away from David. Carol, however, accuses Louise of killing her mother to win him back, then threatens to tell her father about it. Closely following Carol down the hall, Louise strikes her, sending her tumbling down the stairs.

Only when Carol's lifeless body at the bottom of the stairs begins to dematerialize do we realize that the entire incident has been a hallucination. Though the sequence is visually rendered in a straightforward, naturalistic manner until the body "dissolve," its hallucinatory character is foreshadowed by Louise's hypersensitive attention to everyday sounds (a ticking clock, rain falling in an open window),[43] auditory phenomena retroactively triggered by her earlier, fantasmatic recollection of Schumann's *Carnaval*. In the final analysis, Louise is not "possessed by the devil" (as Dr. Willard feebly informs Dean Graham), she's possessed by the tender, lyrical melodies of Schumann which, like the Furies, are tearing her up inside.

Undercurrent (1946) is noteworthy in the context of instrumental source music not simply because it pivots, as in *Possessed*, on classical piano sequences but because it's the only noir starring Katherine Hepburn and directed by Vincente Minnelli. Ann (Hepburn) is the tomboyish, marriage-averse daughter of a chemistry professor, David "Dink" Hamilton (Edmund Gwenn). However, when a young "captain of industry," Alan Garroway

(Robert Taylor), visits to pitch a business idea, he simultaneously strikes a deal with the professor and sparks Ann's interest.

The romantic fire lit in Ann is suggested in an early sequence. After sitting curled up in a chair lost in reverie, she joins her father at the piano where he's playing Brahms's Third Symphony. While Dink continues to play, Ann performs a series of flourishes with her right hand, then exclaims, "How fresh this always is, and new. It always transports me to another world." Her father's response—"Whatever world you were in, you were not alone"—correlates Ann's expansive mood and lively playing with Alan's entrance into her heretofore sheltered life. (Brahms was fifty years old and a bachelor—"Free but happy" [*Frei aber Froh*], to quote the composer's F-A-F touchstone—when he wrote the Third Symphony.)

At the same time, the ambiguity suggested by the bittersweet melody of the third movement of Brahms's symphony—Ann, once married, will all-too-soon be *un*free and *un*happy—introduces a distinct noir note into the seemingly happy household scenario in the form of her future husband as well as the attendant refuge she finds by "falling in love with a dream" in the form of Alan's mysterious brother, Michael (Robert Mitchum).[44]

This dream initially appears in a sinister aspect after the now-married Ann and Alan travel to his ancestral home in Middleburg, Virginia, and she sits down one night at a candle-lit piano to play Brahms. Arriving home from work, Alan hears it and immediately accosts her, "Who was playing? Who was it? You? Why did you play *that* piece? What made you play it?" Still eager to please her new husband, Ann patiently explains that her father taught her the piece because Brahms was his favorite composer, at which point Alan breaks down and confesses his mother "died sitting at *that* piano playing *that* piece."

Although "*that* piece," according to the ever-optimistic Ann, now represents a "bond" between Alan and her, this connection is shattered later that night when the black servant George (Leigh Whipper) tells her "Mrs. Garroway never played no piano." Ann, baffled by her husband's false confession, blows out the candles on the piano to mask her identity and begins playing the Third Symphony again. George comes racing down the stairs and Ann, doubling now as Alan, subjects him to the very same questions her husband subjected her to, "Who did you think it was? Who could it be? Who played that piece? Who used to sit at that piano?" George says "nobody" until, prodded by Ann, he concedes it was Michael. Since she's already begun to suspect that Alan might have killed his brother, this is the nightmare world, one in which Ann's formerly placid marital life reveals unexpected and dangerous "undercurrents."

Michael, however, is still very much alive, having vanished when he realized that Alan had murdered the person responsible for inventing the device —the "long-distance control"—on which the family aircraft manufacturing business has been built. In fact, after Ann accidentally makes Michael's acquaintance at his house (she erroneously thinks he's the caretaker), she begins to feel a strange kinship with this physically absent yet psychically present man who loves "music and books," Brahms and English verse. Meanwhile, Michael, concerned about Ann's welfare, resurfaces in Alan's life and threatens to tell her the truth unless Alan tells her about his dark past. Unable to bear the thought of losing her, Alan imprisons Ann in the family house, then, convinced she's in love with Michael, tries to run her horse off the edge of a canyon. In a poetic twist, Ann manages to survive when her horse, which was once Michael's, kills Alan by repeatedly kicking him in the head.

The classical-musical coda to *Undercurrent* is, like many a forties noir, not without ambiguity. On one hand, the earlier piano scenes set at Ann and Alan's Middleburg home are, as in a symphony, recapitulated and resolved; on the other hand, Ann's pianistic conjuration of Michael renders uncanny the seemingly happy ending. The coda itself opens with the camera tracking from a close-up of a man playing Brahms's Third Symphony to the back lawn of the Hamilton house where Ann, not unlike the Garroways' invalid mother, sits in a wheelchair. An older female friend says, "That's beautiful. Who's playing?" and, since she's now back home, Ann automatically says "My father": "Dink always does well by Brahms." But when her father strolls into the background of the frame, we realize someone else is playing the piano.

It's Michael, of course, whom Ann has sent for, the pianistic conceit that propels *Undercurrent* coming full circle when he begins playing the Third Symphony and Ann, as she earlier did with her father, begins to play along. To quote David Sutton in *Possessed*, they're a duet. The problem with this happy ending is that it's also marked by a "Freudian determinism of the highest order":[45] while Ann's implied romance with and eventual marriage to Michael has a certain symmetry (she's moved on to an "other," not the tyrannical Alan, who's both like and unlike her musically minded father), Michael's fraternal status, not to mention the fact Ann herself has become a double of Mrs. Garroway, underscores the incestuous circuit of desire in which she's trapped.

Chapter 4

Nocturne

If *Nocturne* (1946) can be said to rehearse the psychosexual dynamics of *Undercurrent*, it proffers, even more so than Minnelli's film, a compelling example of the musicalization of noir as a genre. Directed by Edwin L. Marin, produced by Joan Harrison, and executive-produced by Jack Gross who assembled the same creative personnel from the earlier *Johnny Angel* starring George Raft, the score, screenplay, and cinematography for *Nocturne* are by noir veterans Leigh Harline (*The Big Heat, They Live By Night, Pickup on South Street*), Jonathan Latimer (*The Big Clock, The Glass Key, They Won't Believe Me*), and Harry J. Wild (*Murder, My Sweet, Pitfall, His Kind of Woman*).

The opening shot of *Nocturne*, traveling "across a landscape model of the Hollywood Hills and into the window of an isolated house," then "through the window, into the room, and toward a man sitting at a piano," establishes the film's obsessive, voyeuristic point of view.[46] The man, a music composer named Keith Vincent (Edward Ashley), is working on a new song even as he's explaining to a woman why he's breaking up with her, "All right, Dolores, I've been avoiding you. I've been working, trying to finish this song." (The song "Nocturne" was composed for the film by Harline and Mort Greene.)

When Vincent adds that she's been "making a nuisance of herself the last couple of weeks, telephoning, waiting outside his house" and "it isn't doing any good," the camera reverses position: whereas before Vincent was in the near foreground and "Dolores" was sitting in the rear, an indistinct but nonetheless palpable presence, now her legs are clearly visible in the right foreground and he's in the rear sitting at the piano. Although Dolores, who's tamping the floor with her shoe, is literally putting her foot down, the camera reverts to him ("We're finished") as he plays passages—the first Latin-flavored, the second à la "Sun Valley Serenade"—from the popular songs he's previously written for the various women in his life.

After this musical review, a history mirrored by the portraits hung like trophies on the wall ("That one was half-Spanish, followed me all over South America," "I met her in Sun Valley"), Vincent looks over at Dolores and, announcing "This one is yours," begins to sing: "Nocturne, you are my nocturne / For when I see you / Sweet music begins / Yes, the melody begins / And the lyrics start / Like a million violins." Vincent croons the second verse ("Nocturne, you are my nocturne / You are the words I sing / And the notes I play"), then pauses, the camera cutting to a close-up of his

Fig. 12. "Nocturne": Advertisement for Edwin L. Marin's *Nocturne*. See boxed shot of "Hollywood detective" Joe Warne (George Raft) kneeling before pop-music composer Keith Vincent (Edward Ashley) post-mortem at his piano.

hands at the piano as he suddenly becomes lost. Looking for the right words to match the notes he's playing, he hums until—in a flash—the ending comes to him, "But it's over and done / You're no longer the one / For that was yesterday."

A performance in every sense of the word, Vincent's act of composition is a "sublime" example of sublimation. While it's difficult to tell whether women are mere sexual objects for him or a genuine source of musical inspiration, the trite lyrics and generic theme of "Nocturne" (he's no Chopin) suggest the former. Humming again, Vincent picks up a pencil and, as he continues to compose, talks directly to Dolores—"If you need money I'll be glad to hel . . ."—when a gunshot explodes offscreen and he slumps to the floor. Vincent's composition remains unfinished (significantly, he doesn't get the last word), but like the music of Schumann in *Possessed* or Brahms in *Undercurrent*, "Nocturne"—"its moods, colorations, and intonations"[47]—haunts the film's narrative as well as its working-class protagonist, Joe Warne (George Raft).

After Joe investigates the crime scene where he notices one portrait is conspicuously missing from the series on the wall, he returns to the apartment he shares with his mother who, in a bit of comic relief, is an amateur sleuth. Sitting at the family piano "trying to figure out Vincent's last song," he plinks the keys with one finger and, hearing him, Mrs. Warne remarks that he hasn't "sat down at that piano since [he was] seven years old." If Joe at this point is symbolically regressing in the service of the ego—that is, in the service of his investigation (the police have officially ruled Vincent's death a suicide)—the fact that Halberson, the lead detective on the case, brags at one point "I'm no musician, I'm a detective," hints that Joe's musical sensibility aligns him more with Vincent than with the strict letter of the law.

This particular motif is musically reiterated when Joe goes off to bed and his mother begins playing "Nocturne," a reprise (she's played it once before) that bridges a dissolve to him fast asleep in bed dreaming. On the sound track, the piano music modulates into an orchestral version of "Nocturne," succeeded by an increasingly dissonant passage reflecting Joe's agitated state of mind as portraits of Dolores flash before his eyes like cards. Joe's clearly becoming obsessed with the case; it's also clear he has an unusually intimate relationship with his mother. While she performs "Nocturne" on the family piano, he dreams of one Dolores after another, searching for the one who holds the key to his investigation.

Unsurprisingly, given the sexually charged nature of the investigation,

Joe's obsession begins to manifest itself in overtly aggressive behavior. Thus, when he goes to a restaurant looking for Dolores and rips out a piano roll to play "Nocturne" for a waitress who he thinks may be her, he gets hell from his chief, "You've been batting your brains out on a thing no court would accept as evidence—an unfinished song." Mocking Joe's "musical" intuition, Halberson chimes in, "Still, it keeps running through his head," a remark that emphasizes the difference between the two men: although Halberson has already forgotten about the case, Joe can't let it go.

After Joe visits a dancing school where the female instructor comments on how badly he dances (an inside joke given Raft's earlier reputation on vaudeville and Broadway as "The Fastest Dancer in the World"), his next stop is the appropriately named Keyboard Club. The featured performer there is a piano player by the name of Fingers (Joseph Pevney), but Joe's initial focus is on the blonde vocalist he accompanies, Carol Page (Virginia Huston). While she sings "A Little Bit Is Better Than None" ("If you haven't got a lot of trouble / Then you are the luckiest one"), Joe confides in her older sister, Frances (Lynn Bari), that he became a detective because he likes getting into a little bit of trouble. The self-reflexive character of the number is further accented when the musical muscle, Torp (Bernard Hoffman), wheels the piano over to a table and another woman asks Fingers to play "I Couldn't Sleep a Wink Last Night," a reference to Joe's Dolores-haunted sleep.

Later, Torp pushes the piano over to Joe and Frances's table where Carol has just joined them, but when Fingers asks, "Blues or Beethoven?" instead of performing either, he begins to play "Nocturne" from the manuscript Joe has given him. As he picks his way through the number ("What did your friend do, run out of notes?"), Joe's gaze is firmly fixed on Frances even though Carol visibly reacts to the music. Fingers comes to the end of "Nocturne," then turns to Joe and inquires, "Vincent?" The subsequent exchange between the two revises even as it complicates the earlier musician-detective conceit (the vehicle now is painting):

> JOE: How did you know?
> FINGERS: How do you know a Picasso?
> JOE: I don't.
> FINGERS: You're not a painter.

If the class differences between Joe and Vincent, the cop and the composer, are figuratively reiterated here, the painterly conceit nevertheless suggests that Joe's obsession with the late composer involves not simply sexual prowess but, like the title of a song that Vincent and Fingers once composed, a whole "champagne" way of life.

After Joe discovers the hanged body of the photographer who shot the portraits for Vincent as well as the missing picture of Dolores (a picture of Carol as a brunette), he returns to the Keyboard Club where, searching Carol's dressing room, he's physically attacked by Torp. In an extended fight scene choreographed by Fingers's piano music that recalls the violent interludes with which this chapter began, the two beat each other senseless. Joe eventually manages to get the better of Torp by throwing a pot of hot coffee at him (cf. *The Big Heat* [1953]), then goes out to the main room and sits down at one of the tables, the mural behind him—an oval of a dancing woman set in a criss-cross pattern—pointing to the spider woman at the heart of *Nocturne*'s crooked web.

Carol comes over to his table and Joe shows her the photograph of herself as a brunette. Although she admits she was at Vincent's home the night he was killed, she insists she didn't do it and that all the "hocus pocus" has been because of her sister Frances, who's been trying to protect her. "It's a nice story," Joe says, "except I have a tune stuck in my head." Joe now believes that Frances is Vincent's killer until Fingers starts playing "Nocturne" offscreen and, in a rhyme of the long traveling shot that opens the film, the camera glides across the room until it stops on the pianist, trapped by the upturned chairs on the tables around him. Fingers concludes the piece in high, dramatic fashion, but when Joe walks over and stands by the piano, he starts playing in a more subdued register, explaining he killed Vincent because he couldn't bear to see his ex-wife Carol treated so badly.

Not unlike *Fallen Angel*, *Nocturne* ends on an oddly anticlimactic note when Joe disarms Fingers after he retrieves a gun from under the piano lid and Halberson, whom Joe has previously alerted, hauls off the offending trio of Torp, Carol, and Fingers. In a predictably romantic turn of events, Joe also absolves Frances, even though she was an accessory to the crime, announcing he has a "mother who's anxious to meet [her]." However, as in *Undercurrent*, this happy ending is severely qualified by the fact that Joe has just sent up his future wife's kid sister. Moreover, as a working detective (see the montage where Joe walks from one establishment to another searching for information about Dolores), he'll no doubt be spending his future nights not with his new wife but back on the streets, tracking down leads in the gyms and clubs, backrooms and juke-joints of the dark city.

From this "beat" perspective, Marin's film, especially as inflected by what Howard Hawks called a "certain impassive quality" about Raft's persona, moodily evokes Joe Warne's defining element, a nightmarish modality that's closer to Vincent's hard, fast, and, ultimately, not-so-beautiful life than the romantic, "slow and dreamy" world associated with the classical nocturne.[48]

5

Singing Detectives and Bluesmen, Black Jazzwomen and Torch Singers

A Cappella

The death of Keith Vincent in *Nocturne*, murdered while he's composing a popular song, is unique in classic noir, but singing itself is not uncommon in the genre. For example, *The Naked City* (1948), an early semi-documentary that derives from the work of Robert Flaherty and based on the book of the same name by the famed crime photographer Weegee, features a singing detective.

Despite Mark Hellinger's booming voice-over narration and William Daniels's Academy Award–winning photography, it's also something of an anomaly due to the casting of Barry Fitzgerald, an actor now primarily remembered for his musicals, as Detective Lieutenant Dan Muldoon. Before making *The Naked City*, Fitzgerald had appeared in *Duffy's Tavern* (1945), two Betty Hutton vehicles, *Incendiary Blonde* (1945) and *The Stork Club* (1945), and, of course, *Going My Way* (1944) as the aging pastor of Saint Dominic's, Father Fitzgibbon.

Fitzgerald's amiable, "musical" persona is mobilized early on in *The Naked City* when we see Lieutenant Dan Muldoon preparing breakfast in his nightshirt and singing an Irish ditty: "Paddy, no matter where you roam / Don't forget your country / Or the ones you left back home. / Write a letter now and then / And send me on again." Ironically enough, Willie Garzah (Ted de Corsia), the object of Muldoon's investigation and a participant in the murder of a pill-popping model that opens the film, is an acrobat-turned-wrestler who plays the harmonica. Hence his nickname, Willie the Harmonica. As one reviewer wrote, Garzah "used to be an acrobat, then they killed vaudeville."[1]

In the wake of Universal's *Naked City*, Twentieth Century-Fox, which had released the ur-semi-documentary *The House on 92nd Street*, began production on a noir-opera-melodrama about an Italian American family from the Lower East Side, the same environs that produced Willie Garzah. (The family, the Morettis, were a fictional version of the Giannini family who founded Bank of America.) Starring Edward G. Robinson, the paterfamilias in the family drama *All My Sons* (1948), and Richard Conte, who had just appeared in *Call Northside 777* and *Cry of the City* (1948), *House of Strangers*, written and directed by Joseph Mankiewicz, includes an *a cappella* sequence that represents a remarkable exhibition of cinematic audiovisuality.

Max Monetti (Conte), having served seven years in prison for his usurious banker-father, Gino (Robinson), is released and proceeds to visit his thankless brothers, his uptown former girlfriend, Irene Bennett (Susan Hayward), and the now-deserted family mansion on the Lower East Side. (The working title of *House of Strangers* was *East Side Story* and the location is marked on the sound track by the offscreen sound of the subway as Max approaches the home's imposing entrance.) After pausing for a moment in the chandeliered foyer, Max walks straight into the living room that's dominated by an inlaid, elaborately framed portrait of Gino and puts on a record of "M'appari" from Friedrich von Flotow's *Martha*.

While Max stands beside the mantel, his head tilted as he listens to the aria, the camera retreats to a master shot of the room before gliding up the wide, carpeted steps to the landing where it stops before a white-curtained window. In a lyrical dissolve that recollects *Fallen Angel* (see chapter 3), the light in the window changes from evening to morning and, as the curtains sway in the breeze, there's a "jump cut" on the sound track from "M'appari" to a man singing robustly off-key to himself. As if compelled by the sheer force of this voice, the camera suddenly tacks left into the master bedroom, moving past a draped bed and into a large bathroom where, beneath a set of monogrammed towels ("GM"), Gino sits in a bathtub performing "La donna è mobile" from Giuseppe Verdi's *Rigoletto* and scrubbing himself vigorously with a washcloth.

The utter disparity between Lawrence Tibbett's recorded and Gino's live voice effects a dynamic shift from the present (Max waxing nostalgic about his father in the family parlor) to the past (Gino singing an aria while he bathes). In fact, the two passages are complementary: in the first phonographic part, Max puts on one of his father's favorite recordings and becomes lost in reverie, the movement of the camera miming his former, rapid upward mobility both as the family attorney and as his father's favored son. In the second part of the sequence, however, the "real drown[s] out the ideal,"[2] Tibbett's rich, orchestra-accompanied baritone yielding to Gino's bellowing *opéra buffa* or, more precisely perhaps, *basso buffa*. Gino's autocratic, overbearing nature is epitomized by his insistence on serving spaghetti for dinner on Wednesday evenings while playing Figaro's cavatina, "Largo al factotum della città," from *The Barber of Seville* at conversation-deadening decibels ("I like it loud"). When we later see Max playing the piano at an Italian restaurant, his subdued, contemplative manner not only contrasts with Gino's bellicose personality but presages his liberatory break from his father's oppressive influence.

Edward G. Robinson's performance as Gino Moretti in *House of Strangers* is grandly operatic. But in *Key Largo* (1948), it's his character Johnny Rocco's moll, Gaye Dawn (Claire Trevor), who offers the most compelling, if pathetic, *a cappella* vocal performance in forties noir. In John Huston's film, adapted from the verse play by Maxwell Anderson, Rocco has commandeered a hotel on the Florida Keys owned by wheelchair-bound James Temple (Lionel Barrymore) and his daughter, Nora (Lauren Bacall), whose husband has died during the Italian campaign. A war buddy, Major Frank McCloud (Humphrey Bogart), has personally come to express his condolences. However, before meeting Nora and her father, he makes the acquaintance of Gaye who's sitting at the bar drinking heavily and listening to the races on the radio. Frank asks for a beer and when one of Rocco's men, Angel, says the hotel's closed, Gaye, in a bit of foreshadowing, orders the man to serve him.

The first signs of conflict occur when Gaye, feeling faint, announces she needs another drink, and one of Rocco's henchmen, Curley, barks, "Boss say you get no more drink." Although Gaye is defiant at first ("He did, did he? Well, this is a free country. I want a drink, I can have one"), Rocco only has to stroll into the room and it's obvious that the hotel, isolated on the Keys by a tropical storm, is not a "free country" and that Gaye's desires mean nothing to him. (Rocco is based on Al Capone after he retired to Florida, but Robinson's character comes across as an earlier, "movie" incarnation of Little Caesar in Mervyn LeRoy's famous film [1931], a gangster who, unlike his criminal peers, renounces both women *and* drink. Trevor's character is based on the real Gay Orlova, the one-time Broadway performer and long-time girlfriend of Lucky Luciano.)

Gaye eventually scares up enough courage to declare in Rocco's presence, "I think I'll have a scotch and water," though the big man, true to his increasingly sadistic persona, categorically says no. Later, after Rocco shoots and kills a local cop, Gaye, desperate for a drink, goes to the bar and pours herself one. Rocco, seeing her shakes, dismissively tosses it on the floor, "Didn't I say no drinkin'? One thing I can't stand is a dame who is a drunk." The ensuing, acrimonious exchange between the two not only offers a compact overview of their relationship but sets up Gaye's subsequent performance of Ralph Rainger and Howard Deitz's "Moanin' Low," a torch song first famously recorded by Libby Holman for Brunswick in 1931 and later by Billie Holiday with Teddy Wilson and His Orchestra in 1937:[3]

GAYE: You gave me my first drink, Johnny.
ROCCO: Oh, so it's my fault now. Everybody has their first drink, don't they? But everybody ain't a lush. Eight years since I seen her. You wouldn't know it was the same dame.
GAYE: You certainly haven't changed one bit.
ROCCO: Meaning what?
GAYE: Nothing. If I'd known you was gonna act this way, I wouldn't have come.
ROCCO: If I'd known what you'd be like, I wouldn't have asked.
GAYE: Gee, honey, you're as mean as can be.

Rocco will go on to show just how mean he can be, but in the meantime, since he gave "Maggie Mooney" her first chance at stardom when he took her out of the chorus and made her a singer (according to Rocco, she once had everything—"voice, looks, plenty of class"), he proposes a deal: a drink for a song.

While the throwaway phrase doesn't begin to do justice to just how cruel this wager is for Gaye, the acerbic dialogue does:

ROCCO: Why don't you give us your old song?
GAYE: You mean right now? I can't.
ROCCO: Oh, sure you can.
GAYE: Please, Johnny, don't make me.

ROCCO: I won't make you do anything. I tell you what. I got a proposition for you. You sing us your song and you can have a drink.
GAYE: Can I have the drink first?
ROCCO: No, the song first and then the drink.
GAYE: Without any accompaniment?
ROCCO: Now, look, do you want a drink or don't you?

Gamely endeavoring to recapture the past when she was all the "rage," Gaye verbally sets the scene: a "low-cut" "gorgeous" gown, no makeup except "some lipstick," and a "baby" spotlight. As the assembled motley crew —Rocco and his goons, Frank and Nora and Mr. Temple—wait without bated breath, Gaye finally begins to sing: "Moanin' low, / My sweet man I love him so / Though he's mean as can be / He's the kind of man needs the kind of woman like me."

Drawing like an aging athlete on her past experience as a performer, Gaye starts out strong, her voice momentarily invigorated by the challenge. Then all the years and all the drinks finally take their toll: "Don't know any reason why he treats me so poorly, / What have I gone and done?" At the end of the verse, Gaye's voice breaks and the camera cuts away to Curley who, shaking his head, looks over to Rocco who mirrors his disapproval.

Thoroughly humiliated by the ordeal, Gaye nonetheless asks for her drink and Rocco refuses, saying she's "rotten." Frank has earlier backed down to the big man, refusing to shoot him when he was offered the chance, "One Rocco more or less isn't worth dying for." This time, however, he lets his actions speak, striding over to the bar and pouring Gaye a drink. Rocco slaps him across the face for his troubles, but the balance of power has subtly shifted. When the hurricane hits, it's Rocco, not Gaye, who'll have the shakes, and no drink or song will be able to save him from his fate: a little big man at the end of the line, dreaming of Cuba as he lies bleeding to death in a fishing boat off Key Largo.

Solo Accompaniment: Guitar

With the exception of Gaye Dawn's "Moanin' Low" in *Key Largo*, a wrenching rendition that can be directly attributed to the Academy Award–winning turn by Claire Trevor, the most memorable vocal performances in forties noir feature music, minimally piano or guitar accompaniment. The musicians are occasionally male, like pianists Al Roberts in *Detour* and Marty Blair in *Black Angel*, but the vocalists, such as Sue Harvey in Ulmer's film and Mavis Marlowe in Roy William Neill's, are almost invariably female. This asymmetry of emphasis is not, needless to say, indicative of American popular music at the time since the 1940s saw the demise of the big band and the meteoric rise of both the male and female "solo" artist. (For example, the top vocalist in 1941, according to the annual *Downbeat* poll, was not Bing Crosby, "who had held the spot for the previous four years," but Frank Sinatra.[4])

Despite the phenomenon that was Frank Sinatra (one thinks immediately of his performances at the Paramount Theatre in October 1944), the conventions of film noir, deriving as they do from the "tough guy" tradition of the American detective novel, were such that the sort of "frail" romantic persona associated with "The Swooner" was not readily available to male protagonists in the genre. Therefore, when a male character sings, the mere fact of his singing says something about his character, perhaps even feminizes him.

A representative film in the context is the 1946 version of *The Postman Always Rings Twice*. In this third adaptation of Cain's novel (which had previously been made by Pierre Chenal as *Le Dernier tournant* in 1939 and by Luchino Visconti as *Ossessione* in 1943[5]), Nick Smith, sympathetically portrayed by Cecil Kellaway, hires a drifter to help him out with his roadside diner. Nick's young and prepossessing wife, Cora (Lana Turner), tries to talk him out of it, and even the drifter Frank (John Garfield) thinks twice about staying, pulling the "Man Wanted" sign out of a trash fire until he gets an eyeful of Mrs. Smith standing outside the entrance to the Twin Oaks in her waitressing outfit: white turban and halter-top, white shoes and white short shorts.

One night Frank is lamenting his inability to get anywhere with Cora (he's already kissed her full on the lips to no discernible effect) when the wooden sign for the Twin Oaks comes crashing down in the Santa Ana wind. Frank, who's still trying to impress Mrs. Smith, persuades Nick to buy a new-fangled neon one that will "give people an appetite," as Frank says. Since Cora has been trying to upgrade the place for some time (her burning desire for upward mobility, sooner rather than later, is reminiscent of Mildred Pierce[6]), the neon sign signals Frank and Cora's first act of conspiracy, an event confirmed—once her husband has left the room—by the match he strikes to light her cigarette.

The subsequent scene begins with a high crane shot, the words "Twin Oaks" blinking on and off in the dusk as Cora and Frank stand admiring it

Fig. 13. Crooner: Nick Smith (Cecil Kellaway) preparing to perform "She's Funny That Way" for Frank Chambers (John Garfield) and Cora Smith (Lana Turner) in Tay Garnett's *The Postman Always Rings Twice.*

together from the steps of the diner. Unlike the previous sequence in the kitchen, a domestic space lit in the familiar M-G-M style that nonetheless imprisons the couple in the bright, high-key light, in the scene outdoors in the ocean-freshened air, their bodies are mottled with shadows. Cora's also dressed differently: swathed in a white summer dress, her platinum hair down, she's open for the first time to Nick's advances.

However, when they go inside to the living room (a space, like the kitchen, associated with domesticity), Nick is sitting in a chair, holding a guitar in one hand and a drink in the other. Cora asks him to sing and he's happy to comply: "I'm not much to look at, nothing to see / Just glad I'm living, lucky to be / I've got a woman crazy for me / She's funny that way." Still strumming, Nick asks Cora to do a "little dance," but she begs off, claiming she feels "silly dancing alone." Cora then suggests they dance together, and Nick in turn demurs ("I prefer to watch"), at which point Frank, who's standing between the two, asks if he can dance with Mrs. Smith.

In fact, Nick has another "idea" and suggests they retire to the next room where the jukebox is. (Of course, there's no little irony here since although Nick thinks the idea for the sign was his, it was really Frank's.) After a tight close-up of Nick inserting a coin into the jukebox, a record begins to spin. While Nick stands in the doorway accompanying the song on guitar, Frank and Cora dance together, the neon light illuminating their bodies as they sway to the Latin beat. Nick's presence eventually makes Cora uncomfortable enough that she brusquely concludes the "tango" by literally pulling the plug on the jukebox, but not before she and Nick have worked up a sweat that ends with a nighttime swim in the Pacific.

After the swim (which, as in the more famous sequence in *From Here to Eternity* [1953], signifies "sex") and an aborted attempt at "eloping" (Cora calls it quits when her immaculate white outfit gets dirtied hitchhiking with Frank), the couple returns to the Twin Oaks where she's left a goodbye note for her husband, "I'm going away—I love Frank." Nick, however, remains none the wiser, showing up after them "higher than a kite," a bundle of laundry cradled in his arms like a child, drunkenly singing "She's Funny That Way."

A week passes and Frank, as he bitterly confesses in voice-over, can't decide whether he should stay or go. After some hard thinking on the beach at night (but without Cora to warm him), he returns to the diner intent on having it out with her. But when he hears music, he goes over to a window and looks inside where Nick's sitting back in his chair playing the guitar and singing "She's Funny That Way" and Cora's lying on a couch meticulously brushing one of her white shoes as if it were a new tooth: "Though she'd love to work and slave for me every day / She'd be so much better off if I went away. / But why should I leave her? Why should I go?" Although Cora looks up and sees Frank in the window nodding his head for her to come out, she shakes her head "no." When he shakes his head more vigorously, she carefully mouths the word again and, for the moment, it's Frank who goes, Frank who leaves. But before Nick can finish singing the Neil Morét and Richard Whiting song (later reprised by Frank Sinatra in *Meet Danny Wilson* [1952]), Cora comes to Nick in his room and broaches the issue of murder, in the process eliding the last line of "She's Funny That Way": "She'd be unhappy without me, I know."

We know from Frank and Cora's previous little talk in the kitchen that she married Nick because she had to fight off *all* the guys *all* the time when what she really wanted, as Frank puts it, was a "gold watch": instead of love or even lust, Cora chose safety and security, those twin pillars of forties domesticity. But if she was glad once just to be living, working and slaving at the Twin Oaks, now she'll never be happy unless Nick goes away for good so she can have Frank *and* the diner. Of course, what the illicit lovers can't know because they're mad about each other (an *amour fou* that no doubt inspired Chenal to make the film) is that the postman always rings twice and, as Jacques Lacan was fond of saying, the letter always arrives at its destination.

Unlike Gaye Dawn's brutally public rendition of "Moanin' Low" in *Key Largo*, Nick Smith's version of "She's Funny That Way" in *The Postman Always Rings Twice* is, relatively speaking, private. As with Lieutenant Muldoon's *a cappella* singing in *The Naked City* and Gino Moretti's in *House of Strangers*, the private setting, not to mention lack of external compulsion, codes Nick's performance as a spontaneous expression of his personality—in this case, that he's a sweet, if benighted man. The fact that he accompanies himself on acoustic guitar contributes to the impression, just as the caretaker Leick Thome's (Chill Wills) novelty song on guitar, "Deedle Deedle, Dum Dum," in *Leave Her to Heaven* contrasts with Ellen Berent's high-strung mood and petulant manner ("Oh, a possum and a top cat had a fight / They fight all day and they fight all night"). Thus, while Nick's obliviousness in the first part of *The Postman Always Rings Twice* tends to mitigate whatever sympathy we might have for him, his later wistful rendition of "She's Funny That Way" not only facilitates our identification with his character but codes Cora, especially after she goes to Frank's bedroom, as cold-blooded and avaricious.

As portrayed by Rita Hayworth, Gilda possesses in spades what Richard Dyer calls "charisma," but the "rhetoric of the private" that governs her initial performance of "Put the Blame on Mame" in Charles Vidor's 1946 film —where, like Nick Smith, she accompanies herself on guitar—generates a "certain pity for [her] character."[7] The scenario is complicated, to say the least. Down and out in Buenos Aires, Johnny Farrell (Glenn Ford) is caught crooking a waterfront craps game and has to be rescued from a holdup by a mysterious gentleman, Ballin Mundson (George Macready). The proprietor of a popular gambling casino as well as the front for a Nazi-affiliated tungsten cartel, Mundson immediately takes a shine to Johnny, hiring him to oversee his club's operations. Gilda's unexpected arrival not only upsets the original trio of Johnny, Mundson, and the nightclub-owner's cane-cum-dagger, it initiates an ever-escalating game of sadomasochistic cat and mouse between Gilda and Johnny in which it becomes virtually impossible to determine who's the cat and who's the mouse.

Although Johnny's plainly unhappy about it, Mundson also asks him to oversee his wife's wanderlust. So when Gilda returns home one night humming "Put the Blame on Mame" with a man who's not her husband, Johnny slaps the man a couple of times, then knocks him down. As for Gilda, Johnny tells her she can go anywhere she pleases, with anyone she pleases, but he'll take her there and pick her up—like Mundson's "laundry." It's then that Johnny's voice-over resumes ("I hated her so I couldn't get her out of my mind for a minute. She was in the air I breathed and the food I ate"), bridging a straight cut from the exterior of Mundson's mansion to the mezzanine casino office where he's trying, unsuccessfully, to sleep.

Gilda, accompanying herself on acoustic guitar, can be heard offscreen humming the opening bars of "Put the Blame on Mame" while Johnny, turning in bed, continues his voice-over: "At first I thought I was just dreaming it. I'd been hearing her voice in my sleep for nights anyway." But as soon as Gilda begins to sing the first verse of "Put the Blame on Mame" ("When M[issus] O'Leary's cow kicked the lantern, in Chicago town / They say that started the fire that burned Chicago down"), he sits straight up in bed and flicks on the lighted clock—it's five in the morning—before going to the window that looks out onto the casino where Gilda sits perched on a gaming table. The following shot-countershot encapsulates their twisted relationship ("here's the real low-down"): if the louvers appear to cut Gilda's image into ribbons, miming Johnny's aggressive point of view, the reverse, low-angle shot imprisons him within the very same composition.

There's an uncluttered wide shot, then the camera begins to descend—as if, like Johnny, it can't resist being pulled toward Gilda—while she sings the refrain to "Put the Blame on Mame": "Mame kissed a buyer from out of town, that kiss burned Chicago down / So you can put the blame on Mame, boys, put the blame on Mame." After the crane shot resolves to a medium two-shot with Gilda on the left and Uncle Pio on the right, his face cupped in his palm ("Remember the blizzard back in Manhattan, in eighteen-eighty-six"), Gilda looks over at him and he raises his eyebrows. Unlike Johnny, Uncle Pio—"the wise man of the people"[8]—gets Gilda.

The subsequent close-ups of Gilda, with her chorded fingers visible in the near foreground as she continues to sing ("They say the traffic was tied up and folks were in a fix"), are from Uncle Pio's point of view. They're also intimate addresses to the audience, who are now aligned not with Johnny's superior gaze but with the bathroom attendant's sympathetic, egalitarian one. In fact, in the final part of the number, the camera cuts from a shot of Gilda backlit and singing the intro to the refrain ("That's the story that went around but here's the real lowdown") to a slightly off-center close-up. Unlike the earlier close-ups where Gilda appears to be singing to Johnny or Uncle Pio, here she seems to be lost in thought: "Mame gave a trump such an ice-cold no / For seven days they shoveled snow." The implication is that at some point in the not-so-distant past, Gilda rejected Johnny and now she's paying for it.

Gilda is still singing "Put the Blame on Mame" when Johnny comes storming down the stairs. After she taunts him, "Good morning, how very pretty you look in your nightgown," Johnny, furious, asks her what she's doing, as if he doesn't know. When she coolly replies, "Singing to my friend," he dispatches Uncle Pio, at which point Gilda, laughing, quips, "Put a beggar on horseback" (a reference to Uncle Pio's continuing description of Johnny as a "peasant"), before putting down her guitar and brightly adding, "Well, here's the laundry waiting to be picked up."

I will return to Vidor's film and the second "striptease" version of "Put the Blame on Mame" in chapter 7, but suffice it to say that Gilda's active appropriation of Johnny's demeaning comment about the "laundry," preceded as it is by her musical outcry against men's categorization of women as the cause of all the world's ills, points up her "resistance." Although Johnny repeatedly tries to put her in her place, Gilda refuses to stay put. The fact that she shows up in the casino at night, singing the same song she was humming when Johnny earlier accosted her, speaks to her refusal to remain silent: for Gilda, who was a professional entertainer before she met either Ballin or Johnny, singing, whether while dancing or playing the guitar, is sweet revenge.

In the previous chapter, "Blues in the Night," I discussed the role of African American musicians in forties noir. The number that Mose (Rex Ingram) performs in *Moonrise*, a "blue story" he sings while accompanying himself on acoustic guitar, differs markedly not only from the popular tune that Nick Smith croons in *The Postman Always Rings Twice* but from the sort of "resistance" associated with Gilda's performances in Vidor's film. Since Frank Borzage's film is set in Virginia and Mose has "chosen" to live away from civilization, his character can also be said to comment both on the urban black jazzmen featured in such films as *The Dark Corner*, *Kiss of Death*, and *Force of Evil* and the black female piano-players in *This Gun for Hire* and *House of Strangers*.

Paradoxically enough, the character of Mose is both stock and rounded.

Unlike Pompey in the gothic noir *Among the Living*, a black servant whose reward for being a faithful retinue is to be killed off in the first reel by the wealthy family's insane son, Mose, a black Thoreau who raises bloodhounds, remains a central character throughout the course of *Moonrise*. If the raccoon hunting strikes contemporary audiences as patently offensive, both Ingram's performance and the film's complex narrative effectively problematize this initial impression.

Before being cast in *Moonrise*, Ingram was one of the most accomplished black actors in Hollywood, having appeared as Jim in the 1939 version of *The Adventures of Huckleberry Finn*, the genie Djinn in *The Thief of Bagdad* (1940) as well as, to name only two of his musicals, Adam/De Lawd in *The Green Pastures* (1936) and Lucius Ferry/Lucifer Jr. in *Cabin in the Sky* (1943). If the "essence of black film history," as Donald Bogle has observed à propos of Ingram, "is not found in the stereotyped role but in what certain talented actors have done with the stereotype," Ingram's "dignified, self-contained" performance as the bluesman Mose in *Moonrise* is illustrative.[9]

In order to appreciate the complexity of Mose's soulful rendition of Theodore Strauss and William Lava's "Lonesome," it's useful to situate the song in relation to the film's elaborate hunting conceits. Thus, when Danny Hawkins (Dane Clark) goes to Mose's shack in the swamp after killing Jerry Sykes (Lloyd Bridges) in self-defense, the black man quells Danny's fears about having inherited his father's "bad blood" by relating an anecdote. Once, while working as a brakeman on the railroad, Mose saw a hobo sleeping in a boxcar; instead of throwing him off the train, though, he put a coat over the man because of the "lonesome, cold look on his face." Later, the sheriff "grabbed" his dogs to track the man down, but Mose never felt right about it since, as he says, "it's all right for a dog to chase a coon, but not a man."

When Danny asks what happened to the man, Mose says he was sentenced to fifteen years "for making love to the constable's daughter when she didn't want any," adding that the man went to prison not because he had "bad blood" but because he was "lonesome." Danny points out that Mose is lonesome and he hasn't committed any crimes, whereupon Mose reflects:

> Sure I get lonesome. Man oughta have a woman, friends anyway. Man oughta live in the world with other folks. When I came out here, I thought I would be out of the way, no one shoving me around. What I did was

> resign from the human race and I guess that's about the worst crime there is, only they don't hang you for it.

Worse crimes come to mind than resigning from the human race—like lynching a black man—but Ingram's performance of "Lonesome" may well have been affected by a traumatic incident in the actor's life. In 1948, Ingram was arrested, like Chuck Berry later, for violating the Mann Act: illegally transporting a minor, "a fifteen-year-old white Kansas girl," across state lines for "immoral purposes."[10] Although Ingram had previously "played men who seemed essentially free, slightly heroic, and removed from typical American life,"[11] his career was never the same.

The hunter/hunted conceit of *Moonrise* deepens when Danny, Mose, a deaf-and-dumb boy named Billy Scripture (Harry Morgan), and a small hunting party end up at Brother's Pond, the scene of Danny's crime. In a telling match shot, the film cuts from a tight close-up of Danny as he listens to the hounds barking for blood to the terrified face of a raccoon holed up in a tree, a close-up that's almost immediately reprised when, after climbing the tree, Danny sees the place where he killed Sykes and then has to violently shake the limb to make the raccoon fall. On the way back to Mose's place, the hunting party discovers Sykes's body and, in a fit of rage, Danny kicks one of Mose's dogs. (The film's human/animal metaphors are, importantly, reversible: Mose says it's wrong to use dogs to hunt a man; in fact, he calls them "Mister" because, he says, "there isn't enough dignity in the world.")

The discovery of Sykes's body precipitates Danny's return to Mose's place, the film cutting directly to the black man sitting on his porch and strumming his battered guitar while, in the background, Danny's lying down near the swamp, his hands behind his head, listening: "Lonesome / Lonesome / I want her not to leave me / Want her not to grieve me." Mose stops singing long enough to encourage Danny to see his grandmother in Chinamook and learn about his father ("Daylight coming in the morning / Hanged man waiting on the stone"), then continues: "Don't send me flowers / Don't send me mail / For where I am going / I won't need no mail." Although Danny knows the song is addressed to him ("You're saying something"), Mose says he's "just talking to Mister Guitar."

Finally taking Mose's song to heart, Danny flees through the swamps and makes his way to Chinamook where, talking to his grandmother (Ethel Barrymore), he learns the truth about his father: that he was a happy man until the local doctor left his wife to die after she had given birth to Danny. The next morning, Danny leaves his shotgun at his father's grave and goes out to meet the search party that includes Mose, the sheriff, and Danny's girl, Gilly (Gail Russell). Looking over at the bloodhound that Danny kicked, Mose says, "Mr. Dog, if a man knows how to rejoin the human race once he's resigned, it helps, it helps."

As Hervé Dumont records in his definitive study of Borzage, the director described *Moonrise* as a "moving picture in sound."[12] In fact, the director's unified approach to dialogue, effects, score, and source music exemplifies the complex relation between narrative and "sound design" in forties noir. This "narrative melody" (to echo Borzage) is epitomized by Mose's rendition of "Lonesome," a performance that prefigures Danny's reconciliation with his father's traumatic patrimony even as it recalls the film's bravura opening, an eye- and ear-catching sequence composed of three pieces that interlock like a puzzle.

In the first part, accompanied by the pounding timpani of Lava's score, the final credit ("Directed by Frank Borzage") dissolves to a gray, rain-spattered puddle in which the legs of three men are reflected. The camera tracks in reverse to show the men walking under an overcast sky, the middle man's hands hanging at his sides, then slowly cranes up past a crowd of onlookers standing with umbrellas, eyes raised, to a silhouette of a man putting a brace and noose around the neck of another man. After the camera pans left to a silhouette of a man pushing a lever, there's a cut from the sound of a man falling through the hatch to a baby crying. The baby appears to be reacting to the shadow of the hanging figure, but when the camera pulls back for a wider shot, it turns out to be a doll suspended over a crib.

Dissolve to a high-angle, reverse-tracking shot of little Danny Hawkins swiftly crossing a playground accompanied by the sound of the condemned man's steps mixed with a "mocking rhyme chanted by a chorus of children," "Danny Hawkins's Dad was hanged! Danny Hawkins's Dad was hanged!"[13] Little Jerry Sykes suddenly approaches the camera, his hand around his neck, making grotesque gurgling sounds until Danny—provoked to the point of violence—steps into the frame and knocks him down. Although many years will pass before Danny knocks down Jerry again, killing him with a stone outside Brother's Pond as big-band music plays in the background, here—in the opening moments of Borzage's *Moonrise*—he's already haunted by the figure of the hanging man evoked in Mose's lonesome blues.

Chapter 5

Black Jazzwomen

Cecil Kellaway's, Rita's Hayworth's, and Rex Ingram's guitar-accompanied vocal performances in *The Postman Always Rings Twice*, *Gilda*, and *Moonrise*, respectively, are unusual in forties noir since the more common instrument for solo accompaniment is the piano. While private, strictly instrumental performances can be used, not unlike voice-over, to convey a character's interiority, public performances constitute a primary musical site in the genre. *The Glass Key* and *House of Strangers* are especially suggestive in the context because they feature black female vocal and piano performances that shed light, like the jazz band numbers discussed in the previous chapter, on the representation of African Americans in film noir, a genre that has been historically linked to the cultural discourse of blackness.

Made only one year after *The Maltese Falcon*, Stuart Heisler's *The Glass Key* (1942), a remake of the 1935 adaptation of Hammett's well-known novel starring George Raft, is distinguished not only by its leads, Alan Ladd and Veronica Lake, but also by its graphic depiction of physical violence. In fact, Lillian Randolph's performance of the Jule Styne-Frank Loesser standard, "I Don't Want to Walk without You," which was originally introduced by Johnnie Johnston in the 1942 college "crime" musical, *Sweater Girl*, can be said to deflect attention from the conventional heterosexual romance between Ed Beaumont (Ladd) and Janet Henry (Lake) to the rather more loaded, sadomasochistic relation between Ed and Jeff (William Bendix).

The plot of *The Glass Key* is, true to the genre, thoroughly Byzantine and, with respect to sexual psychodynamics, patently incestuous: Ed works as an aide-de-camp for Paul Madvig (Brian Donlevy), a Great-McGintyesque political kingpin who's a prime suspect in the death of Senator Ralph Henry's dissolute playboy son. When Paul shifts his allegiance from the racketeer Nick Varna to Senator Taylor and his reform campaign, Ed violently disagrees, albeit on strictly political, not principled grounds.

Slavoj Žižek has identified the central conflict of both the novel and film as Ed's ambivalent relation to the paternal figure, a subtext that also informs the Coen brothers' postmodern take on the Hammett novel, *Miller's Crossing* (1990): "when [Ed] consents to collaborate with the enemy, does he really betray Paul or is it all a kind of squared double cross to obtain the much-needed information?"[14] The plot heats up when Ed briefly entertains Varna's offer of twenty grand and control of a gambling casino if he spills his story about Paul's apparent involvement in the death of the senator's son to the publisher of a paper Varna controls. However, when Ed flatly rejects the gangster's offer, throwing the money in his face, Varna has only to say "Jeff" and his right-hand henchman, eyes popping like flash bulbs, knocks him down.

Cut to a dingy little room above the Basement Club where Ed sits up in a bed, moaning with pain, then collapses onto the floor. (Since his shirt is bloodied and in rags, it's clear he's been lovingly attended to by Jeff.) Ed starts to crawl toward the door until Jeff, who's playing poker with Varna's other henchman, Rusty, glances over and remarks, "Sweetheart, you know what I told you." After Jeff lugs Ed back to the bed, he stands him up, saying, "Look, sweetie pie, you oughta lie down. You don't feel so good," then punches him in the face with a right, then a left. Although Rusty sounds a note of caution, "Be careful, you're gonna croak him," Jeff's reply—"You can't croak him, he's tough. He likes it, don't ya, baby?"—suggests he's a direct antecedent of Krause in *Dead Reckoning*, a man who appears to get off beating other men up.

The fun and games continue when Varna shows up with the publisher and, after Ed doesn't respond to having his body dumped in a bathtub with ice-cold water, Jeff starts to beat him again. Ed eventually manages to escape his tormentors by starting a fire, then throwing himself out a window. Later, however, while recuperating in a hospital, he tells Janet he took the beatings for his boss, an admission that explicitly links Ed's slavish relation with Paul to his masochistic one with Jeff.

All this violence is prelude to an extraordinary musical sequence set at the Basement Club. The number opens with Randolph playing the piano and singing to an unidentified woman as Jeff stands by drinking a beer: "Walk without my arm about you, baby / I thought the day you left me behind / I'd take a stroll and get you right off my mind." In a rhyme of an earlier gesture when he knocked down Ed for the first time, Jeff wipes his nose before going to the bar to order another beer.

However, when Randolph sings "Oh, baby, please come back / Or you'll break my heart for me," the film cuts to the stairs where Ed suddenly appears, the camera quickly tracking in as he pauses on a step, a fedora on his no doubt still sore head, his right hand hidden deep in the pocket of his overcoat. The whole place goes dead until Jeff, looking up from a shot of whiskey he's about to down, breaks the silence, "Well, if it isn't sock-me-again Beaumont." Putting one hand on Ed's back while massaging his chest with the other, Jeff offers him a drink upstairs in the same "little room" where they played before. "Excuse us, gents," Jeff announces to the bar, his arms once again about his "baby," "we gotta go up and play handball, me and cuddles."

Due in no small part to Randolph's bluesy, understated performance of "I Don't Want to Walk without You" (her other noir credentials include *Phantom Lady* and *Sleep, My Love*), *The Glass Key* epitomizes the sort of *detournement* that film noir can perform on a standard romantic ballad. Since Jeff is a born sadist (not so much born to kill like Sam Wild but born to take real pleasure inflicting physical pain on others), his day really does brighten when Ed walks into the "gloom" of the Basement Club. As for Ed, who seems more interested in Paul than Janet, his masochistic relation with both his mentor and Jeff has more than a "touch of the homoerotic."[15] Of course, in a touch worthy of the Paramount musicals Ladd and Lake appeared in together such as *Star Spangled Rhythm* (1942) and *Variety Girl* (1947), Ed also ends up in Janet's arms and with Paul's blessing, although one can't help but wonder whether he'll ever forget his walk on the wild side with Jeff.

Dolores Parker, who sang with Fletcher Henderson's band in the forties, then with Duke Ellington's Orchestra as one of "The Rhythm Debs," performs a trio of songs at the piano in *House of Strangers*. But the real difference between her role and Randolph's in *The Glass Key* is that her songs are allotted an unusual amount of screen time. While Parker, like Randolph, is not the main focus of the sequence, her diegetic presence, reinforced by her conversational delivery and low-key playing, not only sutures the sequence but bestows on her character the status of a narrator. In fact, the three songs Parker performs can be said to constitute a cycle that charts the progression of Max and Irene's rapidly deteriorating romance, a relationship that nonetheless represents a positive counterweight to Max's all-consuming battle with the three brothers who have betrayed him.

Even as Max has been conducting an extra-engagement affair with Irene, he's agreed—during a meeting his father has brokered—to marry his longstanding Italian-American fiancée, Maria (Debra Paget). Later that night, he's back on the town with Irene. (There's a telling match cut from Max kissing Maria in the family living room to him dancing cheek-to-cheek to "Honey" with Irene at the Club Gala.) When Irene storms off, sensing Max's mind is elsewhere ("You're not dancing with me"), Max follows her out to the street where he pulls her into an alley that's the stage entrance for a theater. Irene makes it perfectly clear that the terms of their affair have changed (he's engaged *and* now she's in love with him), but Max

Fig. 14. End of an Affair: Dolores Parker performing "Can't We Talk It Over?" in Joseph Mankiewicz's *House of Strangers*.

announces—"just like that"—he's hungry and Irene agrees to go to dinner with him.

The film dissolves to an Italian restaurant where, in the background, a bartender is serving a table of six and, in the foreground, Parker is playing the piano and singing Victor Young and Ned Washington's "Can't We Talk It Over?" (originally recorded by Bing Crosby). In the course of the song, the camera follows the bartender as he picks up a glass from a drunk who's passed out in a booth ("Can't we get together and figure / Whether this is the right thing to do?"), serves a drink to an older man with a cigar stuck in his mouth talking to a young woman in a hat ("I hate the thought of spending nights all alone"), and extinguishes a candle with an empty glass ("Missing the thrill of nights that we've known"). After the bartender serves Max a drink (Irene's "not drinking tonight") and unceremoniously empties an ashtray onto the floor right in front of them, the song comes to its bittersweet conclusion: "Before you whisper goodbye / Goodbye, forever / Let's talk it over, dear." Although the lyrics are all about longing and romantic tristesse, the bartender's actions suggest that Max and Irene's romance is in fact over.

Parker, meanwhile, begins to croon the Sidney Clare–Sam Stept number "Please Don't Talk about Me When I'm Gone" (recorded by Gene Austin in 1931 and later covered by Count Basie, Louis Armstrong, and, most importantly in the context, Billie Holiday): "Please don't talk about me when I'm gone / Oh, honey, though our friendship ceases from now on / And, listen, if you can't say anything real nice / It's better not to talk at all, that's my advice." In this, the second part of the song cycle, the action is primarily an extended exchange between Max and Irene framed in a classic medium two-shot as he drinks his drink and she tells him to enjoy it because it's their last night together.

The overt meaning of the scene, however, is complicated by the camerawork, the film cutting first to the booth where the older man appears to be trying to console the young, hatted woman who's now crying, and then to the bartender, a cigar stuck in his mouth, who's playing chess with a patron at the bar. If the first scenario appears to be about an unsuccessful seduction, the second one mirrors the intricate game of chess between Max and Irene, one that, as his thinly veiled discourse of frustration suggests, Irene appears to be winning, "You can turn it on or off. Character, that's what you got. Plenty of character."

Max continues to try to woo Irene, kissing her on the ear, then full on the mouth, but she looks straight ahead, face blank, arms crossed. The coup de grâce occurs when she pulls out a compact and, reapplying her lipstick, says she'll take *him* home. Defeated ("Boy, you're loaded with character tonight"), Max, who's been playing the whole time with a matchbook, crumples an empty pack of cigarettes—a sign, like the emptied ashtray before, their romance is dead—and goes to the bar to bum a smoke. As he stands there making small talk ("Got a nice place here. Lots of atmosphere. Full of characters"), the bartender says in passing, "Your lady friend's leaving," and a resigned Max can only rejoin, "She left me four hours ago."

Max and Irene's exit song, "Was That the Human Thing to Do?," written by Sammy Fain and Joe Young and recorded in 1931 by Guy Lombardo and His Canadians, completes the cycle: from the still burning desire for reconciliation to the bitter reality of separation. While the song's address remains ambiguous since it could refer to either Max or Irene, the fact that Irene leaves Max standing at the bar (before he catches up with her outside) suggests it's from his disenchanted point of view. This interpretation is confirmed by the conclusion of *House of Strangers* when, the phonograph needle skipping on the recording of "M'appari," the opera-motivated flashback ends and Max, recognizing the new beginning that Irene represents, breaks with his father's memory and the restrictive, patriarchal tradition it embodies.

From this changed point of audition one can also begin to appreciate the difference between Gino's music of choice—Italian opera—and Max's. It's not simply that Max plays the piano, an activity that links him with Parker's character; rather, it's that the popular American songs Parker performs represent a native, indigenous tradition, whether understood as jazz or blues, which contrasts with the classical Old World discourse of opera: compared to the Rossini Gino imposes like a prison sentence on his extended family every Wednesday evening, Parker's interpretations of the great American songbook are not only irresistible but altogether liberating.

The Right Angle

Lillian Randolph and Dolores Parker, the black female performers in *The Glass Key* and *House of Strangers*, are anomalies in forties noir not simply because the majority of vocalists in the period are white but because they're not subject to the interested gaze of their employer or, as in *Gilda*, his right-hand man. The restive relation in *I Walk Alone* between Kay Lawrence (Lizabeth Scott) and Noll Turner (Kirk Douglas)—the female entertainer and male proprietor—in fact reflects a cardinal trope or topic of the genre. Of course, there's a particular historical irony at work since, if the nightclub understood as the public sphere represents an escape for women from the vicissitudes of the home, the male nightclub owner frequently attempts to exercise all the prerogatives of the traditional forties husband. In this, the nightclub becomes a displaced site where the problems and anxieties of the domestic sphere play out in musical form.

This tension between entertainer and proprietor is not immediately apparent in *I Walk Alone*, a noir-inflected crime film that's remarkable for its unabashed "ambiance of romanticism."[16] This "romantic nuance" is personified by the character of Kay Lawrence, an entertainer at the Regency Club whose "singing is warmly evocative of postwar idealism."[17] Although there's the proverbial set piece where Kay performs backed by an orchestra, the difference between Scott's performances in *I Walk Alone* and her earlier one in *Dead Reckoning* is that in both the first and third numbers, she accompanies herself, like Lily Stevens in *Road House*, on the piano.

In fact, Kay's performances are woven into the very fabric of Haskin's film, as in the early scene where, enjoying a massage, Noll picks up a phone to hear that his ex-bootlegging partner, Frankie Madison (Burt Lancaster), has entered the club and piano music can suddenly be heard offscreen. After the camera cuts to a close-up of a woman playing "Don't Call It Love," the camera pulls back to show Kay at the piano as Frankie, walking into the background of the shot, remarks in passing, "So you're the famous Kay Lawrence. It takes so well to coach you." Intrigued, Kay asks the bartender about Frankie and he tells her Frankie was "before [her] time."

While Kay's response when she gets up from the piano appears to be unmotivated ("All the songs sound alike these days"), it's crucial to the plot of *I Walk Alone* since if Frankie's associated with the good old days before gangsters like Noll became corporate businessmen, Kay's preference for thirties, prewar music suggests a certain commonality of character. (The sound track of *I Walk Alone* is littered with songs from the period: Yip Harburg and Johnny Green's "I'm Yours" [1930]; Robin, Whiting, and Chase's "My Ideal" [1930]; Richard Rodgers and Lorenz Hart's "It's Easy to Remember" [1930]; Fred Hollander and Ralph Freed's "You Leave Me Breathless" [1938]; and Frank Loesser and Hoagy Carmichael's "Two Sleepy People" [1939].) The romantic import of Kay and Frankie's mutual attachment to the past emerges in the "welcome-home dinner" that Noll stages for Frankie to "soften" him up. Kay initially protests she's only "paid to sing," but she ultimately agrees to the plan—"the trio playing soft and sweet, candlelight and good champagne"—because she believes Noll genuinely wants to make it up to Frankie.

Once the two are ensconced in the club's lavish private dining room, Frankie, hearing the trio, says, "Funny, all the new songs sound alike," then adds, "For a song to stick, you gotta be with a girl when the music's playing." Kay asks what sort of song he's thinking about, and when he mentions Rodgers and Hart's "Isn't It Romantic?" she requests it from the band, The Regency Three, a black trio that serenades them throughout dinner. Later, they dance to her request, Loesser and Carmichael's "Heart and Soul" ("Heart and soul, I fell in love with you / Heart and soul, the way a fool would do"),[18] but the trio stops playing when Frankie tells her that he hasn't been "overseas with the marines" as she's been led to believe, but in prison and, as Frankie angrily emphasizes, "not just in prison, fourteen years in prison."

The musical climax of *I Walk Alone* recapitulates the opening piano sequence but with a subtle vocal difference. This time, when Frankie shows up at the club, his rag-tag gang is already planted at the bar and Noll's not supine on a massage table but ready and waiting behind his desk. Frankie sets off for Noll's office for what he mistakenly thinks will be the big showdown, but before he does so, he exchanges a glance with Kay, who's earlier warned him that violence isn't the answer. Unlike Frankie, Kay knows the score: in 1933 (the same year as the champagne served at the welcome-home dinner), Frankie and Noll agreed that if either of them was ever arrested, the remaining partner would continue to run the club, then share half the profits when the other one was released.

In the intervening years, however, years in which Frankie has languished in jail while his partner has lived the high life, Noll has transformed what was once a small-time bootlegging organization into a complex business enterprise that Frankie can't even begin to comprehend. (The scene where Dave outlines the club's corporate structure is breathtaking in its intricacy.) Worse yet, Noll's only "prepared to split the profits . . . on the old nightclub *before* it was sold."[19] Since Noll himself is now only a figurehead, Frankie, embittered but impotent, takes out his rage on the club's books, then Dave, before the doorman Dan (Mike Mazurki)—who, like the bartender Ben, once worked for Frankie—puts him in a stranglehold and takes him outside to be beaten, as instructed, "senseless."

The concluding musical number of *I Walk Alone* occurs on the heels of the above, catastrophic series of events. If in *Gilda* and *Road House* the female entertainers are overseen by a proprietor whose power, like his gaze, is absolute (in *I Walk Alone* Noll is, as his club's name suggests, a regent), this theme —the proprietor as overseer—is explicitly dramatized in the mise-en-scène of *I Walk Alone*. The sequence opens with Kay offscreen singing and accompanying herself on piano as Noll, having disposed of Frankie, regally walks the floor greeting customers: "Don't call it love / If it's not a thing / That's strong enough to start / An earthquake in your heart."

As Kay starts into the second verse ("Don't make a fool / Out of someone who cares"), the camera cuts to a wide shot of the club's main room with Noll in the left raised foreground watching Kay sing in the background: "Don't let it be one of those impromptu affairs / If you don't feel what I'm conscious of." On the tail of this, the final verse of the song, there's a dramatic cut to a high overhead shot of Kay attacking the piano, the spot-lit brightness of the white piano and her white evening dress offset by an encroaching black shadow.

Noll suddenly slips in behind Kay, who's still at the piano:

KAY: Where is he?
NOLL: Oh, Frankie's not for you, kid. He's been in prison.
KAY: I've been in prison for the past four years. I'm just getting out, so I know how he feels.
NOLL: Oh, flat on that note.
KAY: Where is he?
NOLL: I had him thrown out into the alley where he belongs.

The lights come up and, as Noll smiles and applauds along with the audience, Kay goes to Frankie whose hopes for recouping the past have, like his body, been brutally crushed.

The third and final diegetic performance of "Don't Call It Love" is significant because, like the initial instrumental one when Kay first meets Frankie, she accompanies herself on piano. This performance is in stark contrast to the second time she performs the Allie Wrubel and Ned Washington song (Scott was dubbed by Trudy Stevens) where she's backed by the club's orchestra which, like The Regency Three, is associated with Noll. The aftermath of Kay's second orchestral version of "Don't Call It Love," which she performs without accompanying herself on piano, is also significant: when she asks the patrons if they have any requests, Noll's rich-bitch mistress, Mrs. Richardson, loudly asks for "I Lost My Man"—twice. A consummate professional, Kay apologizes for not knowing the words, but when Noll's mistress snaps, "You ought to learn them," Kay answers back, "Perhaps I better start right now," then goes looking for Noll to confront him about the affair. (Noll, who—to paraphrase another noir—has a dollar sign where his heart ought to be, explains that he intends to marry Mrs. Richardson not because he loves her but because, as a "blue blood," she "puts the club in the upper bracket.")

Previously in *I Walk Alone*, Kay told Frankie, "I've been singing around here for six years. In that time I've learned more than just how to put a song over. I've learned to play every kind of angle but the right angle." The third time Kay performs her signature song—accompanying herself on piano and right before she walks out on Noll for good—is, however, the charm: she's finally learned the right words *and* angle.

Road House

Despite the fact film noir is regularly associated with low rather than high musical culture as in the jazz backstory of *The Man I Love*, opera, paradoxically enough, is not only "on air" but is part of the backstory of another canary-and-club-owner melo-noir, *Road House*. (In the context of opera, see also the brilliantly expressionist, Alton-helmed sequence in *Hollow Triumph*, otherwise known as *The Scar*, where John Muller [Paul Henreid] murders his double, the Wagnerian enthusiast Dr. Bartok [Henreid].) If the "rustic-moderne" look of *Road House* can be attributed in part to Jean Negulesco who, before directing the early noir, *The Mask of Dimitrios* (1944), worked as a sketch artist and stage decorator,[20] the vocal numbers are indebted to musical director Lionel Newman whose original compositions, "Again" (with Dorcas Cochran) and "The Right Kind" (with Charles Henderson and Don George), provide the basis for the film's amorous theme.

In fact, the melodramatic trappings of *Road House* derive as much from the tension between the musical numbers and the obviously artificial sets as it does from the romantic triangle of Jefty (Richard Widmark), Pete Morgan (Cornel Wilde), and Lily Stevens (Ida Lupino). While Widmark reprises the "histrionics" he patented in *Kiss of Death*,[21] the film is Lupino's not simply because her fiancé-to-be Collier Young purchased the rights to the source material especially for her but because her gutsy performance as the torch singer Lily Stevens carries the picture.[22] (Lupino of course was that rarity in classic Hollywood, a female director, helming, among other films, *The Hitch-Hiker* for RKO in 1953.[23])

In *Road House* Lily is a rough-around-the edges singer-piano player whom Jefty brings back from Chicago as the "new attraction" for what she calls his "moose trap." (Although she doesn't know it at the time, her mordant description of Jefty's nightclub/bowling alley/cocktail lounge becomes prophetic when, at the very end of the film, Lily and Pete are hunted down by the seriously unhinged Jefty.) A male customer's passing appraisal of Lily —"If she sings like she looks"—sums up her character: dressed to kill and with a voice that sounds likes gravel (she's the Tom Waits of forties noir), she's the sort of woman that Jefty, even though she's not remotely interested in him, just can't resist and that Pete, who's long since tired of having to dismiss his partner's "entertainers," would rather not have anything to do with. But if Pete's put off by Lily the moment he walks into his office and catches her sitting behind his desk, he's even more perturbed when she exits leaving a cigarette burning a hole into the top of it. (This is Lily's signature, a "scar" that suggests just how tough she is.)

Unlike Jefty, Pete is duly wary of Lily and only grudgingly begins to change his mind once he's seen her sing. (While he runs the financial end of the business, Jefty literally handles the talent.) Before she performs for the first time, he sees to it, per Jefty's instructions, that she gets the proper setting. As he kills the lights and a female patron wonders out loud, "When she's supposed to give out?" (a question that speaks to the sort of place Jefty's road house is), her male companion, having appraised Lily's figure, blurts out, "She reminds me of the first woman that ever slapped my face." After a smattering of applause, Lily strolls over to the stage from the bar, a drink in one hand, a cigarette in the other—she's the queen of this love shack—and, to Pete's continued dismay, sets a burning cigarette on the piano lid.

Sporting a pixie haircut and a black sequined off-the-shoulder dress, cigarette smoke encircling her face, Lily huskily begins to half-talk, half-sing Harold Arlen and Johnny Mercer's "One for My Baby": "It's quarter to three / There's no one in the place except you and me / So set 'em up, Joe / I've got a little story you oughta know." Although this bar ballad with its "bone-simple piano part" and "off-beat blues" was first sung by Fred Astaire in *The Sky's the Limit* (1943) and then covered by Jane Russell in *Macao* (1952),[24] it's long since come to be associated with Frank Sinatra, who first recorded it in 1947 and later reprised it in *Young at Heart* (1954).

However, Lupino's version in *Road House*, which charted and which at least one critic has called the film's "most memorable moment,"[25] radically changes the song's point of view: "You'd never know it / But, buddy, I'm a kind of poet." Unlike "Moanin' Low" in *Key Largo* where the camera frequently cuts away from Gaye Dawn to show how discomfited Frank and Nora are, the camera stays firmly on Lily as she sings, a focus that highlights her idiosyncratic "charisma." Her voice might be a wreck, but partly because of her playing (Lupino studied music for years), you can't take your eyes off her. Consequently, the only cutaways—for example, on the word "code"—are to Pete whose widening eyes suggest he's starting to fall, like Jefty, under Lily's spell.

The subsequent close-up of Lily fingering the keys of the piano not only evinces her feral, almost tactile sense of sexuality but her equally palpable sense of self-possession. This sense of autonomy and "being there for herself"—which, as Dyer has argued, is usually reserved for the male characters in film noir—is accented by the fact that Lily, like Gilda, accompanies

Fig. 15. Torcher: Lily Stevens (Ida Lupino) behind the piano and "backed" by Jefty (Richard Widmark) and Pete (Cornel Wilde) at Jefty's "moose trap" in Jean Negulesco's *Road House.*

herself.[26] Moreover, and notwithstanding the pervasive sailing and cigarette imagery in *Road House*, Lily, unlike Elsa Bannister in *The Lady from Shanghai*, is no siren. As in Lupino's other noirs in which she plays "stoic females caught up in a web of intrigue and danger, usually caused by a lover" (here Jefty), Lily may be as hard as they come, but she's got a heart and, as we later learn (if it isn't already obvious from her singing), soul.

Although Lionel Newman no doubt chose "One for My Baby" for Lily to perform in *Road House* because of the reference to the "road" and Lupino's so-called "whiskey-throated" voice (in the film she drinks Scotch straight), the song's "wandering" form—it has forty-eight instead of the usual thirty-two bars—has real resonance in Negulesco's film. This resonance, which appears for the first time after Lily tells Pete she's staying after slapping him in the face *and* taking the two-hundred bucks he's just given her to go away, resurfaces in the aftermath of her performance of the Arlen and Mercer number. Pete and Susie (Celeste Holm) have reassured Jefty about his new chanteuse: Pete concedes she's good, then burns a finger on a lighter, while Susie says "she does more without a voice than anybody I've ever known." As a bartender busies himself cleaning tables and Lily runs through an instrumental version of "Again," Pete comes over to apologize, but when she asks him if he still wants to run her out of town, he leaves in a huff.

The film dissolves from Lily asking Jefty if there's someone who can teach her how to bowl (bowling being like "swimming" in *Gilda*) to a tight shot of her playing the opening bars of "Again" before a packed house, the camera tilting down to a close-up of the piano lid where a lit cigarette lies next to a series of finger-length burn marks: "Again, this couldn't happen again / This is that once in a lifetime / This is the thrill divine." The difference between Lily's performance of "One for My Baby" and "Again" is that during the latter number, she only looks this time to the left where Pete's standing —crucially, without Susie. A bar still shadows his torso, but it signifies not so much that he's ambivalent about Lily as that he's somehow barred from being with her. The reason of course is Jefty who, exercising his male prerogative, has already claimed Lily despite her manifest independence.

Accordingly, when Lily comes to the line "Mine to hold as I'm holding you now," Pete retreats to the bowling alley. Lily can still be heard singing offscreen ("We'll have this moment forever / But never, never again") as Pete, tearing off his jacket, throws a split. The pinboy's comment—"Sore about something, Pete? You hit them like you mean it"—is echoed in the film when Pete tries to teach Lily how to bowl, then when Jefty, who's just back in town, unexpectedly brings her breakfast in bed the next morning and she's "sore" from bowling. (Lily's "soreness" does not bode well for Jefty, especially when—in a telling reversal—she later wakes up Pete by bowling, then brings *him* breakfast in bed.)

The final song of *Road House*, "The Right Kind," is striking in that, unlike the regressive song sequence in *House of Strangers*, it marks the progression of Pete and Lily's relationship: "There's only one kind of lovin' / That I've been missin' / The right kind." Although Lily performs the number with real brio (she's absolutely buoyant about her new relationship with Pete), the mood quickly changes when the camera cuts to a wide shot that encompasses the back of the bar where, sitting in the dark beneath a set of stuffed deer heads, a large man can be seen swigging a beer and wiping his mouth.

When Lily glances his way, Dutch, mistaking her look, staggers over and stands hulking next to her: "I want a man who's my kind of man / Daddy, oh where can you be?" The lights go down to signal the end of Lily's performance, but after a man who's been trying to discourage Dutch puts a hand on his arm, Dutch swats him off his chair. A mêlée ensues in which Lily's injured and Pete has to pin Dutch down until the police arrive. (In retrospect, the bear-like Dutch is a double for Jefty who, when he discovers Lily's in love with Pete, is wild with resentment.)

Once Dutch has been hauled off to jail, Pete goes to his office where Lily's already retired to put ice on her bruise. The two share a shot of whiskey and she turns on a radio. It's "Elsa's Dream" from Wagner's *Lohengrin*, an aria that comments on both Lili's dream of becoming an opera singer and, not unlike Elsa, her present, debased status as an object of Jefty's accusations. Pete sits down next to Lili on the couch, and she tells him the sort of story that the speaker in "One for My Baby" never gets around to telling:

> Competition. I guess my old man wanted me to sound like that. "Lil, some day you're gonna sing at the Met." He'd say to me, "You gotta practice, study hard day and night." So, in the daytime I worked in a factory, at night I'd study. . . . By the time I got good enough to sing *Madame Butterfly*, what do you know, I lost my voice.

While we never do learn how Lily lost her voice, the one she has, which in some ways is no voice at all, is a perfect instrument for the sort of torch songs she sings in *Road House*. It's literally a long way from singing *Madame Butterfly* at the Metropolitan Opera to Jefty's joint, but by the end of the film, having dispatched him with a shotgun, Lily has escaped Elsa's fate and is off with Pete to the Pacific Northwest where, unlike the narrator of "One for My Baby" ("This torch that I've found / Must be drowned / Or it soon might explode"), her torch can burn as brightly as her heart's desire.

6

The Big Number (Side B)

KILLING THEM SOFTLY

It's safe to say that the musical numbers one remembers most from classic—in this case, forties—noir are those in which a woman sings while backed by a combo or orchestra. Although there's something to be said for female performers who accompany themselves, whether on guitar (as Rita Hayworth does in *Gilda*) or piano (as Ida Lupino does in *Road House*), there's also something about a woman who's free to move while she sings, unencumbered by an instrument,

One way to frame this sort of performance would be to argue, as Laura Mulvey does in "Visual Pleasure and Narrative Cinema," that, freed of instrumentation, female performers can be better shown as spectacular objects of desire. Men look, so the argument goes, and women in all their corporeality are "to-be-looked at." In other words, male spectators, not unlike their ideal masculine counterparts within the diegesis, derive fetishistic and voyeuristic pleasure from contemplating the female form, even and especially its parts—say, a leg. (Consider, for example, the striking shot of Gilda's leg, stuck up into the air like a baton, as she dresses for the Carnival in Vidor's film.)

While there's clearly more than a grain of truth to the critique of the spectacular, stereotypical construction of women in forties noir, what does it mean if a woman is singing or dancing? Even if a woman is "only" singing, what does this act of performance say about her? Is it possible that the musical number is a dramatic site in film noir, a place where women "speak," as it were, with a certain discursive authority?[1]

The Crooner and the Black Blueswoman

Before I turn to two features that, like the Hayworth vehicle *Gilda*, constitute significant exceptions to the standard white female figuration of the "big number" in forties noir, I want to open with a film, *Bewitched* (1945), that provides another, audiovisual frame of sorts.

Written and directed by Arch Oboler who began in radio like Orson Welles and helmed the first 3-D picture, *Bwana Devil* (1952), *Bewitched* features neither a siren nor big number, but it does invoke what Eric Lott calls "whiteface dream work."[2] Joan Ellis—"young, pretty, alert"—has fled her parents' home after hearing voices and fainting at her engagement party to hometown boyfriend Bob. When she hears voices again at the zoo while visiting the tiger cage, she wanders the city alone at night pursued by her "evil" alter ago Karen, who keeps jabbering in her head, "Crazy crazy crazy." (The eerie sound effects were dubbed by M-G-M maestro Douglas Shearer, and Karen was voiced by noir staple Audrey Totter who appears in such forties noirs as *The Set-Up*, *High Wall*, *The Unsuspected*, and *Lady in the Lake*.)

Seeking sanctuary in a concert hall, Joan sits on the stairs leading up to the loggia where she listens to a white female vocalist, accompanied by a pianist, performing a faux-operatic version of "Nobody Knows the Trouble I've Seen," a spiritual covered in 1938 by Louis Armstrong with the Decca Mixed Choir: "Nobody knows the trouble I've seen / Nobody knows but Jesus / Nobody knows the trouble I've seen / Glory hallelujah." Although the high-angle shot of the singer standing in a circle of light on the darkened stage below is not from Joan's POV, the lyrics clearly reference her troubled existence.

The implicit connection between Joan's personal hell and the travails of African Americans is made even more explicit in the second number, "My Old Kentucky Home,"[3] the Stephen Foster standard performed here in its original, unexpurgated version: "The sun shines bright in the old Kentucky home / 'Tis summer, the darkies are gay." According to Krin Gabbard, black magic refers to the "enchanting effect that black music . . . [has] on movie characters more often than not when the characters onscreen are white."[4] But if it's true that "Nobody Knows the Trouble I've Seen" offers Joan a momentary stay against madness, "My Old Kentucky Home" and its sunny, bird-sung vistas are no match for the "dark" voices that assail her.

After the first two consolatory lines of the chorus for "My Old Kentucky Home"—"Weep no more, my lady / Oh, weep no more today"—the fleeting communion between Foster's song and Joan's fragile ego is superseded by the "call and response" between two voices, a childlike one that repeats in a rising, singsong cadence "Crazy, crazy, crazy" and a more "mature" one that first tells her to "go away," then, id-like, "You need a man." Not unlike Paul Raden in *Among the Living*, Joan, hands over her ears, rushes toward the exit. By the end of the film, she'll have murdered her hometown boyfriend with a pair of scissors.

Although Joan is arrested and sentenced to death, she's saved by a kindly psychoanalyst, Dr. Bergson (Edmund Gwenn), who convinces the governor to stay her execution on the grounds she's enslaved by another, completely different personality. The proof is quite persuasive: under hypnosis, Joan's two personalities materialize like ghosts and stand on either side of her slumped body until Bergson puts Karen and her dark, libidinal drives to sleep and reawakens the "normal, happy, young girl" locked inside. The doctor exhorts Joan, "You are free, free forever!" We, however, sense that this last-minute exorcism, like Foster's nostalgic vision of a "lost antebellum world,"[5] is as fantastical as the special audiovisual effects and that Joan's "troubles" are certain to return, sooner rather than later.

No unlike "My Old Kentucky Home" in *Bewitched*, the "sweet" romantic ballad performed by the white male big-band leader in *Moonrise* can be said to answer the "blues" associated with black music. That is to say, whereas Mose's song "Lonesome" in *Moonrise* acts as chorus and catalyst, commenting on Danny Hawkins's plight and encouraging him to come clean about his dark past, Ken Williams's (David Street's) rendition of "It Just Dawned on Me" projects a utopian scenario that contrasts with Danny's frequently tormented existence.

The "Moonrise" sequence begins after Danny, studying himself in a restroom mirror, notices the deaf-and-dumb boy, Billy Scripture, has found the pen-knife that Danny inadvertently left behind at the scene of the crime and is now standing right behind him with a compact mirror. Since Danny has just defended Billy, taking the compact mirror away from another young man who's been teasing him with it, the mirror-within-mirror shot reflects Danny's ultra-outsider status. When Danny returns to the club, the camera follows him from the band's slightly elevated point of view as, alone, he crosses the length of the dance floor. His sense of isolation is also reinforced by the fact that everyone else, with the exception of the musicians in the foreground, seems to be coupled up and dancing as well as by Ken's salutation, "Lost your girl, Danny?" Danny's social status, which has previously been alluded to (the banker's son Sykes tells him that Gilly Johnson is "out of his class"), is referenced when Ken asks him if he wants to join in a game of "bourbon and poker" after the dance, and Danny answers, "Not me, I can't afford that kind of poker."

Turning away from Danny, Ken starts to sing the first verse of William Lava and Harry Tobias's "Moonrise": "It just dawned on me / That there's magic in the moonrise." Danny disappears until midway through the second verse of the song ("A serenade of silver strings / From dreamy violins") when he abruptly cuts in on another, unidentified young man who's slow-dancing with Gilly. Although she chastises Danny for his rudeness ("You're not very courteous"), he forcefully takes the lead and continues dancing with her: "It just dawned on me / That life is filled with romance / Let's give love a chance." Gilly, looking at Danny as if for the very first time, asks, "What's come over you?" Danny doesn't answer, but as the music diminuendos and the camera tracks in to the couple for a classic medium two-shot, he tells her, "You're not dancing with anyone else tonight."

Given the song's self-reflexive lyrics and the "moony" couples who, facing the stage, appear to be more interested in listening than dancing, the above musical scenario would appear to be stereotypically romantic. In other words, the spectacle of a male vocalist as opposed to female one can be said to foreground Danny's point of audition: it's just dawned on Danny that even though Gilly's dancing with one young man and engaged to another, she's destined to be with him. Once the song ends, however, this high romanticism is shadowed by another, darker scenario, what one might call the romance of violence. After Gilly explains to Danny she only danced with him because he'd been drinking and, as a school teacher, she can't afford to fight in public, he tells her—again, brooking no argument—that she's leaving with him. When she tries to break away ("I'm certainly not!"), he threateningly adds, "Or I'll carry you out."

While the moonrise-inspired conclusion of Borzage's film retroactively codes Danny's aggressive behavior as romantic, it also reveals a troubling pattern of violence: Mose's anecdote about the tramp who raped the sheriff's daughter, his father's murder of the country doctor for failing to attend to his wife after she'd given birth to Danny, and Danny's own killing of

Sykes in self-defense, an act that is itself a belated response to the history of violence Jerry has perpetrated against him since childhood. From this vantage point, the high-romantic promise of "Moonrise"—"Two hearts will sing in harmony / Just like a symphony"—seems at best like a dream or, at worst, a delusion.

A similar dynamic or dialectic haunts *They Live by Night*, although the musical number in Nicholas Ray's film performs an overtly dystopian, disenchanting function, in the process exposing the heavy wages of fear. *They Live by Night* is distinguished by a striking use of sound effects, a "stylized echo of ordinary, everyday noises" such as door knocks and train whistles.[6] The aural originality of Ray's film is not limited, however, to these sonic elements since, according to Ray's biographer, it was only in putting the sound track together, supplementing the image track with an evocative world of song and music, that the first-time director "revealed his mastery."[7] For example, Woody Guthrie's "Going Down the Road Feeling Bad" can be heard on the radio in the getaway car after the Zelton robbery, and the film itself, not unlike a Hollywood musical, was originally named after a popular song, "Your Red Wagon." (The studio also strenuously objected to the film's other working title, *Thieves Like Us*, which Robert Altman later used for his 1974 version of the Edward Anderson novel.)

In fact, Ray had just finished directing *Beggar's Holiday* on Broadway and, reflecting on the experience, commented, "If you've done musicals on Broadway, and you go out on the road with eighteen songs, knowing you're going to come in with fourteen, you make your selection on the basis of whether the song advances the story or not."[8] Thus, unlike the excised dance-hall scene in which the New Orleans expression "your red wagon," meaning "it's your business," was originally first heard, the nightclub sequence where Marie Bryant performs the Richard Jones, Don Raye, and Gene de Paul song not only survived the final cut but represents, according to the director, the "climax of [Bowie and Keechie] being real people."[9]

This musical climax also builds on another, excised scene. In Ray's initial treatment, Bowie (Farley Granger), in the aftermath of the car accident in which his fate is sealed when his fingerprints are found on a gun, tells Keechie (Cathy O'Donnell) he has "all the blues rolled up in one," crooning: "I'm a stranger here / I'm a stranger everywhere / I would go home, but / I'm a stranger there." Bowie's blues, reflecting his utter estrangement from all those folks who live by day, is the absent musical pretext for Bryant's performance of "Your Red Wagon." In other words, the black female singer articulates what both Bowie and Keechie cannot say to each other or, if they are to continue as a couple, admit to themselves.

The immediate context of the song illustrates the lovers' desperate predicament. After being forced by a suspicious plumber to leave the sanctuary of the Lambert Inn, "clean away from everything except the sky and trees," Bowie and Keechie light out for the open road. Later, after staying overnight at a hotel, the female proprietor brings them sweet-potato pie in the morning and they decide to "make a day" of it with, as Keechie says, "music and all that—just like other people." Dressed in their Sunday best, Keechie in a gray-flannel suit, Bowie in a double-breasted one, they stroll through a park where people are boating and playing ball.

Cut to a "respectable," "brightly lit" nightclub where an all-black sextet (bass, drums, trumpet, trombone, piano, clarinet) is playing jazzed-up blues while Bowie and Keechie sit in the foreground, happy just to watch other people dancing.[10] A true innocent because he's grown up in prison, Bowie can no more understand why people might want to dance—"I think it's silly, switchin' around like that, gettin' all het up"—than he can understand them "pattin' around a ball." It's in this "innocent" context that Bryant makes her entrance: "Your business is your red wagon / What's in it is all your own / So don't load it up with trouble / 'Cause you draggin' it all alone." Bryant, still singing, steps down from the slightly elevated stage ("If you wanna play horses and blow your dough / Don't ya run to me if they don't show"), Bowie talks to Keechie about going to Mexico where they can live "like a couple of real people." Keechie, however, doesn't take him seriously. Having earlier kidded him about a Mexican girl he was so absorbed in watching that he forgot to light her cigarette, she thinks his mind's still on "Mexican girls."

At this point in the number—the cue is the "cigarette" exchange—Bryant directly addresses Bowie and Keechie, the lyrics of "Your Red Wagon" reiterating the film's "fire" motif (the couple first met when Bowie helped Keechie with the stove at her father's garage) and hinting that Bowie's dream of escaping to Mexico is just a dream to chase the blues away: "Now you finally learn / That you get burned / When you play with fire." Bryant approaches Bowie and Keechie's table for a tip, but when Keechie taps Bowie, a drunk crashes into their table—an ominous sign, like the knock on the door they've been warned about, that their time is up. Although Bryant says "No trouble," the damage has been done. The momentary refuge that the couple has found in this nightclub, listening to music just like other

Fig. 16. Lounge Time: Marie Bryant, tips in hand, singing "Your Red Wagon" to Bowie (Farley Granger) and Keechie (Cathy O'Donnell) in Nicholas Ray's *They Live by Night.*

people, is abruptly shattered like the Christmas ball Chickamaw (Howard Da Silva) breaks at their "country cabin retreat."[11]

As they hurriedly exit the club, Bowie and Keechie briefly split up when he goes to the men's room to buy some cigarettes for her. While the band continues to play in the background, a man in a dinner jacket recognizes him as "Bowie the Kid" and tells him he's got "about an hour, maybe less, to get out of town." A scuffle ensues and after taking Bowie's .45, the man points it at him, saying, "We don't want a lot of trigger-happy hillbillies around here. This is a nice cool town. Business is good." Whereas the fire imagery in *They Live by Night* has previously been connected with Bowie and Keechie's budding romance, it's associated here, as in the scene where Bowie, Chickamaw, and T-Dub (Jay C. Flippen) burn their getaway car, with their "hot," criminal status. Suddenly, Bryant can be heard singing again offscreen ("So just keep draggin' / Just keep draggin'") and, in another reversal, the man in the dinner jacket gives Bowie back his gun along with a pack of cigarettes: he's not the law, he just doesn't want "The Kid" heating up the town. The sequence ends on a dark, jazz-infused note with a straight cut to a shot of Bryant singing directly into the camera, her scatting of the last few bars of "Your Red Wagon" italicizing the song's message for these young lovers on the lam: it's *your* red wagon.

Bryant's performance of "Your Red Wagon" in *They Live by Night* is, in the context of forties noir, an exceptional one. It's not simply that, as with Lillian Randolph in *The Glass Key* and Dolores Parker in *House of Strangers*, a black woman has been cast in a crucial musical role but that the song itself, as in the Hollywood musical, is a full-length number and advances the story. Bowie and Keechie have been expelled from the paradise of everyday life and are desperately trying to act like ordinary people. However, because Bowie's exploits have been publicized on the radio and in the newspapers (to the bitter dismay of Chickamaw, who's been nicknamed "One-Eyed Mobley" by the press), even a nightclub during the day cannot offer them safe haven. The newly married couple's "red wagon" is now so top-heavy that no amount of running or dreaming will lighten the load. In fact, not unlike Paul and Millie Baxter in *When Strangers Marry*, Bowie and Keechie "have even less power and control over their lives than the black singer."[12] The good news, especially given how badly things will end, is that they don't know where they're going.

Fol-de-Rol

The performance in *They Live by Night* by Marie Bryant, whom Ray recruited from *Beggar's Holiday*, is the sort that most people associate with classic noir: a solo female vocalist backed by a band and playing to a nightclub audience. The difference, of course, is that the singer is black and that it's day, not night. Which is to say that the paradigmatic vocal performance in forties noir features a white female singer and occurs, true to the genre and the title of Ray's film, at night.

Because it's an iconic performance and features a white female vocalist accompanied by a small combo, a good place to begin is a film that is by all accounts a canonical noir, *The Big Sleep*. In Howard Hawks's film, Vivian Sternwood (played by Lauren Bacall) sings "And Her Tears Flowed Like Wine" at a gambling casino owned by mobster Eddie Mars while observed by private detective Philip Marlowe (Humphrey Bogart). Bacall had already made a considerable impression on audiences huskily singing "Am I Blue?" and "How Little We Know" with Hoagy Carmichael on piano in Hawks's *To Have and Have Not* (1944).[13] However, in *The Big Sleep*, her performance of Stan Kenton, Charles Lawrence, and Joe Greene's "And Her Tears Flowed Like Wine"—which is not, despite the conventional wisdom, dubbed—is not only a meta-performance (since it's meant to distract Marlowe) but advances a narrative that's as convoluted as any in classic noir.[14]

The song in fact occurs at a pivotal point in the action. Marlowe has apparently solved General Sternwood's problems: Arthur Geiger has been blackmailing the general with incriminating pictures of his wayward daughter, Carmen (Martha Vickers), but he's now dead, having been killed by Joe Brody. (Just don't ask who killed Owen Taylor.) Although Vivian tells Marlowe the case is "completely closed," Marlowe, playing a hunch, decides to visit Mars's club. As he walks up to a "rusticated ranch house,"[15] music can be heard inside. Checking his hat and coat, Marlowe tells a cigarette girl he's there to see Mars and, in one of the ongoing conceits of the film, she checks him out. (He catches her eye, as David Thomson pertly puts it, "as easily as a suit picking up fluff."[16])

While Marlowe wanders off to check out the bar where "men in flashy singing cowboy getup" and a "pair of young women in riding breeches" are circulating,[17] a woman is singing offscreen: "He was spending on the ponies / He was spending on the girls." (The first verse recollects Marlowe and Vivian's previous, seriously risqué repartee, set to a diegetic piano rendition of "I Guess I'll Have to Change My Plan," about "horse racing.") Marlowe's ears prick up and, turning on his heel, he goes to the other room where Vivian, her back to the camera, stands singing.

Slipping inside the door, Marlowe stands watching her, his back against a wall, smoke wafting around him. As Vivian continues to sing ("But when his wife said 'Sweetie, / What did you get for me?' "), the camera cuts to a two-shot with Marlowe in the background framed by the door and Vivian in the foreground surrounded by singing patrons and a trio of musicians (bass, guitar, and Stan Kenton on piano). Vivian waves hello to Marlowe and, as the chorus repeats the lyric ("Yes, her tears flowed like wine"), he salutes back. There's another exchange of verses ("She's a real sad tomato / She's a busted valentine"), then the chorus comes in behind Vivian on the line "Mama done told her" before she sings the "kicker": "That a man is darn unkind."

The last verse is the prompt for a musical routine. The cigarette girl reappears—where there's smoke, there's a cigarette girl—leaning in to tell

Fig. 17. Valentine: Italian lobby card of Vivian Sternwood (Lauren Bacall) singing "And Her Tears Flowed Like Wine" and Philip Marlowe (Humphrey Bogart) giving her the two-finger salute in Howard Hawks's *The Big Sleep*.

Marlowe that Mars is ready to see him. While the chorus and Vivian continue their call-and-response ("I'm a-telling you, mister / She was a sob sob sister"), the camera cuts away to Vivian who unabashedly looks the girl up and down. In the reverse shot, the cigarette girl, dressed in a tight sleeveless black outfit with a white collar and black bow-tie, puts her hand on her hip. Marlowe looks down at her body ("Lying on a pillow / Weeping like a willow"), then, nodding his head in approval, looks back at Vivian who nods in return: "My, oh my, how that baby could cry." Finally, after taking a sip from a patron's drink, Vivian nods again, sending Marlowe on his way before, in a reversal of the first refrain, she comes in behind the chorus: "Yes, and her tears flowed like wine."

In his BFI book on *The Big Sleep*, Thomson comments that it's a "gorgeous exchange, superbly timed and cut."[18] It's also, like the notorious racing exchange where Vivian wonders whether Marlowe's a "front-runner" or "comes from behind," rife with suggestion. Part of the scene's enormous appeal derives from the consonance between the song and the play of looks between Vivian and Marlowe. The song itself, which was a hit in 1944 for Anita O'Day and the Stan Kenton Band, is a paradox, albeit one familiar in popular music, with the tension coming from the counterpoint between the up-tempo music and downbeat lyrics. The implication is that unlike the "sob sob sister" in the song, Vivian has no use for the crying game: she's rough and ready, just like the guys.

Vivian's independence—she's no "busted valentine"—is also expressed in how she comannds the play of looks. Although she's initially the object of Marlowe's gaze, she initiates, even as she's singing, his frank appraisal of the cigarette girl's body. In other words, while she deflects Marlowe's gaze onto the cigarette girl, an act that mirrors her earlier attempt to evade his interrogation (What *does* Eddie Mars have on her?), she also arguably sexualizes the encounter. In this, she plays the femme fatale, mobilizing the discourse of sex to distract the private eye, using the music and lyrics to catch his ear in addition to turning his look back on itself, as if to say: *You want a cigarette girl, there's a cigarette girl.* Although it's not clear at this point in the narrative who Vivian is (Is she a femme fatale or comrade-in-arms?), it's clear she's no cigarette girl.

The opening and closing credit sequences of *The Big Sleep* are instructive here. In the opening credit sequence, Marlowe and Vivian are standing in silhouette and, after he lights her cigarette, they set their cigarettes down in a glass ashtray. This visual conceit is later fleshed out in the body of the film when Marlowe is bound but not gagged in Geiger's house and Vivian lights his cigarette for him. Since his hands are tied, she puts it in his mouth and, after he takes a drag, removes it. The sexual implications of this scene as well as the opening credit sequence are raveled at the very end of *The Big Sleep*. Marlowe is busy tying up the loose ends when Vivian interrupts him, "You've forgotten one thing—me." Playing along, Marlowe asks, "What's wrong with you?" and Vivian smartly replies, "Nothing you can't fix." Cut to two cigarettes sitting pretty in a glass ashtray.

As more than one critic has observed, Eddie Mars's nightclub in *The Big Sleep* is based on the Clover Club, "one of several elite gambling joints in Los Angeles" (that, not so incidentally, had a "large gay clientele").[19] Since nightclubs in classic noir run from "dank, darkly lit bars" to cafés and cabarets that are, like the self-made men who own them, citadels of "leisure, luxury, and self-indulgence,"[20] the "glee club" atmosphere of Mars's casino comments on both Vivian and its owner. While Vivian could be a co-ed, Mars, with his "easy manners, clean-shaven good looks, and slick-backed hair," looks as if he just stepped out of a "photograph of Oxford graduates at a class reunion."[21]

It probably goes without saying that not every nightclub or, for that matter, musical number in forties noir is quite so collegiate. For a prototypical locale and performance, one need look no further than *Scene of the Crime*, a little-known noir starring Van Johnson that was produced at M-G-M in 1949, a year in which "Metro" released a number of other, equally gritty noirs such as *Act of Violence* and *Border Incident*. To be sure, it may seem a "bit incongruous" that the film's star is Van Johnson, who appeared the same year opposite Judy Garland in M-G-M's *In the Good Old Summertime*, but this sort of anomaly was in fact "typical of the short-lived noir series produced at M-G-M during the Dore Schary years."[22]

In *Scene of the Crime*, as in Roy Rowland's later *Rogue Cop* (1954), the impeccable production values that epitomize the M-G-M look have been jettisoned for the "dark streets and back rooms of old warehouses."[23] The credit sequence, jump-started by André Previn's martial score, sets the scene. After an opening high-angle freeze frame of a gun lying next to body sprawled on a sidewalk, the camera comes alive, cutting to a policeman sticking a pencil into the barrel of a revolver. The ensuing montage, in which we watch LAPD lab technicians testing the gun by shooting it into a box, retrieving the bullet, then examining it under a microscope, is capped by a blowup of the bullet under magnification and, in a final semi-documentary flourish, a shot of the ballistic report from the "Scientific Investigative Division."

As this compact, *CSI*-style sequence suggests, *Scene of the Crime* is a police procedural: a street cop, Edward Monigan, has been gunned down outside a bookie joint by a man with a disfigured face and twisted left hand. However, since $1,000 has been found on his person, ex-partner Mike Conovan (Johnson) has been recruited to find out—as his superior, Captain Forster (Leon Ames), quips—"how a man assigned to crying babies got himself killed." The musical elements of the film come dramatically to the fore when Mike decides to cozy up to one of the suspect's mistresses, Lili (Gloria DeHaven), a "sizzler" with a "figure like champagne and a heart like the cork." (In addition to teaming with Johnson in *Two Girls and a Sailor* [1944], DeHaven appeared in a string of M-G-M musicals in the 1940s, including *Best Foot Forward* [1943], *Broadway Rhythm* [1944], *Step Lively* [1944], and *Summer Holiday* [1948].)

Mike has found out about Lili from a private eye who, specializing in matrimonial matters like Jake Gittes in *Chinatown*, has just taken a beating from yet another unhappy customer. "I'm no Humphrey Bogart," he laments, rubbing a brand-new shiner, "He gets slugged and he's ready for action. I get slugged and I'm ready for pickling." Determined to exonerate his former partner, Mike sets off for the Fol-de-Rol where "Mar-le-ne" (Jean Carter) —"famous," according to the marquee, for her "Dying Blond Swan" dance —is beginning her routine.

Sporting long white gloves, long bleached platinum-white hair, and a white stole wrapped around her shoulders, Mar-le-ne shakes and shimmies as the Joe Enley Quintet vamps in the background: "I'm a goody goody girl / And I like my gentlemen refined / If you never try to stop / Then you better get your brakes relined / You can see that I'm refined / And, my dear, that's all you're gonna see." The film quickly cuts away from Mar-le-ne when Mike glimpses Lili, but the catcalls and bump-and-grind music tell us everything we need to know about the Fol-de-Rol. Lili herself says that Mar-le-ne "builds them up" and Mike completes her thought, "Then you come in for the kill." While it's clear from Mike's dead-pan response that Lili does not so much get men off as off them, he nevertheless asks her to go to the movies with him where, he says, they'll hold hands and eat six-cent candy.

Since Mike's angle is to treat Lili like a lady in order to win her trust, he does just as he promises, taking her to the movies, holding her hand, and buying her six-cent candy. In fact, when he doesn't hit on her afterwards, she expresses genuine surprise, "Nobody ever took me to the movies to look at the movies." Later, still wearing her lipstick on his face, Mike tells his wife Gloria (Arlene Dahl) that Lili "seems OK," although Gloria's reply ("Nice innocent sizzler") momentarily punctures his good-girl fantasy.

Still confident he has Lili where he wants her, Mike returns to the Fol-de-Rol for the "kill"—to ask her straight up about Turk's role in the shooting death of Monigan. However, just as she's about to go on stage, Lili pleads with Mike not to watch her act. (Meanwhile, the MC can be heard offscreen priming the mostly male audience, "Here to entertain you the way you're here to be entertained.") Mike agrees to Lili's request (which he construes as just another sign of her inherent goodness), then she slips him the key to her apartment, "I wanna make talk with you." A past-master at the bait-and-switch, Lili here shows just how smart she is: even as her double entendre conveys that she wants to do more than "talk," that she's no "goody goody girl," she's simultaneously playing on Mike's desire to see her as "nice" and "innocent." (Gloria, of course, has no such illusions.) Mike, in turn, doesn't want to see Lili get up on stage and strip because such an act would violently conflict with his sentimental notion of who she is.

After entertaining the clientele at the Fol-de-Rol, Lili returns to her studio apartment to find Mike lying on the bed, a posture that belies his overt refusal of her offer of a cigarette and kiss ("I've had one"). In fact, it's only now, when he's manifestly compromised, that Lili admits she lied about knowing Turk, telling Mike that although she met him at the Fol-de-Rol over a "glass of phony champagne," she's no longer seeing him because "he laughs at the wrong things." (This enigmatic remark alludes to the private detective's earlier, passing answer to Mike's question about how Turk was getting his "laughs." Answer: he had three "giggles" on the side.)

Mike's ambivalence about being a cop—the girl-as-"giggle" conceit hints Mike might well be jealous, like Joe Warne of the composer Vincent in *Nocturne*, of Turk's sexual freedom—is compounded by the fact that Gloria, fearful about becoming a widow, desperately wants her husband to quit the police force. To this end, she arranges for Mike to meet Norrie, an influential, multi-millionaire ex-beau who's still enamored with her, at a swanky dinner club. Whereas the Fol-de-Rol is dark and cramped and the only "dancing" occurs on stage, the dinner-club is light and expansive as well-dressed couples slowly revolve to sweet big-band music. Gloria's hopeful mood is dashed, though, when Mike rejects Norrie's offer and "Glory," Mike's pet name for her, can only rue the day she became a cop's wife:

NORRIE: Got ya, hasn't he?
GLORIA: Like a song spinning around in my brain.
NORRIE: How do the lyrics go?
GLORIA: Every day I see him dead, and I die a little myself. The Glory blues.

The subsequent straight cut from the champagne and candlelit tables at the dinner club to a dim, nondescript office at police headquarters confirms Mike's preference for that other, darker world. The camera tilts down from a neon-splashed window to a bunch of cops with coffee cups listening to a tape recording of Turk bragging about Monigan's death to a drunk woman. Mike, who's completely disgusted, exits without a word, leaving his elder partner, Piper (John McIntire), to explain his action to rookie C. C. Gordon, "In every case there's a move you have to make and this is it."

Finally making a "move" (the word itself is suggestive), Mike forces Lili to listen to the tape recording so she'll be "sore" at Turk and set up his buddy, Lafe (William Haade). Mike apparently has Lili just where he wants her: "It worked good," she says, her voice cracking, "This is why you went after me. It worked swell. Because now you've really got me." Mike's now on the verge of solving Monigan's murder, but in a surprise twist he hands in his badge because Capt. Forster refuses to move on the case.

Circumstances, though, almost immediately force him to return when Piper, suffering from poor eyesight and facing that dreaded thing for a street cop, a desk job, is tipped by Lili and goes to meet the man with the "twisted left hand." Meanwhile, Mike's out dancing again at the swanky dinner club —without, it seems, a care in the world—when Gordon shows up with his badge to inform him that Piper's been killed. Only then does Mike realize just how badly Lili has duped him, the "eyesight" conceit underscoring his utter inability to see through her act. (In this specular context, the opening "microscopic" sequence takes on additional significance.) As in the song "Goody Goody Girl," Mike is the "refined gentleman" and, precisely because he's made the mistake of thinking Lili's "refined" too, he's been taken for the biggest ride of his life.

His eyes opened for the first time, Mike returns to the Fol-de-Rol where Lili, attired in long black gloves and a short spaghetti-strapped dress, is singing "I Call Myself a Lady" (composed, like "I'm a Goody Goody Girl," by Previn and William Katz) while doing her "Dance of Enchantment," and it's an eyeful: "I call myself a lady / I'm a belle with a delicate air / For my gown is a tatter / It really doesn't matter / Disregard the clothes I wear." After this "tease," the camera cuts to a low-angle wide shot as "Lady" Lili, her black-stockinged legs fully on display, begins to discard her clothes one provocative piece at a time: "My hat is yours / My gloves are yours / How generous we ladies are." In a revealing bit ("That's all I've got / For boys I'm not / A charity bazaar"), Lili concludes her number with a reverse strip, unrolling her shorts to form a skirt. Is she a bad or goody goody girl, a lady or *la belle dame sans merci*? Having sufficiently enchanted the audience, Lili steps down from the stage and, as the camera cuts from a shot of her leg to Mike's face (she hasn't seen him in the audience), he says with obvious disdain, "You look a little surprised."

In the car ride back to the police station (a scene that rhymes with an earlier one where she lies about agreeing to set up Turk), Mike's belated explanation—"All the time I was using you against Turk, Turk was using you against me"—is curtly undercut by Lili's matter-of-fact response, "It was a cinch." Even after she offers a tribute to the vicious Turk ("He'll kill anybody who touches me. He takes my breath away"), Mike continues to rationalize his blinkered vision, "When a girl has the looks you have, it's hard to see her." If, as Captain Forster says, one cop's drunk, every cop's a drunk, then Mike is blind, at least when it comes to "generous" women like Lili. In the final exchange between the two, Lili, who's hard as a champagne cork, asks Mike what they'll do to her and, after he answers "Throw the book," she writes the ending to their brief romance, "There's a crime on every page for me." Unlike Vivian Sternwood in *The Big Sleep*, whose problems can be fixed by Marlowe, Lili is incorrigible: she knows that when the law's done with her, the Dance of Enchantment will still be waiting for her at the Fol-de-Rol.

Valse Brillante

The featured musical performer in *Mildred Pierce* is also, like Lili, a femme fatale, but unlike the "B" girl in *Scene of the Crime*, she's the hyper-class-conscious daughter of the film's seriously upwardly mobile protagonist, Mildred. Veda, portrayed by Ann Blyth in a performance that's as compelling as Crawford's Academy Award–winning one, is the ultimate demon seed, the bad little other of the more than good enough mother. Veda, in fact, is "everything that Mildred is not: deceitful, promiscuous, greedy."[24] In Cain's novel, Mr. Treviso, who's been teaching Veda the fine art of opera singing, tells Mildred in his broken English that "Dees girl . . . is snake, is bitch, is coloratura."[25]

Although Veda does not pursue an operatic career in Curtiz's film, her performances, first on the piano, then on stage, reflect Treviso's observation that one of the things she lives for is "make a mother feel bad." (The other related thing is, of course, to "get back wit' all a rich pipple.") The baleful nature of the mother-daughter relationship in *Mildred Pierce* is apparent early on when Mildred, having vacated the beach house where ex-husband Monte Beragon has been shot and killed, walks down a pier contemplating suicide until a policeman stops her. Walking back down the pier, she passes a waterfront club owned by her ex-partner, Wally Fay (Jack Carson), who, seeing her outside in the rain, asks what she's doing "slumming" there, then invites her in for a drink on the house—"for free." The band's playing Harry Warren and Johnny Mercer's "You Must Have Been a Beautiful Baby" ("You must have been a beautiful baby / You must have been a wonderful child") and the music couldn't be more ironic since it's Veda, not Mildred, who has just killed Monte: Veda may have been a beautiful baby, but she's become her mother's worst nightmare.

Unlike Mildred, the audience sees Veda for the ungrateful, hopelessly spoiled daughter she is from the very beginning of the film—from, that is, the first voice-over-motivated flashback. When Mildred's first husband, Bert (Bruce Bennett), sees a new dress his wife has just purchased for Veda, he bitterly observes their daughter "has to have a piano and lessons and fancy dresses so she can sit up on a platform smirking her way through a piece any five-year-old can play." Later, after Mildred sends him packing, Veda and Kay (Jo Ann Marlowe) come home from school and Mildred, who's boxing a cake, asks Veda how her piano lesson went. Primly taking off her gloves, she replies, "I'm learning a new piece. *Valse brillante*," then adds, "That means 'brilliant waltz.' " (Veda is referring to Chopin's salon-influenced Waltz in E flat Major for solo piano, or *Grande valse brillante*.) Although Veda's still only a child, it's clear she enjoys shaming her mother, who's far too busy baking cakes to learn French, let alone play Chopin on the piano.

In the novel, Cain writes that Veda not only "employed the full French pronunciation" but "spoke in the clear, affected voice that one associates with stage children."[26] Veda appears on stage in *Mildred Pierce*, but it's not an opera house or concert hall and represents, in fact, the low ebb of her relationship with her mother. (The opening credit sequence with its Max Steiner–scored shot of crashing waves can be said to prefigure this moment.) Before this moment, though, we watch as Mildred begins her climb to the top, becoming a waitress, selling home-made pies, and eventually starting a chain of "fine" fried-chicken restaurants. While she sits at the kitchen table at the end of another grueling day entering figures into her bank book, a brief audiovisual passage epitomizes what she's willing to do for her daughters. Even as she's marking her progress in voice-over ("I was doing fine. I was able to afford an expensive singing teacher for Veda and a good dancing school for Kay"), a shot of Veda standing by a piano and hitting a high note is superimposed over a still shot of the bank book. (This shot is echoed later in Curtiz's film when, at the close of the opening night of Mildred's first restaurant, she sits down to rest her feet as Veda dances gaily with Monte to "Please Think of Me.") Mildred's only real worry: that one day Veda will find out—gasp!—she's a waitress.

The inevitable comes to pass when Mildred returns home one day to find their black maid Lottie (Butterfly McQueen) dressed in a uniform that up until now has been hidden in a closet.[27] Offscreen, Veda is at the piano, operatically singing Jimmy McHugh and Al Dubin's smash hit, "South American Way," from *Down Argentine Way* (1940) while Kay, a bandana wrapped around her head, is mimicking the Carmen Miranda number. (The bandana symbolically links Kay, who will tragically die at a young age, with Lottie.) Mildred sends Kay upstairs with Lottie to change before confronting Veda about the uniform, "What were you doing snooping around in my closet?" Although Mildred dominates the scene, compositionally speaking (she's standing over Veda who's sitting at the piano), Veda immediately puts her on the defensive—"My mother, a waitress." Mildred yanks her up from the piano bench, but Veda lets her have it right between the eyes, "Aren't the pies bad enough, did you have to degrade us?"

It's only later, after discovering Veda has feigned pregnancy in order to extort her fiancé (Wally, the bad surrogate father, gives the couple his blessing at his waterfront nightclub), that Mildred finally, reluctantly kicks her daughter out of the house. But despite the fact that Veda has slapped her mother in the face, knocking her against the staircase, Mildred cannot let her go. As soon as she returns from a Mexican vacation, Mildred tells her best friend, Ida (played by the sensible, wise-cracking Eve Arden), that she wants to take her daughter back. Although Ida is cool to the idea ("Personally, Veda's convinced me that alligators have the right idea: they eat their young"), the women's conversation is interrupted when Bert (who, according to Ida, has been "calling every day for the last month") asks Mildred out to dinner. (Since the two last communicated, he's become gainfully employed; he also tells Mildred that her previous rival, Mrs. Biederhof, is getting married.)

Bert proceeds to take his ex-wife to Wally's "joint," but when Mildred, who's dressed all in black as if she's going to a funeral, asks why he brought her there, he admits, "I thought it was a good idea at the time. Now I'm not so sure." We're sure as soon as we see Mildred's crestfallen face. Up on stage, Veda, attired in a skimpy, midriff-baring, South Seas outfit and backed by a trio, is singing and swaying to Lucien Denni and Roger Lewis's "The Oceana Roll": it's as if the dead Kay has suddenly been reborn in the adult, burlesque form of her older sister. If the tacky décor (see the parrot perched at the side of the stage) contrasts with Mildred's smart appearance (she's dressed in a matching fur coat and hat), the sailors sitting up front whistling at the line "Start that syncopated rhythm lovingly" show just how far Veda has fallen, at least in her mother's eyes. Gone forever, apparently, are Veda's (Or were they Mildred's?) dreams of becoming an opera singer or concert musician.

Now, instead of playing piano at Carnegie Hall or singing an aria at the

Fig. 18. "Sailors Beware": Veda Pierce (Ann Blyth) doing "The Oceana Roll" in Michael Curtiz's *Mildred Pierce*.

Met, Veda's "a-singin'" a "rag" at Wally's waterfront shack: "Each fish and worm / Begins to twist and squirm / The ship starts in a dip / And does a corkscrew turn / Now when the hammock starts a-swingin'." As Veda concludes her number, Bert apologizes to Mildred while Wally, unlit cigarette in hand, appears in a doorway, striking a match on a bamboo post. Mildred looks over and catches his eye, and if looks could kill, he'd be dead. The final indignity comes when Veda, waving a scarf, sings herself off stage and a sailor lets out a long, low wolf whistle in appreciation.

Mildred immediately goes backstage, as we know she must, to plead with her daughter to return home (a fellow female performer, seeing her, remarks, "I didn't know you had a mother"), telling Veda she's redecorated the house in Glendale and even bought a new piano for her. Emboldened by her first sweet taste of independence, Veda, however, is in no mood for compromise: "I want more than that. I want the kind of life that Monte taught me, and you can't give me. The way you want to live isn't good enough for me." Then, since she has to change for her next number, she sends her mother packing.

Ann Blyth's rollicking performance of "The Oceana Roll" in *Mildred Pierce* is something of a one-off in forties noir if only because her character, unlike Vivian Sternwood in *The Big Sleep* or Lili in *Scene of the Crime*, is not directly opposed to a male protagonist (the private detective Philip Marlowe in the former, police detective Mike Conovan in the latter). That is to say, Veda's performance is not addressed to a private dick or police detective but to her own mother, who's forced once again to confront the intractability of her daughter's desires, desires that at once mirror and mock her own. For Veda, the solution is simple: if her mother won't give her the privileged way of life she rightfully deserves, she'll act out on stage the mean, déclassé existence that Mildred has spent her whole life trying to escape.

Saint or Sinner?

Unlike Veda's ersatz South Pacific routine in *Mildred Pierce* and Elaine Gannin's "show" numbers in *Race Street*, a more classically seductive noir performance appears in *The Bribe* scripted by Marguerite Roberts. The town where all the action happens is Carlota—Rigby, the undercover federal agent who narrates the story, says it's the kind of place one goes for "whiskey and quinine"—and Ava Gardner's rendition of Nacio Herb Brown and William Katz's "Situation Wanted" in Leonard's film (Gardner was dubbed by Eileen Wilson) recollects one of the classic musical routines in film noir, Kitty Collins's siren song in *The Killers*. Rigby's situation is not in fact dissimilar to the Swede's in Siodmak's film. Just as the Swede (Burt Lancaster) meets Kitty (Gardner) when his boxing career is ending and his criminal one is beginning, Rigby—a "good cop," as his superior, Gibbs, calls him—has been sent by the American government to investigate a "war surplus racket" and soon finds himself at a major crossroads in his life.

Tug (John Hodiak) and Elizabeth Hintten (Gardner) are an American couple making big, undeclared money—Gibbs references the IRS at one point—off airplane motors disguised as "scrap." However, after Rigby becomes acquainted with Elizabeth, he begins to question his identity as a cop as well as the meaning of the word "honor" which, he muses, is "just a word with a fancy necktie on it": "Say it enough and it's not even a word anymore." In the opening voice-over sequence before the film flashes back, Rigby's about to send off a wire ("Have located evidence. Send chief of police to fly me to Carlota soon as storm allows for immediate raid") that will mean the end of both the case and his fast-developing relationship with Elizabeth.

Although this chapter and the following one focus on the "big number," there are any number of forties noirs (*Journey into Fear*, *Body and Soul*, *Calcutta* [1947]) in which a "canary" or siren, although peripheral to the main action, elucidates not only the intimate relation between the femme fatale and female musical performance but between the canary and male proprietor.

For example, in Jean Negulesco's *Nobody Lives Forever* (1946), the canary-as-siren in the person of Toni Blackburn (Faye Emerson) first earns, then betrays the trust of the antihero, Nick Blake (John Garfield). This complex dynamic also informs *Race Street* (1948), a late forties noir that, like Edwin L. Marin's *Nocturne*, reveals the director's flair for audiovisual spectacle. In *Race Street* (the reference is to horse racing, not "race music"), Dan Gannin (George Raft) is an independent bookie like Leo Morse in *Force of Evil*. Since a syndicate operated by Phil Dickson is starting to make waves, Dan is considering quitting the gambling business because, as his boyhood friend, Hal (Harry Morgan), reminds him, he's got a steady girl and a new club that's about to open.

In fact, the entertainment at the appropriately named Turf Club will be provided by Dan's sister, Elaine (Gale Robbins), and her song-and-dance partner, Mike Hadley, whom we see rehearsing Jimmy McHugh and Harold Adamson's "I Saw You First" at the beginning of the film. Mike quips, "If vaudeville ever comes back again, we'll kill it again," and Dan's girlfriend, Robbie Lawrence (Marilyn Maxwell), rejoins, "Well, I didn't keep it alive. Used to do a little hoofing myself." In addition to its contemporary evocation of the slow death of vaudeville, *Race Street* is memorable among forties noirs for its elaborate, visually dazzling staging of the first, full-length musical number.

The narrative pretext for "I'm in a Jam with Baby" is that Hal can't get out of the gambling racket, even though Dan offers him a "piece of the club," because Dan has looked after him ever since he injured his leg in a truck accident when they were playing ball as kids. The film cuts from Dan giving Hal his signature goodbye, "Stick with it," to a piano-accented exterior shot of the Turf Club followed by a straight cut to Elaine, posed against a cirrus-clouded background, singing the opening verse of "I'm in a Jam with Baby" to a restrained big-band sound: "Why am I in the sky / When I ought to be walking around on the ground / Down where I belong?"

Suddenly, Elaine begins to descend through a circular space in the false ceiling to a room packed with customers. Amazingly enough, even as Elaine sings suspended in mid-air, she continues to glide above the audience. After she catches the eye of a male customer sitting at the bar who tips his glass in recognition, the horns brashly come in and the song metamorphoses into a burlesque: "I'm in a jam with baby /

Baby won't talk to me / Looks like someone has been lying / I guess a friend of mine is trying / Trying to take my baby from me." Finally touching down, Elaine slips onto the dance floor where she sings the final verse of "I'm in a Jam with Baby": "I don't know this game of love too well / I don't know where I am / I only know I'm in a jam."

Although "I'm in a Jam with Baby"—composed by Ray Heindorf, Moe Gerome, and Ted Koehler—is a racy divertissement, the lyrics assume dramatic significance when Dan realizes that Hal hasn't shown up at the club, then goes to their apartment building (Dan and Hal live on separate floors in the same building) where he discovers his friend's body at the bottom of a steep staircase. Later, after Elaine and her fiancé Mike perform Gene de Paul's "Love That Boy" at the Turf Club with Dan and Robbie in attendance, another of Dan's childhood friends, Lieutenant Barney Runson (William Bendix), dances with Elaine so he can warn her about the "jam" Dan's in. That night, after dropping Robbie off, Dan is kidnapped by Dickson's henchmen and taken blindfolded to the big man, who flatly tells him that he's "either coming in or going out."

Dan already suspects his girlfriend Robbie is somehow involved (like Rip Murdock in *Dead Reckoning*, he smells her perfume right before he's sapped), although the film takes an unusual musical turn when Barney unexpectedly guides Dan to an old vaudeville house, The Golden Gate, for a cup of coffee. (Note the movie musical playing on the screen when they enter.) While Pop makes the coffee, Barney opens his scrapbook in order to show Dan the "only black mark on his record": a picture of Dickson, dressed in tails and top hat, posing with his blonde wife, Robbie.

Unlike Nick Blake in *Nobody Lives Forever* who lives for another day *and* gets the "good girl," Dan dies in a shootout with Dickson when he takes a bullet meant for Barney. Like Hal's fatal tumble, it's quite a fall. At the beginning of *Race Street*, Dan Gannin is living the high life, but he's brought down to the ground, to quote "I'm in a Jam with Baby," by former hoofer-turned-femme fatale Robbie Lawrence who, like Toni Blackburn, seems to confirm Barney's "moral" that all showgirls are "bad," a proposition that an early, classic film noir like *Murder, My Sweet* fully endorses. At the same time, Dan's close working relationship with and unconditional support for his sister Elaine presents a familial, non-proprietary model of canary and club owner that's rare in classic noir. Elaine's duet with Mike also proffers, as in the Hollywood musical, an optimistic, companionable view of marriage. In fact, in *Race Street*, Marin —aided by Roy Webb's score, J. Roy Hunt's camerawork, and former hoofer George Raft's quietly moving performance—showcases the backstage musical beating at the dark heart of film noir.

Still recovering after she's drugged him, he stands before his reflection in a rain-streaming window and acknowledges that, after all these years, maybe he's got a price too. Then he rips up the wire, wondering what changed him and, as his reflection in the window turns into Elizabeth's, asks himself, "Is she guilty or innocent?"

This dark interrogative situation, flush with desire, is the pretext for the beginning of the flashback where we watch as Rigby, having flown down to Carlota, goes to a nightclub called Pedro's looking for suspects. He dryly remarks in voice-over that the "entertainer" there is an "unknown quantity" until she appears, then he hastily corrects himself, "One look and you thought you knew the quality." What has Rigby seen that would make him change his mind so quickly? A flute sounds in the dark (a musical echo of the rumba sequence in *Criss Cross*) and, after the entertainer strikes a match and fires up a cigarette, the house lights come up on a woman standing next to a piano, a cigarette burning in one hand, her pale face and bare white shoulders offset by her dark hair and sleeveless black top.

After the "dark woman" sings the first few verses—"I placed an ad in a paper / You'll find it there today / The words reveal the way I feel"—the film cuts on the word "reveal" to a revealing full shot of Elizabeth Hintten dressed, not unlike Veda in *Mildred Pierce*, in a tight, midriff-baring top. Then, taking a drag on a cigarette, she sticks it in the mouth of a male patron and begins to tell her "story": "I'm not a saint or sinner / I walk the middle ground / I'll stay right on the level / Too smart to play around." Elizabeth coyly places a braceleted hand on a balustrade near another male patron's hand, but when the man reaches over to touch her, she withdraws it and dances away. Coupled with the sensual, languorous music (composed, in addition to the flute, of piano, bass, and drums), it's a real act of provocation, not least because, as we learn when Rigby goes to her dressing room after the show, she's completely devoted to her husband, a "lost cause" who suffers from a bad heart.

The situation becomes even more complicated when J. J. Bealer, whom Rigby has identified as a suspect (and who, as played by Charles Laughton, has a "physical and iconographic presence" as a heavy in noir[28]), makes his appearance. In fact, as Elizabeth continues to sing her way around the room, Bealer's "pie-shaped" figure can be seen trailing her. Hence the brief cutaway to Rigby watching intently from his table. The second cutaway to Rigby ("Getting tired of waiting / Getting kind of blue") introduces yet another level of complication. When Elizabeth pauses by a column, an eye-line match links the two until, still singing ("Love is all that matters"), she approaches Rigby's table where she meets his gaze.

If the spotlight on Rigby and Elizabeth's faces suggests an affair between them is a fait accompli, the bull-fighting tapestry on the back wall also suggests it will not be without consequences: "Now you know my story / What am I do? / Situation wanted with someone / But who?" The irony, of course, is that Rigby doesn't really know Elizabeth's story—doesn't, in fact, know anything about her, whether she's saint or sinner, guilty or innocent. He just knows he wants her. Accordingly, when Elizabeth turns away, Rigby turns around in his chair to watch her sing herself back to the stage where, after a flute player, basket in hand, leaps down to catch the shower of coins, she thanks him ("Gracias, señor") and looks him in the eye a final, tantalizing time.

Although Gardner's sultry performance of "Situation Wanted" is the only musical number in *The Bribe*, it colors our initial reading of her character, as does her costume—in particular, the jet-black, strap-lined top that reveals her midriff and shoulders—which codes her, even more so than Kitty's off-the-shoulder dress in *The Killers*, as a femme fatale. At the same time, her off-stage manner—she's brusque to the point of rudeness to Rigby—contradicts the highly sexualized persona on display in her musical routine. In this sense, Elizabeth Hintten's not unlike numerous femme fatales, complex, multifaceted women who are extremely difficult to read and, as such, the very embodiment of undecidability.

This ambiguity or duality is explicitly thematized in *The Bribe*. When Rigby goes to her dressing room after the show, music plays softly in the background and he bluntly asks her, "Tell me something. Which is real, the hot tonsils out there or the string music in here?" (Such are the conventions of the genre it somehow never occurs to Rigby that both sides of Elizabeth —the sexual and romantic, domestic and theatrical—may well be genuine.) This duality is also reflected in Elizabeth's change of costume. As she goes to a closet to change, she tells Rigby in no uncertain terms to leave, but when she reemerges and he's still there, she's wearing a simple top and pocket skirt, the sort of "daytime" clothes one imagines she dons to do her "housekeeping." Still later, when Bealer tells Rigby Elizabeth's involved in what Gibbs calls the "graft of public assets" because her husband's boat is "registered in her name," Rigby repeats the simple, mutually exclusive opposition that fuels his initial, conflicted voice-over, "Guilty or innocent? Nothing in between."

This oppositional logic drives the lead characters' behavior until Rigby, even though he realizes Elizabeth may be involved in her husband's racket, decides to sell out, choosing desire over duty: "I never knew a crooked road could look so straight." The way is still crooked, however, not simply because Elizabeth has agreed to Bealer's plan to drug Rigby, but because her seemingly unforgivable act of betrayal is itself the consequence of another, ulterior—and, in the context, understandable—motive: she doesn't want her husband, who's heart-sick in both senses of the word, to die in prison. (As in *The Crooked Way*, the war is crucial to Tug and Elizabeth's backstory: her husband's alcoholism, she explains to Rigby at one point, is the result of flying one too many missions. And as Rigby himself acknowledges, "A lot of those kids had nerves—with reason.") Consequently, it's only after her husband has been murdered, smothered in bed by the mercenary ringleader Carwood (Vincent Price), that Elizabeth is free to commit herself to Rigby and reveal her true motivations, a revelation that anticipates his later, ad hoc resignation. (In a climax set during the fireworks display for the Fiesta de Carlota, Rigby corners Carwood, but when the "crook" tells the "cop" he has no jurisdiction there, Rigby resigns on the spot in order to arrest and eventually, when Carwood resists, shoot and kill him.)

Rigby appears to emerge victorious at the end of *The Bribe*, but not unlike Mike Conovan in *Scene of the Crime*, he's narrating—according to Robert Porfirio in his entry in *Film Noir*—from the "noir position of defeat and betrayal."[29] Or is he? Since the film's dénouement occurs *after* Rigby's voice-over flashback, it's entirely possible that his moral compass up to this point has been too schematic—in other words, that *before* meeting Elizabeth, Rigby couldn't function effectively in the complicated, postwar world because he was merely a "good cop." As for the dark object of his desire, Elizabeth Hintten is—to sample the music of the period—simultaneously "hot" *and* "sweet." Just as her stage act is no act (she's neither saint nor sinner), so Rigby is a "bad cop" (but all the better for being so). According to this crooked logic, *The Bribe* is a film gris, eschewing "mono," black-and-white scenarios for complex, stereophonic shades of gray.

Cinderella with a Husky Voice

Like Ava Gardner and Lauren Bacall, Lizabeth Scott is one of the most iconic female musical performers in forties noir. Her breakthrough appearance as

Toni Marachek in *The Strange Love of Martha Ivers* initially established her as a "good-bad girl," a young woman in trouble with the law but, as Eddie Heyman and Miklós Rózsa's "Strange Love" underscores,[30] ultimately sweet. However, her role as Coral Chandler opposite Humphrey Bogart in *Dead Reckoning*, produced the same year she made *Variety Girl* (1947), codified her as a classic siren à la Kitty Collins in *The Killers*.

Although this coding remains problematic even within the restricted genre of film noir (the ultra femme fatale of *Too Late for Tears* [1949] can be said to be countered by the "good-bad" girls of *Desert Fury* [1947] and, more importantly, *Pitfall* [1948]), Scott's role in *Dead Reckoning* can nevertheless be seen as a "composite of various star-images of the period."[31] It's not just that Scott replaced Rita Hayworth in *Dead Reckoning* (after *Gilda*, Hayworth was assigned by Harry Cohn to make *The Lady from Shanghai* instead); Columbia also "capitalized on certain similarities between Scott and Bacall."[32] In fact, Hal Wallis regarded Scott as a "direct replacement" for "The Voice," an ill-conceived strategy that led to his heavy-handed moniker for her, "The Threat."[33] Despite the studio's unsuccessful attempt to make Scott into a simulacrum of Bacall, she's not without her charms. For example, her performance as Coral Chandler in *Dead Reckoning* brings out something in Bogart's character that remains occluded in his roles with Bacall (from *To Have and Have Not* to *Key Largo*), isolating a certain psychic volatility characteristic of the "tough loner," the man who knows too much.

The opening of *Dead Reckoning* institutes, as the title betokens, a fatal and fateful itinerary. After Johnny Drake skips out on Rip Murdock (Bogart) on their way to D.C. to be decorated (Johnny doesn't want his photo to be taken because of something in his past), Rip travels to a town "he's never heard of," Gulf City, to contact Johnny's girlfriend, Coral Chandler. Unable to get any news on the radio at his hotel, he accidentally changes it to the police frequency and, while lying in bed, hears a disturbing report: "There's a burned sedan in the ravine. Body in it charred beyond identification. Send morgue wagon." Later, at the morgue, Rip meets a homicide detective who shows him a body "crisp as bacon" that even "his own mother wouldn't know."

Devastated, Rip returns to his hotel room where he stands before an open window and reflects in voice-over on his loss, "I remembered him in Berlin, crazy song he always sang. I used to say, 'You drive me nuts with it.' Yeah, I used to say to him. . . . Let's just say I remember Johnny laughing, tough, and lonesome. Let's just say that." As in the brutal "song-and-dance" routine in which Krause beats up Rip to the sound of big-band music on the radio, the homoerotic undercurrents of Rip and Johnny's relationship are suggested by Rip's overtly romantic remembrance of his paratrooper buddy's "crazy singing." Thus, the paradox of the morgue scene, which graphically reinscribes Johnny's body when he was still alive—for example, at the very beginning of the film when, naked from the waist up, he's washing himself in the train compartment in full view of Rip.[34]

Determined now more than ever to locate the woman who sang that "crazy song," Rip goes to the Sanctuary Club, a plush nightclub complete with white tuxedoed waiters and an Old South, *Gone with the Wind*–style mural with the requisite showboats and palatial, Greek Revival architecture. While the ambiance is Southern Comfort, the orchestra is playing an instrumental version of "Amado Mio" (a Latin number that's also featured in *Gilda*). Rip's trying to glean some information from the bartender (whose dead body he'll soon be saddled with) when a woman starts to speak offscreen. As the camera slowly pans up her bare leg (revealed by the slit in her dress) to her lap (where she takes a cigarette from a purse) to, finally, her profiled face, a hand enters from offscreen to light her cigarette and Rip cracks, "Cinderella with a husky voice."

It's Johnny's girl, Coral Chandler, and once Rip has parried her questions ("Where have we met?") with more japery ("In another's guy's dream"), he begins to interrogate her in earnest, "You still haven't told me whether you sing that song he likes. You remember it, don't you?" It's then that Krause intercedes on her behalf, inadvertently answering Rip's question, "Boss said to ask you as a special favor. Will you sing that song you made the big hit with when you were with the show here?" Although Rip appears to be calm and collected, he suddenly unburdens himself in voice-over, "I hated every part of her. I couldn't figure out yet. I wanted to see her the way Johnny had. I wanted to hear that song of hers with Johnny's ears. Maybe she was all right and maybe Christmas comes in July, but I didn't believe it." Rip is, to say the least, ambivalent about Coral: on one hand, he hates her because he thinks she may have been involved in Johnny's death; on the other hand, he clearly wants to see and hear her just like his dead buddy did. And, as Ballin Mundson wickedly observes in *Gilda*, "hate can be a very exciting emotion."

After Rip baits Coral again, asking her if she's seen Johnny ("I saw him"), the lights go down, there's a brief fanfare, and the bandleader announces a "special treat": "As a great favor, the little lady who not so long ago was our

Fig. 19. "Custard": Coral Chandler (Lizabeth Scott) singing "Either It's Love or It Isn't" in *Dead Reckoning*.

own star attraction has agreed to give us once again the song she made the sensation of the South." The band starts into a lush, string-embellished rendition of Allan Roberts and Doris Fisher's "Either It's Love or It Isn't," the camera cutting to Coral still in her seat illuminated by a single spotlight, Rip sitting across from her pensive in the darkness: "Either it's love or it isn't / You can't compromise / Either it's real or it isn't / There's no otherwise." (As in *I Walk Alone*, Scott was dubbed by Trudy Stevens.)

Coral stands up and strolls toward the center of the dance floor while Rip continues to sit in the dark, eyes downcast, fingering his drink. Now that he can finally see and hear her, he somehow doesn't want to. Is he thinking of Johnny or is he afraid that, listening to Coral sing her siren song, he'll fall for her too? After a wide, brightly lit view of Coral singing to a male customer ("Either you're true or you aren't / There's no in between"), the film cuts to a low-key, dramatic shot of her with her hands on her hips ("If you've been lied to by someone / You'll know what I mean"), then to Krause twisting the arm of the bartender who's just agreed to meet Rip to give him the letter that Johnny left for him.

Coral returns to the table where Rip ruefully acknowledges, "I see what

Johnny meant." The band slips into an instrumental version of "Either It's Love or It's Isn't" and, as couples get up to dance, Rip—spurred by Coral—reminisces about his relation with Johnny:

> CORAL: You and Johnny, you were together all the time, weren't you?
> RIP: We fought together, two-man team.
> CORAL: And spent all your leaves together, London, Paris, Rome.
> RIP: Me with a gal always, Johnny without one, just a picture of you in his eyes.

However, after Coral inquires one too many times about Johnny, Rip asks her to dance while disclosing his motives in voice-over, "I wanted her in my arms when I told her. My right hand on her spine would feel the shock if there was any." As the two turn in circles on the dance floor, Rip continues to parry Coral with questions ("He used to call you Dusty, it was sort of a love name between the two of you, wasn't it?") before "slugging" her: "In a slab in the morgue burned to a crisp." Coral passes the test, her body turning "soft as custard" in Rip's arms, though he remains incredulous, thinking, "She had to know something."

Rip eventually figures out who's responsible for Johnny's death—Martinelli pulled the trigger of Coral's gun—but it's not until she accidentally shoots her secret husband with a bullet with Rip's name on it that he's able to answer the riddle of Coral Chandler, a "problem in algebra" Johnny the college professor couldn't solve. (Rip joking to Johnny on the train, "Say, when you get on again as a professor at some college and I'm back running my cabs in St. Louis, send me up a problem in algebra once in a while.") For Rip, the answer to the question about Coral is simple—she's bad as they come—a judgment that's confirmed when, as he's driving her to the police station, she threatens to shoot him and, in order to stop her, he smashes the car into a telephone pole.

Since Coral doesn't think twice about shooting Rip even though she claims she loves him, it's not surprising that Andrew Spicer calls her the "archetypal siren."[35] However, if Coral is clearly a torch singer with the accent on "torch,"[36] the ambiguity surrounding her status as a femme fatale manifests itself in her performance of "Either It's Love or It Isn't." While the song's lyrics insist "there's no in between," the film's narrative, like *The Bribe*'s, suggests "otherwise." Thus, numerous men die, whether directly or indirectly, because of Coral (Johnny, Chandler, Martinelli), but—unlike, say, Jeff Bailey in *Out of the Past*—Rip survives the car crash. More importantly, Coral herself survives long enough to be redeemed by Rip.

Given this last-minute transubstantiation, Coral's performance of "Either It's Love or It Isn't" sheds both light and heat on the film's insistent reiteration of hard-boiled masculinity. Johnny died in a fiery car "accident," so the immediate context—Coral's driving and she's just let her hair down—is noteworthy:

> RIP: I've been thinking. Women ought to come capsule-size, about four inches high. When a man goes out of an evening, he just puts her in his pocket and takes her along with him and that way he knows exactly where she is. He gets to his favorite restaurant, he puts her on the table and lets her run around among the coffee cups while he swaps a few lies with his pals.
>
> CORAL: Why?
>
> RIP: Without danger of interruption. And when it comes to that time of the evening when he wants her full-sized and beautiful, he just waves his hand and there she is—full-size.

I don't think it's too much to submit (to invoke one of the seminal sci-fi films of the fifties) that *Dead Reckoning* is all about the incredible shrinking woman. For Rip, this fantasy is the solution to any woman who asks "too many questions": you simply shrink her down to size, then slip her into your pocket so you and your "pals" can get on with your "lies."

The importance of this fantasmatic scenario in the context of Coral Chandler's character is that it retroactively reframes her performance of "Either It's Love or It Isn't." It's not simply that her singing interrupts Rip's "sadistic" line of questioning or even that, by standing up, she refuses to be reduced to the terms of his calculus; rather, the song self-reflexively poses one of the fundamental questions of film noir: Is she or isn't she? In other words, is she a "good girl" or a "bad girl"? Although in the final analysis Coral Chandler is arguably a "good-bad girl," John Cromwell's film, unlike *The Bribe*, can only really answer this question by turning her into one of the guys, "Mike," thereby reducing her very being to a zero. In fact, in *Dead Reckoning*, the elision of femininity is an elemental operation. Which is to say, it's not algebra, it's simple math.

7

The Big Number (A Side)

SIREN CITY

Six Songs an Evening

Unlike Coral Chandler, who's responsible for the deaths of both her husbands, Nora Prentiss (Ann Sheridan) in Vincent Sherman's 1947 film of the same name is selflessly devoted to her husband to the bitter end. (In this, her character's estimable, albeit very nearly masochistic, commitment to her spouse, like Elizabeth Hintten's in *The Bribe*, no doubt allayed male postwar fears about marital infidelity and female promiscuity.) If one difference between *Nora Prentiss* and *Dead Reckoning* is that the former film, like *Gilda*, revolves around a woman who lives to sing another day, the fact that Nora and Coral perform their songs while backed by an orchestra indicates that, unlike Veda in *Mildred Pierce*, they enjoy a certain level of professional success. (Ann Sheridan, the "Oomph Girl," had appeared in numerous musicals in the ten-year period from the 1934 *Murder at the Vanities* to *Shine on Harvest Moon* in 1944.) Certainly, one cannot imagine either Nora or Coral spending her downtime, as Elizabeth Hintten claims she does, doing housework. It's therefore surprising when Nora assumes this domestic persona early in the film, although it's plainly coded as a performance.

Richard Talbot (Kent Smith) is a successful San Francisco doctor who, according to one synopsis, "leads an unsatisfying and ordinary life with his wife and two children."[1] It might be more accurate to say, however, that

Talbot's ordinary life is relatively satisfying until he meets Nora after she's hit by a car outside his office where he professionally attends to her knee. Identifying herself to a street cop as a nightclub singer (he translates this to "entertainer"), Nora tells the good doctor she watches him come and go every day from her apartment (Talbot, it's important to note, is initially the object of *Nora's* gaze) and sets her watch by him. After Talbot applies a bandage ("That doesn't look bad"), Nora, her leg crooked like a pin-up's, asks "The bandage or the leg?" (she later apologizes for being "fresh") then, rejuvenated by a drink and cigarette, exclaims, "Feel like a new man."

Things take a romantic turn when Nora goes back to the doctor's office to see if she can return to work and Talbot, who's been repeatedly rebuffed by his wife, asks about the nightclub where she sings. Her response—"If it's food you want, stay away. But the singing's good, if it's singing you want"—is suggestive both because it bespeaks self-confidence (Nora knows she's a good singer) and because it simultaneously recognizes Talbot's tentative feelings for her and sets limits, at least for the moment, on what she's willing to offer him (singing, not sex).

The ensuing night shot of the waterfront outside Dinardo's club is alive with the sound of tugboats and its bustle contrasts with the earlier schedule-bound scenes set at the doctor's house. Inside, a trio of lettermen introduces Nora who, isolated by a spotlight as she sits at the bar holding a flower and backed by a big band, recites the first, extravagantly deprecatory verse of Moe Jerome, Jack Scholl, and Eddie Cherkose's "Would You Like a Souvenir?": "How can I make history / When no one's ever heard of me / I've never done a thing that should be noticed / No one ever fought for me."

After depositing the flower with the bartender, Nora, like Elizabeth Hintten in *The Bribe*, starts to make her way around the room, pausing at a table to return a cigarette case to its male owner and ruffling another man's hair as she continues to sing: "Would you like a souvenir / Some memento / That will always keep our dreams in touch? / Darling, it means so much." When Nora spots Talbot sitting at a table, she sings her way over to him, then sets her elbows on the top of a chair ("If your conscience hurts / Don't let it / I'm a get it / While it's here") before returning to the bar where, concluding her routine, she picks up the flower, "You'll be making no mistake if you take a souvenir."

As the music segues into a piano-bar version of "Would You Like a Souvenir?" Nora returns to Talbot's table and remarks, "I can't help wondering what a married man with a strict routine is doing in a place like this."

Fig. 20. That's Entertainment: Nora Prentiss (Ann Sheridan) performing "Would You Like a Souvenir?" in Vincent Sherman's *Nora Prentiss*.

Talbot says his wife's out of town, but Nora immediately sets him straight, "I may not have been handled with care, but I'm not shopworn." Although Talbot apologizes and stands up to leave, Nora, realizing she's overreacted, apologizes in turn and asks him to stay. In a key exchange, Phil Dinardo (Robert Alda), the nightclub owner and an intimate of Nora's, comes over to the couple's table and she introduces Talbot as "Robert Thompson." (The musical cue is Jimmy Van Heusen's "Deep in a Dream.") When Dinardo leaves, Talbot tells her she didn't have to cover for him, but Nora explains "In a place like this, names aren't important," a comment that, given her earlier characterization of Dinardo's, suggests she's ambivalent about her life there as an "entertainer." This is confirmed in another key exchange after Talbot tells her she doesn't belong there and Nora responds, "The next thing to ask is how did I get into this kind of life." The real question, of course, is where does Nora belong if not singing in a nightclub like Dinardo's?

Suddenly, the orchestra begins to play an up-tempo version of Jerome and Scholl's "Who Cares What People Say?" and Nora once again takes the lead, asking Talbot if he wants to dance. As Dinardo watches thoughtfully from the sidelines (where he'll remain until the end of the film), Nora and

Talbot join the dancing couples and, when the doctor puts his arms around her, she momentarily breaks into song: "As long as he desires his arms about me / Who cares what people say?" It's an extraordinary moment for both of them since if Talbot is "off schedule" for once, Nora has finally met a man who sees something in her besides her obvious physical charms. (As she later tells him, most men she meets are "amateur wrestlers looking for a partner.") Moreover, the fact that Nora's singing while she's dancing with Talbot can be said to momentarily marry her two selves: the career woman who works as an entertainer and the other woman who dreams of another, different—perhaps better—life. The irony is that if Talbot already has the bourgeois life Nora dreams of, Nora herself enjoys the sort of fast life the doctor appears to be experiencing for the very first time.

Both Nora's dream of domesticity and Talbot's desire for her are actively fanned when she goes off with him to his cabin in the woods. We've earlier seen him propose just such a getaway to his wife only to be flatly refused due to other, more pressing social engagements. (In *Nora Prentiss*, Mrs. Talbot is the very embodiment of carceral time, which she gets, as her husband reminds her, from her doctor-father.) While Nora and Talbot are not on the lam like the young lovers in *They Live by Night*, nature is a refuge for them just as it is for Bowie and Keechie in Ray's film, a place where they can explore their hidden, repressed selves. Talbot acknowledges this utopian aspect when he announces upon entering the cabin, "I haven't been here in a long time," and Nora expresses her own secret, nurturing side when she notes all the dust, "So much you can plant flowers in it." (The botanical reference refashions the "souvenir" that she uses as a prop in her nightclub routine, in addition to associating her, not unlike Ruth Berent in *Leave Her to Heaven*, with the natural order of things.)

In a gesture that surprises Talbot but not the audience, Nora takes off her overcoat (she's now wearing a striped wool sweater and *below*-the-knee wool skirt) and cheerfully announces, "We can get it cleaned in no time." Although Nora's enthusiasm suggests she doesn't spend much time actually doing housework, this enthusiasm also points up just how different it is from the sort of work she does for a living. However, the subsequent straight cut from Nora ordering Talbot to get to work ("Yes, M'am") to a roaring fire—a fire from which Nora plucks a twig to light a cigarette—subtly changes the tenor of the scene. As Nora reclines on a pillow, Talbot sits at a piano playing Chopin's *Berceuse* in "B flat Minor" or, as he corrects her, "D flat Major." The fact that the Chopin is a "lullaby" or "cradle song" reflects Talbot's paternal character. The "serious" (his word) nature of the music also underscores the increasing seriousness of their relationship as well as the utter disparity between their worlds: the quiet, orderly life of a physician as opposed to the noisy, irregular life of an "entertainer." In fact, Nora, reflecting on this idyllic scenario and obviously day-dreaming, confesses—not without sadness (and as the minor-key score sneaks in)—that it's a "little different from most of [her] evenings."

Picking up on the pathos in her voice, Talbot comes over and sits down next to her, then asks the ultimate question (one that Freud himself, at least when it came to women, couldn't answer), "What do you want?" Dinardo is moving to New York and wants her to accompany him (Nora once dreamed of being "sent" to New York or Hollywood), but she insists that's not what she wants. Then, after she observes without regret that "dreams last only so long," she preemptively rejects Talbot's pity and, in one of the most memorable passages in the film, forcefully affirms who she is, "I like me just the way I am. Nora Prentiss. Six songs an evening with an occasional drink with the better customers."

Later, Nora and Talbot are about to return to the city when a kiss—appropriately enough, on the threshold—seals their romance. The subsequent "happy" montage—Talbot buying flowers, the couple dancing intimately in a club—quickly yields, however, to the inevitable "unhappy" scenario of the doctor, enveloped in Venetian-blind shadows, returning home in the dead of night to his sleeping wife. If this plot turn is the stuff of melodrama, the desperate, on-the-spot resolution that Talbot devises is noirish as they come. Unable to tell his wife he wants a divorce (Nora's already decided it would be best for both of them if she followed Dinardo to New York), he assumes the identity of a man with a heart ailment who accidentally dies in his office one night. (In one of those coincidences on which many a classic noir turns [see, for example, *Hollow Triumph*], Talbot bears a striking resemblance to the dead man and, in yet another classic twist, he puts the corpse in a car and pushes it off a pier.)

In New York, the once well-respected doctor is so fearful of being recognized in public that he becomes a virtual shut-in while Nora, who's not privy to his secret, plays records and reads the books he compulsively brings her like flowers. ("If this keeps up," she wanly jokes at one point, "I'll get a liberal education.") Finally, after months of being sequestered in separate apartments, Nora voices her desire to be married and have a real home, "like other people." In the meantime, they go to Dinardo's new club, The

Sea Gull Café, in order to "hear some music" ("Who Cares What People Say?" is playing when they enter) and the next thing you know, Nora's back where she began, singing for her supper or, more to the point, *their* supper since the fugitive Talbot will never again be able to practice as a doctor.

Dressed all in black and standing motionless like Jackie Lamont in *Christmas Holiday*, Nora reprises "Who Cares What People Say?," which she danced to with Talbot in happier times and which now is less a proclamation of their love than an elegy to it: "We've built our dreams too high / Why should we let them all come tumbling down / I know that he and I / Will keep our love alive / Though we're the talk of the town." On this, the final verse of the song, the camera pulls back from a shot of Nora singing on the verge of tears, then cuts to Talbot standing, like Nora earlier, at an open window. The dissolve to Ed Sullivan's "Little Old New York" column ("Nora Prentiss, Phil Dinardo's star warbler, is catching on") completes the cycle: since Nora's too busy rehearsing for a new show to take her husband's phone call, Talbot can only sit by the phone, unkempt as a bum, and fume.

The conclusion of *Nora Prentiss* is as fantastic in its own way as Talbot's earlier adoption of a dead man's identity. After he attacks Dinardo at his club for giving Nora a bracelet, he manages to escape in the club-owner's car only to end up in a flaming wreck that leaves his face severely disfigured. Although there appears to be a silver lining when the corrective plastic surgery promises à la *Dark Passage* to give him a new identity, the police arrest him for murdering himself. As he says matter-of-factly to Nora while in prison awaiting execution, "I killed Robert Talbot." In a final twist, Talbot decides to go quietly to his death for the sake of his wife and children, making Nora promise she'll keep his secret. The film ends on a somber note with a high shot of Nora walking away from the courthouse in the darkness, Dinardo trailing her like a shadow. Unlike the dénouement of *The Man I Love* in which Petey (Ida Lupino) strides toward the camera, smiling through the tears, Nora, her dream of being a doctor's wife dashed, is fated to return to her life as an "entertainer," singing six songs an evening and, on a good night, having a drink with the better customers.

Bait and Switch

In *This Gun for Hire*, a film that Borde and Chaumeton rightly view as central to the "formation of the noir style," Ellen Graham—played by "V-bomb"

Veronica Lake—is a professional female entertainer.[2] While she's unlike Nora Prentiss in that she adopts various personae—"faithful fiancée, undercover agent, entertainer, confidant"—in the course of Tuttle's film, her character is similar to various "mysterious undercover female operatives" in "spy crime thrillers" of the period who were "multifaceted career women."[3] Reflecting the massive and momentous entry of women into the war-time workforce, Ellen not only "Dons Boy's Garb" (to quote the pressbook) but is working, unbeknownst to her police detective fiancé, Michael Crane (Robert Preston), on behalf of the United States government to bust a domestic spy ring masterminded by Alvin Brewster.

The other villainous male figure in *This Gun for Hire* is Willard Gates (Laird Cregar), an "overweight, unctuous epicure"[4] who first has sexual, then murderous designs on Ellen. However, unlike Lily in *Road House* and Gilda in Vidor's film (two film noirs in which a nightclub owner directly threatens the female entertainer's life), Ellen, to quote Kay Lawrence in *I Walk Alone*, has the "right angle" on him. Although we're not in on the secret at the beginning of Tuttle's film and are therefore as unwitting as Gates, we do know that the "fat wolf" is a gourmand (he pops peppermints) and fancies himself a ladies' man. For example, at a restaurant where he pays off Philip Raven (Alan Ladd) in ten-dollar bills for eliminating a blackmailer and his mistress, he roughly grabs a waitress by the wrist when she tries to take away his dessert before he's finished. If Gates's reply ("I'm an expert") to the waitress's comment that he reads palms sets him up as the opposite of the abstemious Raven for whom cats are preferable to women, Gates's admission that one of his vices is "backing leg shows" suggests he's a "perfect sucker," as he later describes himself to Ellen, for her legerdemain.

After Gates complains to the police about Raven, thus betraying his duplicity (he marked the ten-dollar bills), the film cuts to a rehearsal hall where he's reviewing acts for his nightspot, The Neptune Club. Gates is singularly unimpressed by the first act, a man using a whip to snip the end off a cigarette stuck in a female assistant's mouth (a trick that foreshadows a similar stunt in *Gun Crazy*), but when the promoter announces "This is the girl" and the orchestra begins to play Frank Loesser and Jacques Press's "Now You See It, Now You Don't," he's all ears and eyes.

Cut to a woman's white-gloved hand extended from behind a bare white column. After one egg, then another materializes between her fingers, Ellen appears dressed in a white form-fitting gown that matches her pale complexion and long, platinum-blond hair. As she begins to sing (Lake was

Fig. 21. V-Bomb: Ellen Graham (Veronica Lake) pulling an ace of spades out of the air while singing "Now You See It, Now You Don't" in Frank Tuttle's *This Gun for Hire*.

dubbed by Martha Mears), the eggs magically disappear one by one: "Have you ever seen a love light in a lady's eyes / And then suddenly watch it vanish away?" Approaching a male customer in the front row who's wearing a hat, Ellen slips her hand inside his coat and, when she withdraws it, the eggs are wedged again between her fingers: "If there's trouble in your love life / Well, my friend, get wise." After a series of tricks—pulling a card out from behind Gates's ear ("Now you see it") and making it disappear ("Now you don't")—Ellen touches his lapel and, when he turns up her palm ("One moment she's making you see"), a canary flies off: "Canaries in the air."

Next, she taps her heart ("Next moment instead of her heart") and the "ace of spades is there."

For Ellen's most elaborate trick, she unstraps a watch from Gates's wrist and, unspooling a silk handkerchief from another man's pocket and placing the watch inside, drops the handkerchief on the floor and steps on it, "That's love." Picking up a glass of water that another man's about to drink, she snaps her fingers and tosses the contents into his face: white confetti flutters out and falls like snowflakes. Finally, taking a peacock fan from a table, Ellen returns to the center of the stage and disappears behind it ("You get blinded by that moon of bright gold above"), then, as the fan drops to the floor, she reappears behind the white column with Gates's watch in her raised hand, "That's love."

Ellen's magic act is a seductive mix of singing and conjuration, but the coda to the scene—occurring, as it does, off stage—reveals just how artful she is. After the promoter tells Gates Ellen's number is perfect for his nightclub, Gates asks her to dinner and Ellen asks a monkey named Magillacuddy whether she should go. Although the monkey shakes its head, Ellen, pulling a flower out of the air, sticks it in Gates's pocket, adding that she doesn't always listen to her "manager." It's an impressive, impromptu bit of business, not least as it's only after the fact that we realize this "monkey business" has all been done to hook Gates. (In retrospect, Ellen's magic act is not so much a spectacle for Gates's sexual gaze as an index of her considerable performative powers.)

The reason for this subterfuge is revealed in the very next sequence when the promoter takes Ellen to a rendezvous with Senator Burnett who, after explaining that a handful of Benedict Arnold–like "heels" are trying to "sabotage the country's defense," actively enlists her assistance: Ellen's mission is to find out who Gates is working for, but—and this is the catch—she's not allowed to tell anyone, including her police detective boyfriend, Michael. The disturbances that Ellen's new, "secret" occupation as a federal agent produce in her relationship with her fiancé surface in a subsequent scene set at an arcade and scored by an instrumental version of "Now You See It, Now You Don't." Both Michael and Ellen, who is first seen fanning a deck of cards, have good news. After Michael shoots a sling-shot at the Play-the-Scale booth (a game that, to the owner's dismay, he regularly wins), he states they can get married now because he's been assigned to a new case. However, Ellen's good news—that she's got a job that will take her away—so surprises him he completely misses the target. It also throws a real wrench into his wedding plans, "What does it take to get you to darn my socks, cook my corned beef and cabbage, and sort of confine your magic to one place and one customer at a time?"

Ellen dutifully tells her boyfriend what he wants to hear—"I want my guy. I want a home and some kids"—but their passionate, protracted kiss is interrupted when a police officer waiting for Michael in a patrol car repeatedly hits the horn after being notified via the radio that the "girl is expected at the store." The couple's engagement is further jeopardized when Ellen tells Michael that if he wants to marry her, it'll have to be in Los Angeles and, moreover, that she can't tell him why. The last plot turn is significant not simply because it puts Michael in the same benighted position as Gates but because it underscores her job comes first, which Michael himself acknowledges when he ruefully says, "Nice start."

On the train to Los Angeles Ellen finds herself sitting next to Raven who, when they arrive, forces her to help him escape from the police. (In a pregnant scenario, Ellen pretends to be Raven's wife and, using a piece of luggage wrapped in a train blanket, carrying their baby.) Once they're free of the police, Ellen tells Raven she has a "dress rehearsal" to attend, but he forces her to accompany him to an abandoned building: just as he's about to shoot her, a noise momentarily distracts him and she escapes. Ellen's passing comment about the "dress rehearsal" acts as a bridge between a scene set at Brewster's office at the Nitro Chemical Corporation and the second, "fishing" number. After Brewster's second-in-command tells him "everything's prepared for the gas mask rehearsal," Gates reports that he saw Raven with a woman, the same one he just hired to perform at his nightclub.

With its reclining mermaids and built-in goldfish bowls, the mise-en-scène of The Neptune Club recalls the earlier audition sequence. The difference between the two musical numbers becomes apparent, however, as soon as Ellen appears: picked out by a single spotlight and backed by a big band, she's dressed in a "shiny," skin-tight black outfit and wielding a fishing pole like a whip. As Ellen sings Loesser and Press's "I've Got You," she casts her line at a male customer, then, reeling it in, drops live goldfish one by one into a glass bowl: "I've got you right where I want you / Dangling on my line / I've got you / And I'm enjoying it fine."

The lyrics take on additional significance when Ellen crosses the room and casts the line at Gates who's been ordered by Brewster to figure out what she's up to: "I was one out of fifty in your address book / Oh, what a spot you had me in / But today you're the sucker for the shiny hook /

And you never wiggle off / You can bet your bottom fin." For her final trick, Ellen takes a small glass aquarium from a female assistant. After a male assistant fills it with water from a pitcher, she tilts it and, presto!, it's filled with live goldfish: "Cause I'm not yours anymore / You're mine." Although the song's conceit is familiar enough—the angler is male and the women are fish—the situation here is reversed: Ellen's the angler and Gates is the "fin."

Writing about the importance of musical numbers in film noir, Deborah Thomas remarks that the very "best example" of performative pleasure is the initial "Now You See It, Now You Don't" routine in *This Gun for Hire*, a routine that represents a "marvelous combination of song, music, [and] magic."[5] The key for Thomas is "Lake's own obvious enjoyment and play with the audience within the film, and—through her sleight-of-hand—a breakdown in the stability of appearances, all complemented by her almost constant movement."[6]

While the reference to Lake rather than the character is slightly misleading (if only because, as the star recounts in her autobiography, she found the process "agonizing"[7]), the gist of Thomas's argument is that Ellen's song-and-dance number opens up the noir narrative, which tends to be characterized by blockage and repression or, with respect to female characters, containment. This fantasy of containment—the dream of the "incredible shrinking woman"—is, as we've seen, articulated most explicitly in *Dead Reckoning*. It's therefore no surprise, particularly given the sexual politics of the period (Tuttle's film was shot in 1941), that this fantasy also circumscribes the narrative of *This Gun for Hire*. Thomas herself cites the moment when Michael proposes to Ellen ("What does it take to get you to darn my socks . . ."), but a more visual, not to say graphic, image of this recontainment occurs in the immediate wake of the "fishing" number.

The rehearsal's over and Ellen's finally agreed to a dinner date with Gates at his home. However, since Raven has earlier described him to Ellen as a "fat man who likes peppermints," when he offers her a peppermint, she realizes his interest in her is no longer "romantic." In other words, to paraphrase the lyrics of "I've Got You," the tables have turned and now Gates has her right where he wants her. Accordingly, after Gates confronts her about her relation with Raven, he has his "assistant" Tommy tie her up and gag her, the erotic character of which bondage is accented when Gates, looking down at Ellen laid out on a couch, observes admiringly, "Such a lovely body."

If the ensuing scenario can be said to be stereotypical in that Ellen becomes the classic "damsel in distress" who has to be saved by Raven (in yet another sexual subtext, he discovers her hidden in a closet), its transgressive potential can also be measured if one compares the second "fishing" number to the first "audition" one. Whereas in the "Now You See It, Now You Don't" routine Ellen is hatless and adorned in a white flowing dress, in "I've Got You" she's dressed in matching black pants and hat and sporting a phallic, whip-like fishing pole. In fine, in the second routine, Ellen appears in the guise of the "bad girl," a dominatrix who recognizes a "bottom fin" like Gates when she sees one.

The appeal of the second, "black" magic number as opposed to the initial "white" one is the way it impacts the remainder of the narrative. After rescuing Ellen, Raven takes her back to The Neptune Club (the band is playing an instrumental version of "I've Got You"). However, when he sees Gates and Michael together, he absconds with her again, although this time Ellen leaves a trail of monogrammed magic cards. Later, after becoming trapped in a "dynamo" plant, Ellen and Raven escape yet again to a shack in a freight yard. (Note the capture-and-escape pattern that characterizes Ellen and Raven's relationship, which reenacts on a narrative level the logic of prestidigitation associated with her act.)

In an echo of the film's famous opening scene, the magical appearance of a cat disrupts the narrative as well as threatens to dynamite the film's projection of "cool" masculinity. After Raven confesses he's haunted by bad dreams, he tells Ellen about his traumatic past: when his parents died, he was taken in by a relative who regularly beat him because of his "bad blood," an aunt whom he later knifed to death when she hit him with a "red-hot flat iron." (The reference to a "knife" recollects both the restaurant scene at the top of the film when Raven pricks Gates and the "rescue" one at the mansion when he uses the same knife to cut the ropes that bind Ellen.)

As in *The Dark Corner*, the masochistic scenario that Raven elaborates is crucial to the sexual economy of *This Gun for Hire*. It not only elucidates the sexual chemistry between Ellen and Raven, it also suggests, like Ellen's second number, that they're doubles of each other. In other words, if Ellen can be said to be an angel with a "figure like a dream [and] looks to kill," Raven is her dark alter ego, what Borde and Chaumeton, remembering Baudelaire, call an "angelic killer."[8] This symbiotic twinning of traits is reflected in Ladd and Lake's remarkable physical resemblance, "a pair of diminutive and sullenly pretty blonds" whose incestuous coupling also explains why the relation between them can never be consummated.[9]

Instead, Ellen is bound, true to the film's "happy ending," to wind up in Michael's arms. Forget that she's earlier donned Raven's hat and trench coat in order to help him escape, after which (can Michael ever forgive her for this?) he shoots and kills a police officer. Forget that, in a rhyme of Ellen's role-playing, Raven himself dons a gas mask in order to infiltrate Brewster's organization, forcing the old man to sign a confession at gun point before shooting Gates. In the black masque that is *This Gun for Hire*, Raven must die so that Ellen can marry Michael, her "hocus pocus" and wanderlust forever confined to one place and customer, her bad behavior written off as so much patriotic duty. The audience, however, knows better: the real magic is between Ellen and Raven, the fatal angler and angelic killer, the feline magician and cat-loving assassin.

"Where's the Canary?"

If musical numbers—as in *This Gun for Hire*—can be said to disrupt the classic noir narrative of containment, Rita Hayworth's performances in *Gilda* are arguably the most significant in the genre. While critics, beginning with Richard Dyer, have focused on "Put the Blame on Mame," all three musical numbers in Vidor's film deserve detailed attention. In fact, the second song, Gilda's rendition of "Amado Mio" ("My Loved One"), not only represents an antithesis to the first, "acoustic" version of "Put the Blame on Mame" but provides a musical transition to the third number, Hayworth's celebrated "striptease" rendition of the same song.

In terms of the film's narrative, the "Amado Mio" routine constitutes a literal and figurative moment of escape. Ballin Mundson has apparently died in a plane crash and Johnny Farrell has subsequently married Gilda. The marriage, though, is merely Johnny's pretext, as he explains in voice-over, to continue to punish her for publicly stepping out on her former husband: "She hadn't been faithful to Ballin when he was alive, but she was going to be faithful to him now that he was dead." Gilda's first reaction to Johnny's machinations is to locate a former dance partner, Gabe Evans. (Earlier in the film when Johnny, at Mundson's behest, interrupts them dancing, Gilda says, "Maybe you didn't notice I was dancing. I've never been able to finish a dance yet.")

Since Gilda can't find Evans, she turns to other, anonymous men, but Johnny's henchmen regularly intervene. Her predicament is encapsulated in a brilliant shot outside the Hotel Centenario: after yet another man has been hijacked, Gilda sits bewildered in the back of a taxicab as the driver turns down the fare sign, which reads "Libre." It's at this point, locked in what Johnny calls her "private prison," that Gilda flees Buenos Aires for Montevideo. There, because of her "ability to sing and dance, to perform professionally," she's briefly able to "lead another life than [the one] Johnny wants her to lead."[10]

In fact, Gilda's past life as a performer is evoked early on in Vidor's film when, in a passage that foreshadows her contretemps with Johnny over Evans, she's dancing with Captain Delgado and the band is playing an instrumental version of "Amado Mio." Johnny, who's sitting next to Obregon, is watching from a table Mundson has just vacated and we the audience —but not, significantly, Johnny—are privy to her conversation. Delgado compliments her, "You could be a professional dancer," and Gilda replies, "I am, I mean I was." After she admonishes him for holding her too closely ("That's against our union rules"), their conversation returns to the topic of dancing:

DELGADO: How is that I've never seen you?
GILDA: I didn't dance here.
DELGADO: Where?
GILDA: America.
DELGADO: This is not America?
GILDA: I mean, New York.

Delgado's remark about "America," which appears to be Pan-American rather than, say, anti-imperialist in sentiment, subtly references Hayworth's Latin heritage. (Although Hayworth and her mother were both born in the United States, her father, Eduardo, of the famed "Dancing Cansinos," was born in Spain.[11])

If Gilda once had a career as a dancer in the United States, now that she's married to Mundson, she doesn't have to—dance professionally, that is. When Mundson returns (he's left to attend to some Nazi business), he orders Johnny to get Gilda off the dance floor and Johnny does as he's told, informing Gilda that "her husband is showing." Gilda's response is typically tart, "I always say there's something about Latin men. For one thing, they can dance. For another thing . . . ," at which point she turns to Delgado and inquires, "What's your telephone number?" To paraphrase Eddie Muller in *Dark City*, *Gilda* is a tango of tropes where, among other things, dancing is a figure for sex.

Dancing, literally speaking, is also one of the things that differentiates the "Amado Mio" number from Gilda's first performance of "Put the Blame on Mame." While Johnny narrates the action in voice-over ("She got a job singing in a nightclub"), the film dissolves on action from a tight shot of Gilda sitting in the backseat of a cab in Buenos Aires to a wide shot of her dressed in a "white beaded two-piece" offset by a bare midriff and "slit skirt," striding toward the front of a darkened stage in a Montevideo nightclub.[12] When the lights come up, the contrast between the two numbers is palpable: whereas in the first sequence Gilda is singing at five o'clock in the morning with only Uncle Pio and, eventually, a disgruntled Johnny as her audience, now she's backed by an orchestra and performing before a packed club. In other words, this is very much a public performance.

At the same time, it's not strictly public since after Gilda sings the opening verse ("I'm in a dream world / Of sweet delight"), the camera pulls back to reveal a man sitting at a table watching her. The song's address is confirmed when the film cuts away from Gilda, who's now danced to the edge of the stage, to a formally dressed man, a cigarette in one hand, absorbed like a lover in Gilda's performance: "Many times I've whispered 'Amado mio' / It was just a phrase / That I heard in plays / I was acting a part." In the larger context of the narrative, this verse is especially apposite because it suggests that Gilda's actions do not always coincide with her emotions, a proposition that's articulated by Obregon when he addresses Johnny near the end of the film: "Gilda didn't do any of those things you've been losing sleep over. It was just an act. Every bit of it."

Once Gilda steps down from the stage ("But now I whisper / 'Amado mio' "), the camera, paralleling the lyrics, cuts to a more intimate, medium shot, then back to a wide shot—the widest in the sequence, comprising the tables and audience in front of the stage—of her public admission of love: "Can't you tell I care / By the feeling there / For it comes from the heart." Gilda here is wearing her heart on her sleeve, the mobile tracking camera capturing her every move, eventually returning to a medium shot that acts as a caesura of sorts before the dance break.

If the above confessional verse speaks to one part of Gilda's persona, the romantic or emotional part, the up-tempo "rhumba" music—cued by a cow bell and performed on piano, trumpet, and castanets—speaks to another, equally authentic aspect of her personality, the sexual or erotic part. It's not for nothing that Borde and Chaumeton in their panoramic survey of classic American noir assert that Gilda is a "worthy representative of a certain American eroticism," the new "Lola-Lola of the 'atomic age.'"[13] (The allusion is to Marlene Dietrich's cabaret-singer in *The Blue Angel* [1930].) Drawing on the subtextual play in Hayworth's persona between her Latin and American identities—between, as it were, "Carmen" and "Rita," the "hot" and the "sweet"[14]—the song-and-dance routine of "Amado Mio" mediates Gilda's private and public performances of "Put the Blame on Mame."

Embedded within the lyrical space of "Amado Mio," the dance break, like the concluding version of "Put the Blame on Mame," also exemplifies Gilda's freedom of movement within the frame. This freedom of movement—in which, not so incidentally, she appears to "control" or "direct the camera"[15]—is linked to her sexuality, a charisma that is itself a form of eros in the best, largest sense of the word, a veritable life-force or *élan vital*. Which is to say that Gilda appears to be most alive when she's dancing. The paradox is that, precisely because of this sexual charisma, men want to possess and domesticate—or, in Johnny's case, punish—her.

This curtailment is explicitly thematized at the end of the "Amado Mio" number when the man sitting at the table, a lawyer named Tom Langford, tells Gilda he's "very much in love with her." Langford persuades her to return to Buenos Aires to get an annulment so that she can be "utterly free" of her past ("It will never do any good to escape"), but he turns out to be an agent of Johnny. The nadir for Gilda occurs when she enters what she thinks is her bridal suite at the Hotel Centenario with Langford and sees Johnny sitting there smoking a cigarette: "There's no such thing as an annulment in Argentina." As Gilda slumps crying to the floor, the camera tilts down, recording her utter abjection: instead of dancing up on a stage, the very embodiment of self-possession, she's now down on her knees, begging Johnny to let her go.

Johnny's dominance—signified by a low-angle shot of him lording it over Gilda—is, however, ephemeral: the slave, as Hegel knew, will have its revenge. When Johnny returns to his mezzanine office, the detective Obregon's already there (he's turned on the audiovisual surveillance) and notifies him that the casino has only been allowed to remain open because he's hoping Johnny, the "little thief," will lead him to the "bigger crime." In fact, after Obregon tells Johnny he's "breaking up in little pieces," music wafts up from the casino and, in an echo of the first "Put the Blame on Mame" sequence, Johnny goes over and opens the blinds. (Note the deco statue in front of the blinds, an antelope with horns that recollects the pre-Carnival scene where Uncle Pio comes to Johnny's office with two masks in his hands, asking him whether he wants to go to the party as a bull or a clown.) The camera cuts on action to a wide shot of a spotlighted Gilda, dressed in a strapless, "slit-to-the-thigh" black satin evening gown (designed by Jean Louis and inspired by John Singer Sargent's *Portrait of Madame X*[16]), striding onto the casino floor to the audience's applause, regally tossing away her cape like a bull-fighter who no longer fears the bull.

This dynamic entrance, in which Gilda appears in all her kinetic glory, invokes her first, spectacular appearance in the film. Johnny has gone to Mundson's house to welcome him home from a trip. Ballin invites him upstairs and, pausing at the landing, Johnny asks, "Where's the canary?" Opening the door to the master suite, Mundson, dressed in a jet-black smoking jacket, replies, "Come. This is where the canary is." Suddenly, a woman can be heard offscreen humming along to a song on the radio. "Quite a surprise to hear a woman singing in my house, huh, Johnny?" The song is "Put the Blame on Mame" and, as Johnny follows Mundson through a darkened anteroom to the bright threshold of the boudoir, the camera cuts on action to a close-up of Gilda tossing her hair like a whip into the empty space of the frame. When Mundson asks his spanking-new wife, "Are you decent?" Gilda, quick-witted as ever, replies, "Me. Sure, I'm decent."

Gilda's final, calculated performance of "Put the Blame on Mame" also evokes the earlier Carnival party sequence, which concludes with Johnny returning to Gilda's bedroom and the two kissing, a passionate embrace that's interrupted by the sound of Mundson leaving the house for the airport. The Carnival sequence proper opens with a shot of the casino band leader prepping the musicians on how to play "Put the Blame on Mame": "Wait a minute, fellas, let's . . . make it a little cleaner." Later, during the costume ball, things get a little dirtier when Gilda and Johnny share a slow, masked dance to "Anywhere" (reprised from Hayworth's *Tonight and Every Night* [1945]). Gilda can't stop talking, first praising Johnny, "Nobody could ever dance like you," then affectionately mocking one of his sayings, "Talk or dance, but don't do both at the same time." However, when Johnny stumbles, she immediately pricks him with her rapier, "You're out of practice—aren't you? Dancing, I mean? I could help you get in practice again, Johnny. Dancing, I mean."

Fig. 22. Love Me or Leave Me: Gilda (Rita Hayworth) putting the blame on Mame in Charles Vidor's *Gilda*.

All of the above sexual and gestural subtexts are activated in Gilda's "striptease" version of "Put the Blame on Mame." For starters, Gilda's performance, what Thomas calls "performance as retaliation," is anything but "decent."[17] In fact, it's a positive affront to both her dead husband's memory as well as Johnny's attempt to honor it. (In addition to the scene where Mundson asks Gilda whether she's "decent," there's also the sequence where the married couple return to their new apartment and, in the midst of another passionate embrace, Gilda sees a portrait of Mundson. Although she's appropriately horrified—"Johnny, that isn't even decent"—Johnny's reaction—"That sounded funny coming out of you"—is the first indication their marriage is a farce: Johnny has wed her not as she hopes or believes, out of love, "but to keep her out of circulation."[18])

If in the Carnival scene Johnny tells Gilda not to dance and talk at the same time, here—in front of the whole world, as it were—she's singing *and* dancing and, propelled by the brash, big-band horns, making a complete spectacle of herself. And what a spectacle it is: "One night she started to shim and shake, that brought on the Frisco quake." Easing into a bump-and-grind routine (one that Hayworth "could do in her sleep better than anybody awake in the world"[19]), Gilda punctuates the first line with a toss of her hair and the second with a "shake" of her derrière. Tossing her hair again, she sings the song's tag-line, the camera cutting to Johnny who's rushed down from his office to watch from the bar and who, to paraphrase Obregon in the film's epilogue, proceeds to be a "great audience" for her.

Now piling her hair on top of her head and raising her arms in the air, Gilda proceeds to peel off one of her long-sleeved black gloves, "Folks were puttin' the blame on the lady known as 'Lou.'" Twirling the gloves, she dances first toward, then away from the camera ("Put the blame on Mame, boys") until, holding them high above her head between her outstretched hands, she turns her back and shakes her derrière again, "That's the thing that slew Magrew."

After the audience and orchestra erupt in applause, Gilda, having tossed away one glove, tosses the other to a man sitting table-side who stands up and shouts "More, more." Free, finally, of her gilded cage, Gilda strips off her necklace and tosses it to another man before beginning to undress, giddily announcing, "I'm not very good at zippers." Two men rush over to help her until Johnny's right-hand man, Casey, steps in and escorts her off stage where she screams at Johnny, "Now they all know what I am. The mighty Johnny Farrell got taken and he married a . . ." Slap.

Despite the fact that, as the studio publicity suggested, Gilda seems to get around ("Gilda used men the way other women use makeup"), the lady is no tramp.[20] Later, sitting at the bar in the now empty casino, she decides to return home and Johnny, prodded by Obregon, belatedly comes to his senses and tells her he wants to go away with her. Although Mundson appears out of nowhere like a vampire to reclaim what's his ("I want my wife"), Uncle Pio kills him with Ballin's "little friend," his cane-cum-sword. Obregon, a surrogate for the audience, confesses he's a "pushover for a love story," and Gilda and Johnny set off for "America" where, on a clear day, you can presumably see forever.

Notwithstanding this "happy ending," *Gilda*, like Hayworth's next film, *The Lady from Shanghai*, flaunts its performative contradictions. Consider the tension between number and narrative in Vidor's film, a tension that has a determinate historical component. John Kobal has remarked that the "elation of wartime musicals gave way to perverse thrillers studied with disenchantment,"[21] but Vidor's film belies this simple chronology. On one hand, Gilda's "big number," her near-striptease—a black-and-white routine in which she sings and dances—allies her with the femme fatale and, by extension, film noir: "Rita Hayworth's performance as a sex siren translates into one of the great all-time femme fatales."[22] On the other hand, the bad-girl abandon of "Put the Blame on Mame" is all but muted by an ending that, in its willful insistence that Gilda's a "good girl," is closer to the canonical Hollywood musical than film noir.

Critics are fond of citing Marjorie Rosen's empathetic characterization of Hayworth in *Popcorn Venus* (1973)—" 'This is my body. It's lovely and gives *me* pleasure. I rejoice in it as you do' "—but her assessment of Hayworth as the "golden girl, the beautiful All-American hooker," is equally germane.[23] In other words, *Gilda* is "great" not because it's a "progressive" text; rather, its greatness derives from the dynamic play of its contradictions, the way in which Gilda performatively embodies at one and the same time the "good" and "bad girl," the "golden" songbird and the "beautiful American hooker" next door.

Stereophone Siren

"Please Don't Kiss Me" in *The Lady from Shanghai* may not be a "big number" in the conventional sense, but I want to end with this musical sequence not simply because it was modeled on Hayworth's routines in *Gilda* but because, together with Vidor's film, *The Killers*, *The Big Sleep*, and *Dead Reckoning* (to cite a recent source),[24] it's one of the most recognized vocal performances in classic noir.

Although "Please Don't Kiss Me" was composed by Allan Roberts and Doris Fisher, the same team who wrote the songs for *Gilda*, it's accumulated a rather more complex reception over the years. One reason has been Welles's highly vocal dissatisfaction with the studio-imposed final cut as well as, in particular, the sound track. "The *preview* title music was written by a first-rate composer, George Antheil," Welles remonstrated in a famous nine-page memo to Harry Cohn, and possessed an "atmosphere of darkness and menace combined with something lush and romantic."[25] Instead of Welles's "clear-cut blueprint for music and effects," however, Cohn's version of *The Lady of Shanghai* was severely lacking in "*sound atmosphere*"—for example, in the sequences aboard the yacht—and Heinz Roemheld's music effectively "Disneyfied" the picture.[26] The result is a film that "must be discussed in terms of what might have been, rather than what it is: another mutilated torso."[27]

The last verdict, which has become something of a consensus, is by Simon Callow who nevertheless concludes that *The Lady from Shanghai* is a "remarkable . . . and highly personal work."[28] I would only add Welles's film is also a meditation on the antonym of a mutilated torso: the impossible physical perfection of the "pin-up girl" or ideal woman as femme fatale. In fact, as the term "femme fatale" implies, the complexity of Elsa's performance of "Please Don't Kiss Me" involves Welles's attempt to estrange the "B" pulp fiction, Sherwood King's *If I Die before I Wake*, on which his screenplay was based.

Roemheld's score, according to the director, "destroyed the quality of *freshness* and *strangeness* which is exactly what might have saved *The Lady from Shanghai* from being just another whodunit."[29] In other words, in its original conception at least, Welles's film was not a "whodunit" but a "satire" or "dark parody" of a "Columbia program picture."[30] A close reading of the extant film, mutilated as it is, reveals the contours, if not the corpus, of Welles's intentions. True to the intricate give-and-take between studio and auteur, such a reading also suggests, heresy of heresies, that several of Cohn's contributions to the picture—for instance, his insistence that a song be inserted for Hayworth to sing—are, in retrospect, more felicitous than not.

The first narrative pretext for Elsa's performance occurs (I bracket here Roemheld's score, which draws heavily on Roberts and Fisher's song) after Michael O'Hara (Welles), an itinerant merchant marine, has rescued her from some thugs in Central Park. Her crippled husband, Arthur Bannister (Everett Sloane), "the world's greatest criminal lawyer," has gone to a hiring hall to find Michael who, as he theatrically narrates in voice-over, is working on a novel while "waiting for a ship." (The megaphone with which the house-master summons him—"Michael, please step to the bulletin board, a man wants to see you"—is a familiar, Wellesian sonic touch.)

The film dissolves from the hiring hall where Michael has inveigled Bannister into buying drinks for his mates, Jake and Goldie, to a tight shot of a jukebox. The recording, which ends just as the sequence begins, is "Please Don't Kiss Me" as sung by a male vocalist. (Callow claims that a "barely audible Frank Sinatra can be heard on the jukebox,"[31] though I'm not convinced it's Sinatra.) Bannister, who's drunk and getting drunker by the minute, brags that "Mike saved my wife's life" and, as if on cue, Goldie asks a man who's just walked up to the jukebox to play "Please Don't Kiss Me" again, "Would you mind insertin' these coins. Number four, that's what we like." As the song commences, Bannister claims "Mike's quite a hero, quite a tough guy," blandishments that are sharply undercut by the song's lyrics ("Please don't kiss me"): Bannister is kissing up to Michael, but for the moment at least, he isn't buying.

Jake, echoing Michael's mock-heroic voice-over ("I start this story out as a hero, which I most certainly am not"), interjects that a tough guy's a "guy with an edge." Pointing to his larynx, Jake asks, "What makes him sing better than me?," then answers his own question, "What makes it [the voice] loud? A microphone. That's his edge." After Jake elaborates on his conceit (an edge, whether it's a gun or knife, razor or nightstick, is "something the other guy ain't got"), Bannister darkly warns Michael—"You hear that, Black Irish?"—before passing out. The "saloon" sequence concludes with Goldie asking Jake "But what makes him sing prettier than you?," a question which intimates that Jake's discourse, not unlike Michael's voice-over, has been almost entirely circumlocutious: that Michael may not have an "edge" on Bannister—may, in fact, be less like the "tough guy" he thinks he is or appears to be and more like the crooner on the jukebox.

After Michael takes the drunken Bannister back to his yacht, he agrees, despite his earlier protestations, to be a boatswain on the *Circe* as it navigates its way via the Panama Canal to San Francisco. Later, while the yacht's moored in the West Indies, we watch as the sirenic Elsa, outfitted in a sleek black bathing suit, dives from a cliff and suns herself on a rock like a "Sternbergian Circe."[32] (The allusion here, as in Borde and Chaumeton's reference to Gilda as "Lola-Lola," is *Der blaue Engel*.[33]) The voyeuristic view is from Bannister's law partner George Grisby's (Glenn Anders) binocular point of view, but once Grisby appears to leave, Elsa comes on board for lunch, telling Michael that "ever since that night in the park" when she wrapped one of his cigarettes in a handkerchief, she's been "learning to smoke." She then asks Michael to call her "Rosalie," but when she moves in to kiss him, he slaps her across the face and, trembling, she lights her own cigarette, the smoke clouding her face like a veil.

Michael and Elsa eventually kiss, but Grisby's stentorian *bon voyage* ("So long, kiddies!") catches him, if not her, unaware and sets up the ensuing musical sequence. The number, which opens with the sound of Grisby playing "Please Don't Kiss Me" on the piano, recollects the previous "saloon" sequence, albeit with a difference: instead of Michael entertaining Bannister with his mates, now Bannister is interrogating Michael. The initial four-shot reflects the latter's increasingly compromised position: Michael, dressed in white jacket and cap, is standing in the middle ground; Bannister is sitting in the left background with his "back against the mainmast, looking toward the stern"; Grisby, his "back against the cabin wall, looking to port," is sitting at Elsa's feet "like a faithful dog"; and Elsa is laid out on top of the cabin, her body doubled by the boom above her.[34]

The overlapping dialogue—Bannister telling Michael he's just heard something from Grisby; Michael replying, "Yes, sir"; Elsa singing "But if you kiss me"; Bannister sharply telling her that his news "really concerns [her] more than anyone else"; Grisby, the frog to Elsa's scorpion, croaking "Don't take your arms away"—is dizzying in its polyphonic play. When Bannister announces "Michael is anxious to quit," Grisby croaks another line, "Comes a change of weather," and after Bannister tells him to shut up, the camera cuts to a wide horizontal shot of Elsa: motionless as a calendar girl,[35] she isn't "doing" anything, although everything revolves around her, the prime mover.

While Bannister mocks Michael's independence ("money cannot bring you health and happiness, et cetera"), Elsa hands Grisby a cigarette and asks for a light. Since Grisby doesn't have one, Michael lights a cigarette with a match even as Bessie (Evelyn Ellis) is serving Bannister coffee. The subsequent, overhead tracking shot shows Grisby handing the lit cigarette to Elsa: Bessie serves Bannister, Grisby serves Elsa, and "Michael serves Elsa through Grisby."[36] This circuit of lust and avarice, domination and enslavement, is fleshed out in *The Lady from Shanghai* by way of the film's insistent metaphor of "smoking guns,"[37] a conceit that recollects the cigarette-and-gun exchange in Central Park (Elsa, despite the fact she claims she doesn't smoke or shoot, takes a cigarette from Michael and he finds a gun in her purse) as well as foreshadows the Chinese theater sequence near the end of the film (where the smoking men in the audience contribute to the Brechtian *Stimmung*).

Before Michael, who's had quite enough of Bannister's lecture, heads below, he glances at Elsa who takes a drag on her cigarette then, at Arthur's request ("Sing it for us again, Lover"), starts to sing: "Please don't kiss me / But if you kiss me / Don't take your lips away." Safely below deck, Michael tells Bessie she should quit, but she tells "Mr. Poet" she needs the money and someone has to take care of that "poor little child."[38] (Since Elsa does not appear to be either poor or especially childlike, Welles's characterization of Bessie as a "mammy" is no doubt intended to comment, however crudely, on Michael's romantic and economic naiveté.)

Cut to a canted close-up of Elsa, her cigaretted hand resting on her

Fig. 23. Like a Siren: Elsa Bannister (Rita Hayworth) on the cabin roof of the *Circe* singing "Please Don't Kiss Me" in Orson Welles's *The Lady from Shanghai.*

breast bone, beginning the second verse of "Please Don't Kiss Me" ("Please don't hold me"). The camera tracks in close to her face ("But if you hold me") before cutting away to Michael pacing below, looking up as Goldie's accompaniment on guitar suddenly becomes audible on the sound track: "Comes a change in weather / Comes a change of heart / And who knows when / The rain will start." Michael listens for a moment, then, drawn by Elsa's voice ("So I beg you"), starts up the ladder, the camera rapidly tracking across a tangle of rope. The following shot, an extremely low-key close-up of Michael's face bisected by a line of rigging in the foreground, is the dark visual prelude to a final canted "choker" shot of Elsa: "Then don't take your lips or your arms or your love away."

If the obstructed shot of Michael suggests both his fascination with Elsa and his knowledge he's caught like a fish in a net and the bigger fish, the sharks, are circling—"living on a hook," as he says—the longing in Elsa's voice, combined with her liquid eyes (which, crucially, only the audience can see), conveys her vulnerability. In fact, her distant gaze connects her, like her voice, with the sea and reflects her deep desire for oblivion, a desire that's signified when she gradually closes her eyes at the end of the song.

In her definitive book on Hayworth, Adrienne McLean, comparing the musical performances in *Gilda* and *The Lady from Shanghai*, contends that Welles's film is a "more or less standard example of how musical performance functions in film noir. There is one song only . . . [and] we probably would not miss it if it were gone."[39] (Speaking only for myself and not the audience, I for one would miss it, dearly.) As I hope has become clear in the course of this book, there are any number of noirs, from "obscure" films such as *Rio* (1939) to canonical ones such as *This Gun For Hire*, that feature more than one song. (Brahm's *Rio* has four.[40]) I also think it's fair to say (and here I speak for the audience) that even those films that have only one musical number, such as *The Big Sleep* or *The Killers*, would be poorer without them. Imagine, for example, Hawks's film without Vivian Sternwood seductively singing "And Her Tears Flowed Like Wine" or Siodmak's *The Killers* without Kitty Collins purring "The More I Know of Love" to the Swede.

McLean herself has persuasively argued that "significant action takes place in many musical numbers, *particularly* when the numbers are in non-musical films."[41] Musical numbers in film noir, in addition to complicating the genre's narrative of containment, can be said to advance the action and, in the case of Welles at least, comment on that action. Thus, while much has been made of Welles's contentious relationship with Cohn, the inclusion of "Please Don't Kiss Me" in *The Lady from Shanghai* not only suggests the "old monster [Cohn] knew a bit after all" but is "clear proof, if any were needed, of [Welles's] extraordinary sensitivity to music."[42]

This sensitivity to music and its various, diegetic modes of transmission (radio, jukebox) remains audible in the "studio" version of *The Lady from Shanghai*. Consider the "Glosso Lusto" passage that succeeds the "Please Don't Kiss Me" number. On the image track, Michael, dressed in a black cap and jacket, stands in the left foreground at the wheel of the *Circe* looking back at Elsa who, dressed in a black bathing suit and cap, is holding her dachshund. On the sound track, a commercial is playing on the portable radio that rests next to Michael and Elsa on the deck: "Rub / Rub / Put Glosso Lusto in your hair / Keep it Glosso Lusto bright / G-L-O-double S-O L-U-S-T-O is right / Glosso [whistle] Lusto." There's another "wolf" whistle, then the male announcer burbles, "Remember, ladies, please your hair, please the man you love."

Now, inasmuch as the "Glosso Lusto" commercial is about hair, it's obviously about Elsa's "butch," topaz-blonde coiffure (as well as, by implication, Hayworth's famously loose, "fiery" red mane). While it's been widely repeated that Harry Cohn was furious at Welles about the haircut, Doris Fisher recounts that Cohn summoned her to his office and exclaimed, "We're going to revolutionize the movie industry. We're going to cut Rita's hair. . . . Every woman will go out and cut her hair and be a blonde."[43] A production in every sense of the word, the "cut" was also presided over by Welles, who was keen to satirize Hollywood's notion of beauty and, in particular, the "pin-up girl that Rita Hayworth was in real life."[44]

Of course, Hayworth's hair, especially the style created for *Gilda* by Helen Hunt, was a "prominent aspect" of her popular appeal.[45] The color of Hayworth's hair has in fact a history—from jet-black (her first "B," Columbia film, *Criminals of the Air* [1937]) to black with a bleached streak (*Only Angels Have Wings* [1939]) to auburn (*Gilda*) to platinum (*The Lady from Shanghai*). The significance of the last "white" color is seriously overdetermined in Welles's film since Elsa, unlike Hayworth, was not born in the U.S.A. but in Cheefoo and not from Irish-Spanish but from White Russian parents. Moreover, Elsa not only hails from Macao and Shanghai—two Chinese cities with a distinct noir pedigree—but is hailed as Xinlin Zhang and "red-haired foreigner."[46] Given that Michael O'Hara is also called Black Irish in the film because of his participation in the Spanish Civil War, the cut and color of Elsa's hair in *The Lady from Shanghai* is, it's safe to say, a "real" signifier: Elsa is a "butch," platinum-White Russian Asian femme fatale singing "what could be an old *Gilda* tune" on the deck of the *Circe*.[47]

When the film cuts from Elsa singing the last line of "Please Don't Kiss Me" to the radio commercial, it's clear even in the bowdlerized version of *The Lady from Shanghai* Welles intended this "jump sound" to function, like Hayworth's hair on the image track, as a sonic "shock" or "alienation effect." But if Elsa's performance of "Please Don't Kiss Me" is a lure, "as much an advertising pitch for Michael's devotion as the radio commercial,"[48] its emotional allure is also, paradoxically enough, real. It's important to reiterate this apparent contradiction because the figure of the siren, despite its mythological association with singing, has all too often been *viewed* merely as a stereotype and solely in terms of, to invoke Mulvey, "visual pleasure." For example, McLean insists "we know what Elsa is because of how she looks," a "stereotypical femme fatale" like Barbara Stanwyck in *Double Indemnity*, Claire Trevor in *Murder, My Sweet*, and Lana Turner in *The Postman Always Rings Twice*.[49]

Phyllis Dietrichson in Wilder's film, Velma Valento/Helen Grayle in Dmytryk's, and Cora Smith in Garnett's can be viewed, it's true, as femmes fatales, although none of these characters is a performer in the strict sense of the word.[50] Elsa's also distinguished from the above femmes fatales not simply by the fact that she sings but *how* she sings. Hence the difference—a performative, audiovisual one—between the vulnerability of her "little voice" (dubbed, as in *Gilda*, by Anita Ellis) and the hard, "fluorescent" façade of her persona.[51] To wit, just as Welles's estrangement of "Please Don't Kiss Me" alters the commercial thrust of Cohn's original intent, Hayworth's performance exceeds the "sadistic" drive of the narrative, offering via her eyes and voice a fleeting glimpse of another, non-fatal, more sympathetic Elsa.

Consider, in this audiovisual context, the issue of voice-over. Although *The Lady from Shanghai* has been regarded as a monophonic text because of Michael's first-person narration, this device, as in *Gilda*, is not nearly as monolithic as it appears. In "*Film Noir*, Voice-Over, and the Femme Fatale" Karen Hollinger argues that "first-person voice-over can act as an authoritative evocation of the text's implied author"; however, when combined with such classically noir elements as flashback, "sound becomes dislocated from image," triggering a proliferation of competing perspectives.[52] Hollinger references the embattled relation between male voice-over and the powerful visual presence of the femme fatale, but films such as *Gilda*, *The Bribe*, *Dead Reckoning*, and *The Lady from Shanghai* pose a slightly different issue: that between male voice-over narration and female vocal performance.

From this performative perspective, the musical numbers in film noir are loci of audio-vision where canaries or sirens can be said to speak back—within the diegesis—to the fantasmatic image of them constructed by male characters. Thus, the received critical wisdom today is that Gilda, despite Johnny Farrell's withering voice-over remarks about her, is—at least at the end of Vidor's film and in the wake of her second performance of "Put the Blame on Mame"—not so much a siren as a canary: a woman trapped in a metaphorical coal mine by Ballin Mundson and his slavish protégé, Johnny Farrell.

The same might be said for the allegedly unredeemable, utterly fallen woman, Elsa Bannister, in *The Lady from Shanghai*. While she implicates Michael in a "sinister murder conspiracy," her involvement is clouded by "indications that she is as much a victim of Bannister and Grisby's evil designs as Michael is."[53] In fact, it's possible to discern another, institutional subtext here, one where Elsa's sirenic aspect is a displaced figure for Hayworth's tenure at Columbia, caught like the canary Gilda between two men: Harry Cohn, a Bannister-like figure whose office was modeled on Il Duce's and who repeatedly refused Hayworth's requests to study singing,[54] and Welles, himself caught between the autocratic Cohn and his own hyperbolic, O'Hara-like sense of independence.

With this stereophony in mind, the "most intriguing mystery" in *The Lady from Shanghai* turns on the extent to which Elsa feels the "sentiments expressed in her theme song": "Is she *tempted* to throw away her husband's fortune and run off with poor Michael. . . . Or is she cynically committed to manipulation from beginning to end?"[55] If the latter scenario is true, Elsa is ultimately a stereotype—her moments of vulnerability and suicidal despair mere pretense—and Hayworth, accordingly, a "glorious martyr," as Bazin famously put it, to Welles's misogyny.[56] But if it's virtually impossible to answer the above questions in the course of "listening" to *The Lady from Shanghai*, it's arguably impossible to do so in the end, a terminal ambiguity or undecidability from which Hayworth's character is not exempt.

Welles's film concludes with two spectacular set-pieces. In the first, Chinese theater sequence, the bewildering "polyphony of sounds"—Michael's mock-Irish brogue and Elsa's English-accented Cantonese, the Chinese opera voices as well as string and percussion instruments—is vertiginously reflected in the film's various visual planes and spaces (stage, backstage, auditorium).[57] Thus, even as Elsa's backstage making a call to Lee Gong (note the male performer putting on a headpiece), Michael's sitting in the audience, surrounded by "smoking" old men, watching another male performer singing on stage. When the police arrive looking for Michael, the opera—about the "trial of a woman accused of being a sinner by a judge"[58] —continues apace. (The opera itself, it goes without saying, is a *mise-en-abîme* of *The Lady from Shanghai*.)

Echoing "Please Don't Kiss Me," Elsa tells Michael, "Put your arms around me," and as Lee Gong and his men enter the theatre, the two pretend to kiss. While the actors on stage and the stagehands in the wings watch the action unfold like a play (within a play) before their startled, heavily made-up eyes, Michael, still embracing Elsa, finds a gun in her purse—"You killed Grisby"—before passing out like Bannister in the hiring hall. Later, after woozily coming to and tumbling down the slide in the Crazy House, Michael confronts Elsa in the Magic Mirror Maze where she explains why she killed Grisby: "He lost his silly head and shot Broome." In this scene as well as in the subsequent one where she talks about going off into the sunrise with Michael, Elsa—eyes vacant, face masked—speaks in a "comatose monotone" as if she were mad or, faithful to Welles's own vision of the film, somnambulant.[59] Michael parrots the Chinese proverb Elsa first cited on the deck of the *Circe* when, in the wake of the "Glosso Lusto" jingle, Michael asked her whether she believed in love, "One who follows his nature keeps his nature in the end."

Suddenly, the hollow sound of his canes preceding him, Bannister appears gun in hand and shoots Elsa and, as the shattered glass rains down like hail, Elsa, returning the favor, shoots and kills her husband. Even though Elsa lies dying on the floor like Broome ("I made mistakes"), Michael, his hands in his pockets, continues to parrot her ("You said the world's bad and we can't run away from the badness. . . . But didn't the badness deal with you and make its own terms in the end?"), concluding righteously, "We can't lose only if we quit." Elsa's response, right before she collapses, is swift as it is sardonic, "And you're not going to quit?" It's only when she sees Michael standing by the exit ("Closed") and is finally face to face with her own death that the hardness abruptly vanishes from her voice and we hear the sound of the woman singing softly to herself on the deck of the *Circe*, "Michael, please . . ."

In the end, Elsa may keep her nature, may well be a bad bad girl—siren and femme fatale and seductress supreme—but, in the penultimate scene at least, the camera stays by her side. As for Michael, brave Ulysses, *poet manqué*, good boy turned bad then good again, he leaves her to expire in the house of fun, walking away into the morning sunrise, forever taking away his lips and arms and love.

Epilogue

SILENCES

This book, *Siren City*, has been all about sound effects and source music and, to some extent, dialogue and voice-over and scores. It's also been, if only tacitly, about silence since none of these sonic phenomena would exist without it. Silence is the ultimate source, the matrix and fountainhead, of the audible. However, even in silent film, not to say in noir, it's a relative thing. Which is to say, there are different kinds of silence.

Take, for example, the silence that graces the ending of *Out of the Past.* It is darkest night and the film dissolves from a policeman with a flashlight opening a car door, Jeff Bailey's bullet-ridden body tumbling to the ground like a sack of grain, to a brilliantly sunny day in Bridgeport. Jim the game warden is escorting Ann out of the courthouse past a simple wrought-iron fence and the townspeople who have gathered to gossip. The shadow of a flag flaps against the white façade of the courthouse, the whisper of voices mixed with Jim and Ann's footsteps echoing in the crisp autumnal air. While Jim is dressed in neutral colors, Ann, her blond hair pulled back, a scarf and purse in one hand, is wearing a black beret. Jim, as if still smarting from Marny's earlier comments in the diner, complains, "Too many people, too much talk," then proposes, "Let's get in the car and get away from it. I won't talk to you, Ann, I just want to be with you."

If the audience can't help but remember Jeff and Kathie Moffat have just died suddenly and violently in the previous scene, Ann no doubt can't forget the last time she took a car trip with a man who just wanted to talk. "Thanks, Jim, I can't." Then she breaks free from him and she's walking over to Jeff's gas station where the Kid's sitting alone on a bench. Ann sits down and, as music begins to thrum in the background, she puts her hand on his arm and says, "You can tell me. You knew him better than I did." When the Kid looks away, she asks him point blank, "Was he going away with her?" There's a brief pause, then, when the Kid looks back up, she asks again, "Was he going away?"

In the first two-shot, the camera's on Ann, but in the reverse shot it's close in on the Kid who, after a considerable pause, nods. Heart-broken, Ann pats his arm, then gets up and walks back to the car with the state of California insignia where Jim's waiting for her, will always be waiting for her. The crowd outside the courthouse has dispersed. Ann gets in the car and, in an echo of the film's opening sequence, the camera slowly pans to the right as the car disappears down the main street of Bridgeport toward the foothills in the distance. No names are written in the cloudless sky, but as if buoyed by Webb's score, the film cuts back to the Kid looking up at the sign outside the gas station that says "Jeff Bailey." He salutes it, then turns and walks away, slipping his right hand into his pocket as if he's done signing for the day.

Although the ending to *Out of the Past* was tacked on by RKO (Daniel Mainwaring relates that the "front office" said, "Jesus, you can't end it with them dead there"[1]), this is one of those not-so-rare cases where the studio got it right: the film wouldn't be the same, nor as fine, without it. Thus, if it's true that the Kid's nod frees Ann to "marry her small-town childhood sweetheart" and the salute signals he's "done Jeff's bidding in releasing Ann from her obligations to him," it's equally true that the ending is marked by a veritable "confusion of signs."[2]

The first thing to be said about the rather severely qualified happy ending of *Out of the Past* is that it explicitly rhymes with the film's beginning, in particular Stefanos's retort, sharply revising Marny, that the sign above Jeff Bailey's gas station is "big" or, at least, big enough for him to have noticed it while passing through town. If the sign, unlike the world, were smaller, Stefanos might not have noticed it and Jeff, as he promised Ann at the lake before heading back to see Whit Sterling's messenger, would have built his dream house and lived happily there with Ann. So: no sign, no story.

The second thing to be said about the storied conclusion to Tourneur's film is that the Kid may in fact know Jeff better than Ann does, but he

Fig. 24. The Long Goodbye: The Kid (Dickie Moore) saluting the gas-station sign in *Out of the Past.*

can't expatiate on the subject—assuming he could or would or that Ann, like Jeff, can read sign language. In fact, the Kid's a double of Jeff who, unlike Jeff's big-talking partner Fisher or the loquacious Marny, is a man of few words. (The torrent of language Jeff unlooses in the card ride to Lake Tahoe with Ann is meant, it's clear, to exorcise once and for all his traumatic past.)

The third thing to be said about the dénouement of *Out of the Past* is that it's simultaneously true and false or, more precisely perhaps, true in the way that all fiction, although false, is true. Hence the exchange between Ann and the Kid about Jeff's ultimate destination ("Was he going away with her?"). The Kid knows Jeff loved Ann and wasn't going off with Kathie, but he lies to Ann so that she can get on with her life—so that, in an especially fine irony, she's not haunted by the past as Jeff was. This aporia is marked in the brief space of time that elapses between when Ann first asks the Kid about Jeff and, after having dropped his head, he lifts it, having decided sometimes it's best not to tell the truth, sometimes it's better to lie.

Finally, there's the matter of the Kid's salute, which is a sign addressed to a sign by a person who signs. It's here the play of signs in *Out of the Past* becomes exorbitant since the Kid himself lacks a proper name (though, after everything that's happened, he's arguably no longer a "kid") and the name on the sign, "Jeff Bailey," is itself an alias, a lie of sorts. Jeff's proper last name is in fact Markham, a name associated with a fugitive past that, at the beginning of the film, Jeff Bailey mistakenly believes he's put completely behind him.

In fact, once upon a time, Jeff Bailey was Jeff Markham, a man compelled by circumstances to assume a new identity and occupation. Jeff Bailey, a perfectly nondescript, albeit quintessentially All-American name. Gas-station proprietor, a curious occupation for a big-city shamus whose métier once involved being able to leave on a moment's notice in order to track down a big op's mistress in Mexico. Now the former Jeff Markham is living in a small town, courting a small-town girl, and his travels, it appears, are restricted to the surrounding countryside. Jeff Bailey. He could be a character in a Frank Capra movie or a Thornton Wilder play.

All of this remains unsaid in Tourneur's film. Between the lines. Like when the Kid salutes the sign and we're meant to understand that while he's told Ann what Jeff *Bailey* would have wanted him to say—that he'd gone back to his former life as Jeff *Markham* because he couldn't forget about a woman named Kathie Moffat—the "real" Jeff is the one with his name up on the sign. The real truth, of course, is harder still: that no amount of signing can ever recoup the past or redeem the present. Fisher, Stefanos, Whit, and Kathie dead, and Jeff Bailey, too, as if in penance for his former life as Jeff Markham. Ann and the Kid still standing, although Ann knowing deep down inside, no matter what the Kid says, that she's lost the love of her life, the Kid minus a man good enough to have been his father. In the end, as the Kid knows better than anyone else and despite the consolatory chords provided by Webb's haunting score, there's only silence.

Notes

PREVIEW

1. On some of the audiovisual elements of *Chinatown*, see my "Audio Noir: Audiovisuality in Neo-Modernist Noir," in *Neo-Noir*, ed. Mark Bould, Kathrina Glitre, and Greg Tuck (London: Wallflower Press, 2009), 28–43.
2. Walter Murch, in Vincent LoBrutto, *Sound-on-Film* (Westport, CT: Praeger, 1994), 91.
3. Ibid.
4. Raymond Chandler, *The Little Sister* (New York: Vintage Crime/Black Lizard, 1988), 50.
5. Marc Vernet, "Film Noir on the Edge of Doom," in *Shades of Noir*, ed. Joan Copjec (London: Verso, 1993), 25.
6. Steve Neale, *Genre and Hollywood* (New York: Routledge, 2000), 173.
7. Ibid., 174.
8. James Naremore, *More Than Night: Film Noir in Its Contexts* (Berkeley: University of California Press, 1998), 7.
9. With respect to noir as a mythology, I'm echoing Naremore here, who in *More Than Night* calls noir a "kind of mythology" (7). For the Cowie, see "Film Noir and Women," *Shades of Noir*, 121.
10. On the singing cowboy, see, for example, Peter Stanfield, *Horse Opera: The Strange History of the 1930s Singing Cowboy* (Urbana: University of Illinois Press, 2002).
11. Neale, *Genre and Hollywood*, 249 and 5.
12. See my "Noir Musical: Gene Kelly, *Cover Girl*, and the Pierrot Noir" (forthcoming).
13. Thomas Leitch, *Crime Films* (Cambridge: Cambridge University Press, 2002), 17.
14. Raymond Borde and Étienne Chaumeton, *A Panorama of American Film Noir: 1941–1953*, trans. Paul Hammond (San Francisco: City Lights, 2002), 83.
15. Paul Schrader, "Notes on Film Noir," in *Perspectives on Film Noir*, ed. R. Barton Palmer (New York: G. K. Hall, 1996), 106.
16. Andrew Spicer, *Film Noir* (Harlow, UK: Pearson Education, 2002), 45.

17. On international noir, see, for example, *European Noir*, ed. Andrew Spicer (Manchester: Manchester University Press, 2007); and Jennifer Fay and Justus Nieland's *Film Noir: Hard-Boiled Modernity and the Cultures of Globalization* (New York: Routledge, 2010). As for "Hitch," I bracket his forties films here if only because so much has already been written about them, including their sound tracks. However, for the case against Hitchcock's films as noirs in the "parochial" context of American cinema in the 1940s and 1950s, see James Naremore, "Hitchcock at the Margins of Noir," in *Alfred Hitchcock: Centenary Essays*, ed. Richard Allen and S. Ishii-Gonzalès (London: BFI, 1999), 263–278. On Hitchcock's sound and music, see, respectively, Elisabeth Weis, *The Silent Scream: Alfred Hitchcock's Sound Track* (Rutherford, NJ: Fairleigh Dickinson University Press, 1982); Jack Sullivan, *Hitchcock's Music* (New Haven: Yale University Press, 2006); and Murray Pomerance, " 'The Future's Not Ours to See': Song, Singer, Labyrinth in Hitchcock's *The Man Who Knew Too Much*," in *Soundtrack Available*, ed. Arthur Knight and Pamela Robertson Wojcik (Durham, NC: Duke University Press, 2002), 53–73.
18. For a recent discussion of hard-boiled masculinity, see Philippa Gates, "The Hard-boiled Detective," in *Detecting Men: Masculinity and the Hollywood Detective Film* (Albany: SUNY Press, 2006), 81–88.
19. Richard Dyer, "Resistance through Charisma: Rita Hayworth and *Gilda*," in *Women in Film Noir*, ed. E. Ann Kaplan (London: BFI, 1998 [1978]), 81–89; Robert Porfirio, "The Dark Age of American Film: A Study of American Film Noir (1940–1960)" (Ph.D. diss., Yale University, 1979); Porfirio, "*The Killers*: Expressiveness of Sound and Image in Film Noir," in *Film Noir Reader*, ed. Alain Silver and James Ursini (New York: Limelight, 1996), 177–188; Porfirio, "Whatever Happened to the *Film Noir*? *The Postman Always Rings Twice* (1946–1981)," in *Film Noir Reader 2*, ed. Alain Silver and James Ursini (New York: Limelight, 1999), 85–97; Porfirio, "Dark Jazz: Music in the Film Noir," in *Film Noir Reader 2*, 177–186; David Butler, *Jazz Noir: Listening to Music from Phantom Lady to The Last Seduction* (Westport, CT: Praeger, 2002); Helen Hanson, "Sound Affects: Post-Production Sound, Soundscapes, and Sound Design in Hollywood's Studio Era," *Music, Sound, and the Moving Image* 1, 1 (2007), 27–49; Hanson, "Sounds of the City: The Sonic Fabric of *Film Noir*," in *The Cambridge Companion to Film Music*, ed. Robyn Stilwell and Peter Franklin (forthcoming); and Jans Wager, "Jazz and Cocktails: Reassessing the White and Black Mix in Film Noir," *Literature/Film Quarterly* 35, 3 (2007), 222–228.
20. Michel Chion, *Audio-Vision*, trans. Claudia Gorbman (New York: Columbia University Press, 1999), 145.
21. Ibid.
22. For an earlier take on Mulvey, see my "Audiophilia: Audiovisual Pleasure and Narrative Cinema in *Jackie Brown*," in *Roll Over Adorno: Critical Theory, Popular Culture, Audiovisual Media* (Albany: SUNY Press, 2006), 91–119.

INTRODUCTION

1. Janey Place and Lowell Peterson, "Some Visual Motifs of Film Noir," in *Film Noir Reader*, ed. Alain Silver and James Ursini (New York: Limelight, 2000), 68.

2. Paul Schrader, "Notes on Film Noir," in *Film Noir Reader*, 63.
3. Chion, *Audio-Vision*, xxvi.
4. Ibid., xxv.
5. Sergei Eisenstein, "The Music of Landscape," in *Nonindifferent Nature*, trans. Herbert Marshall (Cambridge: Cambridge University Press, 1987), 355.
6. Eisenstein, quoted in David Bordwell and Kristin Thompson, *Film Art* (New York: McGraw, 1993), 293.
7. Chion, *Audio-Vision*, 6.
8. See James Lastra, "Sound Space and Classical Narrative," *Sound Technology and the American Cinema* (New York: Columbia University Press, 2000), 180–215.
9. David Sonnenschein, *Sound Design* (Studio City, CA: Michael Wiese Productions, 2001), 196.
10. Chion, *Audio-Vision*, 66.
11. Ibid., 221. For a provocative take on the "acousmatic problem," see Murray Pomerance, "A Call from Everywhere," in *The Horse Who Drank the Sky: Film Experience Beyond Narrative and Theory* (New Brunswick, NJ: Rutgers University Press, 2008), 110–138.
12. Rick Altman, "Deep-Focus Sound: *Citizen Kane* and the Radio Aesthetic," in *Perspectives on Citizen Kane*, ed. Ronald Gottesman (New York: G. K. Hall, 1996), 109.
13. See James G. Stewart's recollection of rerecording *Citizen Kane* in "The Evolution of Cinematic Sound," in *Sound and the Cinema: The Coming of Sound to American Film*, ed. Evan William Cameron (Pleasantville, NY: Redgrave, 1980), 53–55. See also in general, Phyllis Goldfarb, "Orson Welles's Use of Sound," in *Perspectives on Orson Welles*, ed. Morris Beja (New York: G. K. Hall, 1995), 107–115; and François Thomas, "*Citizen Kane*: The Sound Track," in *Orson Welles's Citizen Kane: A Casebook*, ed. James Naremore (New York: Oxford University Press, 2004), 161–183.
14. Steve Neale, *Cinema and Technology: Image, Sound, Colour* (Bloomington: Indiana University Press, 1985), 48.
15. Chion, *Audio-Vision*, 58.
16. Sergei Eisenstein, V. I. Pudovkin, G. V. Aleksandrov, "Statement," in *Film Sound: Theory and Practice*, ed. Elisabeth Weis and John Belton (New York: Columbia University Press, 1981), 84.
17. Herbert Eagle, "Introduction," *Nonindifferent Nature*, xv.
18. Eisenstein, "The Music of Landscape," 277.
19. Altman, "Evolution of the Sound Track," *Film Sound*, 48.
20. The so-called "double system sound-on-film," in which there was a second, separate strip of film for sound, prevailed from 1929 to 1951.
21. Stephen Handzo, "Glossary of Film Sound Technology," in *Film Sound*, 400.
22. Mobile sound vans were also equipped with full-size film recorders and mixing consoles. For an illustrative account of some of these innovations, see Ken Cameron, *Sound and the Documentary Film* (London: Sir Isaac Pitman and Sons, 1947), in particular 31 and 33.
23. Handzo, "Glossary of Film Sound Technology," in *Film Sound*, 422.
24. Tony Gibbs, *The Fundamentals of Sonic Art & Sound Design* (Lausanne, Switzerland: AVA Publishing, 2007), 91; Stephen Prince, *Movies and Meaning* (Boston: Pearson, 2004), 173.

25. Chion, *Audio-Vision*, 145.
26. Ibid.
27. Roger Hickman, *Reel Music* (New York: Norton, 2006), 183.
28. With respect to forties noir, other notable composers include André Previn at M-G-M (*Border Incident, Scene of the Crime*); Paul Sawtell at RKO and Eagle-Lion (*Born to Kill, Desperate, T-Men*); Franz Waxman at Warners (*Possessed, Dark Passage, Nora Prentiss, The Unsuspected*); Leigh Harline at RKO (*Johnny Angel, Crack-Up, Nocturne, They Live by Night*); David Buttolph (*The House on 92nd Street, Somewhere in the Night, Kiss of Death, The Brasher Doubloon*) at Twentieth Century–Fox; Mockridge (*The Dark Corner, Nightmare Alley, Road House*) also at Fox; Hans Salter (*Phantom Lady, Scarlet Street, The Strange Affair of Uncle Harry*) at Universal; Frank Skinner at the same studio (*Black Angel, Ride the Pink Horse, The Naked City*); as well as composers not affiliated with a particular studio such as Dimitri Tiomkin (*When Strangers Marry, The Dark Mirror*) and Alfred Newman (*Leave Her to Heaven, Cry of the City, Thieves' Highway*).
29. Royal S. Brown, *Overtones and Undertones* (Berkeley: University of California Press, 1994), 133.
30. Miklós Rózsa, *A Double Life* (New York: Wynwood Press, 1989), 111.
31. *The New Grove Dictionary of American Music*, quoted by Kathryn Kalinak, in *Settling the Score* (Madison: University of Wisconsin Press, 1992), 160.
32. David Raksin, quoted by Kalinak, *Settling the Score*, 167.
33. Kalinak, *Settling the Score*, 178.
34. Raksin, quoted by Kalinak, *Settling the Score*, 166.
35. For a comparison between Rózsa and Steiner, see Mervyn Cooke, "*Film Noir* and the Psychological Drama," in *A History of Film Music* (Cambridge: Cambridge University Press, 2008), 108–112.
36. Timothy E. Scheurer, *Music and Mythmaking in Film* (Jefferson, NC: McFarland, 2008), 98.
37. Ibid.
38. William Darby and Jack Du Bois, *American Film Music: Major Composers, Techniques, Trends* (Jefferson, NC: McFarland, 1990), 267.
39. Ibid.
40. Rózsa, *A Double Life*, 101.
41. Richard R. Ness, "'A Lotta Night Music': The Sound of *Film Noir*," *Cinema Journal* 47, no. 2 (Winter 2008), 52–53.
42. Christopher Palmer, *The Composer in Hollywood* (New York: Marion Boyars, 1990), 166.
43. For analyses of Webb's score for *Murder, My Sweet*, see Palmer, *The Composer in Hollywood*, 167–169; Scheurer, *Music and Mythmaking in Film*, 82–83, 89–91, 94–96; and Ness, "'A Lotta Night Music,'" *Cinema Journal*, 63–66.
44. Palmer, *The Composer in Hollywood*, 169.
45. Ibid., 170.
46. Will Friedwald, *Jazz Singing: America's Great Voices from Bessie Smith to Bebop and Beyond* (New York: Da Capo Press, 1996), 198.
47. Robert Sickels, *The 1940s* (Westport, CT: Greenwood Press, 2004), 165.
48. Degen Pener, *The Swing Book* (Boston: Little, Brown & Co., 1999), 25.

49. Gunther Schuller, *The Swing Era: The Development of Jazz, 1930–1945* (New York: Oxford University Press, 1989), 9.
50. Ibid., 6.
51. But, as Krin Gabbard notes, in a famous scene in *The Big Combo* a "hoodlum refers to a drum break as 'real crazy' before he blasts it through a hearing aid and into the ear of a policeman he is torturing" (*Jammin' at the Margins: Jazz and the American Cinema* [Durham, NC: Duke University Press, 1996], 123).
52. David Butler, *Jazz Noir*, 2.
53. Arthur Knight, "*Jammin' the Blues*: The Sight of Jazz," in *Disintegrating the Musical: Black Performance and American Musical Film* (Durham, NC: Duke University Press, 2002), 198.
54. Schuller, *The Swing Era*, 9.
55. Gabbard, *Jammin' at the Margins*, 20, 27.
56. See Robert Porfirio, "*Among the Living*," in *Film Noir: An Encyclopedic Reference to the American Style*, ed. Alain Silver and Elizabeth Ward (Woodstock, NY: Overlook Press, 1992), 11; Geoff Mayer, in Mayer and Brian McDonnell, *Encyclopedia of Film Noir* (Westport, CT: Greenwood, 2007), 189.
57. Mayer, in Mayer and McDonnell, *Encyclopedia of Film Noir*, 89.
58. For a comparison of these sequences, see Hanson, "Sound Affects," 28–30 and 42–46.
59. Ibid., 89.
60. On the representation of African Americans in (neo-) noir, see Eric Lott, "The Whiteness of Film Noir," in *Whiteness*, ed. Mike Hill (New York: New York University Press, 1997), 81–101; Manthia Diawara, "*Noir* by *Noirs*: Toward a New Realism in Black Cinema," in *Shades of Noir*, 261–278; and Julian Murphet, "Noir and the Racial Unconscious," *Screen* 39, no. 1 (1998), 70–77. It's striking that although Diawara references rap and, in particular, funk in neo-"noirs by noirs," the notion of black musical performance does not figure in Lott's assessment of classic noir and only in passing in Murphet's ("Nor should the common, pulsing background aural accompaniment of jazz be too innocently understood" [30]).
61. Knight, *Disintegrating the Musical*, 225.
62. Elliott Carter, cited by Kenneth J. Bindas, *Swing, That Modern Sound* (Jackson: University Press of Mississippi, 2001), 15.
63. Donald Bogle, *Toms, Coons, Mulattoes, Mammies and Bucks* (New York: Continuum, 1994), 53 and 56.
64. On *Jammin' the Blues*, see Knight, *Disintegrating the Musical*, 195–230; and Gabbard, *Jammin' at the Margins*, 111. On the dismissal of vernacular (black) dance culture in the discourse of jazz, see Robert Crease, "Divine Frivolity: Hollywood Representations of the Lindy Hop, 1937–1942," in *Representing Jazz*, ed. Krin Gabbard (Durham, NC: Duke University Press, 1995), 207–228. The connection between *Jammin' the Blues* and forties noir is implicit in Gabbard's account of the film: "*Jammin' the Blues* adopted many of the expressionistic camera techniques. . . . regularly featured in the work of Hollywood craftsmen such as Fritz Lang, Billy Wilder, and Jacques Tourneur" (*Jammin' at the Margins*, 110).
65. Friedwald, *Jazz Singing*, 69.

66. See, for example, Buzzy Jackson, "Jazz Noir: Billie Holiday," *A Bad Woman Feeling Good: Blues and the Women Who Sing Them* (New York: Norton, 2005), 81–133.
67. William Ruhlmann, *Breaking Records* (New York: Routledge, 2004), 89.
68. *The Big Book of Swing*, ed. Bill Treadwell (New York: Cambridge House, 1946), 84.
69. Linda Mizejewski, *Ziegfeld Girl: Image and Icon in Culture and America* (Durham, NC: Duke University Press, 1999), 187. On the chanteuse associated with Poetic Realism, see, for example, Kelley Conway, *Chanteuse in the City: The Realist Singer in French Film* (Berkeley: University of California Press, 2004); on the German cabaret singer, see Linda Mizejewski, *Divine Decadence: Fascism, Female Spectacle, and the Makings of Sally Bowles* (Princeton: Princeton University Press, 1992); Richard W. McCormick, "The Cabaret of Humiliation," in *Gender and Sexuality in Weimar Modernity* (New York: Palgrave, 2001), 113–129; and Alan Lareau, "The Blonde Lady Sings: Women in Weimar Cabaret," in *Practicing Modernity*, ed. Christiane Schönfeld (Würzburg: Königshausen & Neumann, 2006), 191–217.
70. Friedwald, *Jazz Singing*, 68.
71. Lewis Ehrenberg, *Swingin' the Dream: Big Band Jazz and the Rebirth of American Culture* (Chicago: University of Chicago Press, 1998), 85.
72. See, for example, Janey Place's "Women in Film Noir" where the emphasis is on myth and the "two poles of female archetypes," the "spider woman" and the "nurturing woman" (*Women in Film Noir*, 47–68). I remain indebted to Place's argument, especially her valorization of image, spectacle, and iconography versus, say, narrative. However, as will become apparent in the course of this book, I'm less interested in the mythic or "archetypal" *nature* of the femme fatale than in her performative specificity. For the original, contemporary account of the "good-bad girl," see Martha Wolfenstein and Nathan Leites, *Movies: A Psychological Study* (New York: Atheneum, 1950), 25–47. For a wide-ranging reconsideration of the figure of the femme fatale in terms of, inter alia, "Victorinoir," see Julie Grossman, *Rethinking the Femme Fatale: Ready for Her Close-Up* (London: Palgrave Macmillan, 2009).
73. Richard Dyer, "Resistance through Charisma," in *Women in Film Noir*, 120.

PROLOGUE

1. James Naremore, *More Than Night*, 201.
2. In the end credits for *Out of the Past*, the character played by Paul Valentine is simply listed as "Joe." There are numerous spellings of his last name in the extant literature ("Stefano," "Stefanos," "Stephanos"), but I have opted for "Stefanos" as that's how the character's name is spelled in *Build My Gallows High*. See, for example, the introduction of the "little Greek" in the first chapter of Geoffrey Homes's novel (New York: William Morrow, 1946), 7.

1. HOUSE SOUND

1. Richard B. Jewell with Vernon Harbin, *The RKO Story* (New York: Arlington, 1982), 8.

2. Ibid.
3. Ibid., 9.
4. Sheri Chinen Biesen, *Blackout: World War II and the Origins of Film Noir* (Baltimore: Johns Hopkins University Press, 2005), 33.
5. Jewell, *The RKO Story*, 19.
6. Ibid.
7. Ibid., 120.
8. Ibid., 150.
9. Biesen, *Blackout*, 22. Arthur Lyons contends that "1939 was actually the year that inaugurated the film noir with the release of three prototypical films: *Let Us Live*, *Rio*, and *Blind Alley*" (*Death on the Cheap: The Lost B Movies of Film Noir* [New York: Da Capo Press, 2000], 35).
10. Robert Porfirio, "*Stranger on the Third Floor*," in *Film Noir: An Encyclopedia Reference to the American Style*, 269.
11. Carl Dreher, "Sound Personnel and Organization," in *Recording Sound for Motion Pictures*, ed. Lester Cowan (New York: McGraw-Hill, 1931), 344.
12. Ibid., 349.
13. John Michael Weaver, "James G. Stewart: Post-Production Pioneer," *Mix* (July 1991), 66.
14. In 1937, Stewart designed RKO's "first master console, which was one of the most sophisticated sound-recording operations for its time" (Weaver, "James G. Stewart," 72). Stewart and his assistant, Terry Kellum (who would later work on a number of noirs such as *Nocturne*, *Crack-Up*, and *The Window*), also encouraged RCA, RKO's parent company, to begin "manufacturing a compressor designed specifically for re-recording purposes" (ibid.). This device was instrumental in securing the . . . wide-spread acceptance and long-term viability" of RCA's variable-area optical-sound recording system (ibid.).
15. Robert Carringer, *The Making of Citizen Kane* (Berkeley: University of California Press, 1985), 103.
16. James G. Stewart, "The Evolution of Cinematic Sound," *Sound and the Cinema*, 47.
17. Carringer, *The Making of Citizen Kane*, 102.
18. Stewart, "The Evolution of Cinematic Sound," 48.
19. My emphasis. Ibid., 49.
20. Carringer, *The Making of Citizen Kane*, 103.
21. Ibid., 102.
22. Alexander Ballinger and Danny Graydon, *The Rough Guide to Film Noir* (London: Rough Guides, 2007), 19.
23. Sarah Kozloff, *Invisible Storytellers: Voice-over Narration in American Fiction Film* (Berkeley: University of California Press, 1988), 33.
24. Maureen Turim, *Flashbacks in Film* (New York: Routledge, 1989), 172–174.
25. Frank Krutnik, *In a Lonely Street* (London: Routledge, 1992), 47.
26. Biesen, *Blackout*, 25 and 31.
27. Turim, *Flashbacks in Film*, 173.
28. Mary Anne Doane, "The Voice in the Cinema," *Film Sound*, 168.
29. On *Let Us Live*, see Lyons, *Death on the Cheap*, 35 and 113.

30. Biesen, *Blackout*, 26.
31. Krutnik, *In a Lonely Street*, 48.
32. Ibid.
33. Ibid., 48–49.
34. Noël Carroll, "Lang and Pabst: Paradigms of Early Sound Practice," *Film Sound*, 275.
35. On the sound "pre-lap," see Murray Pomerance, "As Time Goes By," *The Horse Who Drank the Sky*, 139–148.
36. Biesen, *Blackout*, 23.
37. Krutnik, *In a Lonely Street*, 49.
38. See Biesen, *Blackout*, 24–25.
39. Like Lang's *M*, *Stranger on the Third Floor* mobilizes the problem of insanity (a real, censorable issue for the Breen office at the time) but identifies it, precisely, as a *social* problem. For example, The Stranger tells Jane that he was "hurt" at the asylum from which he has escaped: they put him in a "shirt with long sleeves" (clearly, a straitjacket) and doused him with "ice water."
40. Biesen, *Blackout*, 115.
41. Jewell, *The RKO Story*, 141.
42. Jennifer Langdon, *Caught in the Crossfire: Adrian Scott and the Politics of Americanism in 1940s Hollywood* (New York: Columbia University Press, 2008), 72.
43. Ibid.
44. Eddie Robson, *Film Noir* (London: Virgin, 2005), 52.
45. Edward Dmytryk, quoted in Gene D. Phillips, *Creatures of Darkness* (Lexington: University Press of Kentucky, 2000), 33.
46. Ibid.
47. Ibid., 34.
48. John Paxton, quoted by Stephen Pendo, *Raymond Chandler on Screen: His Novels into Film* (Metuchen, NJ: Scarecrow Press, 1976), 34.
49. Edward Dmytryk, *It's a Hell of a Life but Not a Bad Living* (New York: Times Books, 1978), 59.
50. Dmytryk, quoted in Phillips, *Creatures of Darkness*, 40.
51. Paxton, quoted in Langdon, *Caught in the Crossfire*, 77.
52. Ibid.
53. Film noir, to sample a recent volume on the genre, "is the cinema of paranoia" (Wheeler Winston Dixon, *Film Noir and the Cinema of Paranoia* [New Brunswick, NJ: Rutgers University Press, 2009], 1).
54. Jonathan Buchsbaum, "Tame Wolves and Phony Claims: Paranoia and Film Noir," in *The Book of Film Noir*, ed. Ian Cameron (New York: Continuum, 1993), 93 and 97. On the relation between paranoia and Jewishness as well as homosexuality, see also Vincent Brook, *Driven to Darkness: Jewish Émigré Directors and the Rise of Film Noir* (New Brunswick, NJ: Rutgers University Press, 2009), 95 and 116–117.
55. Buchsbaum, "Tame Wolves and Phony Claims," 93.
56. Carroll, "Lang and Pabst," *Film Sound*, 268.
57. J. P. Telotte, "Effacement and Subjectivity: *Murder, My Sweet*'s Troubled Vision," *Voices in the Dark: Narrative Patterns of Film Noir* (Urbana: University of Illinois Press, 1989), 99.

58. Buchsbaum, "Tame Wolves and Phony Claims," 96.
59. John Paxton, quoted in Edward Dmytryk, *On Filmmaking* (Boston: Focal Press, 1986), 139.
60. Ibid., 159.
61. See Dennis Broe, *Film Noir, American Workers, and Postwar Hollywood* (Gainesville: University Press of Florida, 2009), 145 note 24.
62. Dmytryk, *Cinema: Concept and Practice* (Boston: Focal Press, 1988), 99. For Dmytryk's programmatic thoughts on sound, see *On Filmmaking*, 275–278.
63. On Mazurki's career, see William Hare, *Early Film Noir: Greed, Lust and Murder Hollywood Style* (Jefferson, NC: McFarland, 2003), 48–51.
64. John Paxton's script for *Murder, My Sweet*, quoted in Dmytryk, *On Filmmaking*, 137.
65. Buchsbaum, "Tame Wolves and Phony Claims," 96.
66. Kelly Oliver and Benigno Trigo, *Noir Anxiety* (Minneapolis: University of Minnesota Press, 2003), 29.
67. On the "private ear," see Robert Miklitsch, "Audio Noir: Audiovisuality in Neo-Modernist Noir," in *Neo-Noir*, 33–36.
68. Dmytryk, *On Filmmaking*, 526.
69. Ibid., 528–529.
70. For an analysis of the dream sequence, see Dmytryk, *On Filmmaking*, 526–529.
71. Ibid., 528.
72. R. Barton Palmer, "*Murder, My Sweet*," *Hollywood's Dark Cinema* (New York: Twayne, 1994), 78.
73. Robson, *Film Noir*, 58.
74. William Luhr, *Raymond Chandler and Film* (New York: Frederick Ungar, 1982), 119.
75. Ibid.
76. Palmer, *Hollywood's Dark Cinema*, 81. On the "female sleuth" films and the "formation of the companionate couple," see Helen Hanson, *Hollywood Heroines* (London: I. B. Tauris, 2007), 20–32.
77. Chion, *The Voice in the Cinema*, 96.

2. SONIC EFFECTS

1. See, for example, Peggy Thompson and Saeko Usukawa, *Hard-Boiled: Great Lines from Classic Noir Films* (San Francisco: Chronicle Books, 1996).
2. Tom Flinn, "Daniel Mainwaring: An Interview," in *The Big Book of Noir*, ed. Ed Gorman, Lee Server, and Martin Greenberg (New York: Carroll and Graf, 1998), 66.
3. Eddie Muller, *Dark City: The Lost World of Film Noir* (New York: St. Martin's Griffin, 1998), 78.
4. Robson, *Film Noir*, 105.
5. Turim, *Flashbacks in Film*, 171.
6. Ibid.
7. Paul Schrader, "Notes on Film Noir," in *Perspectives on Film Noir*, 104.
8. On the "big city" sound, which I discuss in terms of Walsh's *City of Conquest* (see "Note on Text"), see also Hanson, "Sounds of the City."

9. Christopher Palmer, *The Composer in Hollywood*, 203.
10. Edward Dimendberg, *Film Noir and the Spaces of Modernity* (Cambridge, MA: Harvard University Press, 2004), 61.
11. David Thomson, *The Big Sleep* (London: BFI, 2000), 49.
12. On "footsteps in the dark," see also Hanson, "Sounds of the City."
13. Chris Fujiwara, *Jacques Tourneur: The Cinema of Nightfall* (Jefferson, NC: McFarland, 1998), 75.
14. See Eric Somer, "The Noir Horror of *Cat People*," in *Film Noir Reader 4*, ed. Alain Silver and James Ursini (Pompton Plains, NJ: Limelight, 2004), 191–205.
15. Kim Newman, *Cat People* (London: BFI, 1999), 48.
16. Ibid.
17. Jacques Tourneur, quoted in Newman, *Cat People*, 49.
18. Joan Cohen, "*Nightmare Alley*," in *Film Noir: An Encyclopedic Reference to the American Style*, 209.
19. Tom Gunning, *The Films of Fritz Lang: Allegories of Vision and Modernity* (London: BFI, 2000), 303.
20. Thomas C. Renzi, *Cornell Woolrich: From Pulp Noir to Film Noir* (Jefferson, NC: McFarland, 2006), 252.
21. On the noir returning serviceman, see Robert Francis Saxe, "Kiss the Blood off My Hands," in *Settling Down: World War II Veterans' Challenge to the Postwar Consensus* (New York: Palgrave Macmillan, 2007), 83–115.
22. Cohen, "*Nightmare Alley*," 210.
23. Nicholas Christopher, *Somewhere in the Night* (New York: The Free Press, 1997), 93.
24. Muller, *Dark City*, 120.
25. Robert Sickels, *The 1940s*, 208.
26. Christopher, *Somewhere in the Night*, 94.
27. Frank Enley's confession recalls, as Wheeler Winston Dixon notes, John Ford's *Informer* (1935) as well as the "then-current HUAC hearings in Washington" ("*Act of Violence* and the Early Films of Fred Zinnemann," in *The Films of Fred Zinnemann*, ed. Arthur Nolletti, Jr. [Albany: SUNY Press, 1999], 48 and 52). On the theme of "survivor guilt" in *Act of Violence*, see also Brook, *Driven to Darkness*, 207–210.
28. Dimendberg, *Film Noir and the Spaces of Modernity*, 160.
29. Ibid., 161.
30. Sickels, *The 1940s*, 211.
31. Robert Porfirio, "*Crack-Up*," in *Film Noir: An Encyclopedic Reference to the American Style*, 66.
32. Ibid.
33. The DP is Robert de Grasse and the editor Frederic Knudtson; the score is by Leigh Harline and the sound by John L. Cass and Terry Kellum.
34. Robert Ottoson, *A Reference Guide to the American Film Noir: 1940–1958* (Metuchen, NJ: Scarecrow Press, 1981), 43.
35. Blake Lucas, "*Border Incident*," in *Film Noir: An Encyclopedic Reference to the American Style*, 39.
36. Jeanine Basinger, *Anthony Mann* (Boston: Twayne, 1974), 54.

37. Stephen Handzo, quoted by Robert Ottoson in *A Reference Guide to the American Film Noir*, 27.
38. Ibid.
39. Basinger, *Anthony Mann*, 72.
40. Ibid.
41. Ibid.
42. Jonathan Auerbach, "Noir Citizenship: Anthony Mann's *Border Incident*," *Cinema Journal* 47, no. 4 (Summer 2008), 116.
43. Although Murphy is on record making derogatory comments about Mexicans, he nonetheless credited his initial success in the Senate to his experience making *Border Incident*. See George Murphy with Victor Lasky, *"Say . . . Didn't You Used to Be George Murphy?"* (New York: Bartholomew House, 1970), 2–3.
44. Muller, *Dark City*, 185.
45. Anthony Mann, quoted by Ottoson in *A Reference Guide to the American Film Noir*, 27.

3. AUDIO TECHNOLOGIES

1. Nicholas Christopher, *Somewhere in the Night*, 90.
2. Ibid., 104.
3. Ibid., 105.
4. Lutz Koepnick, "Berlin Noir," in *The Dark Mirror: German Cinema between Hitler and Hollywood* (Berkeley: University of California Press, 2002), 180–181.
5. James M. Cain, *Double Indemnity* (New York: Vintage, 1978), 120.
6. Ibid.
7. Richard Schickel, *Double Indemnity* (London: BFI, 1992), 59.
8. Ibid.
9. Ibid.
10. Ibid., 44.
11. Ibid., 9 and 31.
12. J. P. Telotte, *Voices in the Dark*, 93.
13. Billy Wilder, quoted by Schickel, in *Double Indemnity*, 50.
14. David Mercer, *The Telephone: The Life Story of a Technology* (Westport, CT: Greenwood, 2006), 82.
15. Alfred Hitchcock, quoted in David Thomson, "Telephone," *Film Comment* 20, No. 4 (July/August 1984), 26.
16. Thomson, "Telephone," 28.
17. Jack Shadoian, "*Force of Evil* (1948)," in *Dreams and Dead Ends* (Cambridge, MA: MIT Press, 1977), 143.
18. Christopher, *Somewhere in the Night*, 120.
19. Abraham Polonsky, *Force of Evil: The Critical Edition*, ed. John Schultheiss and Mark Schaubert (Northridge, CA: Center for Telecommunications Studies, 1996), 116.
20. Jean-Luc Godard, quoted in Thomson, "Telephone," 27.
21. William Nadel, "Radio Noir," *The Big Book of Noir*, 34. For a very fine reading of, among

other things, the radio and film versions of *Sorry, Wrong Number*, see Amy Lawrence, "The Problem of the Speaking Woman," in *Echo and Narcissus: Women's Voices in Classical Hollywood Cinema* (Berkeley: University of California Press, 1991), 130–145.

22. Foster Hirsch, *The Dark Side of the Screen: Film Noir* (New York: Da Capo Press, 1981), 152.
23. Ned Schantz, "Telephonic Film," *Film Quarterly* 56, no. 4 (Summer 2003), 30.
24. For an excellent analysis of the discursive character of *Sorry, Wrong Number*, see Telotte, "Tangled Networks and Wrong Numbers," *Voices in the Dark*, 74–81.
25. Palmer, *The Composer in Hollywood*, 101.
26. Sickels, *The 1940s*, 185.
27. Lewis Coe, *Wireless Radio* (Jefferson, NC: McFarland, 1996), 185.
28. Shadoian, *Dreams and Dead Ends*, 191.
29. Carlos Clarens, "Shades of Noir," *Crime Movies* (New York: Da Capo Press, 1997), 226.
30. Dimendberg, *Film Noir and the Spaces of Modernity*, 228.
31. Robert Porfirio, "*He Walked by Night*," in *Film Noir: An Encyclopedic Reference to the American Style*, 121.
32. On Cross's crossed identity (i.e., Christ-figure and Wandering Jew), see Brook, *Driven to Darkness*, 99.
33. Caryl Flinn, *Strains of Utopia: Gender, Nostalgia, and Hollywood Film Music* (Princeton: Princeton University Press, 1992), 165.
34. Robert Porfirio, "*The Unsuspected* and the Noir Sequence: Realism, Expressionism, Style," in *Film Noir Reader 4*, 76. See also Porfirio's "The Noir Title Sequence," in *Film Noir Reader 4*, 69.
35. Porfirio, "The Noir Title Sequence," 69.
36. Christopher, *Somewhere in the Night*, 211.
37. Porfirio, "*The Unsuspected*," *Film Noir Reader 4*, 279.
38. Spencer Selby, *Dark City* (Jefferson, NC: McFarland, 1997), 62.
39. Roland Gelatt, *The Fabulous Phonograph, 1877–1977* (New York: Appleton-Century, 1977), 298.
40. Kathryn Kalinak, *Settling the Score*, 160.
41. Ibid.
42. Gunning, *The Films of Fritz Lang*, 335.
43. Ibid., 318.
44. Renzi, *Cornell Woolrich*, 223.
45. Quoted in Geoffrey O'Brien, *Hardboiled America: Lurid Paperbacks and the Masters of Noir* (New York: Da Capo Press, 1997), 100.
46. But, as Philippa Gates notes, *Black Angel* ends with "Marty and Cathy on the cover of the sheet music for their hit song, 'Time Will Tell'" ("The Maritorious Melodrama: Film Noir with a Female Detective," *Journal of Film and Video* 61, no. 3 [Fall 2009], 36).
47. Alec Wilder, *American Popular Song: The Great Innovators, 1900–1950* (New York: Oxford University Press, 1990), 423.
48. Wheeler Winston Dixon, "1946: Movies and Postwar Recovery," in *American Cinema of the 1940s*, ed. Dixon (New Brunswick, NJ: Rutgers University Press, 2006), 162; Kerry Segrave, *Jukeboxes: An American Social History* (Jefferson, NC: McFarland, 2002), 160.
49. Segrave, *Jukeboxes*, 133.

50. On the production of *The Blue Dahlia*, see James Naremore, *More Than Night*, 107–114; and Sheri Chinen Biesen, *Blackout*, 197–203.
51. As Julie Grossman notes, Joyce Harwood doubles Johnny's "bad-girl" wife when she "repeats Helen's earlier habit of picking petals off the blue dahlias" (*Rethinking the Femme Fatale in Film Noir: Ready for Her Close-Up* (New York: Palgrave Macmillan, 2009), 32–33.
52. Turim, *Flashbacks in Film*, 150.
53. For a recent, revisionary account of the production of *Detour*, see Glenn Erickson, "Fate Seeks the Loser: Edgar G. Ulmer's *Detour* (1945)," *Film Noir Reader 4*, 26.
54. Naremore, *More Than Night*, 147.
55. Flinn, *Strains of Utopia*, 123.
56. Flinn, *Strains of Utopia*, 124. Indeed, when Al takes the wheel of Haskell's car, he glances into the rear-view mirror, a subjective shot that dissolves into Sue dressed in a "shimmering sequin gown" singing "I Can't Believe That You're in Love with Me" and "very much the star of the show" (Noah Isenberg, *Detour* [London: BFI, 2008], 59).
57. Flinn, *Strains of Utopia*, 125.
58. On the process of male projection and female resistance in *Detour*, see Grossman, *Rethinking the Femme Fatale*, 23–25.
59. Bob Baker, "*Fallen Angel*," *The Book of Film Noir*, ed. Ian Cameron (New York: Continuum, 1993), 185.
60. Ibid., 184.
61. Stanley Green, *The Encyclopedia of the Musical Film* (New York: Oxford University Press, 1981), 87.
62. Jane Lenz Elder, *Alice Faye: A Life Beyond the Silver Screen* (Jackson: University Press of Mississippi, 2002), 176; Foster Hirsch, *Otto Preminger: The Man Who Would Be King* (New York: Knopf, 2007), 128. On Linda Darnell and *Fallen Angel*, see also Ronald L. Davis, *Hollywood Beauty: Linda Darnell and the American Dream* (Norman: University of Oklahoma Press, 1991), 89–90.
63. On the "Judeo-Christian synthesis" of Eric Stanton and June Mills, see Brook, *Driven to Darkness*, 153–155.
64. Elder, *Alice Faye*, 179.
65. Gerald Pratley, *The Cinema of Otto Preminger* (New York: Castle, 1971), 74.

4. BLUES IN THE NIGHT

1. Manohla Dargis, *L.A. Confidential* (London: BFI, 2003), 74.
2. Robert Porfirio, "*Born to Kill*," in *Film Noir: An Encyclopedic Reference to the American Style*, 40.
3. Ibid.
4. Geoff Mayer, "*Born to Kill*," in *Encyclopedia of Film Noir*, 117.
5. See, for example, Dan Flory, "Introduction," *Philosophy, Black Film, Film Noir* (University Park: Pennsylvania State University Press, 2008), 32.
6. Borde and Chaumeton, *A Panorama of American Film Noir*, 66.

7. Alain Silver, "*Ride the Pink Horse*," in *Film Noir: An Encyclopedic Reference to the American Style*, 243.
8. Borde and Chaumeton, *A Panorama of American Film Noir*, 66.
9. Roger Tailleur, "*The Pink Horse*, or the Pipe Dream of the Human Condition," in *Perspectives on Film Noir*, 243.
10. Naremore, *More Than Night*, 122.
11. On Adorno's position on popular music, including jazz, see, for example, Robert Miklitsch, *Roll Over Adorno*, 43–59. On the transformation in the film version of *Crossfire* from the topic of homosexuality to anti-Semitism, see Robert Corber, *Homosexuality in Cold War America: Resistance and the Crisis of Masculinity* (Durham, NC: Duke University Press, 1997), 75–104. In the last context, see also Peter Stanfield who remarks with respect to *Crossfire* that "pop" big-band music, at least when played in an all-male "domestic" environment, has a feminine and even homosexual aura (*Body and Soul: Jazz and Blues in American Film* [Urbana: University of Illinois Press, 2005], 149).
12. Michael Tanner, *Wagner* (Princeton: Princeton University Press, 1995), 23.
13. Ibid., 19.
14. Abraham Polonsky, *Force of Evil: The Critical Edition*, 108.
15. Nicholas Christopher, *Somewhere in the Night*, 132.
16. David Butler, *Jazz Noir*, 61.
17. Ibid.
18. Michael F. Keaney, *Film Noir Guide* (Jefferson, NC: McFarland, 2003), 116.
19. Andrew Spicer, *Film Noir*, 92.
20. Christopher, *Somewhere in the Night*, 119.
21. Ibid.
22. See Robert Porfirio, "Aural Structure and Effects in a Sequence from *The Dark Corner*," in *Film Noir Reader 2*, 184–187.
23. Frank Krutnik, *In a Lonely Street*, 102.
24. Ibid., 103.
25. See David Meeker, "Kiss of Death" (#1791), in *Jazz in the Movies* (New York: Da Capo Press, 1982). Jo Jones can also be seen playing on the number "I Got Rhythm" in the nightclub sequence in *The Unsuspected* (Meeker, "*The Unsuspected*" [#3473], in *Jazz in the Movies*).
26. Jack Shadoian, *Dreams and Dead Ends*, 132.
27. Carl Macek, "*Brute Force*," in *Film Noir: An Encyclopedic Reference to the American Style*, 46.
28. Frank Krutnik, "Something More Than Night: Tales of the Noir City," in *The Cinematic City*, ed. David B. Clarke (London: Routledge, 1997), 96.
29. Ibid., 98.
30. Jans B. Wager, *Dames in the Driver's Seat* (Austin: University of Texas Press, 2005), 57. See also William Luhr, *Raymond Chandler and Film* (Tallahassee: Florida State University Press, 1991), 127–128; and Naremore, *More Than Night*, 241.
31. Sean McCann, "Dark Passages: Jazz and Civil Liberty in the Postwar Crime Film," in *"Un-American" Hollywood: Politics and Film in the Blacklist Era*, ed. Frank Krutnik, Steve Neale, Brian Neve, and Peter Stanfield (New Brunswick, NJ: Rutgers University Press, 2007), 120.

32. Jans Wager, "Jazz and Cocktails," 223–224.
33. Ibid., 224.
34. Paula Rabinowitz, *Black & White & Noir: America's Pulp Modernism* (New York: Columbia University Press, 2002), 61–62.
35. James Harvey, *Movie Love in the Fifties* (New York: Knopf, 2001), 29.
36. Gary C. Thomas, "Men at the Keyboard," in *Beyond the Soundtrack: Representing Music in Cinema*, ed. Daniel Goldmark, Lawrence Kramer, and Richard Leppert (Berkeley: University of California Press, 2007), 279.
37. Meredith Brody and Lee Sanders, "*Leave Her to Heaven*," in *Film Noir: An Encyclopedic Reference to the American Style*, 170.
38. Maureen Turim, *Flashbacks in Film*, 158.
39. Ibid.
40. R. Barton Palmer, *Hollywood's Dark Cinema*, 155.
41. Franz Waxman, "Franz Waxman on Film Music," in Tony Thomas, *Film Score: The Art and Craft of Movie Music* (Burbank, CA: Riverwood Press, 1991), 40.
42. Robert Porfirio, "*Possessed*," in *Film Noir: An Encyclopedic Reference to the American Style*, 231.
43. For a reading of this scene in the context of "medical discourse," see Mary Ann Doane, *The Desire to Desire: The Woman's Film in the 1940s* (Bloomington: Indiana University Press, 1987), 57–58.
44. Blake Lucas and Elizabeth Ward, "*Undercurrent*," in *Film Noir: An Encyclopedic Reference to the American Style*, 300.
45. Spencer Selby, "*Undercurrent*," *Dark City*, 47.
46. Alain Silver, "*Nocturne*," in *Film Noir: An Encyclopedic Reference to the American Style*, 212.
47. Christopher, *Somewhere in the Night*, 205.
48. Howard Hawks, quoted in Lewis Yablonsky, *George Raft* (New York: McGraw-Hill, 1974), 73; Jane Bellingham, "Nocturne," in *The Oxford Companion to Music*, ed. Alison Latham (Oxford: Oxford University Press, 2002), 838–839.

5. SINGING DETECTIVES AND BLUESMEN, BLACK JAZZWOMEN AND TORCH SINGERS

1. Cecelia Ager, "Hellinger Film Is a Love Song to NYC," *PM Daily* (March 5, 1948), quoted in Carl Richardson, *Autopsy: An Element of Realism in Film Noir* (Metuchen, NJ: Scarecrow, 1992), 99.
2. Bernard F. Dick, *Joseph L. Mankiewicz* (Boston: Twayne, 1983), 79.
3. As Peter Stanfield remarks, Gaye's performance—"both wretchedly grotesque and unbearably beautiful"—"signifies her age: it is anachronistic, locating her personal history and performance style in the past" (*Body and Soul*, 135).
4. Sickels, *The 1940s*, 166.
5. On *The Postman Always Rings Twice* in an international context (Renoir's *La Bête humaine* [1938] and Visconti's *Ossessione*), see Fay and Nieland, *Film Noir*, 2–28.
6. For a counter-reading of Nora Smith as a femme fatale in terms of "both her ambitions and fears," see Julie Grossman, *Rethinking the Femme Fatale*, 45–47.

7. Dyer, "Resistance through Charisma," in *Women in Film Noir*, 119.
8. Ibid., 118.
9. Bogle, *Toms, Coons, Mulattoes, Mammies, and Bucks*, xxiii.
10. Ibid., 71.
11. Ibid., 70.
12. Hervé Dumont, *Frank Borzage* (Jefferson, NC: McFarland, 2006), 339. In this context, see also the "hanging" song in Charles Laughton's *The Night of the Hunter* (1955).
13. Dumont, *Frank Borzage*, 336.
14. Slavoj Žižek, *Enjoy Your Symptom!: Jacques Lacan in Hollywood and Out* (New York: Routledge, 1992), 158.
15. Robert Porfirio, "*The Glass Key*," in *Film Noir: An Encyclopedic Reference to the American Style*, 114.
16. Blake Lucas, "*I Walk Alone*," in *Film Noir: An Encyclopedic Reference to the American Style*, 143.
17. Ibid.
18. Frank Loesser and Hoagy Carmichael's "Heart and Soul" and "Two Sleepy People" were both composed in 1938, reflecting *I Walk Alone*'s emphasis on the popular music of the thirties. On Loesser's partnership with Carmichael, see Thomas L. Riis, *Frank Loesser* (New Haven: Yale University Press, 2008), 34–35.
19. Jonathan Munby, *Public Enemies, Public Heroes: Screening the Gangster from Little Caesar to Touch of Evil* (Chicago: University of Chicago Press, 1999), 132.
20. Barry Gifford, "*Road House*," in *Out of the Past: Adventures in Film Noir* (Jackson: University of Mississippi Press, 2001), 138.
21. Robert Ottoson, "*Road House*," *The American Film Noir*, 150.
22. William Donati, *Ida Lupino: A Biography* (Lexington: University Press of Kentucky, 1996), 139.
23. See, for example, Lucy Ann Liggett Stewart, *Ida Lupino as a Film Director, 1949–1953: An Auteur Approach* (New York: Arno, 1980); *Queen of the 'B's: Ida Lupino Behind the Camera*, ed. Annette Kuhn (Trowbridge, Wiltshire, UK: Flicks Books, 1995).
24. Wilder, *American Popular Song*, 277.
25. Ottoson, "*Road House*," 150.
26. Dyer, "Resistance through Charisma," 118.

6. THE BIG NUMBER (SIDE B)

1. I am echoing the conclusion of the first chapter of Amy Lawrence's *Echo and Narcissus* here, "Can a woman ever be said to 'speak' in classical cinema?" (32). My working thesis is that when women sing in noir, they are frequently expressing what cannot be spoken and that, even if the men in the film refuse to listen, the audience can hear between the lines.
2. Eric Lott, "The Whiteness of Film Noir," 90.
3. On "My Old Kentucky Home" in the context of, inter alia, theatrical productions of *Uncle Tom's Cabin*, see Eric Lott, *Love and Theft: Blackface Minstrelsy and the American Working*

Class (New York: Oxford University Press, 1993), 187–188, 218; Michael Rogin, *Blackface, White Noise* (Berkeley: University of California Press, 1996), 40–41.

4. Krin Gabbard, *Black Magic: White Hollywood and African American Culture* (New Brunswick, NJ: Rutgers University Press, 2004), 6.
5. Rogin, *Blackface, White Noise*, 41.
6. Bernard Eisenschitz, *Nicholas Ray: An American Journey*, trans. Tom Milne (London: Faber and Faber, 1993), 101.
7. Ibid.
8. Ibid., 102.
9. Ibid.
10. David Butler, *Jazz Noir*, 3.
11. Geoff Andrew, *The Films of Nicholas Ray: The Poet of Nightfall* (London: BFI, 2004), 30.
12. Ibid., 4.
13. On Carmichael and *To Have and Have Not*, see Krin Gabbard, "Nat King Cole, Hoagy Carmichael, and the Fate of the Jazz Actor," *Jammin' at the Margins*, 261–264; and Sean McCann, "Dark Passages: Jazz and Civil Liberty in the Postwar Crime Film," in *"Un-American" Hollywood*, 121–122.
14. For another, different reading of this musical number, one that emphasizes its "spectacular" character, see Peter Larsen, *Film Music* (London: Reaktion Books, 2005), 104–105.
15. Kevin Hagopian, "'How You Fixed for Red Points?': Anecdote and the World War II Home Front in *The Big Sleep*," *Film Noir Reader 4*, 39.
16. David Thomson, *The Big Sleep*, 43.
17. Hagopian, "'How You Fixed for Red Points?,'" 39.
18. Thomson, *The Big Sleep*, 46.
19. Hagopian, "'How You Fixed for Red Points?,'" 39.
20. Nicholas Christopher, *Somewhere in the Night*, 122.
21. Ibid., 124.
22. Robert Porfirio and Alain Silver, "*Scene of the Crime*," in *Film Noir: An Encyclopedic Reference to the American Style*, 249.
23. Ibid.
24. Pam Cook, "Duplicity in *Mildred Pierce*," in *Women in Film Noir*, 77.
25. James M. Cain, *Mildred Pierce* (New York: Vintage, 1989), 253.
26. Ibid.
27. In "The Whiteness of Film Noir" Lott has remarked that Mildred's trajectory, the "rise and fall of an independent woman," "is shadowed at every step by her black maid . . . who figures the proletarian fate Mildred is driven to beat and whose doubling likeness suggests Mildred's darkest dread" (197).
28. Robert Porfirio, "*The Bribe*," in *Film Noir: An Encyclopedic Reference to the American Style*, 43.
29. Ibid.
30. Blake Lucas, "*I Walk Alone*," in *Film Noir: An Encyclopedic Reference to the American Style*, 268.
31. Frank Krutnik, *In a Lonely Street*, 257 note 12.
32. Ibid.
33. Ibid.

34. On the "homosocial" components of *Dead Reckoning*, see Richard Dyer, "Postscript: Queers and Women in Film Noir," *Women in Film Noir*, 127.
35. Spicer, *Film Noir*, 101.
36. As Christopher notes, Coral is both a "torch singer" and an "incendiary" figure in *Dead Reckoning* since she's not only responsible for the death of Johnny, who's "incinerated behind the wheel of a car," but is figuratively linked with the "torrid," "infernal" space of Gulf City (*Somewhere in the Night*, 131 and 127, respectively).

7. THE BIG NUMBER (A SIDE)

1. Robert Porfirio, "*Nora Prentiss*," in *Film Noir: An Encyclopedic Reference to the American Style*, 213.
2. Borde and Chaumeton, *A Panorama of American Film Noir*, 29.
3. Biesen, *Blackout*, 49.
4. Robert Porfirio, "*This Gun for Hire*," in *Film Noir: An Encyclopedic Reference to the American Style*, 291.
5. Deborah Thomas, "Psychoanalysis and Film Noir," *The Book of Film Noir*, 81.
6. Ibid., 80.
7. See Veronica Lake with Donald Bain, *Veronica* (New York: The Citadel Press, 1969), 98–100. But see also Jeff Lenburg's *Peekaboo: The Story of Veronica Lake* where Jan Grippo, a professional magician brought in by Paramount to help Lake with her act, recounts that "he was so impressed by her cooperation and professional ability that he considered forming a magic act with [her]" ([New York: St. Martin's, 1983], 93).
8. Borde and Chaumeton, *A Panorama of American Film Noir*, 38.
9. Naremore, *More Than Night*, 73.
10. Ibid., 158.
11. On *Gilda*'s reception in Spain, see Rob Stone, "Spanish Film Noir," *European Film Noir*, 188.
12. Biesen, *Blackout*, 152.
13. Borde and Chaumeton, *A Panorama of American Film Noir*, 56.
14. On the tension between the Spanish and American aspects of Hayworth's star image, see Adrienne L. McLean, *Being Rita Hayworth: Labor, Identity, and Hollywood Stardom* (New Brunswick, NJ: Rutgers University Press, 2004), 32–39, 44–52. As Mark Bould observes of "Put the Blame on Mame," "the first performance, private and low-key, works to undermine this equation [women are to blame for the world's disasters]; the second, public and spectacular, seems to confirm it" (*Film Noir: From Berlin to Sin City* [London: Wallflower, 2005], 90).
15. Place, "Women in Film Noir," *Women in Film Noir*, 56.
16. Ballinger and Graydon, *Rough Guide to Film Noir*, 95.
17. Thomas, "Psychoanalysis and Film Noir," 81.
18. John Kobal, *Rita Hayworth: Portrait of a Sex Goddess* (New York: Berkeley, 1977), 155.
19. Ibid., 156.
20. Biesen, *Blackout*, 152; Kobal, *Rita Hayworth*, 156.

21. Kobal, *Rita Hayworth*, 151.
22. Biesen, *Blackout*, 145.
23. Marjorie Rosen, *Popcorn Venus* (New York: Coward, McCann & Geohegan, 1973), 211.
24. Heather Laing, *The Gendered Score: Music in 1940s Melodrama and the Woman's Film* (Aldershot, UK: Ashgate, 2007), 101.
25. Orson Welles, in Orson Welles and Peter Bogdanovich, in *This Is Orson Welles*, ed. Jonathan Rosenbaum (New York: HarperCollins, 1992), 194.
26. Ibid., 195.
27. Simon Callow, *Orson Welles: Hello, Americans*, Vol. 2 (New York: Viking, 2006), 361.
28. Ibid., 365.
29. Welles, in Welles and Bogdanovich, *This Is Orson Welles*, 195.
30. Joseph McBride, *Orson Welles* (New York: Viking, 1972), 108.
31. Callow, *Hello, Americans*, 368.
32. James Naremore, "*The Lady from Shanghai*," *The Magic World of Orson Welles*, 160.
33. On *The Blue Angel*, see Paul Coates, "The Cold Heaven of the Blue Angel: Dietrich, Masochism, and Identification," *The Gorgon's Gaze: German Cinema, Expressionism, and the Image of Horror* (Cambridge: Cambridge University Press, 1991), 62–72.
34. Randy Rasmussen, *Orson Welles: Six Films Analyzed* (Jefferson, NC: McFarland, 2006), 112.
35. Naremore writes that Welles dresses Hayworth "in near parodies of calendar-girl fashion" (*The Magic World of Orson Welles*, 160).
36. Rasmussen, *Orson Welles*, 112.
37. See the section on "smoking guns" in McLean's " 'I Told You Not to Move—I Mean It!' " *Being Rita Hayworth*, 150–156.
38. Oliver and Trigo, *Noir Anxiety*, 58.
39. McLean, *Being Rita Hayworth*, 156.
40. Part of the interest of *Rio*, in addition to its neon-blinking climax and pre-*Gilda* Carnival sequence, is its recurring recourse to musical performance: the Parisian chanteuse Irene (Sigrid Gurie) performs a song cycle that chronicles her roller-coaster romantic life—"Love Opened My Eyes," "Heart of Mine," and "It Seems to Be Spring"—and two male characters, Manuelo and Roberto, also duet on the comic number "Si, Si, Si."
41. McLean, *Being Rita Hayworth*, 155.
42. Callow, *Hello, Americans*, 368. Welles's responses to Bogdanovich's questions about "Please Don't Kiss Me" in his interview with the director are, however subjective, pertinent in the context. Bogdanovich: "Why did you have Rita sing in the picture?" / Welles: "How could she not?" / Bogdanovich: "And you recorded it rather lovingly?" / Welles: "How could I not?" (*This Is Orson Welles*, 192). The Roberts and Fisher number was added, of course, "at the request of Cohn," whom Welles in the interview also acknowledges that he "rather liked" (*This Is Orson Welles*, 193 and 195).
43. Doris Fisher, quoted in Kobal, *Rita Hayworth*, 171.
44. Telotte, *Voices in the Dark*, 67.
45. Kobal, *Rita Hayworth*, 57.
46. Oliver and Trigo, *Noir Anxiety*, 69. I'm referring to Sternberg's *Shanghai Express* (1932) and *The Shanghai Gesture* (1941) as well as *Macao* (1952).

47. Kobal, *Rita Hayworth*, 175.
48. Rasmussen, *Orson Welles*, 114.
49. McLean, *Being Rita Hayworth*, 151.
50. According to Laing, the femme fatale as siren, "rather than being 'regarded' by the nondiegetic score," "self-consciously adopts the powerful position of the performer" (*The Gendered Score*, 101).
51. In *Rita Hayworth* Kobal comments that Anita Ellis's voice, when separated out from the musical sequences, "is a little voice because that's the way Rita was" (159). Oliver and Trigo, *Noir Anxiety*, 70.
52. Karen Hollinger, "*Film Noir*, Voice-Over, and the Femme Fatale," *Film Noir Reader* 2, 247.
53. Ibid., 257.
54. Although Hayworth sang, among other things, on radio, "it was to become a source of gnawing resentment to her that Columbia who starred her in a succession of musicals did not make the effort to train her so she could sing for herself" (Kobal, *Rita Hayworth*, 103). See also Rosen who, after commenting on Hayworth's "ripe directness" in *Gilda* (" 'This is my body . . .' "), concludes: "In reality, Rita's rejoicing met with constant obstruction. One of these was studio boss Harry Cohn" (*Popcorn Venus*, 211).
55. Rasmussen, *Orson Welles*, 113.
56. See, for example, Lucy Fischer, "*The Lady from Shanghai*," *Shot/Countershot* (Princeton: Princeton University Press, 1989), 33–49. André Bazin, *Orson Welles*, trans. Jonathan Rosenbaum (New York: Harper Colophon, 1972), 94.
57. Oliver and Trigo, *Noir Anxiety*, 70.
58. Ibid.
59. Ibid., 71.

EPILOGUE

1. Tom Flinn, "Daniel Mainwaring: An Interview," in *The Big Book of Noir*, 67.
2. Krutnik, *In a Lonely Street*, 111–112.

Index